SELF-ESTEEM

SELF-ESTEEM

Paradoxes and Innovations in Clinical Theory and Practice

Richard L. Bednar, PhD, and Scott R. Peterson, MSW

SECOND EDITION

AMERICAN   PSYCHOLOGICAL   ASSOCIATION
Washington, DC

Published by the
American Psychological Association
750 First Street, NE
Washington, DC 20002

Copies may be ordered from
APA Order Department
P.O. Box 2710
Hyattsville, MD 20784

In the UK and Europe, copies may be ordered from
American Psychological Association
3 Henrietta Street
Covent Garden, London
WC2E 8LU England

Typeset in Palatino by PRO-Image Corporation, Techna-Type Div., York, PA

Cover designer: Michael David Brown, Rockville, MD
Printer: Edwards Brothers, Inc., Ann Arbor, MI
Technical / production editor: Miria Liliana Riahi

Library of Congress Cataloging-in-Publication Data
Bednar, Richard L.
     Self-esteem : paradoxes and innovations in clinical theory and practice / Richard L. Bednar, Scott R. Peterson. — 2nd ed.
         p.   cm.
     Includes bibliographical references and index.
     ISBN 1-55798-305-4 (hardcover).—ISBN 1-55798-290-2 (softcover)
     1. Self-esteem.   2. Adjustment (Psychology)   3. Psychotherapy.
     I. Peterson, Scott R.   II. Title.
     RC489.S43B43   1995
     616.89'14—dc20   95-16098
                                                                         CIP

British Library Cataloguing in Publication Data
A CIP record is available from the British Library.

Printed in the United States of America
Second Edition, First Printing

Table of Contents

Preface to the Second Edition

We are glad for a second edition—not because we are unhappy with what we said in the first one, but because of all the things that we did not include. We always understood that our treatment model was deceptively simple, but we never realized how wide the gap would be between understanding the model conceptually and implementing it practically. In the five years since the first edition, we have had conversations with hundreds of colleagues in workshops and seminars that proved to be enlightening for us. We heard about the most common problems arising from the use and misuse of our model that require clarification. So, we have added a new chapter titled "Treatment Caveats and Conundrums." This new chapter discusses the most frequent practical difficulties and conceptual mistakes that practicing clinicians seem to encounter as they go about the business of trying to understand and, then, implement a new treatment model.

We have also added a new chapter on marital therapy titled "Marital and Family Therapy: Primary and Unique Considerations." Many with whom we talked in training sessions had already traced out many of the implications of our model for treating couples and families. Therefore, there was more than enough interest in this topic for us to include it in a new chapter. We have maintained our emphasis on patterns of coping and avoidance as well as on self-description and self-evaluative thoughts, but in this chapter, we placed these elements in a larger social context to accommodate couples and families. This new chapter is longer than most of the others and is certainly different from other approaches to family treatments, sometimes radically different. That is why we have included detailed examples and therapeutic dialogues to illustrate as well as to explain.

Finally, we are indebted to friends and colleagues who read our first drafts and then asked us critical questions that we could not answer. They made us think harder and write more clearly. They alerted us to research that was not available five years ago, and they asked how we were doing when we were not doing so well. Our thanks and appreciation to friends and colleagues whose critical and incisive reactions were only exceeded by their desire to help us improve our work.

RICHARD L. BEDNAR
SCOTT R. PETERSON

Preface to the First Edition

Self-esteem is considered by many to be a central component of personality that affects and is affected by most any psychological difficulty. However, it is so interwoven in the personality that it is seldom the focus of psychotherapy. Most therapeutic models assume that treatment will indirectly modify the client's low self-esteem. The client's improved feeling about self comes, it is supposed, as a by-product of the therapy activity, not as a directly attended effort.

On the other hand, Jerome Frank (1981), in a major address on the common elements of successful psychotherapy, considered low self-esteem to be a nearly universal ingredient in the demoralization experienced by clients seeking psychotherapy. He asserted that the restoration of client morale (and, therefore, the improvement of self-esteem) is the sine qua non of successful treatment. In Frank's view, the restoration of morale depends more upon the quality of the therapeutic relationship than upon any specific treatment technique or model of therapy involved.

The concepts presented in this book represent a radical departure from the expectation that self-esteem will improve simply as a by-product of symptom resolution or a good therapeutic relationship. Herein, we describe a therapeutic process that strategically shifts the balance of focus: making self-esteem the central issue of concern. One's overall evaluation of self, it is suggested, is the natural consequence of a person's tendency to consistently cope with or avoid that which one fears.

The therapeutic approach described in this book is deceptively simple. It does not teach self-affirmation or positive self-talk. Instead, it intervenes in the natural, raw moments from which self-evaluations are constructed by the individual. Although the therapeutic relationship is essential, the renewed, vital sense of self is fashioned by the client, not by the force of the verbally persuasive therapist. We suggest that an enduring and deeply felt sense of self-approval is the inevitable consequence of learning to cope consistently with that which one tends to avoid. As a result, not only does self-esteem improve, but other psychological symptoms may disappear as well.

RICHARD L. BEDNAR
M. GAWAIN WELLS
SCOTT R. PETERSON

Acknowledgments

Special thanks are extended to Melissa Peterson for her exceptional skill in typing, proofreading, and editing this manuscript. However, her real contribution to the development of this book is less obvious and more profound: She took upon herself many clinic responsibilities that were clearly beyond her job description so that we would have more time to write. We truly appreciate her thoughtfulness and her skill.

Special thanks are also extended to Jay Behrman for his critical reviews. The value of his penetrating criticism is exceeded only by the quality of his discerning eye. Both of these people are valued friends and colleagues.

We are also grateful to the following sources for permission to reprint previously published material:

Pp. 24–25: Alfred Adler, *Superiority and Social Interest,* edited and translated by H. L. Ansbacher and R. R. Ansbacher. © 1964, 1970 Northwestern University Press. P. 28: *George Herbert Mead on Social Psychology,* edited by A. Strauss. © 1964, University of Chicago. P. 31: Gordon allport, *Pattern and Growth in Personality.* © 1961 Holt, Rinehart & Winston. Rights have reverted to Robert B. Allport. Pp. 32–33: Rollo May, *The Discovery of Being.* © 1983 W. W. Norton & Co. Pp. 35–36: Carl R. Rogers, *Client-Centered Therapy.* © 1951 Houghton Mifflin Co.

Pp. 38–39: Ruth Wylie, *The Self-Concept: A Review of Methodological Considerations and Measuring Instruments* (Vol. 1, revised edition). © 1974 University of Nebraska Press. P. 39: H. Markus and E. Wurf, "The Dynamic Self-Concept: A Social Psychological Perspective." Reproduced with permission from the *Annual Review of Psychology,* Vol. 38. © 1987 by Annual Reviews, Inc. Pp. 43–44: B. R. Schlenker, "Identity and Self-Identification," in *The Self and Social Life,* edited by B. R. Schlenker. © 1985 McGraw-Hill. P. 50: Stanley Coopersmith, *The Antecedents of Self-Esteem.* © 1967 W. H. Freeman & Co.; p. 52: Excerpts from *Influences on Human Development,* Second Edition, by Urie Bronfenbrenner and Maureen Mahoney, © 1975 by The Dryden Press, a division of Holt, Rinehart and Winston, Inc., reprinted with permission of the publisher. P. 54: Excerpt from *Self-Worth and School Learning* by Martin V. Covington and Richard G. Beery, © 1976 by Holt, Rinehart and Winston, Inc., reprinted with permission of the publisher. P. 74: Carl R. Rogers, "A Theory of Therapy, Personality, and

1

Self-Esteem:
Paradoxes and Contradictions

Although relatively little is known about self-esteem, it is generally considered to be a highly favorable personal attribute, the consequences of which are assumed to be as robust as they are desirable. Books and chapters on mental hygiene and personality development consistently portray self-esteem as one of the premier elements in the highest levels of human functioning (Allport, 1961; Korchin, 1976). Its general importance to a full spectrum of effective human behaviors remains virtually uncontested. We are not aware of a single article in the psychological literature that has identified or discussed any undesirable consequences that are assumed to be a result of realistic and healthy levels of personal self-regard. Certainly, some have confused authentic self-esteem with such undesirable personal attributes as arrogance, self-centeredness, egotism, and an exaggerated sense of self-importance, or with other dysfunctional behavior, but these views are generally more emotive than substantive. They seldom warrant the attention of even the most elementary student interested in self-esteem.

Conversely, the absence of a healthy sense of self-appreciation seems to be one of the basic warning signs of a dysfunctional personality, and it is an assumed condition in virtually all contemporary models of disordered behavior. Professionals in clinical practice also suggest the same conclusion. Clinical patients commonly complain of low self-esteem, lack of self-approval, and lack of self-confidence. When patients have failed to acquire even the most modest sense of personal self-approval, these complaints are often elevated to self-hatred and a pervasive sense of despair. However, it would be uncommon, if not impossible, to find people with high levels of personal self-esteem immobilized in a similar way.

The purpose of this book is to describe a new model of self-esteem in the hope of clarifying the origins and consequences of this important psychological attribute. The model that will be discussed had its conceptual origins in a graduate seminar that we taught several years ago. The purpose of the seminar was to assemble a small group of capable graduate students to spend a year considering two of the most fundamental questions that mental health professionals might ask. Both questions focus on the "symbiotic" relationship between the diagnosis and treatment of emotional problems:

1. Are there psychological elements common to most emotional and behavioral problems?

This question is part of the larger search for the psychological elements that may be common to most forms of emotional and behavioral disorders. The conceptual and practical benefits of being able to cluster together an assortment of psychological symptoms on the basis of similar underlying elements is undeniable. It could help clarify the complex foundations of psychopathology, psychotherapy, and personality development.

2. If there are common elements that mediate the form and substance of different types of disordered behavior, can these underlying factors, rather than the diverse symptoms that they produce, become the basis for understanding and treating psychological disturbances?

A favorable answer to these two questions creates the possibility of being able to diagnose and treat emotional problems within a unified conceptual framework. Such an achievement would certainly be welcomed by many mental health professionals.[1]

During the seminar, the participants debated research evidence, theoretical arguments, and the clinical lore relevant to these two questions. A variety of competing variables and arguments was considered. However, once the topic of self-esteem came up, it was clear that low self-esteem was associated with virtually all types of emotional and behavioral problems, but it was hardly ever clear whether it was a cause or a consequence of the attending psychological problems. Once we began to consider the possibility that low self-esteem could be both a cause and a consequence of disordered behavior, it gradually became clear that self-esteem could be a fundamental and productive consideration in both the etiology and treatment of many forms of dysfunctional behavior.

As we continued to explore the role of self-esteem in the development and remediation of behavior problems, we came to see its power and usefulness as a major explanatory construct. We gradually formalized our thinking into a new theoretical model of self-esteem. Our hope was to clarify the origins and consequences of this important attribute. As the model began to develop, its uniqueness also became apparent. On many important issues, it showed little allegiance to many of the traditional views and propositions about the origins of self-esteem. Additionally, the principles of psychological treatment that are

---

[1] The limited treatment applications that flow from our current diagnostic labels, as recorded in the *Diagnostic and Statistical Manual of Mental Disorders, Third Edition–Revised (DSM-III-R)*, may well prove to be an unnecessary embarrassment to the applied mental health professions. Other diagnostic schemes are currently available (Millon, 1969) in which psychological symptoms are considered to be a direct extension of long-standing patterns of psychological coping and defense. These patterns play a crucial role in defining disordered behavior and the appropriate goals and procedures for its treatment. We suspect that the most potent forms of psychological treatment will eventually evolve from the most incisive models of disordered behavior.

a natural product of this model were also unusual for the same reason. They seemed to challenge many of the cherished views and values about some of the most basic ingredients assumed to be central to effective psychotherapy.

We have tried to avoid gratuitous praise or condemnation of the work of others in this area. Rather, we have attempted to emphasize and integrate ideas and propositions on the basis of conceptual merit. Obviously, that is a difficult task. Nevertheless, we hope our model can contribute to the gradual evolution of knowledge regarding (a) the psychological origins of high and low self-esteem, (b) some of the underlying dynamics of psychopathology, and (c) the principles of psychological intervention that are useful in the remediation of chronically low levels of self-esteem and some elements of disordered behavior, as well as in the enhancement of self-esteem.

We define self-esteem as a subjective and enduring sense of realistic self-approval. It reflects how the individual views and values the self at the most fundamental levels of psychological experiencing. We have found that individuals, when asked, are able to observe and comment upon differentiated aspects of the self. A detailed inquiry into these different "parts" of the self yields a profile of emotions associated with the various roles in which the person operates. This information is basic to defining and understanding self-perceptions; but it is the affective experience associated with these events that defines the presence or absence of self-esteem. Fundamentally, then, self-esteem is an enduring and affective sense of personal value based on accurate self-perceptions.

Self-Esteem and Success: A Major Paradox

From a commonsense point of view, trying to understand the origins of self-esteem involves several paradoxes and contradictions. *One of the most intriguing is why so many successful, competent people seem to be plagued with problems of chronic low self-esteem.* We will use several classic examples to illustrate this point.

The first is a statement from a 70-year-old man reflecting on his lifetime effort to better the world he lived in:

> My whole life has been a succession of disappointments. I can scarcely recollect a single instance of success in anything that I ever undertook. (Kennedy, 1956, p. 35)

The origins of this statement are not to be found in a life dominated by failure, nor was this person an object of pity and scorn to his contemporaries—nothing could be further from the truth. The writer was John Quincy Adams, who served with distinction as the sixth president of the United States, a senator, a congressman, a minister to major European countries, and a vital participant in many of the early and crucial events influencing the development of the nation. One cannot help but wonder how any person so entitled to an abiding sense of personal satisfaction after a distinguished life could be so plagued with self-disappointment. Somewhere behind the external achievements there must have been an internal filtering device that denied the successes and hoarded the failures and, then, served them to John Quincy Adams as the fruits of his life's work.

The theme of this illustration is not limited to the elite. It is common to many segments of our society. Our other examples are far more typical and therefore more compelling. They seem to represent a ubiquitous psychological treadmill that can be as common to the talented high producer as it is to the typical outpatient clientele of middle-class America.

A young college graduate came to the startling realization that his low level of personal self-esteem was a major determinant in creating his current problems, and that it had shaped many of his other important life experiences. He wrote:

> For the past several years, I have felt that my life was meaningless. This was an ironic state of affairs considering all that I had accomplished. Friends and relatives were always lauding me for my good looks and intelligence. I was the first person on either side of my family to graduate from college,

doing so with honors. I had a good job with an important accounting firm. I had plenty of dates. By all outward appearances, my life was very fulfilling. Yet I was miserable and felt increasingly depressed.

Six months of psychotherapy had helped me to catch an occasional glimpse of the underlying cause of my unhappiness. It always seemed to involve low self-esteem or my disapproval of myself. Somehow, it seemed like I really did have a low opinion of myself, but I found that idea confusing because of all of the success in my life. Finally, I was able to put my finger on the problem. Because I had such a low opinion of myself, I believed others would think of me the same way if they really got to know me. Because of this, I had been unwilling to expose myself to others as the person I really was. I took great pains to sidestep high-pressure situations, to gain the approval of others, and to avoid making decisions that might reveal things about myself that I didn't want others to know. I can see countless examples of this pattern in my life now that I have caught on to my style.

About 10 years ago, I agreed to hear missionary lessons from two young men representing a Christian church. I did so partly because I was interested in a particular girl who happened to be a member of that church. After the missionary lessons were completed, I agreed to be baptized a member. I shouldn't have. I was lying to myself. I had serious doubts about most of the basic concepts and beliefs of this church. I really joined so as not to disappoint the missionaries who had spent so much time with me, and because I hoped now to be more acceptable to the girl who had sparked my interest.

In college, I was interested in music, psychology, English, and physics. So what did I major in? Accounting! Why? Because accounting seemed like a difficult major—a good way to impress my friends. Also, being an accountant was prestigious and held the opportunity to make a lot of money. But prestige and money did not go a long way in making me happy, especially when I was working 8 to 10 hours a day at a job that bored me.

My unwillingness to let myself be known probably caused me the greatest difficulty in my relationships with the women I found the most attractive. My most recent relationship is a good example. After weeks of building up courage, I finally asked her out on a date. It was quickly obvious that she liked me as much as I liked her. I should have been elated, but instead I got scared about really making myself known to this woman. I put up a fake front designed to impress her. I was petrified of becoming too intimate or vulnerable. This led to behavior that was both hot and cold, as I kept testing her to see if I could let down my guard, be myself, and still be liked by her. When we broke up after 8 months, I was terribly lonely. I realize now that the relationship might have had a chance to have been meaningful on a long-term basis if I would have had the courage to risk presenting an honest picture of myself.

I am now amazed at how often I have chosen to avoid facing situations that would expose me to others. All of this because I don't want others to know me and dislike me the way I dislike myself.

Another former client wrote the following description of personal problems that originated in low levels of personal self-esteem:

Dragging Main Street with my friends in a '56 Ford convertible, we would occasionally damn some passerby with, "That guy is an accident looking for a place to happen."

More than a decade later, that statement, altered slightly, came floating back as I examined my feelings of beginning a career as a professor, a new PhD: I've been acting as though I'm a failure looking for a place to happen.

It seemed that whenever I began something new for which I had no experience, no "track record" of success, I expected this might be the place where I would fail. As a high school graduate, waiting for college to begin, I thought, This isn't going to be just like high school, where guys are here because they have to be here. These will be students who are here because they want an education. Can I measure up?

I went to college and found that it wasn't that much different. It was still a matter of completing assignments, taking tests, and writing papers. But, instead of recognizing and accepting that I had the ability, I tended to denigrate my expectations, deciding that there were a lot of goof-offs in college too. But in graduate school, that's where my true colors (inadequate bright yellow) would show.

When graduate school came along, it wasn't that much different: just more reading, more exams, and more papers. But where the sheep get separated from "us" goats was the graduate dissertation requirement—a piece of original research and a contribution to the scientific field. Well, I completed my dissertation, and it wasn't that tough. Did that mean I was that good, and a bona fide doctor of philosophy? No, of course not, it meant that I either fooled them or that the real test was just ahead. Almost anyone can be a student, but how about a faculty member at a university!

Another client provided this description of his reasons for being in therapy:

What am I doing here? I am 33 years old, married with 3 children, and a graduate of a good law school. I have a good position with my firm and a good salary. So why am I so tense and unable to enjoy any of this? And why am I getting psychological treatment?

Maybe it's because I don't know what I want to do for a living when I grow up. I am dragging myself to work every day, and most of the time I can't seem to concentrate. But I've got so much invested in it. Law is interesting to me. Besides, what else would I do if I quit?

When it comes right down to it, it seems like I didn't really choose to be a lawyer. Somehow it just happened. People would ask what I was going to be, and what do you do with a degree in English? So I said I was going to be a lawyer. That was cool and people thought I was hot stuff, so here I am being hot stuff. Except that I'm not a very good lawyer, and while the other guys are raking it in being trial lawyers, I stay back here doing research for the senior partners. My wife is envious of my classmates' salaries, but I'm just not the flashy, competitive type. Sometimes, I feel like I get dumped on by the more aggressive attorneys in the firm, but in the press of the situation, I can never think of what to say.

In each of these three examples, we can see the same thing: the trappings of external success coupled with internal distress.

In each case, we are confronted with the same paradox. By what means do people learn to be so displeased with themselves when the world they live in is so eager to reward and approve of them?

Ingredients of the Paradox

This is an intriguing paradox. Many of the traditional approaches to understanding the origins of self-esteem tend to emphasize social and interpersonal learning. Basically, these views suggest that individuals gradually acquire beliefs about themselves that are a reflection of the way in which they are treated by their social environment (Bandura, 1986). In essence, people come to view and value themselves in much the same way in which they are viewed and valued by others. Of course, there are exceptions to this general orientation. Two notable ones include Rollo May's (1953) emphasis on personal awareness and self-alienation, and Carl Rogers's (1961) emphasis on self-congruence and perceptual accuracy. Yet even in these orientations, an unfavorable social environment is a crucial consideration. In both cases, it is the level of emotional acceptance in the social environment that fosters the conditions under-which individuals become more or less self-accepting and self-congruent. We will review the contributions of all of these theoretical approaches in considerable detail in the next chapter.

For now, we only wish to emphasize that, according to these views, individuals with an abundance of approval and affection from their social environment, particularly from "significant others," are more likely to have high levels of self-esteem than are those coming from less favorable social learning environments. Sullivan (1962) was the first to formalize this view in his classic text *Schizophrenia as a Human Process*. One of his primary propositions was that the self-concept is made up largely of the reflected appraisals of significant others.

With these considerations in mind, the depth of the paradox becomes more apparent. Even the most successful people do not seem to develop any enduring immunity to problems of low self-esteem. Yet, most of our theoretical speculations suggest that this should be otherwise. We need not limit our definition of success to business, finance, and high-status positions for this general statement to have a wide range of applicability. On the whole, it seems reasonable to suggest that a rigorous and objective assessment of the major life events of most people nearly always shows that the absolute number of life successes exceeds the number of failures. In the course of a lifetime, most people manage to stay employed most of the time; have relationships in which they share both emotional and physical intimacy at least some of the time; provide support, sustenance, and direction for growing children or others for whom they have responsibility; keep their bills paid most of the time; and stay out of serious entanglements with the law. With just a moment's reflection, it becomes obvious that many of these life achievements are significant ones, requiring persistence, maturity, self-control, complex judgments, and the ability to endure short-term frustrations while long-term goals are pursued. Certainly, there are exceptions to this general characterization, but, on the whole, the majority of people do seem to endure the trials of life relatively well yet fail to acquire a realistic sense of self-appreciation for their accomplishments. This is the paradox!

The question then is why, with 40 to 50 years of reasonably successful and responsible life experience completed, do so many people fail to acquire an enduring and realistic sense of self-appreciation? Although some individuals do seem to have an easier time of it than do others, in an absolute sense, most people do experience more success in their lives than failure. In spite of this, many people fail to acquire a sense of meaningful and enduring personal self-appreciation that is proportional to their major successes in life. In some cases, it is probably fair to suggest that just the opposite is true. Self-doubts, a sense of personal inadequacy, and, in some cases, self-hatred prevail where self-approval would normally be expected. Without minimizing the difficulties of life all of us are required to contend with, it would seem more reasonable to find substantial numbers of people at midlife with a heightened sense of self-appreciation and approval. This would seem to be a more natural result of enduring and, perhaps, thriving in a society that can be competitive and hazardous at best. It seems paradoxical that such common and fundamental successes at life's primary tasks are not weighted more heavily in the equation that accounts for self-perceptions and self-approval.

Insight Into the Paradox: Internal and External Factors

It should now be clear that we do not consider psychological factors external to the individual (social learning and environmental rewards) to be an adequate basis for understanding the origins of self-esteem. A broader conceptual foundation is needed. However, it would make little sense to deny or minimize the important role these social learning influences play in shaping our self-image. This is particularly true during early childhood, when the organism is so teachable and the shaping power of the social environment so obvious. However, a theoretical position emphasizing only learning factors, which are external to the individual, does not seem to account adequately for the development of self-esteem. We see no necessity to rely solely on factors external to the organism to understand the origins of self-esteem for either children or adults.

There is ample evidence in the child development literature for the power of functionally autonomous reinforcement (Bandura, 1986). Anyone who has watched an infant take those first precarious steps across a room without falling cannot help but notice that the child does not need external reinforcement from parents to recognize and to be pleased with this accomplishment. The parents' pleasure in their child is equally obvious, but it is not the only source of reinforcement for the child. Thus, as we will suggest, any meaningful theory of self-esteem must take into account the individual's self-talk and self-thoughts spoken of in the early writings on the concept of the self (Allport, 1937; Hamachek, 1978; James, 1918).

Aside from having incomplete formulations of self-esteem, the traditional social learning approaches are also not much help to those unfortunate souls chronically plagued by low self-esteem. Even if we grant that these socially transmitted self-images might be more true than false, the reliance on external factors to understand the origins of self-esteem suffers from more serious concerns. If individuals must depend on the affirmation from others to overcome low self-esteem, then part of a clinician's job is to teach the client to be a consummate performer, sensitive to the demands of the audience in order to win plaudits and "atta boys" from others. In our opinion, such a task is as impossible as it is undesirable.

Finally, common sense and clinical experience have led us to believe that high or low levels of personal self-esteem can be the result of events that have nothing to do with the way in which we are thought of by significant others. Children who are so lucky as to have affirming, affectionate, and loving parents should have unquestioning self-confidence. Conversely, children whose parents are harsh and critical should inexorably be victims who gradually internalize the criticisms as the given definition of themselves. Yet, our clinical experience has taught us that this is not always the case. Some individuals coming from abusive and traumatic childhoods are remarkably intact, productive, and self-confident. Others, who come from apparently nurturing, supportive environments, may or may not be equally productive but suffer from debilitating self-doubt and low self-esteem. These observations suggest that more is involved in the development of high or low levels of self-esteem than just external social learning factors.

In summary, we consider excessive reliance on external factors in understanding the origins of self-esteem to be ill-advised for the following reasons:

1. It does not accommodate the common observation that self-esteem does not necessarily vary as a function of numerous external factors such as loving parents, achieving positions of power and status, quality peer relationships, success in intimate relationships, or economic success.

2. It cannot explain the conspicuous absence of high levels of self-esteem in the general population, which probably includes many people who were raised in appropriately loving and nurturing social environments.

3. It denies the role of internal determinants of human behavior and psychological development, which common sense and simple introspection suggest to be valid considerations.

4. It is based on the implicit assumption that the development of self-esteem is a function of a favorable social environment

that can be defined and that exerts uniform learning effects on different types of individuals.

Overview

The model of self-esteem that we are proposing will explain (a) the role of intrapsychic and interpersonal feedback in the development of self-esteem; and (b) the role of cognition, affect, and behavior in cultivating this important attribute. The model is based on assumptions about the role and influence of *interpersonal* and *intrapsychic* feedback. With regard to interpersonal feedback, we make the following assumptions:

> *1. Everyone should expect to receive regular amounts of negative feedback from the social environment, most of which is probably valid.*

> *2. Most people receive and enjoy substantial amounts of authentic favorable social feedback but tend not to believe it.*

These two assumptions about interpersonal feedback have a number of striking implications for the development of self-esteem. One of the most important ones is the recognition that virtually everyone will experience and have to respond to interpersonal rejection. Although we view rejection as a major activating catalyst for other psychological processes that are related to self-esteem, we do not suggest that rejection per se is a major cause of low self-esteem.

Instead, we suggest that individual response styles to rejection will involve varying degrees and mixtures of coping and defense. To the degree that a response style favors coping, it will increase the development of a realistic sense of personal identity. To the degree that a response style favors avoidance, it will increase one's tendency to try and gain the approval of others by *impression management,* that is, pretending to be what we believe is most acceptable to others. When people respond to rejection by impression management, they unwittingly create the conditions that will render most of the favorable feedback received untrustworthy, unbelievable, and psychologically impotent because of their internal awareness of their own facade. Even the most modest tendency to avoid the reality of rejection by making oneself more appealing to others by impression management can create the condition in which the individual cannot believe favorable feedback or questions the validity of unfavorable feedback. We explore the influence of these two conditions on the development of self-esteem in considerable depth.

The next two assumptions about intrapsychic feedback are equally striking:

> *3. Self-evaluative processes are a psychological reality for most people.*

> *4. Self-evaluations can provide a basis for continuous affective feedback from the self about the adequacy of the self.*

Inherent in our discussion of internal feedback is the recognition that self-evaluations regularly accompany virtually any type of human experience. In essence, when there is consistency in one's tendency to cope or avoid conflict, there is a continuous basis for internal feedback from the self about the adequacy of the self. Avoidance motivated by fear and anxiety generates negative self-evaluations because of the inherently undesirable qualities of this behavior. Coping generates favorable self-evaluations because of the high quality of the psychological responses inherent in this behavior. Even though these self-evaluative processes go on at different levels of clarity and explicitness for different people, the effects are a psychological reality for most people. And it is the nature and quality of this internal, affective feedback that defines the nature of the organism to itself. High or low levels of self-esteem, then, are the result and the reflection of the internal, affective feedback the organism most commonly experiences.

Finally, we discuss the role of all of these factors hierarchically and developmentally, suggesting that levels of self-esteem are neither fixed in youth nor uniformly influenced by the same factors across the life span. We do suggest that internal self-evaluations play a more important role in determining the form and substance of self-esteem than do external evaluations—though both are clearly influential.

A brief overview of each of the remaining chapters is given below:

Chapter 2—Conceptual themes: Overview and analysis. This chapter provides a concise overview of the most prominent contributors to the conceptual and empirical development of the current concept of self-esteem, ranging from William James to Rollo May. The common themes and issues inherent in this body of literature are identified and discussed.

Chapter 3—Avoidance and coping: Basic considerations. This chapter discusses the role and function of avoidance in disordered behavior and coping in normal behavior. These concepts are considered in a cross-cultural context and are presented as building blocks for understanding the role of coping and avoidance in the development of high and low levels of self-esteem.

Chapter 4—External and internal feedback: Basic assumptions. The role of feedback in human development is discussed in this chapter. Particular emphasis is placed on clarifying the difference between self-evaluative processes (internal feedback) and interpersonal feedback in the development of personal self-esteem. The psychological mechanisms and assumptions that influence the effects of both forms of feedback are also discussed.

Chapter 5—Introduction to the model. All the major concepts introduced in the previous chapters are now integrated into a conceptual model of self-esteem. This model focuses on both the internal and external determinants of self-esteem and discusses the cognitive, affective, and behavioral considerations that are believed to influence the development of self-esteem. It is suggested that levels of self-esteem are neither fixed in youth nor uniformly influenced by the same factors across the life span.

Chapter 6—Clinical applications: Remedial considerations in psychotherapy. This chapter focuses on explaining and illustrating how the chronic patterns of avoidance that breed low levels of self-esteem can be permanently interrupted. Clinical illustrations and actual therapy dialogues are used to illustrate the application of the principles discussed in earlier chapters.

Chapter 7—Developmental considerations in psychotherapy: Enhancing coping responses. This chapter focuses on the means and methods for actually improving self-esteem. The patterns of coping that are essential to improved self-esteem are defined and illustrated. Numerous clinical illustrations and actual therapy dialogues are used to illustrate the application of the principles discussed in earlier chapters.

Chapter 8—Unique qualities of the therapeutic relationship. Because the model of self-esteem we are proposing departs from many of the traditional views about the origins of self-esteem, our conception of growth-inducing relationships is also different in several important respects. These differences are discussed and illustrated with examples.

Chapter 9—Marital and family therapy: Primary and unique considerations. The unique processes involved in marriage and family therapy are discussed in relation to the self-esteem model, including how couples and families interact in social microcosms. Application of the self-esteem model to avoidance patterns observed in the social context of couples and families is illustrated with clinical examples.

Chapter 10—Family relations and the development of self-esteem in children. The fundamental ingredients in family relationships and child-rearing practices that are essential to the development of self-esteem are discussed. The importance of parental authenticity during stress and conflict is emphasized as a primary means of modeling the coping skills essential to the development of an enduring sense of personal well-being. Several myths about family relationships and child-rearing practices are also identified, discussed, and challenged.

Chapter 11—Treatment caveats and conundrums. This final chapter discusses the levels of intervention contained within the self-esteem model and some of the problems that therapists might encounter when they begin to use the treatment model. Suggestions are offered for predicting and dealing with potential problems.

2

Conceptual Themes:
Overview and Analysis

Like any other model, the propositions in this book have their conceptual ancestors: hypotheses about the nature of self-esteem, its origins and development, and amelioration of low self-esteem. This chapter's purpose is to consider early as well as contemporary contributions that broadly mark the directions taken in using the construct.

The history of self-esteem as a concept began with writings of some of the best known theorists in psychology, but early theoretical efforts were followed by years during which the concept was neglected as being unscientific and "softheaded." Gradually, research began to accumulate, primarily oriented toward the measurement of self-esteem as a global, trait-like entity. Research attempts to measure self-esteem were resoundingly criticized at irregular intervals by Wylie (1961, 1974, 1979). Finally, in the present decade, a new generation of social psychologists has claimed renewed usefulness of the concept through more refined measurement of specific aspects of the self-concept (see Markus & Wurf, 1987).

This chapter reviews four major areas of literature on self-esteem: (a) theoretical contributions, ranging from William James to Carl Rogers; (b) conceptual developments, emphasizing contemporary efforts derived from research; (c) developmental writings, focusing on the antecedents of self-esteem; and (d) therapy literature for treatment of self-esteem problems. Inasmuch as the thrust of our concern is clinical, we emphasize the applied elements in each of the formulations. Following each major section, we compare the authors' concepts to those of the proposed model. The review is not exhaustive, of course. Not only is the volume of literature too large to include it reasonably in a book chapter, but often relevant concepts can be found under other labels, such as self-efficacy, self-evaluation, and self-concept.

Theoretical Contributions

Early Theorists

The concept of self-esteem per se is not discussed in depth but must be sifted from related ideas about the self in the writings of early theorists such as William James, Alfred Adler, George Herbert Mead, and Gordon Allport. Similarly, because the focus is broad in these earlier writings, not much attention is given to questions of clinical concern or their development and remediation. Each thinker is considered briefly here to establish the "prime movers" of the concept.

William James. For James (1890), the self psychologically encompasses all the attributes to which the individual would refer as "part of me": one's body, abilities, and reputation; and even one's children, home, and possessions. If any of those component parts is diminished or enhanced, people respond as though they themselves were diminished or enhanced because they have indeed defined the part as the self. Thus, each person bases what James called self-feeling or self-love on the successes and failures of what has been chosen as being the most true self. All the other equally possible selves not chosen become irrelevant to the individual's self-esteem:

> I, who for the time have staked my all on being a psychologist, am mortified if others know much more psychology than I. But I am contented to wallow in the grossest ignorance of Greek. My deficiencies there give me no sense of personal humiliation at all. Had I "pretensions" to be a linguist, it would have been just the reverse. . . . Our self-feeling

> in this world depends entirely on what we back ourselves to be and do. It is determined by the ratio of our actualities to our supposed potentialities; a fraction of which our pretensions are the denominator, and the numerator our successes; thus, self-esteem = successes / pretensions. (James, 1890, p. 296)

In other words, whatever we choose to define as a goal for ourselves—a reputation by which we would like to be known, or an attribute that we would like to possess—becomes one of our "pretensions." The degree to which we match that hope determines our self-esteem in that particular sphere of experience.

According to James, there are three major constituents of the self from which pretensions are chosen: the material self, the social self, and the spiritual self. The *material self* refers to objects and possessions considered to be one's personal property or with which one identifies: body, clothes, family, home, car, and so forth. If the material realm prospers, the individual feels enlarged, more substantial. If one's possessions are damaged or lost, the person feels smaller, as if the personality had shrunk somewhat.

The *social self* is equated with a person's reputation or share of recognition:

> We have an innate propensity to get ourselves noticed, and noticed favorably, by our kind. No more fiendish punishment could be devised, were such a thing physically possible, than that one should be turned into society and remain absolutely unnoticed by all the members thereof. (James, 1890, p. 281)

A person has many social selves—that self seen as son or daughter to parents, the self that is buddy to friends, the self as student or athlete, and so forth. Here again, the individual's pretensions or goals for which self is most important will depend on age and personality. To a preschooler, recognition from parents will be preeminent, whereas at adolescence, peers' affirmations will be weighted heavily.

The person's *spiritual self* is the inner or subjective being, the individual's recognition that he or she thinks about things and that those thoughts have a continuity over time. Usually, the spiritual self feels as though it were the innermost center of one's being. James and other writers of the period spoke of two elements when referring to the self: The portion that is the *me*, the actor, the doer, the performer part of the self; and the *I*, which is the seat of consciousness, the sense of continuity as an individual over time, and the observer and evaluator of the *me*. As the observer, the spiritual self is not exposed to the successes/pretensions equation of self-esteem. Indeed, it is the interpreter of the outcome of the equation and, therefore, the determiner of the felt sense of self-esteem.

James recognized that self-esteem may have a general and a specific aspect. Although there are individual fluctuations of self-esteem that are dependent upon daily encounters, there is an average tone that the person develops over time that self-esteem seems to return to, almost as if it were a resting level. If a person has succeeded consistently over a period of time or has experienced repeated setbacks lately, the general level of self-trust or distrust may shift.

For James's only comments that could be construed as suggestions for changing self-esteem, we must return to the successes/pretensions ratio. Self-love, he says, can be increased either by increasing the numerator (the successes) or by decreasing the denominator (the pretensions to which we aspire):

> How pleasant is the day when we give up striving to be young or slender. "Thank God!" we say, "those illusions are gone." Everything added to the self is a burden as well as a pride. (James, 1890, p. 297)

The stoic recipe for contentment, he noted, was to dispossess oneself of everything that one could not personally control and to become, therefore, invulnerable to disappointment from others. That kind of person, however, seemed to James to be extremely narrow, actively shunning attachments to others. On the other hand, he observed that some people (he calls them sympathetic people) allow themselves to identify with many others and, indeed, see themselves as part of the world, identifying with the successes and failures of many. In its own way, this tactic would seem to decrease one's personal responsibility for the outcome of the self-esteem equation, creating instead a person distanced from the self.

Commentary. James made no attempt to be a clinician in describing means to overcome low self-esteem. He takes the position that people can be active in choosing and meeting their goals and are, therefore, capable of modifying their self-esteem. Without mention of environmental or parental influence, James describes the self as it exists in the adult. Hence, no comment can be made about his position on the developmental process of establishing self-esteem. Given James's successes / pretensions formula, however, one cannot help but wonder whether he would assume that some pretensions or goals are universal among normal children, such as the desire to be loved and affirmed as valuable to their parents. Similarly, the goals to be affirmed by age-mates may be equally universal. Moreover, James did not address the critical and often terrifying moment of choosing to "back" one's self with a particular pretension. As clinicians, we have seen many clients who, having crashed on the shoals of unmet goals, now experience terrible anxiety about committing to seek new successes. The choice to avoid those goals, of course, exacts its own price on their fragile self-esteem.

Alfred Adler. Adler was a practicing psychiatrist, more concerned with understanding abnormal behavior than other theorists discussed here. His works are considered to be among the forerunners of social psychiatry, emphasizing the impact of family and society upon the individual. Indeed, Adler positioned the goals of cooperation (*social interest*) in work, community, and marriage as being central to the individual's mental health. Thus, even though Adlerian psychology is also known as *individual psychology*, it is not an *individualistic* psychology. His choice of the word was to emphasize a holistic understanding of the individual involved meaningfully with society, in contrast to Freud's and Jung's focus on unconscious determinants of behavior (Ansbacher & Ansbacher, 1956).

Adler was also a phenomenologist, believing that each person constructs his or her unique view of reality through what he called the *creative self*. This self strives to make sense of life and to chart meaningfully a course toward some final goal of completeness or perfection. Adler called the motivation of the creative self *striving for superiority* (a term that means self-actualization or self-fulfillment rather than narcissistic invulnerability).

Early in life, the creative self chooses a *style of life,* that is a "window" through which it interprets events throughout life to reach its final goals. The individual's personal evaluations of reality are so subjectively compelling that he or she acts as if these were the only possible interpretations. If, through proper upbringing, one chooses a lifestyle in keeping with the innate human needs to belong, to be productive, and to be intimate, that person will be healthy. If one mistakenly chooses goals of domination, overweening dependency, isolation, and so forth, the search for a sense of completion and security will be in vain.

Adler was also responsible for the term *inferiority complex.* Feelings of inferiority represent the opposite side of striving for superiority; they arise early in life from the helplessness and imperfection of childhood. Thus, individuals are seen as seeking both to achieve actualization as well as to avoid a *minus situation,* a sense of inferiority or incompleteness. Although all people normally struggle with feelings of inferiority at times, and these emotions may be appropriate motivators for achievement, the inferiority complex, as such, is qualitatively different. The inferiority complex is more pervasive and chronic, the consequence of abdicating the responsibility of living in accordance with social feeling. The individual becomes fearful and complaining, often evidencing physical symptoms of anxiety:

> To be a human being means to have inferiority feelings. One recognizes one's own powerlessness in the face of nature. But in the mentally healthy this inferiority feeling acts as a motive for productivity, as a motive for attempting to overcome obstacles, to maintain oneself in life. Only the oversized inferiority feeling, which is to be regarded as a failure in upbringing, burdens the character with oversensitivity, leads to egotistical self-considerations and self-reflections, lays foundations for neurosis with all its known symptoms which let life become a torture. (Adler, 1979, pp. 54–55)

The neurotic twist on striving for superiority that accompanies the inferiority complex is to use the symptoms to avoid, further and more permanently, the responsibility to respond coopera- tively. Now, the individual is apt to say to the self and others, "Just imagine what I could have accomplished if it were not for my disturbance and these painful symptoms, caused by some- thing (my heredity, my body, my education) for which I am not responsible."

Adler (1979) described the goal of treatment as being basically reeducative. The therapist must discern the client's mistaken choice in lifestyle, wherein the person strives for a socially use- less goal of superiority. The therapist must help the client rec- ognize the mistake and assist in increasing the ability to coop- erate and to accept and become involved in the elements of social interest. Therapy becomes a process of helping the client to mature belatedly.

Commentary. Adler did not mention the concept of self- esteem. Indeed, to the degree that self-esteem became a self- absorbing goal, he considered it to be a source of neurosis. Perhaps a more appropriate Adlerian term would be *self-ac- ceptance* (the courage to be imperfect, to use a contemporary Adlerian slogan):

> The patient must be guided away from himself, toward pro- ductivity for others; he must be educated toward social in- terest; he must be led from his seclusion from the world, back to existence; he must be brought to the only correct insight, that he is as important for the community as anyone else; he must get to feel at home on this earth. (Adler, 1964, p. 200)

Thus, appropriate self-esteem entails a person's acceptance of the right to belong to humanity and a willingness to contribute to the social interest of the group.

Adler's work introduces a concept of considerable impor- tance to the model to be presented: the issue of coping versus avoiding; that is, Adler described the essence of what we may term the *low-self-esteem person* as the individual who avoids the call to participate in the community's needs. Everyone must deal with feelings of inferiority that come from being immature and observing others who are much more competent. Chronic avoidance of social interest produces the inferiority complex. The low-self-esteem person hides behind symptoms, fearing to give up narcissistic self-strivings for superiority.

Charles H. Cooley. Cooley's (1902) observations on the self take a decidedly more social approach than those of James, albeit a still more personal one than those of George Herbert Mead, whose work is an extension of Cooley's. To Cooley, the self has several aspects, the most importunate or pressing part of which is the social self. This social self, he said, arises from the individual's observations of how others respond to the self, that is, people learn to define themselves by their perceptions of the way others define them, the *looking-glass self.*

> As we see our face, figure, and dress in the glass and are interested in them because they are ours, and pleased or otherwise with them according as they do or do not answer to what we should like them to be; so in imagination we perceive in another's mind some thought of our appearance, manners, aims, deeds, character, friends, and so on, and are variously affected by it. . . .
>
> This is evident from the fact that the character and weight of that other, in whose mind we see ourselves, makes all the difference with our feeling. We are ashamed to seem evasive in the presence of a straightforward man, cowardly in the presence of a brave one, gross in the eyes of a refined one, and so on. We always imagine, and in the imagining share the judgments of the other mind. (Cooley, 1902, p. 152)

Although there are other selves in Cooley's theory, less mention was made of them. The social self is not only demanding, it is also the vehicle by which the internal sense of self develops and is refined. The child who is thrilled about some new achievement must show it to someone else. The other's response either further elates and enlarges the sense of self or, conversely, humiliates or enrages it, casting doubt on the self-perception of worth.

> We live on, cheerful, self-confident, conscious of helping make the world go round, until in some rude hour we learn

that we do not stand so well as we thought we did, that the image of us is tarnished. Perhaps we do something, quite naturally, that we find the social order is set against, or perhaps it is the ordinary course of our life that is not so well regarded as we supposed. At any rate, we find with a chill of terror that the world is cold and strange, and that our self-esteem, self-confidence, and hope, being chiefly founded upon opinions, attributed to others, go down in the crash. Our reason may tell us that we are no less worthy than we were before, but dread and doubt do not permit us to believe it. (Cooley, 1902, p. 216)

There are three steps in the momentary process by which the social self gathers its delightful or bitter food from the minds of others:

1. the individual's perception of how he or she must appear to the other person,

2. the individual's interpretation of how the other person evaluates him or her on the basis of that interpreted perception, and

3. the individual's personally experienced affective response to the perceived judgment.

In other words, translated into a first-person scenario, the elements could be characterized as: "How do I appear to this person," "What does this person think about me (because of my appearance)," and "I feel (gratified or embarrassed or angry) toward myself because of this encounter." The interpretive nature of the elements described is critical. Here, for the clinician, the obvious likelihood arises that many, if not most, individuals project their own images of themselves onto the judging person(s) and then receive them back as objective feedback, confirmatory proof of what each had thought about himself or herself all along. The stronger and more rigid a person's tendency to project feelings, the less likely that person is to accurately attend to the feedback coming from the other individual.

Commentary. At first glance, it would appear that Cooley viewed people as being basically reactive, responding helplessly to others' opinions of them. Rather, he viewed the development of self as proceeding socially but assumed that maturity brings greater self-control to monitor and direct one's own responses, making one less vulnerable to the effects of others' opinions. The mature individual is sensitive to the feelings of others but maintains the stability to choose one's own direction. Cooley does not describe how the internalization takes place.

Like James, Cooley wrote a descriptive, theoretical work. Little is said about changing or enhancing self-esteem. However, he asserted that people should search for a balance between valuing others' judgments and opinions and developing their own stable ways of thinking, which "cannot be upset by passing phases of praise or blame." How one is to approach the correct balance is not mentioned. But Cooley believed that a judicious concern for the self (self-love) is appropriate. The more people understand themselves and prize their abilities, the more apt they are to risk performing in public, assuming that their assessment of themselves will be mirrored in the eyes of others.

George Herbert Mead. As a sociologist, Mead (1934) viewed the development of the self as most pertinent to the process of the individual's becoming an integrated part of a social group. His theory is concerned with the description of appropriate socialization, not self-esteem. As mentioned, Cooley's concept of the looking-glass self is extended in Mead's work. Language and society are essential elements in the development of the self because it is through interaction that individuals come to see themselves in the way in which others see them. Significant others in the individual's life have a determining influence on self-esteem. The socialization process that teaches people values about all other aspects of the world applies to the ways in which they see themselves. Observing the actions and attitudes of parents and significant others, an individual gradually adopts them and internalizes them as one's own, as though one were an external object:

> That process to which I have just referred, of responding to one's self as another responds to it, taking part in one's own conversation with others, being aware of what one is saying and using that awareness of what one is saying to determine what one is going to say thereafter that is a process with which we are all familiar. (Strauss, 1964, p. 205).

Without that socializing process, said Mead, social groups and communities could not function. Even children's games can be carried to some conclusion only because the attitudes of others about the rules of the game are accepted by all and, therefore, govern the activities. Individuals do not become complete selves until they can take the attitude of the groups they belong to as their own, including the attitude of the group toward themselves.

Commentary. Mead seemed to adopt the most passive stance thus far reviewed about the individual's ability to autonomously determine personal self-esteem. He wrote as if we looked at ourselves as objects, without attachment or affective loading toward the person who is oneself.

The implications of Mead's theory are obvious: To have high self-esteem, individuals must have been held in high esteem by significant others. If, as children, they were ignored, rejected, or demeaned, they will view themselves as objects worthy of such spite. They will think of themselves with impatience, derision, and scorn. The therapeutic inference, of course, is that people must find significant others who will validate them, see them as worthwhile, and communicate praise and encouragement. Slowly, people should come to see themselves that way.

Although therapists might object to the pictured helplessness of the person so damaged, many subscribe to the posture wherein the therapist is reparenting the client as the substitute good parent whom the child never had. Indeed, the work of Truax and Carkhuff (1967) asserted that the essential conditions for therapeutic improvement were based on the relationship elements of unconditional positive regard, genuineness, and nonpossessive warmth.

Gordon Allport. According to Allport (1961), the growth of the awareness of a self proceeds along developmental learning lines. From an early recognition of what is *me* and *not me* in the first year of life (a bodily awareness), a sense of continuity of identity over time in the second year, to a sense of self-esteem in the beginning of the third year, the child gradually adds parts to the sense of self. From ages 3 to 6 years, the concepts of self-image and extension of self (as seen in considering one's possessions a part of the self) come into focus. Here, children begin to learn what is expected of them to be considered good or bad persons.

Cognitive maturation in adolescence produces a sense of self as a thinker, for the first time able to be conscious of the self and consider the effects of one's own thought. The ability to consolidate the aspects of self into an individual and cohesive identity is a major task of adolescence. The final task in the developmental maturation of the aspects of the self is a goal-directedness (what Allport called *propriate striving*), a sense of purpose, knowing where one wants to go in life.

Allport named these elements of the self the *proprium*, using a new label to encompass all the aspects a person learns about the object *my self*. These are the parts that the individual knows about the self. There remains the *knower*, the part that has observed and organized the propriate elements into the identity.

Allport's major contribution to the study of self-esteem is the recognition of the part played by psychological defenses. Harking back to James's formula regarding the ratio between aspirations and achievements, he noted that a surprising number of people experience strong feelings of inferiority. He pointed to a study indicating that only 12% of a group of college students does *not* know what it is to suffer the anxiety of inferiority feelings (McKee & Sherriffs, 1957). When one occasionally feels the disappointment of failure, the individual can shrug off the feeling or make adjustments in goals. If, on the other hand, the sense of failure happens frequently, the result is Adler's *inferiority complex*, defined by Allport as "a strong and persistent tension arising from a somewhat morbid emotional attitude toward one's felt deficiency in his personal equipment" (Allport, 1961, p. 130).

At issue for the ultimate development of normal or abnormal personalities are the methods that each individual uses to combat the experience of inferiority. Some will exert greater effort and practice, making the problem become a strength instead of a perceived weakness; others will decide to pursue other goals; and still others will use psychological defenses, such as rationalization or denial, to avoid the pain of recognizing and facing the problem. The critical juncture for neurotic behavior occurs in the use or misuse of the psychological defenses:

The processes making for normality and for abnormality are very different. For example, to *confront* the world and its problems is intrinsically a wholesome thing to do, because it brings about appropriate adjustment and mastery; to *escape* from the world is intrinsically a dangerous and diseased thing to do. Extreme escape is found in the most severe forms of mental disorder, the psychoses. However, do we not all do some escaping? Yes and what is more, we may obtain recreation from it and find our daydreams eventually constructive. Yet, such harmless and even beneficial results can come about *only if the dominant process is confrontation;* left to itself, escapism spells abnormality. (Allport, 1961, p. 153)

The mechanisms of ego-defense are sly devices by which we try to circumvent discomfort and anxiety. These self-protective strategies are common, but they do not, by any means, constitute the normal person's entire repertoire of adjustive actions. Often, the person faces up to his weaknesses and failings and proceeds to cope with them realistically. He meets his guilt, his fears, he blunders head on, and works out a way of life that fully and consciously takes them into account and makes of them building blocks for a more integrated personal edifice. The opposite of defense, then, is coping. The neurotic shows much defense, less coping. In the healthy personality coping ordinarily predominates. (Allport, 1961, p. 156)

Commentary. Allport's theory was an individual psychology, relying on the presumption of learning and choice to explain both the development of the self and the trajectory of the personality toward normality or abnormality. The press of society and interaction was barely mentioned. Parental influences were only alluded to. Of the authors considered thus far, Allport is the first to emphasize clearly the importance of self-discipline, the courage to confront difficulties as the means toward mental health and greater self-esteem. As will be seen, his focus is a central issue addressed in the model to be presented.

Rollo May. In his consideration of *being* and *nonbeing,* May (1983) defined being as more than another name for self. It is one's *pattern of potentialities,* one's sense of one's totality as a separate and unique person. Individuals are aware, some more dimly than others, of their being, and the relationship of awareness to expression of potentialities is the pivotal balance between mental health and neurosis. All people have a fundamental need to remain "centered" in themselves, aware of their being, accepting their right to be, and willing to tolerate the anxiety attendant upon its fragility.

Repression occurs when individuals choose to block off from awareness some part of their being. Yet, for May, the individual still knows, at another level, that the blockage exists and that one's being is denied expression or, perhaps more accurately, existence. Neurotic symptoms appear as a response to an attack upon the individual's sense of existence centered in the self. People adjust to protect their being from attack, but in doing so narrow the range of their behavior, accepting some portion of nonbeing. Neurotic individuals live in a shrunken world, rigidly clinging to symptoms, which both preserves their centeredness and sacrifices other aspects of their being. In our contemporary culture, many individuals suffer a neuroticism that comes from slavish conformity, that is, outer-directed individuals who try so hard to please and identify with others that their own being is denied. The internal conflict between being and nonbeing creates anxiety, a uniquely human characteristic for May, which is different from any other emotion because it signals the individual's vulnerability to the many shades of nonbeing:

> The anxiety a person feels when someone he respects passes him on the street without speaking, for example, is not as intense as the fear he experiences when the dentist seizes the drill to attack a sensitive tooth. But the gnawing threat of the slight on the street may hound him all day long and torment his dreams at night, whereas the feeling of fear, though it was quantitatively greater, is gone for the time being as soon as he steps out of the dentist's chair. The difference is that the anxiety strikes at the central core of his self-esteem and his sense of value as a self, which is the most important aspect of his experience of himself as a being. (May, 1983, p. 110)

On the other hand, the presence of anxiety may also portend the freedom to fulfill a new potentiality. Recognizing the possibility of a new expression of the individual's being disrupts the self's security, calling into question other established patterns and beliefs about the self. Thus, the inherent risk entailed in change fosters a tendency to deny the potentiality, creating the conflict between being and nonbeing and the dread of anxiety.

Guilt, another singularly human emotion, is the inevitable consequence of denying one's potentialities. Thus, no one can successfully evade the responsibility to be, to become authentically oneself, without experiencing the anxiety and guilt associated with low self-esteem. The existential remedy to low self-esteem is clear. The individual must first become truly self-conscious, open to the recognition of one's potentialities and willing to tolerate the anxiety entailed by the conflict it will generate. Finally, a person must have the courage to be, living and accepting these potentialities.

> To the extent that my sense of existence is authentic, it is precisely *not* what others have told me I should be, but is the one Archimedes point I have to stand on from which to judge what parents and authorities demand. . . . The sense of being gives the person a basis for a self-esteem which is not merely the reflection of others' views about him. For if your self-esteem must rest in the long run on social validation, you have not self-esteem, but a more sophisticated form of social conformity. (May, 1983, p. 102)

May's explication of the conditions for self-esteem, embedded as they are in the search for being, emphasized the central importance of those conditions in the person's psychological life. True self-esteem cannot obtain, without authenticity, a person's willingness to express individuality in spite of the fact that others will undoubtedly exert pressure to change or deny it.

Commentary. May's work asserted the central importance of establishing autonomy to self-esteem. Psychological health requires individuality, listening to one's own being, and, therefore, aloneness. The person must repudiate or at least hold in suspicion any aspect of self that may have been defined by an outside source. However, it is also true for May that people need to venture from their centeredness to relate intimately to others. The critical question becomes: "How far can people risk their sense of being to participate with people about whom they care?"

Although May did not describe either the process of the development of being or the appropriate position of parents' nurturing, their place is emphasized indirectly when he speaks of the task of the existential therapist. The essential first task of therapists is to reach across the gap between their existence and that of their clients, to create a communion within which clients can begin to experience safely their own separate but unique existence.

Carl R. Rogers. The personality theory of Carl Rogers (1951) is an inductive summary of his extensive experience as a psychotherapist. Developed gradually from his clinical observations and systematized into 19 propositions, Rogers viewed the condition of the self as being the pivotal factor in determining a person's emotional health. Like existential therapists, he viewed the essential condition for maladjustment to be a schism between what he called the individual's own organismic valuing of events and the values that he or she consciously asserts. More will be said of this later.

Rogers was a phenomenologist, asserting that each person lives in a private and unique world of one's own perceptions, responding to the environment from the window of personal awareness. It is the individual's reality, the perceptual map that one uses to choose actions and interpret others' responses. The developing infant gradually distinguishes between that part of this private world that is *me* and the portion that is *not me*. Within the gradually developing sense of self, the child places a value, negative or positive, on those experiences deemed satisfying and enhancing or, conversely, threatening.

Because all people need acceptance, especially early in development, evaluation from others may violate the child's organismic valuing process. A prototypical example is the child who enjoys experiencing a bowel movement whenever and wherever he or she wishes. Yet, the parents angrily communicate the message that the child is not loved and, therefore, in danger of being rejected for defecating at will. The resultant conflict may coerce the child into distrusting the internal sense of self, seeing it as dangerous and to be repudiated. The child may also adopt or introject the values of the parents and define them as his or her own. For Rogers, *introjects* from parents or others are distorted symbolizations of experience and, therefore, can never match the sensed validity of direct experiencing.

> It is here, it seems, that the individual begins on a pathway which he later describes as "I don't really know myself." The primary sensory and visceral reactions are ignored, or not permitted into consciousness, except in distorted form. The values which might be built upon them cannot be admitted to awareness. A concept of self based in part upon a distorted symbolization has taken their place. (Rogers, 1951, p. 501)

The perceived self grows out of the configuration of the directly experienced self and the distorted introjects. When a perception enters the consciousness that is distinctly at variance with the self as structured, the individual either denies its meaning or further distorts it. In that fashion, the self now channelizes or narrows the range of information and behaviors available to the person, confirming the structure of the self as one's definition of one's identity. If a substantial discrepancy exists between the person's organismic experiencing and the self-concept, tension and anxiety build as a result of the conflict between the organism's effort to satisfy its needs and the conscious self's attempt to remain unaware of those needs. The person may feel "like I'm coming undone."

How does psychological treatment help? Rogers's definition of the goal of therapy is the restructuring of the self. That restructuring process must be accomplished by the individual alone, of course, because the therapist's values would become another introject. The therapist's task is to create an atmosphere of acceptance and desire to understand. Therein, the counselor establishes a *safe place* for clients in which to permit themselves to explore their experience gradually and to compare their own sense of valuing as a process against the static codes of the introjected value system. As clients come to know the real *me*, they can accept into awareness all the aspects of their organismic experiencing, respect and recognize their impulses, and consciously control their responding in a congruent manner. Clients will experience more spontaneity and also more accountability because all of their experiences will be available to consciousness:

> The client finds that it is his own organism which supplies the evidence upon which value judgments may be made. He discovers that his own senses, his own physiological equipment, can provide the data for making value judgments and for continuously revising them. No one needs to tell him that it is good to act in a freer and more spontaneous fashion, rather than in the rigid way to which he has been accustomed. He senses, he feels that it is satisfying and enhancing. Or when he acts in a defensive fashion, it is his own organism that feels the immediate and short-term satisfaction of being protected and that also senses the longer-range dissatisfaction of having to remain on guard. (Rogers, 1951, p. 523)

Rogers anticipated the reader's possible concern that total trust of one's organismic valuing process may lead to anarchy. Rogers's experience as a psychotherapist was that the opposite is true. Because people share many fundamental needs, he found that each individual responds to a personal valuing process with a high degree of commonality. Each person, therefore, creates a unique and personal value system, but one that is genuinely socialized.

Commentary. Like other writers whom we have considered, Rogers's thrust in understanding self-esteem was directed toward an individual's learning to know the self or perhaps, more accurately, learning to know the self that he or she is. Rogers differed in the sense that the self to be discovered is not the self's abilities or interests (the cognitive–achievement domain), but the person's values and even affective preferences. Rogers asserted that each person's most deeply held values are fundamentally beneficent and social. Adler similarly asserted that the biological substrate of all people is socially oriented but suggests that it must be nurtured and trained in order to make itself manifest. Rogers seemed to suggest that the organismic valuing process is the only source necessary for calibration of values.

Summary and Comparison

Let us consider how the early theories address to the issue of self-esteem. How does a person develop high self-esteem? For James, the person chooses an identity, a self, and successfully matches accomplishment to hopes. People become what they have hoped they are. Self-esteem is dependent on outcomes, that is on setting goals and reaching them. For Adler, the person creates a style of life that fulfills the biological predicates of being human, feeling a belongingness, and of contributing to the social interest. The person becomes what personal evolution and appropriate parenting have prepared one to be. Self-esteem is dependent on accepting imperfectness and still striving to complete the goals of a chosen style of life. For Cooley and Mead, the person is fortunate to have an environment that esteems one and the talents to win approbation. People come to see themselves approvingly because others see them approvingly. Self-esteem depends upon winning approbation from significant others. For Allport, the person develops an appropriate goal-directedness and responds to threat with healthy psychological defenses. The individual becomes psychologically healthy by coping with difficulties instead of avoiding them. For May, the person is willing to recognize all of one's being and to respond congruently to that which is the self. One becomes oneself in spite of pressure to deny or distort aspects of being. Self-esteem depends on the courage to allow all of oneself to exist. For Rogers, the person trusts the organismic valuing processes, choosing a life consistent with those deeply held values. Like May, Rogers suggests that high-self-esteem persons become themselves and not the introjects foisted upon them by others. Self-esteem depends upon the courage to become and remain authentic.

Our proposed model will be presented in its entirety in the next several chapters. However, it is useful to compare it briefly to the theories described above. We assert that self-esteem in the adult is an internal process that focuses upon the inherently self-affirming or self-negating evaluations that obtain inexorably from observing oneself respond to psychological threat. Although it is important to be approved of, we suggest that, fundamentally, self-esteem is not dependent on winning approbation, nor does it require the existence of an articulated self dependent on congruent responding. We suggest that the essential construction of self-esteem occurs in the process of exercising coping or, conversely, avoidance responses, not in their outcome as judged by meeting goals.

Recent Conceptual Developments

Self-esteem propositions have emerged from contemporary research in social psychology. Until recently, the study of self-esteem as a focus for research has yielded disappointingly few results. Ruth Wylie (1961, 1974, 1979) comprehensively reviewed the measurement of self-esteem and its relationship to theory. She concluded:

> Internal inconsistency apparently characterizes all personality theories which emphasize constructs concerning the self, although the vagueness of their statements often makes it impossible to identify inconsistencies with certainty. On this score alone, none of these theories, as presently formulated, can be called wholly scientific. Probably these inconsistencies are partly responsible for the poor state of measurement and research design in this area. (1974, p. 322)

Contemporary reviews, however, have asserted that research in self-concept is finally coming of age. In Wylie (1979), the review of measures of self-concept is much more optimistic:

> It is encouraging that there is much more essential and sophisticated information about the instruments reviewed in detail than there was for those reviewed in Wylie (1974). On the other hand, none of those discussed here has been em-

pirically evaluated in all the desirable ways. This should both induce caution among potential users of these instruments and inspire researchers to plan further explorations of the meaning and appropriate applicability of the scores obtained from them. None of the published information warrants using any of the [*sic*] these instruments as tools for diagnosing individuals. (p. 121)

Markus and Wurf (1987) claim the progress has come about through a decision to abandon the attempt to study self-esteem as a global, unidimensional entity. Measurement of the self-concept is becoming increasingly viewed as being influenced both by the self-motives being served as well as the press of the immediate social situation. Researchers have also chosen to examine more fine-grained behaviors. Thus, the self is seen as

. . . a dynamic interpretive structure that mediates most significant *intrapersonal* processes (including information processing, affect, and motivation), and a wide variety of *interpersonal* processes (including social perception; choice of situation, partner, and interaction strategy; and reaction to feedback). (p. 300)

Disparity Models

As illustrated earlier in the book, one of the most intriguing theoretical questions for the clinician is, "How is it that so many apparently successful people privately experience such negative self-esteem?" As suggested above, we propose that the answer lies in the individual's choosing to avoid difficult situations rather than coping with them and doing so in a manner that is, at some level, unacceptable to the self. The individual's self-evaluations are, therefore, negative in spite of the possibly laudatory judgments of significant people in one's life.

Other authors have suggested the importance of disparity to explain negative self-esteem. Higgins (1983) and his associates (Higgins, Klein, & Strauman, 1985) hypothesized three classes of self-conceptions: the *actual* self (the doer or performer of tasks), the *ideal* self (representing the attributes that, in fantasy, the person would like to possess as an ideal conception), and the *ought* self (representing characteristics that the person reasonably expects to achieve). Discrepancy among classes of self produces discomfort. Thus, Higgins et al. (1985) found that depression was correlated with disparities between the actual and ideal selves, whereas anxiety was more likely to be associated with disparities between the actual and ought selves. Higgins and other researchers (Moretti & Higgins, 1990) have also shown that both positive ideal–actual self discrepancies and negative ideal–actual discrepancies significantly predict self-esteem. Chronic discrepancies between the actual and ideal self may make it difficult for the individuals to integrate positive feedback into their construction of the self (Moretti & Higgins, 1990). Generally, it is widely assumed that chronic disparities of either kind yield a pervasive sense of negative self-esteem.

Rosenberg's (1979) major study of adolescent self-esteem posited a similar classification of selves: the extant self (as one privately views oneself), the desired self (as one would like to be), and the presenting self (the self one attempts to disclose to others). It must be remembered, Rosenberg cautions, no one knows the real self, but each individual creates and interprets images of the self. There is no way to know who we really are. People must impose a construction on their acts without ever truly being able to verify their assumptions. Still, many people attempt to get verification of their worth from others.

Within the extant self, Rosenberg differentiated between self-confidence and self-esteem. Self-confidence is closely related to Bandura's (1977) concept of *self-efficacy* (the expectation of successfully meeting challenges and overcoming obstacles, and a general sense of control of self and the environment). Self-esteem is more an affective sense of accepting one's self and feeling self-worth. Thus, self-confidence may contribute to self-esteem, but the two are not synonymous. A person may expect to succeed at any task and still not accept such accomplishments as *counting* or being worthy of self-respect.

Like Higgins's (1983) conceptions of the self described above, Rosenberg described the desired self as having an idealized component and a *committed* component, which is that part of the desired self that we really think we can become. A third component is the *moral self*, which is more or less a set of standards and values to which the individual feels obligated rather than to an actual image. Its particular importance in self-esteem is the condemnation that follows violation of one's standards. The experience of self-condemnation seems to represent more direct damage to self-esteem than other failures. Rosenberg cites the example of the soldier who commits suicide because he fled under fire. Ironically, he kills himself *as punishment for being afraid of being killed.*

The importance of the presenting self, or self as shown to others, appears in the attempts that people make to manage the impressions that they create. Herein, the theoretical issue of disparity conflict becomes particularly meaningful. The moral self may be discrepant from the image that the individual holds privately and may, therefore, conflict with other components of the self-concept. It may view one's attempt to impress others as putting on an act and, therefore, as duplicitous and shameful. Moreover, because any positive feedback one receives is attributed derisively to an acting ability, a person cannot believe what may be sincere praise. A second possibility is that the extant self may view one's pretensions as committing one's self to a performance standard about which the person may not feel confident privately. This self-doubt vitiates the individual's commitment and concentration when there is performance pressure.

Another alternative observed by clinicians is that of an individual who is sufficiently insecure in the verification process of the extant self that one constantly seeks verification from others. This person may be in the vulnerable position of having to convince others about having certain characteristics in order to convince the self about having them. The individual lives in the constant apprehension of not knowing who the self is and that the image just confirmed by one person may be invalidated by another.

Greenwald and Breckler (1985) proposed a developmental sequence by which four facets of the self emerge, viewing the process as analogous to Loevinger's (1976) theories of ego development. The *diffuse* self is actually a preself, a self oriented only to survival and pleasure needs. It is not a true self because it does not represent an object of knowledge. That is, the diffuse self occurs before the child has sufficient self-consciousness to form a concept of self. The *public* self gradually develops out of the realization that many pleasures come from pleasing powerful others. It is sensitive to evaluation from others, seeking to win approval and social verification of worth. The public self provides a forum for the development of values and a gradual definition of self apart from public evaluation, forming the *private* self. The self now has an inner audience for evaluation, creating more sensitivity to its own attitudes and affective states. A final self, the *collective* self, forms as the individual identifies with and internalizes the goals of the reference group. The individual's goals now transcend being concerned about pleasing others or meeting personal needs for achievement; they are focused on advancing the tasks of the group.

For Greenwald and Breckler, the existence of private and public selves suggests the likelihood of private and public self-esteem. Negative self-esteem can occur at any level when failures occur in the face of expected success. However, the additional possibility arises that the goals of the individual's private and public selves conflict, yielding a new source for self-dissatisfaction. In the presence of important others, people may seek to meet needs of social accreditation that, in the privacy of a later hour, they may repudiate as unworthy of the private self's need for achievement.

Situated identities versus general identity. Schlenker (1985) views a central activity of the self as being the identification of self's characteristics and abilities. Comprehending one's identity is integral to self-regulation, making self-judgments about potential success or failure in endeavors, or evaluating accomplishments. Schlenker defines the individual's identity as one's comprehensive theory of oneself, identical to the self-concept. However, there are frequently times when a person may be placed in a social circumstance in which environmental pressures force a *situated identity,* an identity of the moment. This identity may or may not match the characteristics of the generalized identity.

Discrepancies between the situated identity and generalized identity may occur when the individual attempts to construe information about the self in what is perceived to be a more acceptable image or when others influence the person to adopt a distorted identity that meets their desires. Conflict occurs when the individual attempts to create a particular impression of self to one's audience that contradicts the self-as-audience. If the discrepancy continues over time, the conflict between the situated identity and the generalized identity threatens other desired images of the self-concept, particularly one's sense of integrity.

Other events may foster low self-esteem. Failure, which may or may not be the responsibility of the individual, or the consistently negative behavior of others may create an identity image that is worse than the one desired. Again, if the discrepancy persists, such as one might find in a denigrating occupational relationship or a difficult marriage, the situated identity negatively affects the generalized identity over time, producing negative self-reactions and, perhaps, serious personal problems.

Another characteristic of the self-defining identity is the assessment of likelihood of success in reaching goals. If individuals anticipate success, they are apt to concentrate on the task and persist in the face of obstacles, thereby facilitating performance. On the other hand, if individuals assesses their chances of success as being poor, they will avoid the task if possible or give up when they experience difficulty. Schlenker's conclusions about the effect upon the individual who anticipates failure but cannot escape the situation are a fascinating description for the clinician:

> When actual withdrawal is blocked, people become frozen or locked in assessments of self, situation, audience, and the problem. Their minds race with thoughts about the unreachable goal and their inability to attain it; they become self-preoccupied and self-focused, continually reexamining their limitations. The combination of cognitive withdrawal from the difficult situation (e.g., fantasizing about more preferred activities, outcomes, and being anywhere but where one is at the moment) and self-preoccupation produces distraction and further debilitates social performance. Information pro-

cessing declines in effectiveness, reducing sensitivity to ongoing events, and self-monitoring and self-control worsen. . . . People whose personality characteristics and life situations continually expose them to problems in constructing and maintaining desired identities become chronically anxious, fearing the worst in any particular situation and avoiding interpersonal interactions as much as possible, producing a spiral into loneliness. (Schlenker, 1985, pp. 88–89)

Commentary. As suggested earlier, the above models view self-esteem as a component part in the construction of the self. The disparity between different selves or identities is thought to be a major source of low self-esteem. In contrast to the historical theorists, current authors view the selves as being more personalized and capable of conflict. That is, James and Cooley both described different selves but seemed to consider them as simply contributing different sources of information to the total self-concept. Each of the current authors regards the selves as separate entities of the *me*, which, when in conflict, create discomfort and self-denigration by the executive ego, *I*.

Like Allport, Greenwald and Breckler posited a developmental process, but again, they considered the public, private, and collective selves as more complete and personalized than Allport does. Self-esteem for them would seem to hinge on the maturation process, and the particular successes / pretensions tasks would vary correspondingly. Thus, one would expect that while a person is currently in a public-self stage, popularity and praise would be most important for high self-esteem. Later, the importance of praise would wane in favor of private approval for integrity, for instance. Still, the disparity or conflict among the goals of the separate selves is seen as the primary seedbed for low self-esteem.

Self-concept as a self-theory. Others (Greenberg et al., 1992) have shown that self-esteem serves as a buffer against anxiety.

Epstein (1973, 1979a, 1979b), another contemporary theorist, focused on the hypothesized activities of the executive ego, *I*. He proposed that one can gain a meaningful understanding of the self-concept by conceiving of it as a self-theory. The *I* attempts to make sense of the *me*'s abilities and interests as it interfaces with its world to achieve certain ends.

> It is a theory that the individual has unwittingly constructed about himself as an experiencing, functioning individual, and it is part of a broader theory which he holds with respect to his entire range of significant experience. . . . Like most theories, the self-theory is a conceptual tool for accomplishing a purpose. The most fundamental purpose of the self-theory is to *optimize the pleasure/pain balance of the individual over a course of a lifetime.* Two other basic functions, not unrelated to the first, are to *facilitate the maintenance of self-esteem,* and to *organize the data of experience in a manner that can be coped with effectively.* (Epstein, 1973, p. 407)

Although Epstein recognized the commonalities between his conceptualization and George Kelley's (1955) self-as-a-scientist theory, Epstein proposed that the role of emotion is much more central to the functioning of self-theory than that accorded it by Kelley. Indeed, many of the problems attendant upon negative self-esteem are seen as distortions that occur as a result of stress and anxiety. Because no theory is completely valid, the usefulness of the self-theory depends upon its approximation to reality and its ability to self-correct in the face of disconfirming evidence.

As a child develops, his or her self-theory is initially easily overwhelmed by emotions. Over time, however, the individual's cognitive capacities increasingly affect and modulate the power of emotion. Epstein assumes that the individual experiences exhilaration when the self-theory expands by assimilating new information or resolving inner conflict. The experience becomes a motivator to continue to explore and expand the individual's conceptual system.

As might be expected, anxiety occurs when new information is not currently assimilable. This conflict motivates the person either to search more strenuously for resolution or to defend against the anxiety by creating defenses to protect the system. When, because of overwhelming stress to the system, the individual shuts the self off from corrective experiences, the self-theory becomes restricted and less valid, leading inexorably to the defeat of the basic purposes of the theory. Self-esteem is damaged, the individual is exposed to more painful experiences, and the incoming data are distorted, preventing self-correction of the theory. For Epstein, the result is neurosis or, in extreme cases, psychotic retreat from reality.

Chronically low self-esteem provides an interesting paradox in Epstein's model. Given that one of the major purposes of the self-theory is to enhance self-esteem, why do some people act in ways that appear to deliberately destroy self-esteem? Epstein suggests that chronically low self-esteem is preferable to individuals than precipitous disconfirming experiences, which cause a sudden drop in self-esteem. Expecting further assaults upon self-esteem, these people devalue themselves, opting for the dull ache of low self-esteem rather than the sharp pain that comes of hoping for more success, only to be dashed against the shoals of what they assume to be harsh reality.

Some recent evidence supports this view. Tice (1993), for example, has argued that people with low self-esteem attempt to protect themselves by avoiding circumstances that may expose them as failures. Therefore, only situations that carry a low risk of embarrassment are likely to be tried by people with low self-esteem.

Commentary. Epstein has restored the maintenance of self-esteem as a central function of the self's activities. His emphasis, however, is less on the congruence of selves or match between aspirations and achievements than it is on the individual's sense of control. Having confidence in predicting and, then, meeting one's expectations of the self is the source of high self-esteem. Low self-esteem results from inaccurate or distorted perceptions, which create confusion and distrust of one's capabilities. Moreover, he provides an explanation of the psychological economy of the self-hating individual and why such a person actively chooses self-denigration. His description of the resistance and anxiety attendant upon a low-self-esteem person's belief in good things about the self sounds a resonant chord with the psychotherapist.

Summary and comparison. Recent conceptualizations have emerged in response to the inconsistent findings of self-concept research, wherein the self is postulated as a unitary, global construct. Compartmentalization of the self into several selves that may disapprove of one another creates a cognitive mechanism whereby negative self-esteem may be experienced. Similarly, Schlenker uses a cognitive evaluation process by which the self assesses the possibility of success. When the expectation of success is low, but the opportunity for escape is blocked, the affective consequences of the threatening situation include injured self-feeling. Epstein takes the cognitive process one step further, creating a self whose task it is to construct an accurate theory of itself. In the press of anxiety, this scientific self may reach inaccurate conclusions, which are ineffective in reaching the goals of maximizing pleasure and preserving self-esteem. Collectively, it appears that this group of studies addresses more low or negative self-esteem than the conditions for high self-esteem. Moreover, the generic solution to the question of how low self-esteem is created requires a two-stage cognitive evaluation process: (a) different selves or identities within the person create cognitive or cognitive–affective conflict, and (b) the disparity or conflict engenders a self-evaluation that is negative.

By contrast, the proposed model requires no such complex cognitions. Instead, we support the work of Pelham and Swann (1989) who argue that the cognitive approach to alleviating low self-esteem fails to consider affective origins. We propose that the process of simply observing oneself repeatedly avoid a conflict situation inherently communicates, to the self, a cognitive–affective message of some admixture of shame, fear, helplessness, and sense of inadequacy.

To this point, the literature reviewed has considered the nature of adult self-esteem. Indeed, as suggested earlier, many of the conceptualizations of self-esteem would require adult cognitive capacity to perform the operations attendant upon the theory. The immaturity of the developing child has been included peripherally at best. We have found that, although no authors attempt to construct the inner world of the child's self-esteem, several writers have studied the environmental characteristics that foster or inhibit its development. We turn now to their work.

Developmental Considerations

As expected, the child's parents are considered to be the central players on the stage of enhancing or denigrating the child's sense of self; however, it will be seen that some psychologists hold the school environment to be an equally potent contributor.

For most theorists considering the self-concept, there seems to be a generic expectation about the development of the positive or negative quality of self-evaluation: Parents reward or punish the child's attempts to grow and define the self. Gradually, the child internalizes the expectations of parents or of significant others, judging the self by the same standards. As the child matures, the disparate parts of the self coalesce into an identity with expectations of its own about success and failure (which influence its outcome). As self-definition proceeds, the self-concept becomes more resistant to change, protecting itself to maintain consistency. Some of the authors reviewed below have not examined in any great depth the actual course of self-esteem development; instead, their focus has been on this question: What are the characteristics of those significant others who foster negative or positive self-esteem?

Stanley Coopersmith. Coopersmith's (1967) *Antecedents of Self-Esteem*, a well-known work in this area, suggested four major factors that contribute to the development of self-esteem:

1. the value that the child perceives others to have toward the self—expressed in affection, praise, and concerned attention;

2. the child's experience with successes—the status or position that one perceives oneself to hold in the environment;

3. the child's individual definition of success or failure—the aspirations and demands one places upon oneself to determine what constitutes success; and

4. the child's style of dealing with negative feedback or criticism.

Because all people must experience devaluating events, the child's capacity to respond in ways that are not self-denigrating is significant. The central role of parents in each of the factors is obvious.

Coopersmith's (1969) evaluation of parents of high-self-esteem children suggested the importance of three general conditions in the home. First, the parents communicate clearly their *acceptance* of the children, as suggested above. The children know that they *belong* in the family, that they are prized and valued members. Second, parents communicate *well-defined limits* and *high expectations for performance*. The children recognize expectations for mature behavior and their parents' confidence in their ability. Third, parents *respect* the children's individuality, allowing them *latitude* to be different and unique within the general boundaries established. Contrary to the expectation of other writers, Coopersmith finds that high self-esteem and creativity are more likely to follow from well-structured environments, with limits and demands, than from open-ended, exploratory settings. He suggests that appropriately paced demands for greater competence foster improved capacity, that children will recognize their own growth, and that they will take pride (a stronger sense of competence and worth) in their accomplishments.

Parents' own experienced competence and self-esteem are also significant factors. The child observes the parents' confidence, their approach to challenge, and their method for dealing with difficulties or disappointment. The child may observe them evaluate their good points as well as deficiencies in the face of criticism, learning how they operate to define an event as a challenge rather than a threat. Children's positive expectations of themselves are much more likely to be fulfilled if they have observed their parents model those attributes.

Coopersmith found that, when parents communicate the qualities of acceptance, clearly defined limits, and respect for individuality, their children are more apt to be self-motivated. He hypothesizes that the children become confident enough in their own judgment that their self-rewards are more important than the external sanctions of others.

In addition to data regarding parental characteristics, Coopersmith describes other salient attributes of children with positive and negative self-esteem. For instance, he finds that popularity is unrelated to self-esteem, that is, although popularity does predict people's ability to present themselves as poised and confident, favorable attitudes about the self are not strongly affected. Self-judgment of worthiness apparently requires more internally defined qualities, even in children.

Individuals with high self-esteem trust their judgment and decisions, thereby enabling them to pursue personal directions that differ from the group. Coopersmith finds that children with more self-trust are more aware of their own opinions and more willing to express their convictions in the face of opposition. By contrast, children who are insecure in their assessment of their abilities tend to be cautious, unwilling to enter controversy or expose themselves to criticism. Coopersmith hypothesizes that low-self-esteem children are self-critical and, therefore, expect the same criticism from others, accepting negative statements about themselves from others as true, being congruent with their own observations:

> The judgments, being internal, cannot be evaded and hence serve as constant reminders of inferiority. They result in an omnipresent malaise marked by preoccupation with the self and attention to shortcomings and deficiencies. This preoccupation is masochistic in its consequences if not in intent. By dwelling upon their ineptitude and insufficiencies, those low in self-esteem are exacerbating their point of greatest sensibility and, at the same time, reducing their opportunity for obtaining successes. (1967, p. 69)

An assumptive link between the individual's self-doubts and parental practices is the child's experiencing of what Coopersmith calls *power* in relationships. Children sense their own power in the respect given to their opinions and rights. Thus, parents who recognize their children's individuality, giving them greater opportunity to choose their own direction, foster the children's confidence, inoculating them to resist pressure to conform without their own approval. Coopersmith defines the resultant characteristic as *courage* "the attitudinal posture an individual adopts to attain or maintain actions consistent with his beliefs" (1967, p. 56).

Diana Baumrind. Baumrind (1963, 1966, 1971, 1975) did not study self-esteem as such; her search was for *competence* in children. Observing the behaviors of preschool children over a three-month period, Baumrind identified three groups of children who differ in their self-reliance, self-control, happiness, and ability to respond appropriately to adults as well as peers. Then she observed the behaviors of the children's parents to ascertain the parental characteristics of the competent children.

Baumrind (1975) designated the resultant patterns of parental control as *authoritative, authoritarian,* and *permissive.* Those parents whom she describes as authoritative are the parents of children most apt to be competent. The parents are warm, rational, and attentive to the child's expressed needs. They are also controlling and demanding, expressing high expectations for achievement. According to Baumrind, "These parents balanced much warmth with high control, and high demands with clear communication about what was required of the child" (1975, p. 275).

Citing characteristics similar to those noted by Coopersmith, Baumrind described authoritative parents as respecting the child's independent decisions but being firm about a position they have taken. Demands upon the child are accompanied by reasons.

Children who are relatively more discontented, withdrawn, and distrustful experience the parenting style Baumrind classified as authoritarian. These parents apparently value obedience and respect above any other virtues: respect for authority, respect for work, and respect for order and tradition. Authoritarian parents are found to be more detached but controlling, with little interest in explaining their reasoning to their children. While they stress responsible behavior, Baumrind observed that they do not model responsibility to the same degree as the authoritative parents. More concerned with their own ideas and standards, they sometimes neglect the child's interests and welfare. Recent research (Buri, 1988) has further suggested the value of differentiating betweem authoritativeness and authoritarianism as it relates to self-esteem. Buri reported that parental authoritativeness was positively correlated to self-esteem, whereas authoritarianism was inversely related to self-esteem.

The parents of the least mature children are described by Baumrind as permissive. These parents are relatively warm (although less so than the authoritative parents) but lax in discipline, making only weak demands for maturity upon the child. Lacking the attention and training for independence, the children of permissive parents behave immaturely, dependently, and demandingly. They are least prepared to interact or play cooperatively with peers. As a result of her research, Baumrind takes issue with the oft-used concept of unconditional love as being the essence of good modern parenting:

> The parent who expresses love unconditionally is encouraging the child to be selfish and demanding while she herself is not. Thus, she reinforces exactly the behavior which she does not approve of greedy, demanding, inconsiderate behavior. . . . I believe that a parent expresses her love most fully when she demands of the child that he become his best, and in the early years helps him to act in accordance with *her* image of the noble, the beautiful, and the best, as an initial model upon which he can create (in the adolescent years) his own ideal. (1975, p. 278)

Commentary. The work of Coopersmith and that of Baumrind are remarkably similar in their findings regarding the correlation between high self-esteem in parents and competence in their children. The qualities of emotional warmth, high expectations for achievement, and respect for individuality parallel the themes of earlier writers, emphasizing two major dimensions of self-esteem: acceptance and individuality. In addition, their separate studies point to the importance of parental modeling, both of their own self-esteem and of their approach to problems. Thus, parents affect the child both directly, in their expression of acceptance and discipline, and indirectly, when they demonstrate to the child the behaviors that build esteem. The effect that a parent has on a child is probably dependent on the stage of ego development of the child (Isberg et al., 1989) as well as the orientation that the child has toward the adult (Hoffman, Levy-Shiff, & Ushpiz, 1993). Children at lower stages of ego development are more dependent on parents' evaluations than children at higher stages of development. Additionally, the children that value their parents are more likely to be affected by support from them.

A parent reading Baumrind and Carl Rogers for implications about child rearing would, of course, find a fundamental philosophical conflict. Baumrind particularly warns parents that the lack of control and absence of demand for responsible behavior, connoted by unconditional love, will foster immature and confused children. Rogers, on the other hand, reports that individuals who experience what he might call the intrusiveness suggested by Baumrind will become constricted and confused children. There is no easy resolution of the conflict; the controversy represents a centuries-old value choice among philosophers, such as Rousseau's trust of the individual's innate benevolence versus Locke's emphasis on the necessity of training for citizenship.

Martin Covington and Richard Beery. In a small book, *Self-Worth and School Learning,* Covington and Beery (1976) asserted that there are institutional pressures toward low self-esteem so ubiquitous throughout American education as to be unnoticed. Schools have become institutions of evaluation in which an individual's worth is measured by achievement, rather than institutions of learning. Constant evaluation makes children excessively fearful of making mistakes, seeing school grades as a test of one's worth, while worth is synonymous with ability. Surveys indicate that older students devalue success that comes through hard work, whereas success achieved solely on the basis of ability is more highly regarded. Indeed, a comparison between Japanese and American students found that Japanese students believed effort was the most important characteristic to guarantee success, whereas American students chose ability as the best predictor (Covington & Beery, 1976). It is little wonder, then, that self-esteem becomes so bound to the concept of ability. In classrooms in which examinations and grades are seen as evidence of ability, students daily face threat to their self-esteem. Covington and Beery observe:

> Out of such anguish and frustration a fateful decision is often made, unwittingly and without regard for the consequences. In essence, the student may reason that if he cannot be sure of succeeding, then at least he can protect his dignity by avoiding the experience of failure, with its implications for demoting his belief in his ability. (p. 7)

Although there are several identifiable strategies for avoiding failure, the ironic outcome is that usually students must act in ways that eventually foster overt failure in their struggle to avoid the feelings of failure. They may procrastinate, or blame relationships with teachers, or insist that they do not care about the outcome, all in the search for a means to protect themselves from finding out that they may not have the requisite ability. Thus, failure-avoiding students continue to harbor doubts about their ability, experience anxiety in any evaluation situation, and usually need additional assurances of success before risking the effort. The authors insist that the sheer number of threatening evaluation experiences in school may make the institution as powerful a force in shaping self-esteem as that of parents.

Covington and Beery noted a sometimes hidden variation of failure-avoiding (and low-self-esteem) individuals in school, the *overstrivers*. These students seem to be driven to perform, are unable to enjoy their successes, and react immoderately to any signal of failure. The authors note that, frequently, these students set strict, unforgiving self-standards that are almost impossible to achieve, often criticizing themselves unmercifully for mistakes. Why would people needlessly punish themselves so continually? The authors suggest that self-criticism becomes a symbolic expiation for the sin of being less than perfect. Thus, the self-punishment is followed by a sense of relief, reducing anxiety and guilt, which has a reinforcing value for the individual. The behavior is, of course, a vicious circle, setting up more opportunities for failure, anxiety, self-punishment, and so forth. The root cause, fear of negative evaluation, remains intact.

Students who, by dint of early experiences, believe in their ability choose an orientation of striving for success. Presumably, they approach new challenges with greater confidence and less anxiety (and, therefore, greater ability to concentrate), and they persevere longer when faced with obstacles. Their successes teach these students to see themselves as equal to most school tasks. More importantly, when occasional failure does occur, their interpretation of the event is that they did not exert enough effort. Thus, failure does not represent a threat, in that their ability is not impugned in the failure.

Success strivers may receive plaudits from others, but the intrinsic reinforcement that comes from stretching to meet new goals is most powerful. Moreover, for Covington and Beery, these people's acquaintance with success inoculates them against the damage that they might experience when limits are finally reached. Success strivers are better equipped to accept their limits gracefully without devaluing themselves. They, then, can maintain their aspirations for success in other endeavors.

Commentary. Covington and Beery's assertions may be particularly trenchant in light of both theoretical and research findings described earlier. James' basic successes / pretensions formula assumes that people can choose the areas in which they commit themselves to performance. In school, those alternatives are severely narrowed by curriculum demands. Moreover, Schlenker (1985) described the self-defining process as one in which the individual is continually assessing the likelihood of success. If, for whatever reason, children have experienced failure in school evaluations, they will be likely to assess their future chances as poor and threatening. They will attempt to withdraw or by other means defend themselves against the anticipated humiliation, usually setting in motion the events that will later guarantee further failure.

Summary and comparison. The proposed model is directed essentially toward adult self-esteem, assuming, as it does, that the individual has the cognitive ability to observe the self; hence, little comparison can be made directly to the model from the child-rearing and self-esteem literature. Chapter 9 of this volume, however, provides an examination of the implications of the model for child rearing. Our more limited work in the developmental processes for self-esteem corroborates the importance of the findings of Coopersmith and of Baumrind. We suggest, however, that their findings have not been taken far enough, and that the relative emphasis of nurturance, performance expectations, and respect for individuality should shift to match the developmental needs of the child. In addition, we suggest that a frequent parental error may be that children are socialized developmentally only to Loevinger's public self stage, leaving them unprepared for appropriate individuation.

Thus far, we have considered the historical beginnings of a theory of self-esteem, more recent derivations from social psychological research, and environmental antecedents in childhood. The final section of the chapter reviews therapeutic efforts to promote self-esteem or treat problems of low self-esteem.

Therapeutic Remediation of Low Self-Esteem

Apart from the applications suggested by the theorists reviewed earlier (May, 1983; Rogers, 1951), a search of the literature for treatment of low self-esteem finds a dearth of relevant, focused comment. There are, however, some articles that speak directly to the treatment of low self-esteem, including a major thrust by Bandura (1977) in the related concept of self-efficacy.

Bandura (1977) noted the growth of cognitive behavioral therapy and the emerging theoretical importance of cognitive processes in behavior change. Expectations about one's self and one's efficacy in performing particular tasks become a primary mediator affecting outcome. Bandura suggests that individuals ask themselves two questions as they approach any performance challenge: "What behavior will it require to accomplish this task?" and, "Do I have the ability to perform those behaviors?" People's perceptions regarding their own effectiveness will affect whether they will even attempt the task or, having begun, persist when difficulties arise.

People fear and tend to avoid threatening situations that they believe exceed their coping skills, whereas they get involved in activities and behave with assurance when they judge themselves capable of handling situations that would otherwise be intimidating:

> Not only can perceived self-efficacy have directive influence on choice of activities and settings, but, through expectations of eventual success, it can affect coping efforts once they are initiated. . . . The stronger the perceived self-efficacy, the more active the efforts. Those who persist in subjectively threatening activities that are in fact relatively safe will gain corrective experiences that reinforce their sense of efficacy, thereby eventually eliminating their defensive behavior. Those who cease their coping efforts prematurely will retain their self-debilitating expectations and fears for a long time. (Bandura, 1977, p. 194)

The relationship of perceived self-efficacy to self-esteem is obvious. The self-evaluative processes that follow the challenge of any difficult task, interpersonal or object-oriented, are the fundamental contributors to the construction of self-esteem.

Bandura's analysis of the impact of therapy on perceived self-efficacy suggested four sources of influence: performance accomplishments, vicarious experience, verbal persuasion, and emotional arousal. *Performance accomplishments* entail treatments that provide for enactive responding, such as performance exposure, participant modeling, performance desensitization, or self-instructed performance. The task of the therapist is to construct experiences for clients in such a way that they will experience successful coping with the challenge. The accumulation of personal mastery experiences not only affects self-efficacy expectations for that task but also can be generalized to other challenging situations. For Bandura, treatments that promote behavioral accomplishments are the most effective means of promoting feelings of self-efficacy.

Vicarious experience methods, involving both live and symbolic modeling, are also a source of treatment. Herein, the assumed cognition is a social comparison designed to persuade the client that if the model can do it, so can the client. Moreover, the model provides information relevant to the outcome expectancy in that the client observes what behavior is required to achieve the goal. *Verbal persuasion* methods encompass the bulk of extant therapies. Here, the task of the therapist is to convince clients verbally that they can cope successfully with challenges that have overwhelmed them in the past. Clients are to change their perceived self-efficacy because the therapist believes in them or encourages them to modify their self-evaluations in the direction of greater efficacy. Although Bandura marshals evidence to suggest that verbal persuasion is a weak and transitory intervention, he does find that people who are persuaded to believe that they have the capability to meet their particular challenges will initiate new attempts at mastery and mobilize greater effort to succeed. *Emotional arousal* methods, as seen in symbolic desensitization, relaxation training, and so forth, entail altering the physiological arousal states of the individuals facing performance challenge. Herein, the practitioner assumes that heightened anxiety not only debilitates performance but also affects the individual's perception of efficacy. The clients' developing skill in controlling negative arousal states should permit them to enter threatening situations with greater presence of mind, as well as provide them with an experience in mastery that can be generalized to other challenges.

Commentary. Although Bandura's theory was an important addition to the performance component of self-esteem, perceived self-efficacy remains only a portion of the total concept of self-esteem. Too many theorists as well as clinicians have observed the essential contribution of a sense of relatedness and belonging to positive self-esteem to negate it. People need acceptance as well as achievement to feel good about themselves. Moreover, Bandura's methods speak especially well to specific fears. More diffuse anxieties or skill deficits are less amenable to creating performance accomplishments.

As mentioned, few other writers have addressed specifically the problem of treating low self-esteem. Those who have done so either have posited its importance in treatment for particular disorders or have conducted experimental studies that are so brief as to be suspect. Friedenberg and Gillis (1977, 1980) tested the hypothesis that feelings of self-esteem are attitudinal and, therefore, susceptible to attitude change attempts. Their experimental test of a direct persuasive attempt by a warm, high-credibility speaker showed improvements in expressed self-esteem over two weeks' time. Gauthier, Pellerin, and Renaud (1983) evaluated two different cognitive strategies designed to foster greater self-esteem. One group used cognitive restructuring, in which individuals were trained to recognize self-derogatory ideas and modify them with more accurate and affirming thoughts. A second group was trained to focus on and review positive aspects about themselves. Results showed that each group benefited approximately equally from the procedure in comparison to controls. Gains were maintained over a four-week follow-up.

Steffenhagen (1990) proposed *self-esteem therapy* (SET), which assumes that low self-esteem underlies all psychopathology. He argued that any therapy is effective as it amelioriates low self-esteem. SET is a cognitive–behavioral therapy that focuses on helping clients reinterpret their phenomenological world. In essence, SET encourages the "indivdidual to re-evaluate his or her behavior and bring about a change in judgement and expectations" (p. 97). Steffenhagen describes SET as rational emotive therapy (RET) with the added (and needed) component of judgment.

Daly and Burton (1983) evaluated low-self-esteem individuals with the Irrational Beliefs Test (IBT), a measure derived from Ellis's (1962) RET. Although no clinical attempt was made to alter self-esteem, the authors did find a significant negative correlation between low self-esteem and irrational beliefs. Specific irrational belief factors that were better predictors of low self-esteem were (a) demand for approval, suggesting the overwhelming importance of acceptance in the low-self-esteem individual; (b) high self-expectations, the problem of irrationally setting rigid and unattainable standards; (c) anxious overconcern, highlighting an intensive and fruitless tendency to worry; and (d) problem avoidance, illustrating the self-defeating proclivity to avoid confronting and coping with stresses.

Commentary. Although sparse and perhaps too limited in time and scope to reach definitive conclusions, the literature points to the usefulness of several approaches to modify problems of low self-esteem. Perhaps, the most common is simply the accepting, supporting relationship established as a foundation of most therapeutic schools of thought. For Rogers, it was the primary ingredient in successful treatment. The notion of acceptance has been encountered many times throughout this review; so also has the development and encouragement of individuality, which is another issue and often a matter of focus in therapy settings. Here the client learns to deal with the threat of rejection and overcome what may be the irrational fear of declaring oneself. Rollo May's existential therapy concepts were particularly sensitive to the process of individuation.

Finally, the self-efficacy work of Albert Bandura provided an excellent example of the behavioral approach. Without resorting to deeper, more dynamic explanations, his thrust was to build self-confidence by the straightforward teaching of real skills. Clients experience higher self-esteem because they know the important tasks necessary to accomplish goals, and they have experienced performing them or similar behaviors.

Summary and discussion. Although the limited number of studies focusing on the treatment of low self-esteem prevents a detailed comparison, their findings are promising. Bandura's work represents a major thrust in social learning, and the smaller studies suggest the usefulness of a cognitive–behavioral approach. It is important to note, however, that the proposed model is both more similar and dissimilar to Bandura's work than it might appear. In the later chapters on clinical implementation, it will be seen that the therapist deliberately creates an enactive, in-vivo experience in avoidance and coping within the therapy session. The presenting symptom events are used to set the stage for clients to catch themselves avoiding or coping. The therapist assists clients to focus on the consequent self-evaluative process as they encounter it. In that sense, the model coincides with Bandura's work, emphasizing the benefits of enactive learning as opposed to the more traditional verbal persuasion process in therapy. On the other hand, we suggest that the self-evaluative process is less similar to self-talk approaches entailed by cognitive–behavioral therapy. The therapist makes no attempt to identify irrational thoughts; indeed, we assume the accuracy of the client's self-evaluative process.

Unanswered Questions

Throughout the review, we have attempted to present the concepts of the major authors in the self-esteem literature. And, although the chapter's major purpose is to compare the propositions of the model to the relevant theory and research, we hope that it serves as well to acquaint the reader with the field in general. In that hope, we present here questions that have not been addressed in the study of self-esteem:

1. William James and others suggested that people choose the endeavors in life on which they base their self-esteem (what they back themselves to be). The centrality of particular life domains is chosen individually. This activity, then, allows for a reciprocal interaction between people's interests, the encouragements they receive from significant others, and their native abilities in choosing themselves. Yet, to read the humanists Rollo May and Carl Rogers, one has the sense that the individual *discovers* a self that is already there as opposed to *choosing* or *developing* a self, gradually filling with choices the life space called the self. Although Adler allows for a phenomenological creative self, his thesis was that one achieves the most fulfilled self by aligning oneself with the biologically given template of the requirements of social interest. These writers may not agree, of course, with the extrapolation. However, developmental researchers studying temperament or heritability of personality, such as the longitudinal studies of Thomas and Chess (1977), might agree at least that the range of choices of whom we back ourselves to be is limited by some biological proclivities. Thus, the theoretical question is, "Is one's fulfilled self discovered, biologically given, or chosen?"

2. Another theoretical question emerges on the issues of attachment and individuation, addressed briefly in earlier comments. Cooley and Mead emphasized the importance of acceptance and belonging in the development of self-esteem. That is, we learn to prize ourselves as being worthy of respect only if significant others prize and validate us. Rogers views the primary task of the therapist as that of establishing an accepting atmosphere in which clients discover themselves. The under-

side of the argument is that rejection is a universal fear, the malevolent force that destroys self-esteem. Both Rogers and May viewed the process of becoming separated from the self as one in which the fear of rejection provokes the individual to muffle or deny one's own authentic expression. The remedy, explicitly stated by Rollo May, and certainly implied by Rogers, is to abandon the need for acceptance in favor of individuation. Therefore, the second theoretical question is, "In developing self-esteem, what is the appropriate balance between receiving acceptance and establishing individuality?" In other words, is the path to high self-esteem one in which individuals grow up needing acceptance as well as individuality but gradually must give up the need to receive acceptance from anyone besides themselves?

3. Receiving negative feedback is intertwined with the fear of rejection and is presumably a universal experience. Covington and Beery (1976) found that success-striving students were more likely to respond to negative evaluations as an indication of insufficient effort. Failure-avoiding students experienced negative feedback with considerably more anxiety as evidence of lack of ability. Several of the more recent researchers, including Coopersmith, Epstein, and Schlenker, remarked similarly about the potent effect of the attributions attending the receipt of negative feedback. Thus, a significant concern for the clinician attempting to ameliorate low self-esteem is, "What set of experiences can the therapist provide or foster that will effectively inoculate the client against the debilitation of negative feedback?"

4. Although feedback and its interpretation is a vital part of long-term self-feeling, an individual's experience of anxiety and threat in a situation demanding performance is almost surely the initiation point of the events that lead to self-evaluation. Several of the authors reviewed have suggested that the pivotal question for self-esteem in the immediacy of that moment is, "Will the individual react with a coping response or resort to a defensive avoiding behavior?" Allport and Adler wrote that the predomination of coping over avoidance was the essence of psychological health. Rollo May viewed the courage to express one's being in the face of threat as the goal of existential ther-

apy; and Epstein considered the anxious press of performance demand to be the most likely factor in distorting one's self-theory. For the theorist as well as the clinician, then, the question is, "How critical to self-esteem is the coping–avoidance conflict and, if coping is essential, how does the therapist foster habitual choosing of coping responses in the client?"

3

Avoidance and Coping: Basic Considerations

We will begin our discussion of avoidance and coping by describing an experiential learning exercise that we frequently use at professional training workshops on the development of self-esteem. We originally designed this exercise to illustrate quickly and clearly the role and power of what we consider to be the most influential elements affecting self-esteem. We encourage the reader to participate vicariously in the psychological activities that we describe.

Workshop Training Exercise

We generally start this exercise by having 8 to 12 participants lie on the floor in a circle and put on a comfortable blindfold. We have them increase their level of relaxation by using some traditional deep-breathing exercises that last about five minutes. We then proceed as follows.

Phase 1: Avoidance

1. We ask the participants to recall a specific, chronic problem they tend to *avoid* facing. Once the problem has been clearly identified, the participants are asked to recreate the problem situation as clearly and vividly as possible. This includes im-

ages of the people involved, the feelings expressed, arguments that take place, the participants' avoidance behavior, and all of their unexpressed thoughts and feelings. (Note that in our directions we make no suggestion about the type of events that might be avoided, how long ago they may have happened, or what avoidance might mean; all of these meanings are provided by the individual participants.)

2. After the participants have recreated a specific problem event in its entirety, they are asked to relive this event mentally as if they were watching a movie. We ask that they carefully observe the behavior of all individuals in the event, particularly their own. (Again, note that we ask all participants to observe *carefully* without making any suggestions about what behavior might be important or why.)

3. With these preliminaries completed, the participants are asked to identify the three adjectives that most accurately describe *how they feel about themselves* for their behavior in this specific event. It is particularly important that the participants understand that we are *not* asking how they feel about the event, the consequences of the event, or their own general feelings during the event. We are asking them to identify their thoughts and feelings *about themselves* for their behavior during the event. After the participants have had about 2 or 3 minutes to reflect on our question, they write the adjectives on a 3" × 5" card.

Phase 2: Coping

1. Without any discussion of the exercise, the participants put on their blindfolds, lie down on the floor again, and repeat the original deep-breathing exercises. We then ask them to recreate the same problem situation, but this time we ask them to respond as if they were the kind of person they would like to be in this specific situation. (Note that again we make no suggestions about what or how they might want to be; more important, we make no suggestions that the outcome of this situation will change or improve if they represent themselves as the type of person they want to be.)

2. We then ask the participants to recreate the event just as they did before, carefully observing their own behavior as well

as the behavior of all others involved in the problem. When this is completed, they identify the adjectives that best describe how they feel *about themselves* for their behavior in this specific problem situation.

3. The participants write down the adjectives that they have selected, and these are all turned in to the workshop leaders.

Phase 3: Results

Generally, there is an unusually high level of agreement among different participants in the specific words they select to describe their thoughts and feelings about themselves in the avoidance and coping phases of this exercise. The level of agreement is even higher when we look for the level of conceptual equivalence conveyed by different words. In the avoidance phase, the words appearing most frequently are (a) *wimp*, (b) *weak*, and (c) *coward*. These words appear approximately 70% of the time. A variety of other adjectives also appears, but a simple semantic analysis of these terms suggests that most of them are variations on the general theme of personal weakness.

The same type of consensus emerges from the coping phase of this exercise. The thematic message conveyed is altered dramatically, however. The adjectives appearing most frequently are (a) *strong*, (b) *courageous*, and (c) *brave*. Again, the other terms frequently submitted are consistent with a general theme of personal strength or adequacy. Very seldom do workshop participants select adjectives with a favorable self-evaluation for the avoidance phase or with an unfavorable connotation for the coping phase of the exercise.

Interpretive Speculations

After using this exercise in more than 20 training workshops, we began to wonder what the consistency of these results might mean. On the one hand, if this exercise were considered to be nothing more than an entertaining gimmick to liven up a workshop, there would be little point in examining the resultant phenomenon too closely or too frequently. If, however, these results reflect the central dynamics in the development of self-esteem, our training exercise may be a reflection of some fundamental determinants of self-esteem. The potential implications that flow from these results could be far reaching if they are valid. But their validity can be established only by persuasion and logic.

Certainly, a harsh critic could, and really should, point out that the phenomenon that we have identified could easily be an artifact of the training workshop procedures, deriving from cues perceived by the participants as to our expectations about this exercise. This would be a difficult criticism to refute. Situational demand characteristics and the role of expectations in influencing perceptions and actual behavior are well documented (Kazdin, 1980). Because of our own intellectual investment in the point of view that we are developing, we are not immune to these intellectual contaminants and must therefore guard against them.

On the other hand, this exercise was derived from a new model of self-esteem that is based on more than 40 years of cumulative clinical experience, during which time the authors have attempted to observe carefully the role of self-esteem in the development and remediation of various forms of psychopathology. Although we are fully aware of, and appreciate, the crucial difference between the reliability of deliberate clinical observations and rigorous empirical data, we appreciate equally the fact that careful observation is the first step in truly good science (Bednar, Burlingame, & Masters, 1988). Ironically, it is also probably the most neglected aspect in the mental health sciences.

We wish to suggest, then, at least tentatively, that our training exercise does represent a fairly realistic psychological microcosm in which some of the essential elements and dynamics involved in self-esteem come into sharp focus. We ask the reader to consider the following:

1. After a variety of relatively successful individuals are asked to identify how they feel about themselves for avoiding a problem situation, they tend to see themselves as weak and inadequate.

This finding is a little unusual. Most puzzling is the convergence toward unfavorable self-evaluations. Few participants, if any, have ever recognized the value of avoiding some problem situations. When problems are insoluble, and many are, avoidance can be a very adaptive and appropriate response. It seems a little strange that this point of view is not held by many of the participants who have been doing the avoiding! In light of the accompanying negative self-evaluations, perhaps avoidance, regardless of its intrinsic merit in some situations, is a psychologically unsatisfying response because of what it symbolizes.

2. When a variety of relatively successful people are asked how they would feel about themselves if they could cope with the problem situation they usually avoided, the overwhelming majority see themselves as strong and courageous. Again, we must ask why. What is it about facing problem situations that are usually avoided that seems to generate favorable self-evaluations?

Once again we find an interesting paradox. Admittedly, facing a difficult problem situation does require courage; but it also involves fear, anxiety, stress, risk, uncertainty, and sometimes failure. That is why we started wondering why *courageous* emerged as the most frequently cited adjective to describe the self in the face of so many other competing variables that are decidedly less favorable. Certainly courage represents the most socially desirable answer, but if social desirability were such a dominant influence, why did the same people think of themselves as weak and cowardly when they avoided the problem situations in the first scenario? Obviously, other more socially desirable answers were readily available if that is what the participants wanted. Eventually, we started considering an intriguing possibility. That is, the very act of coping with problems that are usually avoided might provide an intrinsically satisfying psychological experience.

Our hunch that avoidance may be the basis for many negative self-evaluations and coping the basis for a good deal of self-approval is not limited to the workshop exercise. Most experienced clinicians have noticed the consistency with which pathologically dependent persons start to experience pride and pleasure as they become more independent. This tends to be true even when that newly acquired independence brings greater burdens of personal responsibility. Similarly, the neurotically underachieving student almost always feels a sense of pride and personal approval for improved performance, even though that performance requires higher levels of commitment, concentration, and inconvenience. In the clinical cases with the most remarkable levels of client change and self-approval, the clients have learned to cope successfully with the very psychological events that they have most avoided in the past.

These observations have led us to ask several questions:

1. By what psychological processes can individuals come to think of themselves as weak or cowardly for *avoiding* certain types of psychological events?

2. By what psychological processes can individuals come to think of themselves as brave or courageous for *coping* with problem situations that might be easily avoided?

3. Is it possible that styles of psychological coping and avoidance are crucial factors in the development of high or low levels of personal self-esteem?

It may be that *what* people do (content and achievements) does not affect the development of self-esteem nearly as much as *how* (process and style) people conduct their lives. This is potentially an important observation for understanding self-esteem in an achievement-oriented society such as ours, in which personal integrity and principles must often be compromised in the pursuit of achievement and success.

Our answers to these three questions provide the crucial elements for the model of self-esteem that we will be proposing, and each of them will be discussed more fully throughout the book. Our immediate task is to discuss some of the fundamental considerations involved in the concepts of avoidance and coping.

Avoidance and Abnormal Behavior

Three questions will guide our discussion of psychological avoidance:

1. What is psychological avoidance?

2. What function does avoidance serve for the personality?

3. Does avoidance influence self-perceptions and self-evaluations?

What Is Psychological Avoidance?

The concept of avoidance has played a central role in general psychological theory. This is particularly true in the areas of psychopathology, psychotherapy, concepts of normality and abnormality, and personality development. We cannot discuss all of the concepts relevant to psychological avoidance because of their diversity and complexity; that would be a different book. We can, however, identify the general elements common to psychological avoidance in different conceptual systems for understanding the etiology and treatment of disordered behavior. To do this, we will adopt a framework suggested by Gordon Allport (1962) to organize psychological theories on the basis of fundamental similarities. He suggested that most theories are based on one of the following three images of human beings:

1. humans as reactive beings (behavioral);
2. humans as reactive beings in depth (psychodynamic); and
3. humans in the process of becoming (humanistic-existential).

Each of these groupings of psychological theory is based on radically different assumptions about the nature of human beings and the preferred methods of clinical intervention.

Humans as reactive beings. This school of thought is anchored to a deterministic view of man in which past conditioning (learning) determines the future. The human being is considered to be one more creature of nature whose behavior, when properly studied, becomes predictable by general laws. The basic vocabulary of this point of view includes such staple psychological terms as *reinforcement, conditioning, drive reduction, stimulus,* and *environmental determinism.* In recent years, this point of view has expanded to accommodate cognitive–behavioral approaches such as those of Beck et al. (1979), Meichenbaum (1977), and Mahoney and Thoresen (1985).

The concept of avoidance has played a prominent role in behavioral formulations of disordered behavior and its treatment

(Rimm & Masters, 1979). These theories explicate the laws of learning by which irrational or exaggerated fears and anxieties are acquired, generalized, and eliminated. Most of these views suggest that once irrational fears are acquired, these fears and all the events with which they become associated are avoided by the client. Supposedly, avoidance of the feared stimulus (object, event, thought, situation, or feeling) becomes a means of preventing the unpleasant experience of fear or anxiety. Successful treatment generally involves the use of a wide variety of treatment techniques, most of which involve introducing a client to the feared stimulus at low levels of psychological distress or anxiety. The ultimate goal, of course, is the elimination of the need to avoid the feared stimulus.

From a learning point of view, then, avoidance is a learned, maladaptive response. It is a response that can be quickly learned and reinforced when it is the means by which stress and anxiety are successfully avoided. Nevertheless, it is a self-defeating behavior pattern because it prevents the individual from reapproaching the feared stimulus and learning that such fears are exaggerated and irrational. From a learning point of view, avoidance is a psychological attribute that one would not wish to possess to any significant degree.

Humans as reactive beings in depth. This psychodynamic tradition is based on an image of man that has been well publicized in the last half-century. Its influence is readily apparent in all of the major mental health professions. Surprisingly, relatively few seem to understand the fundamental similarities between this point of view and traditional behaviorism. Both share a deterministic view, that is, the present and future are determined by the past; in both there is a conspicuous absence of interest in or concern about proactive human behavior; and both minimize the significance of conscious mental activity as a means of understanding the etiology and treatment of emotional disorders. The distinguishing feature of psychodynamic theories is their emphasis on intrapsychic determinants of behavior. It is a form of intrapsychic determinism rather than of environmental conditioning. The most widely recognized terms that emerge from these orientations to describe intrapsychic events include *repression, regression, abreaction, resistance,* and *reaction formation.*

Freud (1924 / 1961) was the first to formalize a theory of neurosis in which avoidance of anxiety played a central role. Among other things, Freud suggested that the core conditions of neurosis are fear and anxiety. The client attempts to avoid these fears by the use of varied and elaborate defense mechanisms, all of which are in the service of the ego to deny, distort, repress, displace, sublimate, or disguise the feared event as a means of avoiding intrapsychic conflicts.

Successful treatment of disordered behavior is accomplished by bringing previously hidden, unconscious conflicts into consciousness, where they do not have to be so fastidiously avoided with various protective strategies. Awareness and insight are the primary means of cure. Both of these conditions imply an absence of avoidance and defensiveness. Fundamentally, then, avoidance plays essentially the same role in psychodynamic formulations of disordered behavior and its treatment as it does in the behavioral approaches: It is the means by which individuals attempt to excuse themselves from facing unpleasant psychological events.

Humans in the process of becoming. The humanistic–existential movement in psychology has explored a wide range of human experience, far too broad be reviewed here in any detail. There are, however, underlying similarities in this array of viewpoints upon which we can comment. The most distinguishing feature of this movement is its optimistic view of man, in which *personal identity, self-direction, personal growth, individual accountability,* and *free will* are dominant considerations. The self-concept, or one's image of oneself, is obviously central to any point of view concerned with qualities such as identity, growth, choice, and self-determination. All of these activities presuppose the existence of a self that guides and directs the activities of the individual in a purposeful and self-fulfilling manner.

Even though humanistic–existential systems are radically different from all other conceptual systems we have discussed, the discussion of avoidance in humanistic–existential systems is virtually indistinguishable from that in the other systems. According to most self-theories, psychological stress is the result of perceived incongruity between actual life experience and the self-concept (Rogers, 1959). For instance, a typically outstanding student who does poorly on an exam would have to deal with the incongruity between this performance and his or her usual self-concept as a high scholastic achiever. Such incongruity is the primary source of psychological anxiety, which can threaten the integrity of the self-structure. Defensive behavior develops as the person attempts to prevent the anxiety from occurring by distorting the perception of real events so that they are more congruent with the existing self-concept. Unfortunately, many of the terms used to describe the dynamics of human behavior can be difficult to understand because of their vague definitions. To illustrate defensive avoidance more clearly, we will cite an example originally provided by Carl Rogers (1959):

> Let us consider for a moment the general range of the defensive behaviors from the simplest variety, common to all of us, to the more extreme and crippling varieties. Take first of all, rationalization ("I didn't really make that mistake, it was this way . . ."). Such excuses involve a perception of behavior distorted in such a way as to make it congruent with our concept of self (as a person who doesn't make mistakes). Fantasy is another example ("I am a beautiful princess, and all men adore me"). Because the actual experience is threatening to the concept of self (as an adequate person, in this example), this experience is denied, and a new symbolic world is created which enhances the self, but completely avoids any recognition of the actual experience. (p. 228)

As with the other conceptual systems we have discussed, the essence of psychological treatment in this system is to provide a means by which the client can abandon self-defeating avoidance behavior (in this case perceptual distortion) and face events more realistically, with less fear and anxiety. The primary treatment consideration associated with self-theories is to enhance the development of an accurate self-concept by means of personal self-exploration in a climate of psychological safety.

Clinical illustration. Perhaps the meaning and function of psychological avoidance are most succinctly revealed in a letter from a former client that vividly describes his intellectual insights into the purpose and extent of his own patterns of psychological avoidance:

> For the past two days I have sat in the library reading your new text, at times filled with laughter at the insights revealed to me about myself and at times on the brink of tears for feeling that a terrible burden was being lifted from my shoulders. During my therapy I kept looking for one underlying aspect common to all of my problems (dislike of job, fear of girls, lack of meaning in life, and so forth) and never really latched onto it until now. I think you underestimated the extent to which my avoidance pervaded all aspects of my life and overestimated my understanding of the "game" I was engaged in. Finally, I see what you were getting at when you asked whether I approved or disapproved of my actions, or how I felt at the end of a session about my behavior during the session. I remember how you would try to get me to answer a simple "yes" or "no," and I would manipulate the terms of the question so that I could answer either yes or no and thereby keep you from ascertaining anything about me.
>
> At the bottom of the whole thing was the fact that I did not want to accept things about myself, so I put up this tremendous impression to fool myself and others about who and what I really was. This style was so consistent that I in fact became totally alienated from myself, or, as I put it, I was "looking out at the world as if from the inside of a box." The whole thing snowballed to the point where my apparent choices did not make me happy and I didn't know why. I think we eventually called it "selling myself out."
>
> My college major is a good example. Chemistry seemed like a prestigious thing to do, and in my mind it was one of the toughest majors. So I tried to prove to myself and others that I was smart and would be successful. Honestly, I think of myself as average or below. I hated my major and I hate my current job. Everyone seems to have sensed it but me.
>
> My dismay over masturbation is because the sexual impulse reminded me that I needed female companionship, which was too big of a step because I would have to expose

myself. The easiest alternative was to get rid of the desire, which made me feel not only cowardly but hopeless about ever having the courage to establish a relationship.

There is more to the letter, but this example provides a highly personal account of precisely the same point the major theoreticians are making about the role of avoidance in disordered behavior.

Summary. We have seen, then, the essential similarity of the role that psychological avoidance plays in different conceptual systems for understanding the etiology and treatment of disordered behavior. In spite of vast differences in basic assumptions, explanatory constructs, and clinical intervention methods, all of these systems consider avoidance to be a protective strategy that may or may not be voluntary. Furthermore, in all of these schools of thought, the very psychological defenses that are used to avoid unpleasant events are frequently the major symptoms of disordered behavior as well as the objects of psychological treatment. In light of all these considerations, it does not seem extravagant to suggest that the concept of psychological avoidance is a staple ingredient in the major psychological formulations of disordered behavior.

What Psychological Function Does Avoidance Serve?

To answer this question is more difficult than it may first appear. Any answer must ultimately be an extension of our current definitions of both normal and abnormal behavior. Although many of us may wish it were otherwise, the mental health professions are far from having robust conceptual models of normal and abnormal behavior. This unhappy state of affairs is hardly surprising given the absence of conceptually adequate definitions of either normal or abnormal behavior. However, our lack of achievement in this area is not because of lack of interest or effort. Attempts to define and differentiate normal and abnormal behavior have been the subject of intense debate in the psychological literature for at least 60 years (Korchin, 1976). Although we cannot review the issues involved in this topic in any depth, we do want to identify the major issues, particularly those that will help us understand the psychological function that avoidance may serve.

At the crux of this knotty problem are four central questions:

1. What are psychological disturbances, and how can their presence be reliably ascertained?

2. What is psychological health, and how can its presence be ascertained reliably?

3. Are there essential differences between psychological health and disturbance, and can these differences be ascertained reliably?

4. Are the attributes that define and differentiate psychological health and abnormality culture bound, or can they be applied on a cross-cultural basis?

These are not easy questions to answer. Particularly difficult are questions three and four. Question three is difficult because it requires not only a definition of normality and abnormality but also the crucial variables that will differentiate these two conditions. Question four is even more difficult because now not only must discriminating variables be identified, but these variables must also be applicable across cultural boundaries. We recognize that there are no definitive answers to these crucial questions in the immediate future, but several fruitful possibilities do exist. Surprisingly, the one consideration that seems to hold a great deal of promise for both defining abnormality and differentiating it from psychological health is avoidance.

Avoidance: A necessary element in abnormality. Differences of opinion about what constitutes abnormality are far from random or arbitrary. Rather, they seem to be a systematic extension of fundamental social values about what constitutes personal well-being. For example, in the affluent and psychologically minded areas of North America, this might include the ability to care for others in intimate relationships, cultivating clear thinking and personal self-direction, or developing a sense of personal identity and personal responsibility. This view assumes that striving for and attaining highly valued, socially desirable attributes is the essence of what it is to be normal (Linton, 1956).

On the other hand, cultural relativists (e.g., Benedict, 1934) have argued that ideals are pertinent only to particular cultural groups and that there are no values or ideals that transcend cultural boundaries. Accordingly, they suggest that the problem of defining normality or abnormality cannot be solved by studying behavior, which varies widely from culture to culture, and just as important, from subculture to subculture. They suggest our understanding of normal and abnormal behavior can best be served by directing our attention to the underlying motivations of behavior.

Wegrocki's (1939) views are a good illustration of this stance. His basic thesis rests on two assumptions. The first is that abnormality cannot be considered to be any behavior that some group considers aberrant. The second is that it cannot be defined in terms of conformity to social standards, values, or expectations; all of these are contaminated by arbitrary cultural considerations, the relevance of which to basic models of human behavior is obviously suspect. However, abnormality can be understood in terms of underlying motivation. Wegrocki points out that virtually any form of human behavior can be considered either normal or abnormal, depending on the function that the behavior serves "in the total economy of the personality." Specifically, he suggests that the quintessence of abnormality is *the tendency to choose a type of reaction that represents an attempt to escape from a conflict-producing situation.* He develops this thesis with a series of cross-cultural analyses of different behavior patterns. These include:

1. The Dobuans of Papua, who are characterized by what we would consider to be an unusual and unnatural degree of fear and suspicion.

2. The Plains Indians, with their religiously colored visual and auditory hallucinations.

3. The Yogis and their trance states.

4. The frequent inclusion of homosexuality as an accepted practice in the religion or social structure of different cultures.

Each of these examples represents behavior patterns that are considered to be perfectly normal in the culture in which they occur, but they would be considered highly abnormal in Western culture. He then cites examples that would be considered normal in Western societies but abnormal in other cultures. These include:

1. The Zuni Indians believe that the individual with undisguised initiative and greater drive than other people is probably a witch and should therefore be hung up by the thumbs.

2. The Northwest Coast Indians would consider Americans more than a little odd because of our disposition to acquire material possessions. For these Indians, the possession of property is secondary to the prestige they acquire when they freely give away all of their possessions in what is called a *potlatch* ceremony.

In the analysis of each of these behavior patterns, the primary point remains the same: to illustrate how deceptive it is to try to understand the meaning of normality or abnormality without taking into account the underlying motivation that lies behind any behavior pattern. The following example illustrates Wegrocki's most basic assumption as it relates to what Western civilization would call paranoid delusions, which are in fact quite normal in the culture of the Northwest Coast Indian. He writes:

> ... the Haida Chief [is a person] in whom the "delusions" of reference and grandeur are externally imposed patterns. A Northwest Coast Indian, if given the opportunity for a naturalistic investigation of the situations that provoke his "paranoid" reactions—as, for example, through an education—could unlearn his previous emotional habits or at least modify them. He is capable of insight; the true paranoiac is usually beyond it. The latter, if he kills the person who he thinks is persecuting him, only temporarily resolves his difficulty; the Indian chief who kills another family "to avenge the insult of his wife's death" achieves a permanent affective equilibration with regard to that incident. His prestige restored, he once more enjoys his self-respect. The Haida defends imagined assaults against his personal integrity only when some violent extra-personal event occurs. The paranoid psychotic defends himself against imagined assaults even though there is no objective evidence of any.
>
> The point that the writer would then emphasize is that the delusions of the psychotic and the delusions of the Northwest Coast Indian cannot by any means be equated. Mechanisms like the conviction of grandeur are abnormal, not by

virtue of unique, abnormal qualia, but by virtue of their *func-*
tion in the total economy of the personality. The true paranoiac
reaction represents a *choice of the abnormal;* the reaction of the
Haida chief represents no such choice—there is but one path
for him to follow. If one of the chief's men showed paranoid
symptoms by proclaiming that *he* really was the chief of the
tribe and that his lawful place was being usurped, the insti-
tutionalization of paranoid symptoms within the culture
would not, I am sure, prevent the rest of the tribe from thinking him abnormal. (Wegrocki, 1939, pp. 169–170)

The essence of this point of view is that abnormality cannot
be defined by any specific pattern of behavior irrespective of its
content or form. Any behavior that is culturally determined and
reinforced simply cannot be considered abnormal in the true
sense of the word. The judgment of abnormality is reserved for
avoidance behavior that is motivated by fear, anxiety, or an in-
stinct to protect the self from intolerable conflicts. Accordingly,
behavior per se is not the index against which normality or
abnormality can be judged. Rather, as we noted earlier, it is the
function any specific behavior serves for the individual that reveals its normality or abnormality. *One of the quintessential qual-*
ities of abnormality is avoidance—avoidance motivated by fear and
anxiety.
   Please note that this conception is remarkably similar to the
general conception of abnormality inherent in most of the major
models of human behavior reviewed earlier in this chapter. It
now becomes more obvious why avoidance is such a central
proposition in our most basic formulations of disordered behavior. It is one of a very few concepts in psychological theory
the underlying function of which seems to be commonly and
almost consensually understood and accepted from a variety of
different perspectives. Granted, different theorists have explained the dynamics of avoidance in different and imaginative
language. But the underlying function of avoidance is virtually
always the same: to defend and protect the individual from
unpleasant or unwelcome psychological experiences. It is a process we engage in that allows us to cling to our childish ideals
by not facing those unpleasant psychological realities that can

expose the fraud and faults in our idealistic self-conceptions. There are, of course, other definitions of avoidance, but our use of the term is restricted to its generic meaning as a defense mechanism common to most disordered behavior.

Avoidance differs from coping in many important ways. Certainly, it is a more primitive response to psychological threat than coping is. It is nothing more than an attempt to evade the threat and, we suppose, pretend that the conflict does not exist before it is understood or resolved. In its most basic form, it is a type of denial. The purpose of the denial is obvious enough: to excuse the individual from the unpleasantness of the threat. However, herein lies a paradox of major proportions (McCall, 1975). The moment in which we choose avoidance over coping, we openly and undeniably announce to ourselves (and to any others who care to observe) that we have detected impulses within that are so unacceptable that they cannot be faced realistically. It is as though we try to say to ourselves that this is too unpleasant to be true and then proceed to act as though it were not. However, there must be some recognition of the possibility of truth; otherwise, there would be no threat that would mobilize the defenses. The threat must be at least partially recognized before it can even arouse defensive instincts. Ironically, then, the very attempt to deny the threat can verify its existence. Obviously, the prospects for personal growth are virtually nonexistent when the individual's response to threat is *to deny that which one has already glimpsed to be true.*

Clinical illustration. The following example of fear-motivated avoidance is a good illustration of the principle under discussion.

A 34-year-old in-house writer for a large corporation was attempting to expand his career on a free-lance basis. He had already completed several small, independent projects but had yet to become involved in anything that would truly test his talent and skills, which were abundant. He had recently submitted a proposal to write a documentary screenplay for a major motion picture studio. The studio accepted his proposal without recommending any changes. This was a significant professional opportunity, but more to the point, one that would require the utmost of his abilities. The prospect of having to produce materials that would be reviewed by established experts that would reveal what he was capable, or incapable, of doing proved to be incapacitating.

This behavior was not entirely puzzling to him. In fact, he responded to this challenge just as he had to numerous other opportunities to establish himself professionally. He was well aware that his fear of this experience was tied to his fear of failure, in this case the fear that his best efforts would be found lacking. In spite of this person's ambition and hunger for success, his attempts at productive work were continually interrupted by television, eating, and other inconsequential activities that he would attempt to construe as important and necessary. Even though he had been endowed with considerable creative and intellectual talents, they remained essentially unused because of the person's fear that his talents would be found inadequate in an authentic test. To this day, the manuscript remains only partially completed. That portion is excellent and the studio remains eager for him to complete his assigned task. It will probably never be completed. By only partially completing the task, the person has again demonstrated the adequacy of his talents to himself in such a way that it cannot be refuted by others.

As one might suspect, a life of mediocre accomplishments and personal dissatisfaction is the only realistic outcome for this person so long as he continues to avoid facing his irrational fear of failure.

Does Avoidance Influence Self-Perceptions?

The importance of this question will probably become obvious if it is asked in generic terms. Considered in this light, the question is really asking whether a person's behavior (which in our view includes thinking, feeling, and overt actions) influences self-perceptions. The answer, of course, must be a resounding *yes*. If one's most intimate knowledge and daily experience with the self do not have a profound effect on self-perceptions, we cannot imagine what else would. Our attention, then, almost automatically shifts to trying to understand how patterns of avoidance influence self-perceptions. We will discuss this problem more fully in a later chapter. For now, we only wish to preview the two major points on how patterns of avoidance can influence self-perceptions. First, it is doubtful whether most people can remain completely oblivious of their tendency to avoid some types of conflict situations. Second, the self-evaluations that accompany patterns of avoidance are mostly negative because of the inadequacies inherent in avoidance responses. In light of both these considerations, we will suggest that patterns of avoidance are a staple ingredient in the psychological mixture that brews chronically low levels of personal self-esteem.

Summary. Our discussion of psychological avoidance has emphasized three primary points. First, the concept of avoidance is implicit in most of the major formulations of disordered behavior. Even though different theories are based on different assumptions and models of man, there is nearly universal agreement that the psychological function of avoidance is to provide an escape from unpleasant psychological events.

Second, one of the quintessential qualities of abnormal behavior is a tendency to choose a type of reaction that represents an attempt to escape from psychological conflict to avoid the fear and anxiety associated with the conflict. Accordingly, we have suggested that the problem of defining normality or abnormality cannot be approached by studying any specific and overt patterns of behavior, which vary widely from culture to culture and, just as important, from subculture to subculture. Instead, we have proposed, as have others, that our understanding of both normal and abnormal behavior can be served best by directing our attention to the underlying function the behavior is serving for the personality.

Third, the psychological processes involved in avoidance are qualitatively different from those involved in coping. Avoidance is basically a form of denial and escape that requires distortions of thinking and perception. These processes virtually preclude the possibility of personal growth and development because of the inadequacies inherent in these responses.

Psychological Coping and Normal Behavior

We now turn our attention to the process of psychological coping and its effects on the development of normal behavior. Our discussion will focus on two basic questions:

1. What is coping?
2. What are the underlying psychological attributes necessary to sustain a process of psychological coping?

In our discussion of psychological coping and the development of normal behavior, it is important to remember that, behind most conceptions of normality, we can usually expect to find a variety of ideological assumptions and values that are assumed to reflect the essential elements of personal well-being. We are now ready to discuss what we consider these most basic ingredients to be. This is a more difficult problem than defining abnormality and, regrettably, one that has received far less scholarly consideration. Numerous essays do exist on the topic (Lynn, 1959; Seeman, 1959; Shoben, 1957). In spite of the quality of these fine essays, it is difficult to find a unifying conceptual thread to bind these diverse views together. We must start our discussion of normality by frankly acknowledging that we know far more about the deviant, the diseased, and the disordered than we do about normal persons. This unhappy state of affairs obligates us to be even more tentative in our speculations and more modest in our hopes for conceptual clarity.

Our views of normality will be guided, at least initially, by our views on abnormality. Let us explain and illustrate. We have already suggested that the essence of disordered behavior is (a) psychological fear and anxiety (b) that lead to avoidance of conflict situations. The antithesis of avoidance would be coping, which is essentially a realistic facing-up to threatening situations. We suggest that just as avoidance is the essence of abnormality, the ability to face psychological threat successfully is the essence of normality. This is not meant to imply that the absence of avoidance constitutes normality. We have higher conceptual aspirations than simply defining normality as the absence of abnormality. Circular reasoning of this type would do little to enhance our understanding of the fundamentals of normality; more important, it would be conceptually misleading.

We will suggest that the ability to cope successfully with psychological threat implies the presence of other psychological attributes (e.g., risk taking, personal responsibility). We consider the process of realistically facing and resolving threatening situations to be essential to personal growth, development, and change. This process is the cardinal, distinguishing feature of normality. To understand normality requires an understanding of the process of coping.

What Is Coping?

Coping involves a candid and realistic facing-up to threatening situations. This usually requires personal introspection, personal honesty, and a willingness to acknowledge openly the imperfections in the self. Even though candid self-evaluation can create high levels of subjective distress, this is not an unreasonable ingredient for a concept of coping that is associated with personal growth and development. We have not read a single sentence that would suggest that the healthiest personalities can be excused from psychological threat and anxiety. Actually, most psychological theories would suggest just the opposite. The healthier the personality, the more anxiety-laden conflicts it can face without being overly influenced by the threat inherent in difficult situations. The anxiety can be felt, but it can also be tolerated without evasive action.

It seems reasonable to suggest, then, that psychological threat is a reality for all of us. Furthermore, its presence implies the existence of some inadequacies in the personality that can either be coped with or avoided. When these inadequacies are faced with candor, they become a unique source of personal growth tailored to each individual. This is the path of psychological insight and reality testing, which are crucial considerations in personal growth and development.

An illustration of coping may help illustrate the fundamental differences between this growth-producing attribute and avoidance. Our example is factual, continuing the life of the free-lance writer whom we have already introduced. This event takes place about 10 months after our first example. He has now successfully completed 6 months of individual psychotherapy and is involved in group therapy on a weekly basis.

> As a result of the understanding and insight our client acquired in therapy about his pattern of avoidance, he re-enrolled in the graduate program he had previously discontinued. He needed only to complete his thesis, but in the face of this specific crucial task, he again started to show the familiar signs of avoidance. A pivotal therapy session occurred when he brought this topic up in a group meeting. He requested assistance from the group members to help him, in his words, "to gain the necessary insight" he needed to motivate him to complete his thesis. The group listened to his story patiently and attentively, as was their custom. When he had finished, they thoughtfully pondered his problem. With unprecedented unanimity, the group members confronted him with the obvious reality that *he didn't seem to really want to complete his thesis, and they were puzzled about why he pretended he did.* In spite of his protestations to the contrary, the group continually and unanimously maintained that they would feel more comfortable with him if he stopped making excuses for what was obvious to everybody—he didn't really want to finish his thesis, and he was probably afraid to try. Frustrated and discouraged, he told the group they had been of no help to him and that he felt let down by them.
>
> At this point the group leader intervened with what proved to be a poignant moment in this man's life. He said, "It sounds as though you're your own man with this one. No one here seems able to provide you with the help you seem to need, though we wish we could. And you don't seem able to get past this barrier on your own. Perhaps it's time to accept the possibility you simply won't be able to finish your thesis."
>
> With that comment, all rationalizations ceased, as did the client's attempts to find reassurance from the words of others. In the absence of these defenses, his acute personal disapproval of self for not even trying began to surface and far exceeded his fear of attempting the task and failing. Not even trying to scale the symbolic wall before him said something about him he found frightening and fundamentally unacceptable. He had no further recourse but to squarely face the

fact that he felt deeply inadequate to the task. Upon closer examination, he decided that if he could not complete his thesis, he probably couldn't complete anything else of importance, either. He now understood and accepted that reality—but more important, he took responsibility for his own failures. His thesis now turned into the explicit test of his adequacy that it had always been implicitly. But now, with his resources mobilized and the meaning of the test clear, he declined the invitation he usually accepted: that is, denying his feelings of inadequacy and avoiding any test of his adequacy. It became important to him to see what kind of work he could actually produce.

Group members applauded his honesty and indicated that if it turned out he couldn't finish his thesis, at least he should "go down fighting the whole way." If he didn't, they would be disappointed in him. They would rather see him give his maximum effort and fail than see him "get by" with another partial effort. Interestingly, no one reassured him that if he tried he would succeed.

His efforts were well rewarded. He completed his thesis and was given more than the usual number of compliments by the faculty. Far more important, he had taken the first major step in removing his incapacitating fear of failure. The small confidence in himself he had acquired was well earned. He is now at a much closer approximation to the free-lance writer he always wanted to be, and with a little luck he may become a successful writer. Though his accomplishments are still few, his sense of personal well-being has increased measurably and is fairly obvious to those who know him. We suspect that his improved state of well-being is not a result of his modest success, though that was undoubtedly helpful. Rather, it was a result of the self-respect he feels for coping with a major personal conflict instead of avoiding it. As a result of that process, he has acquired some realistic reasons to believe that he can trust his talents and abilities when they are most needed. He has also come to understand the personal cost of his tendency to avoid rather than face personal conflict. These two elements constitute major ingredients in a new definition of self the influence of which will probably be undeniable in many future events.

We hope that this example has illustrated how coping with threatening situations, rather than avoiding them, is the means by which individuals can create unique personal learning experiences that teach about the self and its diverse abilities, liabilities, and needs. According to our view, the most accurate self-knowledge is acquired when one tests oneself in real situations. Please note that we did not say that this is the only means by which individuals can acquire self-knowledge, but we do suggest that it is generally the most accurate. Knowledge about the self, when properly acquired, becomes the basis for individuals to orchestrate their lives into a meaningful, satisfying, and self-directed experience for which they readily accept personal responsibility. We will say more about how self-knowledge is "properly" acquired later. Until then, we ask the reader to note that our definition of coping and normality refers more to a process that regulates realistic learning about the self than it does to any specific psychological quality, attribute, or achievement. Coping, then, is a growth-oriented process in which personal development is the inevitable result of facing, understanding, and resolving conflict situations. It is also a process that involves psychological ingredients fundamentally different from those involved in avoidance. The two most important ones are *psychological risk taking* and *personal responsibility.*

Coping: Essential Attributes and Consequences

Just as avoidance is indicative of highly sensitive inadequacies in the personality, the ability to successfully cope is a measure of personal adequacy. Individuals who, when confronted with conflict situations, allow themselves to experience the anxiety inherent in these situations and elect to face and resolve the conflict are on the threshold of a powerful personal learning experience. It is hard to imagine how it could be otherwise. Psychological learning is the inevitable result of facing conflict openly, realistically, and nondefensively. The quality, duration, and depth of this learning, however, is most likely to be mediated by two other important psychological attributes: psychological risk taking and personal responsibility. Both of these attributes play a crucial role in our concept of coping and in the development of personal self-esteem. Let us explain and illustrate.

Psychological risk taking.[1] The notion of psychological risk is difficult to conceptualize. It is a phenomenon by which knowledge by acquaintance may be superior to knowledge by description, probably because psychological risk is such an idiosyncratic experience. It does, however, seem to have certain common properties. It involves the possibility of psychological injury or loss. Some easily recognized risks include the possible loss of self-esteem, injury to one's reputation, loss of approval from others, greater vulnerability, increased anxiety, increased subjective distress as one moves closer to facing unpleasant impulses and emotions, and open rejection by others. Different psychological theories vary in their explanations for these experiences, and they argue about the causes and their meaning. Recognition and acceptance of these experiences, however, is universal.

In general, psychological risk taking involves at least two components that are central to our views on psychological avoidance and coping. One is intrapsychic; the other is interpersonal. There is no reason to suppose that risk taking is necessarily limited to these two areas. However, there can be little question that a great deal of what is called psychological risk takes place within these two domains.

Intrapsychic risk refers to increased exposure to and awareness of unacceptable or feared thoughts and feelings. It is the risk of *knowing*. It can result from introspection, confrontation, or loosening of defensive barricades. The risk is to find out about oneself, to face the possibility that one's greatest fears are, in fact, true or even partly true (e.g., "I am unlovable," "My anger is uncontrollable," and so forth). The more immediate and intense the feelings associated with any intrapsychic event of this kind, the greater the psychological risk that is experienced as the person attempts to cope with rather than to avoid the feared event.

Interpersonal risk is similar in kind but stimulated by different events. It is the risk of *being known*. It involves interpersonal

---

[1] Much of the material included in the Psychological Risk Taking and Personal Responsibility sections was developed by Dr. Richard L. Bednar and Dr. Theodore J. Kaul in an unpublished manuscript titled "Group Psychotherapy: A Comparative Review and Analysis."

perceptions, interpersonal rejection, and having one's psychological secrets exposed to others. Interpersonal risk taking involves increased exposure to and awareness of interpersonal fears. Whereas these two types of risk taking involve fear of different events, the severity of psychological risk is mediated by the immediacy and intensity of emotions associated with the particular psychological event.

These two areas of psychological risk taking are the most important ones in our discussion of coping and defense. They represent the areas in which learning about the self and the development of self-esteem are most central. Obviously, the presence of any enduring disposition to avoid reasonable and appropriate risks in these two areas diminishes the prospect of intrapsychic and interpersonal learning when threat is involved. We might even go so far as to suggest that the greater the risk the personality can tolerate, the more important the psychological learning that can take place. Inherent in this formulation, however, is the inescapable conclusion that coping, as we have defined it, involves personal risk taking, and by implication, personal discomfort. We suggest that the ability or disposition to take psychological risks is a learned attribute that can be enhanced and cultivated.

The role of risk taking in personal growth is illustrated by the following example.

> One of the members in the therapy group we have already mentioned (with regard to our free-lance writer) was a quiet person. Her personal history was one from which risk taking was noticeably absent. Only on the rarest occasions would this woman talk about her personal feelings or views. Neither would she engage in conversation that was personally revealing. Her marriage, though far from being satisfying, was acceptable. But as might be expected, few problem areas were discussed openly, and many sensitive areas were avoided systematically. On the surface, it appeared that this woman had developed a "don't-rock-the-boat" style. Underneath the exterior was a person who worried a lot, experienced a great deal of self-consciousness, and felt as though life was proving to be more displeasing than it really needed to be.

Needless to say, she was not well prepared to deal with the personal and interpersonal intensity that can develop in group psychotherapy. This was a high-functioning group, which only served to heighten her ambivalence about participation. On the one hand, it was fairly obvious that meaningful participation could pay high dividends. The benefits derived by some group members were obvious. On the other hand, the modus operandi of the group was at a level of emotional intensity and immediacy that served only to further frighten her. She was stuck at a major crossroads. She wanted to participate, but her fear and anxiety seemed to be an insurmountable obstacle. After a particular session had ended, she remained to talk with the group leader to explain her dilemma, which the therapist was already well aware of. He quickly stopped her and asked if she would be willing to start the next group session with the conversation she wanted to have with him now. She reluctantly agreed.

At the next group meeting, she bravely initiated her conversation with the group leader. He immediately stopped her and asked if she would be willing to start by telling the group members what it felt like to talk in front of the group. She nervously but bravely responded. She indicated that she had dreaded this meeting all week, her mouth was dry, and she felt a lot of fear and anxiety. She couldn't explain why she was afraid, but it was clear to her that she was. She was actually very articulate in her description.

When she was through talking, the group leader asked if there were other group members who had similar experiences in the group, or if there were members whose participation continued to be limited because of similar feelings. Much to this woman's surprise, over half the group members felt just as she did. She had been so sure she was the only one! In the conversation that followed, this woman and most of the group got to explore their fears of really being known and of knowing others in depth. It was a particularly poignant experience for this woman. She found out that she was not the only one with such basic fears, but more important, she found out what it was like to be closer to people as a result of authentic sharing based on simple honesty with self and others. It came as quite a revelation to her. She had many preconceived notions about meaningful relationships' being based on personal perfection and desirability more than on simple authenticity. Her behavior in the group gradually changed as she became more and more willing to make herself really known to others. As she became more comfortable with herself, she also became more comfortable knowing others, and being known by them. *None of this could have occurred without someone's taking the psychological risks involved in courageously facing the unknown.* As usual, the greatest benefits in this situation were derived by the person who took the greatest risks. With the help of her therapists, this woman was able to create a personal learning situation that was perfectly matched to her particular and idiosyncratic concerns.

Personal responsibility. In psychological circles, personal responsibility generally refers to behavior that is considered to be psychologically responsible. Responsibility to family, society, or nation is seldom discussed. If discussed, it is usually only to clarify the assumption that seems implicit in other presentations, that is, that personally responsible behavior will lead to socially responsible actions, and that one will necessarily follow the other. It is an interesting assumption, but it is not held in all cultures.

Although the concept of personal responsibility is discussed in different terms, two common elements do seem to emerge. The first element common to most conceptions of personal responsibility is the personal attribution of causality or control. Most forms of psychological treatment share the goal of increasing their clients' level of personal responsibility and control over their lives. No approach attempts to persuade clients that they are responsible for the weather, famines, or the existence of evil. Yet, virtually all treatment approaches, in their own way, attempt to increase clients' willingness to see themselves either as causal agents or at least as being able to exert more control in their own lives. This is accomplished by encouraging clients to accept the consequences of their own thoughts and actions. They are shown how their thoughts and emotions can affect their actions, and how their actions influence the actions of others. They are continually encouraged to achieve more symmetry between what they wish to have happen to them and what actually happens.

Also, most discussions of personal responsibility imply or express the view that it involves accurate self-perceptions. High levels of personal responsibility are suggested by insight: nondefensive recognition of impulses, emotions, or thoughts; completely experiencing oneself; and perhaps leading a self-directed lifestyle. Increasingly accurate perceptions and knowledge about the self are at or near the top of the hierarchy of considerations involved in our discussion of normality and coping.

It should be obvious that high levels of personal responsibility are generally indicative of normality, coping skills, and manageable levels of psychological stress and anxiety. It would be an understatement to call this a pleasing and highly desirable trait. This is not meant to imply a tension-free existence. Our existential colleagues have carefully taught us about the anguish involved in personal choices under these conditions (May, Angel, & Ellenberger, 1958); but, functionally, it is more than that. It is a process in which individuals hold themselves accountable for much of what does or does not happen in their lives. The debate about their being or not being causative agents in their own lives has ended. They are! The crucial question is now, "What do I need to do differently so that other things will be different in my life?" Once this is understood, it becomes a powerful incentive to cope efficiently and effectively. It is the means by which individuals can avoid pain, disappointment, and remorse in their lives. It is the most reliable means for improving the quality of one's existence. "After all, if I am the cause, I can also be the cure."

High levels of personal responsibility are illustrated in the following two examples. The first example is based on a client in psychotherapy, the second on a psychologically mature friend whom we have known for a number of years.

> A client had been in therapy for about 3 weeks because of deeply conflicted feelings about his father. The client was 26, married, with no children. In previous sessions, the client reported many favorable perceptions and experiences with his father. All of these seemed to be the result of having a father who was genuinely preoccupied with his family's well-being, being a good friend and provider to all, valuing

family participation more than professional opportunity, and always being available to provide assistance when needed. In this particular session, the client was talking about his conflicted feelings about spending the Labor Day holiday on a family picnic his father had arranged as opposed to getting away with his wife for two days. It was clear this young man preferred to go away with his wife, but felt as though that would be unfair and disloyal to his family in general and to his father in particular.

After carefully listening to the client's remarks, the therapist said, "You seem to have difficulty accepting your feelings of resentment toward your father for smothering you." The client recoiled briskly. Obviously, the therapist's comment was on target but premature. The client wasn't willing or ready to face such negative feelings in such a sensitive area. The therapist asked the client to close his eyes for five minutes, turn inward, and without saying anything, work toward identifying his feelings toward his father at that moment.

Much to the therapist's surprise, the client opened his eyes and announced, "I really do resent him. I didn't realize how much." Though this client found these feelings puzzling, unacceptable, and problematic, they were now his. From then on, the client was able to explore openly what it was about *himself* that made it difficult to become emancipated from his somewhat overbearing father. Though the idea of resenting his father still does not sit well with this client, he makes no attempts to deny this reality to himself.

Our second example is unusual. It is a true story of a no-nonsense, middle-aged man who was being recruited for a prestigious professional position. After the usual preliminary screening was completed on both sides, an interview was arranged. This is what actually happened.

At the end of two days of interviews, group meetings, meals, and professional presentations, the applicant met with the president and his two vice presidents for a farewell luncheon. During this meeting, the president indicated that all had been most favorably impressed and that they wanted to offer him a position. An unusually generous salary was included in the offer. In a totally unpretentious way, the candidate responded to the offer by saying that he appreciated the generous offer, the thoughtful and courteous way he was treated during the visit, and their approval of him as a professional person. However, he felt as though he would be uncomfortable in the position and must decline. Puzzled, the chief administrators pressed him to clarify the reasons they might lose this outstanding candidate. The candidate asked in what depth and at what level of honesty they really wanted to know about his reservations. They insisted on absolute candor. For over six hours, they discussed the company with regard to deficits in moral values, personal integrity, work habits, and simple honesty. The candidate basically informed them that he would find it personally embarrassing to be affiliated with them on a professional basis irrespective of salary or apparent prestige. The company officials so appreciated his views and candor that they offered him a consultantship that would focus exclusively on the development of moral integrity in the organization. This offer was undoubtedly the result of the candidate's impressive ability to present himself as the most obvious expression of his own moral views and values.

Risk and responsibility: Important differences. The concepts of personal risk and responsibility are similar in several ways. They can refer to similar or highly related psychological events in some instances, making it difficult to differentiate the two clearly. In spite of these potential sources of confusion, several points help demarcate the boundaries of these two important concepts and the functions they serve.

A fundamental difference between personal risk and responsibility is contained in their core definitions. Risk taking refers to increased awareness of and exposure to feared psychological events, whereas personal responsibility refers to a willingness to attribute the cause and consequences of one's own behavior to the self. Whereas risk taking is most easily recognized by a willingness to expose oneself to feared situations without a clear understanding of how these events might affect the self, personal responsibility refers to a willingness to acknowledge one's psychological experiences as a direct reflection and extension of the self. In this sense, personal responsibility is a form of psychological ownership: a recognition of the reality that one's thoughts, feelings, and behavior reflect who or what one is.

Summary

Our discussion of psychological coping and normality has emphasized its underlying attributes, which we consider to be psychological risk taking and personal responsibility. We have suggested that these qualities are the foundation on which a lifetime of continual growth and development is based.

We have also suggested that the psychological processes involved in avoidance are qualitatively different from those involved in coping. We have suggested that avoidance is based on psychological processes that deny or distort unpleasant psychological realities. We cannot think of any enduring benefits to be derived by consistently avoiding conflict situations as a way of containing fear and anxiety. On the other hand, we have portrayed coping as the means by which one can acquire an accurate understanding of self and perhaps others. Coping involves facing conflict realistically, learning how to tolerate the distress inherent in these situations, and gradually modifying the personality through personal conflict resolution. We have continually emphasized the favorable social and psychological connotation of coping and conflict resolution. The underlying attributes that mediate personal growth and development are socially valued and, in addition, may stand scrutiny in an absolute sense as well.

Our discussion of psychological coping and defense is central to the model of self-esteem that we will be discussing. It raises two fundamental questions basic to our model of self-esteem:

1. Is it reasonable to assume that a person with a deeply ingrained tendency either to cope or to avoid conflict is, or could be, completely *oblivious* of that fact?

2. Is it reasonable to assume that self-perceptions *will not* be influenced by one's tendency to cope or avoid conflict?

These questions provide the basis for much of our discussion in the next chapter.

4

External and Internal Feedback: Basic Assumptions

The Importance of Feedback

Our model of self-esteem is based on four underlying assumptions, each of which involves *feedback* about personal and interpersonal acceptability. Because feedback is a term that is commonly used and misused in a variety of disciplines, it may be useful to clarify some of the most fundamental elements of this important concept. It was originally postulated as a regulatory mechanism in biological systems by Walter Cannon (1939) in his principle of homeostasis. Since then, it has gradually found application in systems theory, information theory, and cybernetics. Norbert Wiener (1948), a cyberneticist, defined feedback as the control of a machine on the basis of actual rather than expected performance, which required sensory units for such performance monitoring.

The crucial elements in the concept of feedback are (a) it provides a particularly relevant type of information (feedback) intended to monitor, define, and correct undesirable deviations; (b) the source of the feedback can be either internal or external to the system being monitored; (c) feedback can vary from highly intermittent to continuous; and (d) feedback can vary in its potency to correct deviations. In brief, feedback is a special type of information that can describe, evaluate, or influence performance: in our case, human behavior. This complex concept occupies a central role in several major theoretical approaches to personality development, psychotherapy, and psychopathology.

Although he used different terminology, Harry S. Sullivan (1962) was among the first theorists to discuss systematically the role of feedback in personality development. In his classic text, *Schizophrenia as a Human Process,* information about the self from others (interpersonal feedback) plays a preeminent role in personality development. Sullivan maintained that

> There is within the personality a system of experience to which we apply the terms, the ego, or the self. This is built up of all the factors of experience that we have in which significant other people "respond" to us. In other words, *our self is made up of the reflections of our personality that we have encountered, mirrored in those with whom we deal* [emphasis added]. (1962, pp. 249–250)

Sullivan further maintained that interpersonal processes in general and interpersonal feedback in particular play a major role in the development and treatment of disordered behavior. The essence of his view is that feedback from others shapes the formation of the self-concept. If one receives responses from significant others that are essentially negative, this is incorporated into the self-image. The perception and interpretation of many future events is determined by that self-image.

Carl Rogers (1951) and George Herbert Mead (1934) have expressed essentially the same view of personality development, though the specific semantics of their presentations vary somewhat. Rogers (1951), for example, has suggested that feedback is a means of assisting the client to establish congruence between the self and the real world. This is accomplished by the therapist empathically understanding the client's experiential world. The therapist can reflect back to the client perceptions that are intended to increase awareness. Regardless of variations in descriptions, Rogers, Mead, and Sullivan emphasized the role of interpersonal processes in the formation, maintenance, and alteration of personality.

In addition to theoretical speculation, there is a growing body of research literature that further suggests the potency of interpersonal feedback as a primary source of psychological influence (Stockton & Moran, 1982). Yalom (1985) has reported a good example of this type of research. He found that the most significant event for clients in group treatment was the expression of strong positive or negative comments to other group members.

In more general terms, interpersonal feedback is considered to be one of the premier curative factors in group therapy (Bednar & Kaul, 1978; Bednar & Lawlis, 1971; Kaul & Bednar, 1986). Despite the apparent success of the use of feedback in clinical settings, an empirical understanding of the phenomenon is still rather incomplete in two fundamental regards:

1. There is a lack of clarity about what psychological feedback actually is and is not.

2. It is unclear under what conditions and with what type of client feedback can or should be used.

Nevertheless, some general principles about the therapeutic use of interpersonal feedback are emerging in the psychological literature. The most consistent research findings suggest that (a) most people prefer positive to negative feedback, (b) negative feedback is most likely to be accepted by high-self-esteem individuals, or if it is preceded by positive feedback, and (c) most people find it easier to deliver positive rather than negative feedback (Kaul & Bednar, 1986). The generality of these findings is not at all clear because of the usual methodological problems that accompany a young science.

Underlying Assumptions

There are four basic assumptions in our model of self-esteem that involve the delivery of positive and negative feedback about personal or interpersonal acceptability. Each assumption considers feedback from different sources (external and internal) as well as its probable consequences. The first two assumptions focus on feedback originating in the social environment. In these cases, the self-evaluations of *others* are the primary source of the feedback. Assumption 1 explains how and why virtually all individuals receive regular and substantial doses of negative feedback from their social environment. (Ironically, we suggest that most of this feedback is valid, at least from one perspective.) Assumption 2 identifies and explains the dynamics behind the common observation that negative interpersonal feedback tends to be more believable than positive interpersonal feedback.

The remaining two assumptions are based on internal sources of feedback. In these cases, the self-evaluations of the *individual* are the primary sources of the feedback. Assumption 3 suggests that self-evaluations can and usually do take place. This is important in that it makes explicit what most of us implicitly recognize and experience: that we notice, monitor, and evaluate what we do. Assumption 4 suggests that our self-evaluative thoughts provide continuous internal feedback about the adequacy of the self. Each of these four assumptions will be described and illustrated with care, inasmuch as their validity is the most important consideration in our model of self-esteem.

External Feedback

Assumption 1

People should expect to receive regular amounts of negative feedback from their social environment, most of which will probably be valid. This may appear to be an unusual or pessimistic assumption for those constantly hoping for the approval of others. Nevertheless, the following considerations suggest that this assumption may well be the most reasonable of the four.

Individual differences and social acceptability. The field of psychology probably acknowledges more about individual differences than about any other single topic (Tyler, 1978). If this appears to be an overstatement, we can retreat to a more modest position and point out that "differences between people" is one of the very few topics that has been the subject of extensive data collection for 50 years or more. As a result, we know that people differ from each other along almost every conceivable dimension. In the area of personal appearance, we have all noticed the consistency with which people differ in height, weight, and girth. The same is true in less obvious areas, such as special aptitudes for learning, aggressiveness, temperament, and frustration tolerance. Our best evidence (Kolb & Wishaw, 1985) also suggests that the scope and magnitude of these individual differences extend into the biological substrata of human behavior and include such basic factors as brain morphology, sympathetic and parasympathetic reactivity, and neural capacity. The evidence about which people consistently differ from each other (physical appearance, performance, aptitudes and talents, personality attributes, and biological and neurological characteristics) is simply undeniable.

But what does all of this have to do with personal and interpersonal acceptability? If we consider these facts in conjunction with the social nature of human beings, the answer becomes more obvious. Most human activities take place in a social context. We tend to associate together in groups such as churches, neighborhoods, fraternal organizations, families, professional associations, political parties, and employment organizations. Some groups are formed to satisfy our need for interpersonal relationships and togetherness. Others are formed to foster achievement and accomplishment. Still others exist for the benefit of the disabled and bereaved. Each group has its own membership requirements, which may include level of education, designated talents, and special interests. Each has its own norms and approves or disapproves of members according to the degree to which they (a) comply with group requirements and expectations, and (b) enhance the goals for which the group was formed. Group members tend to be recognized and rewarded for their allegiance and contribution to group goals and values.

Because of the number and diversity of admission requirements and role expectations for different groups and because of the divergent nature of human beings, it is simply illogical to expect any one individual to be equally adept at satisfying the varied demands of all groups in which membership is either required or desired. Consequently, we will always be unacceptable to some groups and to some people. More important, our acceptability to the various groups to which we do belong will vary depending on our contribution to the group's goals and values. It is important to notice that group acceptance or rejection is not necessarily attached to any higher set of standards or values; it is usually based on simple compliance with group norms and values. Whether these more restrictive norms and values are desirable is seldom considered in the broader context of social values and their consequences. For example, creativity in some circles is a highly desired and valued trait. This is most likely to be true in areas in which conventional thinking is unlikely to produce answers to unorthodox problems. Under these conditions, creativity will be appreciated and encouraged. Blessed is the group member who, through genetics or social learning, is disposed to view problems and their solutions in divergent and unorthodox ways. Heaven help this same person, however, in a public education system. Research in the 1960s and 1970s (Hetherington & Parke, 1986) has left little doubt that busy schoolteachers with large classes tend to ignore, punish, and reject creative students who are not inclined to respond to classroom instruction in a conventional and convergent way.

Other examples would reveal the same underlying process. Our personal acceptability in the social circle to which we belong, either by choice or by chance, is far from unconditional. It depends on the degree to which we are equipped to contribute to the goals and purposes that the group values. We suggest this process to be as true of the small family that values and teaches personal responsibility to its children as it is of large corporations that value profits and require productivity of their employees.

Ambiguous social evaluations. Most of the difficulties that can be expected in finding an appropriate match between group values and individual talents could be avoided if individuals would seek companionship only from the groups to which they are most suited. Three considerations prevent this, however. The first is that this would require individuals to react to rejection comfortably and move on in search of more accepting peers. This seldom happens, particularly in the formative years, when our reference groups are a major source of self-validation. Rejection from these significant groups can hardly be expected to be taken indifferently. Additionally, we know of no reason to suggest that rejection by our primary reference groups at any time should be responded to indifferently. Such indifference is usually a denial of the strong emotion that is typically evoked by rejection.

Second, membership in many groups is not volitional, and the prospects for moving on to "greener pastures" are nonexistent. Examples of this include membership in families, and to a lesser extent, employment status.

Third and most important, a majority of the appraisals we receive from significant groups or individuals are not entirely rejecting. Rather, they are messages in which disappointment is veiled by expressions of hope that we might do better next time. A loving mother's eagerness to assist her daughter with her first home-cooked meal can also imply an inability to do it alone. Similarly, a friendly reminder of a deadline also suggests that we might forget, and if a teacher singles us out to compliment us on our academic work with the suggestion we apply ourselves more diligently, have we not also been told that our performance is less than desirable? Praise also goes two ways: A parent's delight with a child's latest achievement also creates the possibility of future disappointment. Because most of these evaluations are veiled, they seldom damage the self permanently, but they do alert it to the negative possibilities of what might be said. Rejection is implied; rarely is it stated explicitly. Comments about one's assertiveness, as appropriate in some situations, may also be a reminder of the importance of knowing and keeping one's place.

These are the messages of real life. They are descriptive evaluations having undesirable qualities or lacking desirable ones. Some of these messages are explicit, but more often, they are implicit. Others are almost completely veiled, detectable only by, for example, the strain of a throat being cleared.

Much of what is pertinent to the development of self-esteem and to the larger question of abnormality, depends on the manner in which we respond to these thinly disguised criticisms from our social environment. The two most basic responses to these "mixed" messages are to cope with or avoid the conflicts inherent in them.

Responding to mixed messages. To cope with these veiled criticisms would require the individual to actively seek explicit clarification of the views, feelings, and perceptions behind the messages. This would remove ambiguity and replace it with clarity and precision of language. It would make explicit what message was intended, either intentionally or unintentionally. It would require the messenger to behave at a high level of personal responsibility. All of this involves a high level of personal risk taking. It creates the possibility of finding out that one is seen as inept, lazy, impulsive, dull, or whatever else the self fears finding out.

It also requires a high level of personal introspection and reality testing to see if perceptions by others are fundamentally true of the self. And if they are true, we must also decide how *we* feel about them compared to the reference group. It is entirely possible that being called lazy by a group of obsessive overachievers is not really such a bad thing, or that being called dull by intellectual snobs is a pleasant compliment if properly understood. The most likely consequences of coping are to (a) integrate the perceptions of others into a more accurate self-image if those perceptions are valid, or (b) excuse oneself from the coercive influence of others' perceptions if their evaluations and values are not in harmony with the perceptions and values of the individual.

Avoidance of these complex and threatening issues is the easier course to follow. All we must now do is avoid critical questions and deny any responsibility for our personal views and feelings. As we do this, it becomes easier to mold our behavior so that it is more acceptable and pleasing to the wishes of our reference group. Pretending is the easiest solution. If we appear to be pleasant when we are angry, cooperative when we are belligerent, and entertained when we are bored, there will be few occasions for others to find fault with us. Efforts in the direction of conformity are usually rewarded quickly as our chameleon exterior takes on the colors of those around us. The results of avoidance are (a) an increase in our skill at *impression management*, which is the ability to appear to be what others want us to be, and (b) a gradual decrease in our sense of personal identity and self.

Summary. Contained in Assumption 1 are two essential features in our model of self-esteem. The first is the recognition that, because of the undeniable individual differences among humans, there exists the certainty that all of us will have to deal with rejection. We are not saying that this disapproval is a major source of low self-esteem. Rather, it is a catalyst that activates other psychological processes that influence the development of self-esteem. Second, individual response styles to this rejection will involve varying degrees and mixtures of coping and avoidance. To the degree that a response style favors coping, it will increase the development of a realistic sense of personal identity, self-evaluation, and personal growth. To the degree that a response style favors avoidance, it will increase one's tendency to manage impressions as a means of gaining the approval of others. This inevitably, and even necessarily, contributes to a fundamental alienation of the self and its authentic thoughts, feelings, impulses, and strivings.

Assumption 2

Most people receive and enjoy substantial amounts of authentic favorable social feedback, but they tend not to believe it. In our discussion of the inevitability of rejection, under Assumption 1, we were able to base many of our observations about individual differences and group sanctions on some commonly recognized facts from the social and behavioral sciences. We were glad for the conceptual guidance provided by an existent body of knowledge. Such information helps minimize extravagant speculation; more important, this accumulated knowledge actually helps shape the development of new explanatory constructs and assumptions.

Assumptions are generally considered to be most useful when they appear to be logical extensions of a relatively well-established body of knowledge (Kazdin, 1980). Of course, this is not always the case. In our discussion of self-esteem, it seems most applicable because this topic is only in the formative stages of knowledge development.

Regrettably, the development of Assumption 2 was not influenced by, and cannot be based on, reliable supplementary information as was Assumption 1. Clinical experience, shared observations, and a fair amount of consensual agreement among our colleagues are the basis for this assumption. Again, however, we wish to remind the reader that careful observation is the first step in truly good science (Bednar, Burlingame, & Masters, 1988; Kazdin, 1980). While recognizing the limitations of persuasion by clinical example, we will explain and illustrate our second assumption.

Western society is far from stingy when it comes to giving favorable feedback to others. Compliments usually relate to the appearance of new clothes, cars, furniture, and other material possessions. Our public-relations-minded society requires managers to compliment and reward quality performance in its employees. Improvement is often just as important as outstanding performance, so compliments are hardly limited to the gifted few. Certainly, some of this favorable feedback is not authentic and is appropriately disregarded, but much of it is completely authentic and is still disregarded. Two examples will illustrate this point.

> About 10 years ago I remember reading a very impressive term paper by a first-year student in a clinical psychology training program. I was so impressed by the paper that the first time I saw that student in the hall I stopped and talked with her. It was a short and simple conversation. I told her I had read her paper carefully and was very impressed. I mentioned several of the specific points in the paper that made it so exceptional in my view. I also explained what qualities set this particular paper apart from other first-year papers. It was a brief but pleasant conversation. I delivered a well-deserved compliment and forgot about it. Several weeks later this student came to my office and wanted to talk. It was a difficult conversation for her. She wanted to know what I *really* thought about her academic talents!

Our second example represents an experience we have found to be quite common to psychotherapy groups.

> One of the most common and puzzling experiences in small groups generally takes place the first time group members clearly request direct feedback about how they are seen by other group members. This usually occurs early in the life of the group, and the requests tend to be rather simple and

straightforward. Usually, such a request can be taken at face value; the group members are curious about the type of first impression they make. Seldom is the request made in such a way that would suggest the need for a carefully reasoned and documented character analysis or sweeping value judgment regarding the worth of the individual. It tends simply to be a request for feedback about first impressions.

Nevertheless, such a request frequently generates an inordinate level of anxiety, avoidance, and a misunderstanding of the literal meaning of the request. Seldom do group members show a willingness to share their first impressions of the group members, though such impressions are clearly present. Put most simply, adults tend to be very apprehensive about the prospect of telling others how they really see them. Eventually, and usually with a great deal of tension, someone will start sharing his or her impressions with group members. Gradually, more and more group members get involved in sharing interpersonal perceptions. The initial tension starts to subside, and individuals begin asking more specific questions about how they are seen by others. Once this takes place, an interesting thing happens. If the feedback is generally favorable, people listen attentively and appreciatively. But once the favorable feedback ends, they say something like "Go ahead and tell me about the negative things—I can take it." The implication is that the real truth has been withheld, or worse, the favorable feedback was just a means of "getting ready" for the real truth. Ironically, if the initial feedback is unfavorable, seldom, if ever, have we seen clients ask for feedback about their more desirable qualities.

These are only two of many clinical or social examples we could use to illustrate the degree to which favorable feedback seems to be less believable than unfavorable feedback. This observation raises an interesting question. Why is it that so many people are willing to accept negative feedback from others, which may or may not be valid, while they tend to reject positive feedback, even when it is valid?

The answer lies in our disposition to impression management: to make ourselves appear more acceptable to our peers when we get messages that we are not. Many different fears can be involved in our eagerness to avoid rejection by others.

But all of these fears share a common property—they are all immediate and highly motivating psychological states. In social situations, one of the most frequent expressions of fear of rejection is approval seeking, that is, presenting oneself to others in a way that is congruent with the expectations, values, and dominant interests of others. Earlier in this chapter, we defined this as impression management. The specific term, however, is not as important as the function that this process serves. It is a method of gaining approval by being that which pleases others.

Unfortunately, this process can have two devastating and self-defeating components. The first is rather obvious and has already been discussed in detail earlier in this chapter. That is, the more persons act in ways dictated by external sources, the more alienated they may become from themselves. Far more important, however, are the destructive effects of impression management on new social learning. If people continually present themselves to others in ways that are artificially designed to be pleasing, then any interpersonal feedback about their pleasing qualities will be a reflection of the facade they have presented rather than of the enduring qualities of the personality.

Because most people cannot remain entirely oblivious of their impression management tendencies at all times, they are also aware that much of the feedback they receive is not believable because it is based on the facade they have presented. The effects of such feedback are minimal inasmuch as the limitations on the credibility of the feedback are perfectly understood by the impression manager. This principle is clearly portrayed by common statements such as "If you really knew me you wouldn't think I was such a good friend," or "We'll see what you think of me when you really get to know me." Such statements portray the rejection of favorable interpersonal feedback because of impression management designed to hide other attributes, which are assumed to be less desirable. Similarly, a common curative factor assumed to be operating in most forms of psychotherapy, irrespective of specific treatment techniques, is the endurance of an interpersonal relationship with the therapist, who "knows all" (absence of impression management) and voluntarily stays in the relationship.

An interesting paradox about impression management now becomes obvious. The more individuals engage in it as a means of gaining approval and acceptance, the less likely they are to believe and accept the favorable feedback that they desperately seek. In general terms, it appears that *the greater the impression management, the less believable the favorable feedback.*

Summary. Collectively, then, external feedback is of primary importance for the development of self-esteem in two ways. First, it is the source of abundant unfavorable feedback that is reasonably authentic and potent. And second, if people avoid facing reality by impression management, they create the conditions that render most of the favorable feedback they receive untrustworthy, unbelievable, and psychologically impotent. In fact, most of the feedback from our social environment does not foster good coping skills because of the social pressure to deny the self and conform to social expectations.

Internal Feedback

In psychological circles, feedback is usually thought of as an interpersonal phenomenon. We seldom hear about feedback as an intrapersonal event and, when we do, it is generally referred to as *self-talk* by most behavioral scientists. We will suggest that intrapersonal feedback, or internal feedback, is both a common and influential psychological event for most people. We will attempt to identify and describe this phenomenon in considerable detail and differentiate it from the traditional concept of self-talk. The following three questions will guide our discussion:

1. What are self-evaluations?

2. How are self-evaluative processes different from the various conceptions of self-talk that have become so influential recently (Beck, Rush, Shaw, & Emery, 1979; Meichenbaum, 1977).

3. What role do self-evaluations play in the development of self-esteem?

Assumption 3

Self-evaluations are a psychological reality for most people. We will suggest that self-evaluative processes play a pivotal role in the development and maintenance of either high or low levels of personal self-esteem. As will become clear later, however, we see little structural or substantive similarity between traditional formulations of self-talk and our conception of self-evaluative processes. We will clarify these important differences later in our discussion. Our thesis is that most people are continually engaged in a process of noticing, monitoring, thinking about, and evaluating their behavior and performance. We suggest that these self-evaluations are the primary basis for feelings of personal approval and disapproval *because they frequently reflect the degree to which a person has developed a response style that favors either coping or avoidance.*

What Are Self-Evaluative Processes? Self-evaluative processes involve two basic ingredients: cognitive awareness and affective experiencing. Throughout the book, and in all the examples, it is important to note that all self-evaluations are cognitive–affective events. Both components are equally important and will be explained in greater detail later in this section. We will illustrate self-evaluative processes with an example and, then, discuss the role of cognitive awareness and affective experiencing in self-evaluative processes.

> Several years ago our department hired a young new assistant professor. She was a talented researcher and therapist with a promising future, but her current teaching skills left something to be desired, as did her teacher ratings. We became good friends and talked often. Whenever these conversations touched on her anxiety about teaching, which was often, she would almost always start the conversation with a statement such as "I am doing better," "The last class was horrible," or "I don't think I was cut out to be a teacher." All of these statements are uncamouflaged self-evaluations about performance.

A moment's reflection will reveal that self-evaluations of this type are common to most of us, but not all self-evaluations focus on such obvious and observable behavior, however. For example,

> I once had a client who had developed an interpersonal style designed to minimize interpersonal conflict. She did this by consistently trying to be as acceptable and pleasing to others as possible. This is not a particularly unusual style; it is commonly referred to in psychological circles as that of a "pleaser and placater." As this client became more aware of her avoidant behavior and the function it served for her, she started exploring the feelings she had about herself for being a pleaser at all costs. She thought of herself as weak for needing the approval of others so desperately. She also thought it was inappropriate for an adult to pretend to be something she was not as a means of buying approval from others. As a result of these self-evaluations, her personal feelings about herself were negative and intense. She hated herself for being unable to stand alone, or, as she put it, "to be true to myself." It is important to note that these self-evaluations were anchored to fairly accurate perceptions of her behavior and the function it served.

Cognitive awareness and self-evaluative processes. As we said earlier, cognitive awareness and affective experiencing are major components of self-evaluation. We have no reason to believe that these two attributes are equally distributed in the population. Rather, it seems much more likely to suppose that they are learned attributes, with some people being much more adept than others in either or both areas. *But we have absolutely no reason to believe that people can be completely unaware of their behavior and the function that it serves or the self-evaluations that accompany that behavior.* This could be a controversial point in the minds of some, particularly those who favor an analytic point of view, with its emphasis on repression and denial. We will not even attempt to resolve the question of how complete repression can be. For the purposes of our discussion, however, it is sufficient to point out that even Freud (1915/1937) suggested that repression could not be absolute. Hidden impulse, at a minimum, would find expression in one form or another. Additionally, we wish to remind the reader that anxiety-producing conflicts, no matter how deeply repressed, must be recognized before they can be responded to defensively. Again, we see the possibility that awareness of behavior and its meaning are a psychological reality for most people. Certainly, vast differences in the clarity and precision of this awareness can be expected. But these differences are probably more a question of explicitness than of existence. For some, there can be a high degree of clarity and explicitness in their personal awareness and self-evaluations. For others, the same phenomenon takes place, but at a level of clarity that could only be called vague. The important point is our assumption that self-evaluative processes are a psychological reality for most people and, when necessary, these self-evaluations can be made clearer and more explicit by appropriate methods of observation and inquiry.

For example, it would be unreasonable to expect the woman who was a pleaser in our earlier example to be able to label accurately and succinctly the role and function of her behavior without assistance. However, she would probably not find it difficult to describe the way she acted around people whom she wanted to like her if she were asked such a question. It is equally doubtful that she would find it difficult to speculate about the reasons why she acted that way. Once behavior styles have been identified and described with reasonable clarity, the self-evaluations that accompany these behavior patterns can become obvious to both the client and the therapist. In principle, then, we are suggesting that virtually all self-evaluations can be made reasonably clear and explicit with appropriate methods of observation and inquiry. We will say more about this process in chapter 6.

Affective experiencing and self-evaluative processes. Although cognitive awareness is an essential component of self-evaluation, it is not the most important one. It is imperative that self-evaluative processes not be confused with detached, analytical, or purely cognitive activities. Our conception of self-evaluation is too emotionally robust to be accommodated by such a limited definition. We assume that virtually any human experience will have some affective valence attached to it. Some of these emotions may be more obvious or intense than others, but these are variations in degree, not existence. People regularly notice what they do (cognitions), how they feel (affect), and how they feel about what they are doing (cognition–affect).

Self-evaluative processes are ultimately anchored to what clients see cognitively and experience affectively about themselves as a result of their own most authentic motives and behavior. It is as though individuals were participant–observers of their own lives. This allows individuals to observe their own tendencies to avoid or cope with psychological threat. A coping response, in which the person actively seeks resolution to psychological conflict in spite of fear and anxiety, is a fundamentally self-affirming experience. The favorable, and sometimes intense, affective evaluation that follows is the inevitable consequence of the adaptive behavior. The converse is equally true of an avoidant response. No matter how strategic a retreat from pathological anxiety may appear, it will still evoke a virtually reflexive negative affective evaluation. Self-evaluations are close relatives of primary processes and need little, if any, secondary interpretation.

For example, pleasers and placaters are (or can become) aware of the underlying meaning and motives of their behavior, and they have an affective response (evaluative) to their perceptions. In this case, the lack of psychological integrity implicit in the act of avoiding rejection by pretending to be that which is more pleasing to others can be (a) accurately perceived by the individual at some level of awareness, and (b) the source of considerable affective displeasure for the undesirable psychological qualities inherent in the motives and behavior. We are suggesting a high and continuous level of correspondence between the level of psychological integrity inherent in some response patterns and the affective evaluation it generates.

Brief commentary on self-evaluative processes. At the highest levels of cognitive awareness and affective experiencing, self-evaluations are anchored to identifiable patterns of behavior and motives. We are not talking about specific events or situations; we are referring to "behavioral styles" or "trait dispositions" that transcend events and endure time, and to patterns of motives and behavior that are identifiable and describable.

These patterns of behavior contain varying degrees and mixtures of one's enduring tendency to avoid or cope with anxiety-producing conflict. We suggest that self-evaluations tend to be consistently negative in the presence of patterns of avoidance simply because these patterns are so unflattering. We further suggest that people are, or can become, aware of their avoidance patterns and the personal inadequacies implicit in avoidance strategies. Those perceptions, or psychological realities, are the basis for the negative self-evaluations. They are at least partially reality bound.

Conversely, favorable self-evaluations are the inevitable result of coping. Inherent in coping responses are higher levels of risk taking, personal responsibility, and human growth, which are more satisfying psychological responses to anxiety and conflicts. This could result from social learning factors, which are rather obvious in our society, or from more intrinsic rewards inherent in the process of coping. In either case, favorable self-evaluations tend to accompany coping more than avoidance because coping is a more favorable response.

This entire process may occur at lower levels of clarity and explicitness than we have described. When self-evaluations are not clearly attached to identifiable patterns and motives, they are simply more difficult to understand. They are more general and free-floating. Similarly, when self-evaluations remain vague, it is more difficult to understand feelings of despair and poor self-regard. But, in either case, feelings of approval or disapproval probably accompany coping or avoidance even though people differ in the clarity and explicitness with which this process is seen and understood.

This does not mean, however, that we are suggesting some mystical process that is difficult to understand. On the contrary, we have found very few clients who have had difficulty in identifying, describing, and labeling their most important behavior patterns and the self-evaluations that accompany them. It seems to depend entirely on the desire of the therapist to ask clients to identify and describe selected behavior patterns and the self-evaluations they generate. We will say more about the methods of observation and interviewing essential to this task in chapter 6.

Self-Evaluative Processes and Self-Talk: Important Differences

We see few similarities between our conception of self-evaluative processes and the major conceptions of self-talk.

Accurate perceptions or social learning? We have already indicated that self-evaluative processes are based on a continuous process of noticing, monitoring, thinking about, and directly experiencing the affective consequences of one's enduring patterns of behavior. Our definition of behavior refers to more than observable behavioral acts; it also includes internal events such as thoughts and feelings. Traditional conceptions of self-talk rely almost exclusively on the cognitive elements of personal awareness and evaluation. According to these views, human emotions and behavior are an expression of the attitudes and beliefs that we acquire about ourselves in a social context. Typically, these attitudes are most obvious in the specific sentences that people use when they talk to themselves about themselves.

For example, if students did poorly on an exam, they might say something to themselves such as, "I did poorly on this exam. Boy, am I a dunce." The result would be negative feelings about themselves. Examination of the self-talk involved in this scenario reveals what most cognitive–behavioral therapists would call irrational beliefs in their sentences, which are the proximate cause of their newly acquired psychic distress. The first irrational belief is that they are dunces because they did poorly on the exam. This would be considered irrational because it is an overgeneralized statement. In reality, doing poorly on an exam does not make one a dunce. Few would dispute that fact. Accordingly, eliminating irrational and self-accusatory sentences from self-talk can also eliminate the cause of the negative feelings.

The second irrational belief in this case is more implicit but just as influential and irrational. It is the belief that it is horrible to do poorly on an exam. If a cognitive–behavioral therapist were to examine this irrational belief, a dialogue between therapist and client would probably sound something like this:

Therapist:	You seem a little down-in-the-mouth today. Care to talk about it?
Client:	It's *horrible,* Doc! I just found out this morning that I failed my chemistry exam.
Therapist:	You say you failed your exam, and it's horrible!
Client:	Look, Doc, if I can't pass a simple exam like that one, what'll it be like when I have to take the final? I may as well start packing right now. What's the use?
Therapist:	It sounds to me as though you believe failing that one exam is a major catastrophe.
Client:	Well, that's exactly what it is—a *major* catastrophe.
Therapist:	Okay, Jim, you are telling me how horrible and catastrophic it is that you failed that test, right? Now, I want you to pay careful attention to how you're feeling at this moment. Can you tell me what you're feeling?
Client:	I feel like the door to my future just slammed shut. I feel—well, hopeless is the best word I can think of.
Therapist:	So, you failed an exam, you tell yourself it's horrible, and you feel hopeless. Can you see how labeling that event as horrible causes you to feel hopeless?
Client:	But it really seems that way to me.
Therapist:	Have you ever done poorly on a test before?
Client:	Well, sure I have, a few times. But this seems so much worse.
Therapist:	Can you recall how you felt during those times?
Client:	Well, I guess I felt a lot like I do now.
Therapist:	So it probably seemed horrible then, too. But here you are. You've graduated from high school, been accepted into a fine university, and successfully completed two semesters. That doesn't seem so horrible to me.

Client: Well, when you look at it that way, it doesn't seem quite so bad.

Therapist: And that's precisely the point. As you look at it differently, you'll have different feelings. Now, rather than labeling your test failure as horrible, let's explore some more rational ways of viewing it and see what happens to your feelings.

In essence, then, cognitive–behavioral approaches emphasize the irrationality of human thinking and personal beliefs in the development of emotional distress. All of these approaches share the assumption that the irrational beliefs revealed in self-talk are without foundation: They are simply acquired beliefs that are best disregarded. Additionally, most of these approaches view self-talk as a psychological trigger that activates useless negative feelings that eventually come to serve as inhibitors to human behavior and performance. Consistent with these views is the assumption that negative feelings and emotional inhibitors can be most expeditiously removed by identifying and eliminating irrational beliefs, values, attitudes, and sentences from self-talk.

Self-evaluations, on the other hand, are based on an entirely different set of assumptions and psychological processes. In the first place, they are not considered to be acquired, irrational beliefs. Rather, they are assumed to be at least partially valid self-perceptions. These perceptions have their origins in one of the most fundamental levels of psychological experiencing. They are based on a cognitive awareness of self and the direct affective experience that accompanies that awareness. The most fundamental differences between self-talk and self-evaluative processes should now be more apparent. In the first place, self-evaluations are based on what we consider to be at least partially valid self-perceptions. They are not simply learned, irrational beliefs that are central to the various definitions of self-talk. Second, self-evaluative processes are based on the best elements of cognitive and affective dimensions of human experience, whereas self-talk is primarily a cognitive event; and because the affect in self-evaluations is intimately tied to enduring patterns of behavior, these emotions are generic to the individual and can be quite intense and durable.

Self-Evaluations and Self-Esteem

We maintain that high levels of self-esteem are the product of a response style that favors coping over avoidance. When this is the case, conflicts are faced, understood, and resolved, resulting in self-confidence, personal approval, and feelings of personal well-being. Patterns of excessive avoidance breed just the opposite results. The very act of avoidance, by denial and distortion, precludes any feeling of adequacy. Therefore, the tendency to cope or avoid virtually dictates the positive or negative nature of personal psychological experience.

Finally, it is of utmost importance to note that self-evaluative processes and the levels of self-esteem that they create are based on the *process* of coping and avoidance, not on the *outcomes* that they produce. An amusing example of this comes from one of the writer's clients who was acutely self-conscious about his inability to sing.

> The client avoided any occasion where his lack of vocal talent might be evidenced. Sufficiently exasperated, he resolved to confront his fear once and for all. He did so by responding to an ad in a music trade paper announcing auditions for a professional singer. The client entered the crowded audition hall, stood before the director, producer, and dozens of other auditioning singers, and sang "My Country 'Tis of Thee" without accompaniment. The director smiled, the producer shook his head, and there were several audible coughs and laughs from the onlookers. The client said "thank you" and walked out of the room. The outcome is obvious. The client did not make the callback list, and there was ample negative feedback to verify what he already knew about his singing skills.

However, there were other outcomes that were less discernible. In undertaking this action, the client (a) understood the risks involved in auditioning (potential embarrassment, ridicule), (b) openly acknowledged and accepted those risks, and (c) made his best effort at performing, never denying the possibility of a negative outcome. Although his worst fears were realized in some regards, his ability to approach this long-avoided task produced personal pleasure and self-approval for not letting his fears dictate his behavior entirely. To this day, he tells this story with pride, humor, and fondness.

Assumption 4

Self-evaluative processes can provide a basis for continuous affective feedback from the self about the adequacy of the self. It is time to discuss the role of personal emotions in the development of self-esteem. We consider emotions to be the crowning element in the development of either high or low levels of self-esteem. As discussed earlier, cognitive activity is important to our model because it provides a means to identify and clarify the role and the function that various behavior patterns serve. In this regard, cognitions are in the service of increasing psychic clarity and understanding. However, cognitions per se are not affect laden. Their power to motivate and influence human behavior is limited compared to the power of aroused affect. In our model, self-esteem is not a thought but a subjective and enduring state of realistic self-approval. It is a feeling people experience about themselves. The same thing is true of low self-esteem. We must attempt to explain where these feelings come from!

In our view, in a corrective therapeutic encounter, clients experience their own affect directly in its full intensity. The fact that emotions can be discussed and understood cognitively does not necessarily alter the nature of the feelings or their influence. And the self-evaluative processes we have already discussed provide the conduit for accessing client emotions that are most relevant to the therapeutic process. We will illustrate this point with two clinical examples. The first is a patient suffering from paranoid schizophrenia who was in treatment for seven years. The second is a typical client treated on an outpatient basis. We have included the former to help illustrate this proposition because it represents one of the most difficult clinical situations that we can imagine. In each of these examples, we hope to demonstrate the rapidity with which self-evaluative processes, and the feelings that they represent, can influence the behavior of the individual. We will start with the schizophrenic client.

This particular client was a young woman with exceptional intellectual talents. She was first diagnosed as a paranoid schizophrenic approximately 9 years earlier. She had frequent psychotic breaks, which could only be partially controlled with phenothiazines. However, she was able to remain un-hospitalized as long as she met with her therapist weekly. On those occasions when her therapist was out of town for more than a week she would invariably be hospitalized. She had been in treatment with the same therapist for over 5 years when this particular example occurred. During this time, the client had maintained what must be considered a remarkably good therapeutic relationship, given her diagnosis.

In this particular session, the client arrived and took her customary seat. She was slightly more quiet than usual and obviously preoccupied. After an appropriate silence, the therapist asked if she thought she should be talking about the thoughts and feelings she seemed to be avoiding. She indicated that she didn't know. The therapist then asked how she felt about herself for her avoidance during a therapy session. After an extraordinarily long silence, the client said that she *should* talk about it, but that she was afraid. Her therapist asked her to try to identify what she needed to do during the session so she could approve of herself when it was over. She thought about it and hesitantly started talking about the increasing tensions in her marriage and the growing prospect that her husband might leave her. The prospect of being alone terrified her, mostly because of the implications of her mental health problems. In spite of the distressing content she was discussing, the client gradually became more re-sponsive to herself and her therapist. When the session was over, the therapist asked if she was leaving the session ap-proving of what she did during the hour. She said yes. More-over, she wished she could handle other issues in her life in the same way without the assistance of her therapist.

In this example, we see three areas of self-evaluation and their emotional consequences. The first is the client's personal disapproval for avoiding the issues about which she was most concerned. This disapproval was manifested verbally and by her dysphoric mood and withdrawal. The second area of self-evaluation was her personal approval for facing the issue during the therapy session. This was manifested verbally and by her improved mood and behavior. The effects of this approval seem to have transcended the stress associated with the topic being discussed. The third area of self-evaluation was her disapproval for needing the therapist to help her face problems rather than avoid them.

On the whole, however, this client experienced substantially more self-approval during this hour than disapproval, and the session ended with the therapist fairly confident that she would not need to be hospitalized during the week or call for additional sessions. In the therapist's mind, her attempts at coping with a difficult life issue produced more personal self-approval than could be obtained by hiding from these unpleasant realities. We find that attempts by the client to cope with difficult psychic issues nearly always engender more internal self-approving affect than is necessary to cope successfully with the stress involved. This tends to be true irrespective of the stress and fear associated with some topics, no matter how fragile the client. We suggest that this client found hope in a fairly desperate situation because of the immediate self-approval she *felt* as a result of coping with this difficult situation for the better part of an hour. Although we cannot be absolutely sure that this is the case, it is obvious that her improved mental status was *not* the result of an improved marriage, diminished fears about being left alone, external reassurance, or significant progress toward resolution of a personal problem!

Our second example is more typical.

> This client was a middle-aged, upper-middle-class business-man. A number of therapy hours had already been devoted to examining his tendency to avoid interpersonal conflicts. This client found it less distressing to simply accommodate

the needs and wishes of others than to get into interpersonal confrontations. Regrettably, however, this strategy was as effective at diminishing his self-respect as it was for avoiding conflict. He suffered moderately severe depression, and considered himself to be a coward and hypocrite. In reality, he resented others' demands on him and his inability to resist them. The client finally arrived at the point of understanding that his own personal approval required that he represent himself more honestly in his dealings with others whether this would lead to conflict or not. He promptly went to those with whom he had unresolved issues and expressed his feelings more openly and honestly than usual. While these people were mildly surprised at his feelings, it was hardly a noticeable event in their lives. Even though these behavioral changes made no obvious or appreciable difference in how this man was seen or treated by others, he reported feeling "like a new man." He took great pride in his accomplishments, vowed not to be dishonest in his dealings with others for any reason, and found himself feeling remarkably better.

In both of these examples, we see the possibility of significant personal improvement because of the self-approval experienced by clients in their attempts to cope with problems that they typically avoided.

This entire proposition is based on the assumption that self-evaluative processes can be continuous, and that their affective consequences are immediate. This is particularly true when there are deliberate shifts from avoidance to coping in an attempt to face what is usually avoided. It is important to note that improved self-evaluations and the self-approving feelings they create are more the result of attempting to cope than of achieving any specific outcome. In many cases, even an unfavorable outcome will not negate the psychological benefits of attempting to cope. The effects of the very act of avoidance or coping are assumed to be more potent, consequential, and influential than most of the outcomes that either act will produce.

The prominent role of emotions in our formulation of self-esteem should now be obvious. Ultimately, the development of self-esteem is anchored directly to what clients actually experience affectively *about* themselves as a result of their own behavior. Coping breeds a pleasant and rewarding affective experience. And if the organism has an enduring tendency to cope rather than avoid, the organism's internal, self-evaluative feedback loop will produce favorable affective feedback for the organism. *It is the nature and quality of this internal, affective feedback that defines the nature of the organism to itself.* High or low self-esteem, then, is the result and the reflection of the internal, affective feedback that the organism most commonly experiences.

Summary

We have described a process of internal self-evaluation that we suggest is a central element in the development of either high or low levels of personal self-esteem. In essence, when there is consistency in one's tendency to cope or avoid conflict, there is a continuous basis for internal feedback from the self about the adequacy of the self. Avoidance breeds negative self-evaluative processes, feelings, and perceptions because of the inherently undesirable qualities of this behavior. Coping is associated with favorable self-evaluative processes, feelings, and perceptions because of the high psychological quality of the elements associated with this response. In each case, these perceptions are assumed to be at least partially valid and a direct reflection of the actual attributes involved in coping and avoidance. Even though these self-evaluative processes go on at different levels of clarity and explicitness for different people, their effects are a psychological reality for most people. Finally, we have suggested that internal self-evaluations play a more important role in determining the form and substance of human behavior than external evaluation does, although both are clearly influential.

5

Introduction to the Model

We are now ready to combine the prior concepts that we have discussed with our four assumptions about feedback into a series of propositions to explain the origins and dynamics of high and low levels of personal self-esteem. We will discuss these propositions sequentially and then illustrate the assumed interrelationships among them.

Origins and Dynamics of Personal Self-Esteem

1. Self-esteem is a dynamic attribute. We do not consider self-esteem to be necessarily fixed at any point in the life span. We think it can be either static or dynamic, depending on the changing behavior dispositions of the individual across the life span. Rigid behavior patterns characterized by a tendency to avoid conflict consistently are not likely to be associated with improved self-esteem. This is not because self-esteem is invariant but because the behavior patterns that most readily influence the development of self-esteem are fixed. We believe that feelings of personal worth are highly responsive to authentic, consistent feedback from either the social environment or self-evaluations. Favorable internal feedback is more potent, with longer-lasting benefits, than is social approval for reasons that we have already discussed. Similarly, negative feedback from either source can prove to be devastating. In either situation, however, feelings of personal approval are responsive to the evaluative thoughts of self and others.

We submit, then, that a sense of self-appreciation is primarily a reflection of one's tendency to choose coping over avoidance when faced with conflicts that involve fear and anxiety. It is, secondarily, a reflection of the way in which one is valued by others. Any change in either of these two factors can have a significant influence on one's self-esteem, but how one perceives oneself will always be more influential than how one is perceived by others.

For the remainder of our discussion, self-esteem refers to a psychological attribute that is responsive to consistent, credible feedback from either internal or external sources. We will discuss the potency and consequences of feedback from these different sources more fully in another section of this chapter. For now, we wish only to suggest that self-esteem can move along a continuum from high to virtually nonexistent. Dramatic movement along this continuum, however, is unlikely in the absence of equally dramatic changes in individual response patterns.

2. Psychological threat is unavoidable! In our discussion of the concept of coping, we have repeatedly emphasized that coping is the path of reality testing, insight, and the recognition of imperfections in the self. It should be clear that the very psychological attributes we have used to define the coping response will also guarantee the eventual recognition of personal limitations. In effect, we have a two-edged sword. First, personal limitations must be recognized and accepted openly before they can be faced and dealt with. This creates personal threat and discomfort. Second, learning to understand and face this threat is the basis for the most powerful forms of psychological learning.

In brief, psychological threat is a reality for us all. For some, the frequency and intensity of the threat can be consistently high. For others, it can remain relatively low. However, everyone is vulnerable to psychological threat in some areas, and overcoming this threat is one of the most basic processes involved in personal growth and development. Because of this, we suggest that the frequency and intensity of psychological threat can vary along a continuum from very high to relatively low.

3. *Self-esteem modifies psychological threat.* We suggest that there is an inverse relationship between levels of self-esteem and levels of psychological threat. As self-esteem increases, the frequency and intensity of psychological threat decrease. The converse is equally true. As self-esteem decreases, the frequency and intensity of psychological threat increases. There are two primary reasons for suggesting this relationship. Both are equally important, though one is based on a large body of empirical data and the other on a content analysis of avoidance and coping. We will start with our content analysis.

Coping and avoidance are based on attributes the intrinsic qualities of which lend themselves to either increasing or decreasing psychological threat. The act of avoidance virtually precludes the possibility of new learning. Its primary function is to avoid fear and anxiety. Avoidance does not provide a basis for learning new or more adaptive response patterns, or for reducing the number of areas in which a person's psychological function is impaired; nor does it provide any hope for personal growth and development. If avoidance does anything with surety, it provides people with personal experiences and perceptions of themselves as unable to deal with anxiety, fear, or conflict. Such experiences and self-perceptions can only be expected to impair further the person's ability to respond to threatening situations in the future. The result is an increase in the frequency and intensity of perceived psychological threats.

On the other hand, the act of coping with personal conflict requires risk taking, personal responsibility, and willingness to face personal issues realistically. When this is done successfully, people not only broaden their understanding of themselves and the world they live in, they also experience themselves as able to deal with threatening situations productively. This is a powerful consideration in any definition of self. It allows a person to approach threatening situations in the future with far less fear and anxiety than might normally be expected. High levels of self-esteem not only contribute to the ability to face and learn from threatening situations, they also contribute to people's perceptions of themselves as able to resolve difficult issues. All of these considerations reduce the number of events that a person finds threatening and increase the inclination to respond appropriately when one is threatened.

This content analysis is consistent with a substantial body of research literature. It has been repeatedly demonstrated that self-esteem and psychological health are related to favorable consequences in a variety of psychological situations. High ego strength, for example, is a good indicator of a favorable response to psychotherapy (Garfield, 1986). Not surprisingly, ego strength is related to high self-esteem as well as other measures of personal adjustment (Harmm, 1980). Similarly, individuals with a high internal locus of control as measured by the Rotter Internal/External Locus of Control Scale (I-E) generally have a more favorable response to psychotherapy than those with a more external orientation (Patrick, 1984). Again, we find that high self-esteem is related to an internal locus of control (Fish & Karabenick, 1971; Sathyavathi & Anthony, 1984) as well as to other desirable psychological attributes, such as perceptual accuracy (Steger, Simmons, & Lavelle, 1973), better adjustment to old age (Carp & Carp, 1981), and less conformity (Singh, Prasad, & Bhagalpur, 1973). Finally, high self-esteem has been related to androgyny or sex-role flexibility (Flaherty & Dusek, 1980). Again, we find the same pattern as before. Androgynous people tend to be well adjusted and more flexible in responding to a wide variety of psychological situations (Bem & Lenney, 1976).

Collectively, then, there are both logical and empirical reasons to suggest an inverse relationship between self-esteem and the experience of psychological threat. The evidence from a variety of settings and researchers consistently describes the benefits derived from the psychological attributes typically related to high self-esteem. All of these observations suggest that high levels of self-esteem are associated with reduced levels of anxiety and fear, probably because the attributes associated with high self-esteem allow a person to respond to these situations more realistically and appropriately. Because of this, we suggest that the experience of psychological threat can vary on a continuum from high to low, depending on an individual's level of self-esteem.

4. Self-esteem varies as a function of response styles to threat. We have already discussed the role, function, and consequence of coping and avoidance in detail in an earlier section of this chapter. Our purpose now is only to highlight some of these considerations and describe the assumed relationships among self-esteem, psychological threat, and response styles. We have already suggested that individual response styles to threat can vary in degree from coping to avoidance. We defined coping as a process of realistically facing up to difficult issues that involve such desirable psychological attributes as self-examination, insight, reality testing, risk taking, and personal responsibility. On the other hand, avoidance and defense are based on a process of denial, distortion, and self-deception as a means of avoiding fear and anxiety. We have said that individual response styles contain varying degrees and mixtures of avoidance and coping. To the extent that these response styles favor coping over avoidance, they tend to engender favorable self-evaluative thoughts and feelings. Conversely, patterns of avoidance can be expected to breed negative self-evaluative thoughts and feelings. These evaluations of the self and the feelings they engender can also be expected to vary from intense to mild. The more extreme the avoidance, the more intense the self-disapproval. The greater the risk and responsibility involved in the coping response, the greater the feelings of self-respect and approval. We will say more about these feedback loops shortly. For now, we wish to emphasize our assumption that enduring response styles do exist, that they can usually be identified explicitly, and that these patterns of behavior are the basis for many self-evaluations.

Summary

We have now described the continuum along which self-esteem, personal threat, and response styles can vary. The relationships among these three variables can be summarized as follows:

1. As self-esteem increases, there is a corresponding decrease in the frequency and intensity of psychological threat. This increases the probability of a coping response to conflict, which will usually generate favorable self-evaluations.

2. As self-esteem declines, there is a corresponding increase in the frequency and intensity of psychological threat. This increases the probability of an avoidance response to conflict, which will generate unfavorable self-evaluations.

With the relationship among these psychological variables now defined, we are ready to discuss the means and mechanisms by which feedback from the social environment, or the self, influences each variable. The remainder of the variables and propositions involved in our model of self-esteem are portrayed in Figure 1. Most of these variables define and describe the means and mechanisms by which self-evaluative processes and feedback from the social environment influence the development and maintenance of high or low levels of self-esteem. The following observations about Figure 1 are central:

1. Collectively, there are more sources of negative feedback-than there are positive ones. Of the five feedback sources represented in the figure, two provide distinctly negative feedback (self-generated disapproval and credible negative feedback from the environment), and one provides positive feedback (self-generated approval). Of the two remaining sources, one provides feedback that is moderately positive (credible positive feedback from the environment), but the other is so untrustworthy that it need not be counted (noncredible positive feedback from the environment). Even though the last feedback source appears to provide positive feedback, it constitutes such a fundamental verification of one's impression management tendencies (avoidance) that its net effect is decidedly negative.

In brief, then, the most important source of enduring self-approval is internal positive self-evaluation. Disapproval, however, can be the result of credible negative feedback and noncredible positive feedback from the social environment, or from negative self-evaluations. It appears that there are more sources of negative information about the self than there are positive ones.

2. While external feedback and self-evaluations influence self-esteem, it is important to note that the two sources are not equal in their ability to do so. The relative potency of each source is suggested by the degree to which its lines of influence (the dotted and dashed lines in Figure 1) are extended to the extreme

Figure 1

The Role of Internal Feedback, External/Social Feedback, and Personal Response Styles in the Development and Maintenance of High or Low Levels of Self-Esteem points on the self-esteem scale. Self-evaluations are clearly the most potent. Note that internal self-evaluations touch both extremes of the internal feedback scale, which in turn touches both extremes of the self-esteem scale, whereas feedback from the social environment does not. Credible negative social feedback is not quite as destructive as negative self-evaluations, and positive social feedback is not nearly as potent or uplifting as positive self-evaluations.

The differences in potency become particularly important when there are any inconsistencies between the feedback provided by internal and external sources. Favorable self-evaluations can more than negate the influence of negative social feedback. Similarly, negative self-evaluations can completely negate the influence of positive social feedback. In essence, we are suggesting that authentic high self-esteem *requires* reasonably high levels of self-approving thoughts. External social feedback can be influential, but usually on a supplementary basis, and only so long as the feedback is continuously available and consistent with other, more basic self-evaluations.

3. Based on our earlier discussion describing the relationships among self-esteem, psychological threat, and response styles portrayed in Figure 1, we would expect feedback to be processed as follows:

　　a. Positive feedback from internal or external sources tends to increase self-esteem, lowers the frequency and intensity of psychological threats, and increases the probability of a coping response when threat does occur. This sequence then provides the organism with feedback (1) to the self, (2) from the self, and (3) about the adequacy of the self. This is the internal self-evaluative process that we have suggested to be virtually continuous. This internal feedback influences the current level of self-esteem, sensitivity to threat, and tendency to avoid or cope with conflict as the cycle repeats itself over and over.

　　b. Negative feedback from either source is processed in essentially the same manner. Current levels of self-esteem are lowered, which increases the probability of an avoidance response when threat does occur. When this happens, the organism receives new internal feedback about the inadequacy of the self. Once again, this internal negative feedback and all of its consequences are entered into the cycle as it repeats itself over and over.

The units of time and behavior involved in any cycle can be highly variable, ranging from relatively brief episodes of appropriately assertive behavior to prolonged periods of self-control and restraint; or they could be based on moral transgressions or prolonged periods of self-indulgence. These considerations are unique to each individual and need not be defined by any a priori theoretical considerations. We are proposing a mechanistic model that defines and describes some of the more basic parameters affecting how evaluations by self and others are conducted. This process is assumed to be applicable to a wide range of behavioral considerations.

Finally, it is important to notice that we have deliberately avoided any attempt to provide profiles that would define coping, avoidance, or response styles. We consider our reasons for this to be compelling. The manifestations of each of these concepts are so varied that they cannot, and probably should not, be made more objective. It would simply be misleading. Remember that avoidance is not defined by any observable behavior patterns; it is defined by the function that the behavior serves. We are referring to motivational constructs when we talk about avoidance and coping. One's intention to face conflict realistically and learn from it is the essence of a coping response. Similarly, one's tendency to escape from conflict is the essence of avoidance. Even though these personality dispositions shape behavior patterns, they cannot be identified by any specific behavior.

For example, simple politeness may be the first attempt by one person to become more sociable and overcome a fear of people, but for another person, this same behavior may be the means of avoiding any interpersonal intimacy with others. The only reliable means of understanding human motives is on an individual basis. We consider the preservation of highly individualized and idiosyncratic considerations within a nonthematic framework of general principles to be one of the greatest strengths of this model. We can discuss the general principles involved in the model, but their application on an individual basis requires an understanding of each particular individual. In brief, we suggest that these general principles remain constant with different individuals, but understanding each individual's unique style of coping and defense is required before the general principles can be used. We will discuss this in more detail in chapter 6.

Theoretical Implications

Before discussing the important theoretical implications of this model, we want to provide a detailed case study to illustrate the clinical manifestation of the concepts that we are discussing. We have two reasons for this. First, from past experience, we have learned that it is easy to confuse the simplicity of the model with its subtlety. A clear conceptual understanding of basic principles does not imply a clear understanding of the behavioral manifestations of these principles. Admittedly, the model is not conceptually complex, but the manifestations of its most central concepts can be highly varied and are seldom obvious. Clinical illustrations contribute to a fuller understanding of the model for most readers. Second, clinical examples can also be used to illustrate the major theoretical implications more fully after these clinical examples are described.

Clinical Illustration

Our first case study is of a pregnant, unmarried 20-year-old woman. We will discuss this case with regard to (a) a brief history, (b) presenting complaints, (c) treatment considerations, (d) critical incidents in psychotherapy, and (e) current status of the patient.

Brief history. During high school, this young woman, like so many teenagers from middle-class America, was preoccupied with personal appearance, peer acceptability, and personal self-consciousness. Her fondest memories of high school were of her senior year, when she was a cheerleader. Other than that, her life was more typical than remarkable. She was not particularly attractive, but she was certainly well-groomed and stylishly dressed. She had more friends than many of her peers but not nearly as many as she would have liked. She was, in essence, in the middle of the bell-shaped curve on most qualities, including feelings of inadequacy and inferiority.

She lived with two reasonably caring parents. Their marriage was probably better than most, though far from exemplary. She had a much better relationship with her mother than with her father, whom she described as detached. She had planned on continuing her college education before she became pregnant.

She had been dating her boyfriend for about eight months before she stopped resisting his sexual advances. Actually, she agreed to sex more out of compassion for her boyfriend's frustration than her own sexual passion; it was just too difficult to say no. This was her first sexual experience. Even though her religious and moral values created a great deal of guilt about her sexual behavior, they were not sufficiently influential to curtail the sexual activity. She found out she was pregnant after three months of sex on an intermittent basis. Birth control measures had not been used regularly.

Presenting complaints. In the initial interview, she complained about depression, feeling deserted by her boyfriend, and confusion about what to do with the baby. She had already decided not to have an abortion, but the question of adoption still remained. Her voice was barely audible when she spoke, she avoided eye contact by looking at the floor, and she had a slight tendency to whine when she talked. With careful probing, she admitted to some feelings of anger toward her boyfriend, but she quickly minimized their importance because they would only make him angry. She described herself as always having had very low self-esteem. Her major concerns focused on the confusion that she felt about whether to keep the baby or place it for adoption, and the feelings of despair that accompanied her depression. From a clinical point of view, her symptoms varied from mild to moderate but fell far short of severe.

Treatment considerations. Major elements in the treatment of the client, based on the principles we are discussing, include:

1. The presence and pervasiveness of the client's impression management tendencies had to be ascertained, which was not difficult in this case. It was clear in the initial interview that this

young woman was far more accustomed to gaining approval from others by impression management than by making herself known to those around her. Her proclivity toward impression management was repeatedly suggested by

   a. her preoccupation with peer acceptance and approval;

   b. denial of her feelings of anger toward her boyfriend because they would be unacceptable to him;

   c. excessive and almost unquestioning conformity to conventional social standards (clothing styles, appearance, and value placed on being a cheerleader); and

   d. a diminished sense of identity, as revealed by her willingness to engage in sexual intercourse in the absence of any intrinsic motivation to do so.

Future interviews provided additional evidence that she was a consummate impression manager and had been for many years. This was most evident in situations in which anger and conflict could be avoided by denying her own thoughts and feelings or when acceptance could be enhanced by being what would be most pleasing to others.

2. Once her impression management tendencies had been clearly identified, it became important to understand the role and function of this behavior. Given that her impression management tendencies were far from isolated events, it was reasonable to assume the presence of some underlying motives that would account for the consistency of this behavior. Again, the answer was fairly obvious in the initial interview. It was part of a pattern that she had developed to make herself more pleasing to others, and at the same time, avoid interpersonal conflict. She was, in essence, a person who had developed an interpersonal style of being a pleaser and placater. This is one of the most common conflict-avoidant strategies, and the only thing unique about it in this case was its embeddedness. She appeared to be so preoccupied with her personal acceptability to others because of low self-esteem that she had virtually no sense of self or personal self-direction. The following comments from the initial interview were consistent with this view:

   a. She appeared to be just as concerned about how others would see her because she was pregnant as she was about such critical considerations as (1) adoption, (2) finances, (3) sin and guilt, and (4) the implications of all of the above for her future.

b. She was more willing to provide sex to her boyfriend than to argue about it.

c. She wanted to avoid conflict with her boyfriend's parents, even though it meant allowing them to mistakenly believe that she had seduced their innocent son.

3. Given the evidence that this young woman had developed chronic avoidance strategies, a major treatment consideration would be for the client to increase her awareness of her interpersonal style, the role and function it served, and the negative self-evaluations it generated. Generally speaking, as the role, function, and self-evaluations associated with avoidance patterns become more explicit, the behavior patterns themselves become more unacceptable to the patient for reasons that are fairly obvious. They are, for the most part, behavior patterns that are seldom cherished or held in high personal esteem. Making patterns of avoidance more explicit to the client only tends to make them more obviously unacceptable.

4. Finally, and most important, a major treatment consideration for this client would be to actually engage in a series of coping behaviors during therapy sessions in response to the actual stress and conflict that the therapy process will inevitably generate. This is probably the most reliable means of increasing a client's awareness of what a coping response is, what it feels like, and what self-evaluative thoughts and feelings are associated with facing rather than avoiding problems. Fortunately, this is not as difficult as it may at first appear. The very act of asking clients to realistically identify, describe, and label their avoidance strategies and the self-evaluations that they generate is a *primary coping response*. It requires most of the psychological attributes we used to define coping, such as risk taking, reality testing, insight, and personal responsibility. Undoubtedly, this process can be extremely upsetting to the client. When properly understood, however, this distress is as inevitable to the therapy process as it is beneficial to the client. In the first place, the distress signifies that clients truly grasp the significance and consequences of their prior avoidance patterns. This is usually well worth being upset about. The presence of intense distress

also verifies that clients are facing their own unpleasant psychological realities without resorting to their usual primitive methods of denial, distortion, and self-deception. Second, intense emotional distress becomes a powerful incentive for personal change provided that clients clearly understand that it is the result of their own avoidant behavior, which they have already identified, described, and labeled.

Once these events have happened, *it is imperative* that the therapist assist clients in identifying any new behavioral elements present in their response to conflict. Identification of the self-evaluations that accompany any new behavior is equally central. We will say a great deal more about this process in the next chapter. For now, we will only illustrate this principle with examples of what a therapist might say to accomplish this purpose. Several alternatives are listed below.

1. "How do you feel about yourself for being able to talk openly about some problems that you have always avoided discussing in the past?"

2. "Even though you seem very upset about what we are talking about, how does it feel to be honest with yourself?"

3. "Have you noticed that you have been behaving differently for the last half hour or so? What differences have you noticed, and how do you feel about yourself when you act that way?"

Critical incidents in therapy. After about 30 minutes into the first therapy session, the patient was asked to describe her way of presenting herself to the therapist. She passively resisted. After a short pause, she was asked to describe her voice, eye contact, and willingness to talk openly about her situation. She described each of these characteristics accurately. After another short pause, she was asked what impression she was conveying about herself. Again she resisted answering. She was now obviously uncomfortable. The therapist waited patiently, maintained eye contact, and eventually commented on her discomfort. The therapist said that she seemed to find his questions unsettling and it appeared that she wanted to avoid him. She nodded affirmatively. He asked whether she typically tried to avoid unpleasantness. Again, she nodded affirmatively. The therapist indicated that he would still like her to try to answer his question and wanted to know whether she would try. She said yes. After a long pause, she said that she probably appeared weak and helpless. She was complimented for her incisiveness and was asked to explain in more detail precisely what she thought would make her appear weak and helpless.

When she finished, she was much more relaxed. The therapist wanted to know if she was as weak and helpless as she was acting. She said NO, as if insulted by the question. (Actually, very few people would say yes to a question phrased this way.) The therapist thanked her for her honesty and indicated that he agreed with her. He asked her to think of an adjective that captured the essence of how she created the impression of being weaker and more helpless than she actually was. A big smile came over her face as she said, "By acting like a dodo." The therapist smiled back and said, "Let's call this your dodo routine, then."

The task of identifying the self-evaluations generated by the dodo routine started at the beginning of the second session. She was asked to tell the therapist more about her routine, how she developed it, how well it worked, from whom she learned it, when she was most likely to use it, and how good she thought she was at it. Actually, all of these invitations for introspective speculation were preparation for a more fundamental question that could not be asked yet. Eventually, the therapist was able to bring it up: "How do you feel about yourself for acting like a dodo so often?" The client paused, more out of thoughtfulness than resistance. Tears formed in her eyes before she said, "Ashamed." The therapist wanted to know more. Other adjectives were added, all of which were embarrassing and uncomplimentary. The client was allowed, and at times gently pushed, to experience the shame generated by her own self-evaluative thought. It was a difficult session for her, and she left with a severe headache.

In future sessions, the therapist saw less and less of the dodo routine. The client also reported using it less frequently with others. Of course, there were occasional lapses in the session. When these occurred she was quickly asked if she meant to do her routine again. She almost always said no, but not always. The therapist faithfully asked how she felt about herself for allowing the dodo routine to reappear, either intentionally or unintentionally. "Ashamed" and "embarrassed" were the adjectives used most frequently to describe her feelings. There was also some resentment toward the therapist for catching it so quickly.

Two other basic avoidance patterns were also identified. These were described and labeled with equivalent care, as were the self-evaluations that they generated. She called one "wimpy," which was nothing more than a simple extension of the dodo routine. The other was called "pleaser," which was her primary method of avoiding conflict.

About two-thirds of the way through the second hour of therapy, the therapist asked whether she was using any of her dodo routine in this session. She paused thoughtfully and said she did not think so. The therapist pointed out that she had maintained eye contact with him a good portion of the time, spoken up much more clearly, discussed her situation more openly, identified the concerns she was most worried about, and expressed many thoughts and feelings she usually kept private. He wanted to know if she had noticed the change. Because of the seriousness of her concerns and the stress they had created, she had not. This was not unusual. She was asked to reflect on her actual behavior for the past 30 minutes and identify everything that was new or not common for her. Most of her answers focused on being more honest with herself and feeling more upset about her situation than usual. She was asked if she approved of herself for being that way in spite of the distress it caused. She was not sure. However, when asked if she thought the session was good for her, she answered yes with no equivocation. Even though she was emotionally on edge, she reported feeling a bit more hopeful about her ability to solve some of the serious issues with which she was now confronted. When the therapist asked whether she thought it would make much difference if she could learn to behave on a daily basis, the way in which she acted in therapy, she talked at length about how hard it would be and the difference that it could make.

The remaining ten sessions covered a variety of different topics. They included such basic and consequential matters as adoption, personal identity, anger, and plans for her future. In spite of the differences between these sessions, they all had two underlying similarities. The first was the therapist's continuing attention to the dominant style used by the client when considering these issues. The second was the client's experience of continually being asked to behave only in ways that she could personally approve of.

Current status of the client. Therapy ended just prior to the birth of the client's daughter, who was put up for adoption. The client will always regret not having her daughter, but she believes any other choice would have been irresponsible. This way, her child will have a father. The client is actually proud of her ability to consider the well-being of her baby above her own wants and wishes. Giving up her baby may well prove to be one of the most difficult things she will ever have to do, but in spite of this, she does not regret her decision.

Her depression is virtually gone. She is sad about many things from her life but not depressed. She is also quite determined not to make the same mistakes again. She clearly understands that her dodo routine and being a pleaser are the real reasons for her becoming an unwed mother. In conflict situations, she now forces herself to be more honest with others. This has made life more complicated and stressful than it used to be, at least on an immediate basis. She is still waiting to see whether the long-term benefits are worth it. For example, she terminated her relationship with her old boyfriend for the best of reasons, but now she is lonely. She has also talked with her boyfriend's parents and clarified their mistaken belief that their son was an innocent victim of her seductive talents. She is pleased with herself for all of these difficult accomplishments, but deep down, she seems to wish that there were an easier way to feel good about herself. She will continue to see her therapist on a once-a-month basis for about six months. The goal of treatment is to strengthen the linkage between her new behavior patterns and the feelings of personal approval that are clearly emerging. Ironically, now that she has earned the respect of her parents, her therapist, and the parents of her boyfriend, she seems surprised that it is less important than it used to be.

Implications of the Model

Four primary theoretical implications that flow from this model should be identified:

1. Because high or low levels of self-esteem are the result of behavior patterns that have varying degrees and mixtures of coping and avoidance, one's enduring tendencies to cope or avoid will have a profound, long-term effect on the development of self-esteem. Remember that we have suggested that coping not only increases self-esteem, but increased self-esteem increases the probability of more frequent coping responses. Obviously, the converse is equally true. Avoidance not only decreases self-esteem, but lowered self-esteem increases the probability of more frequent avoidance response. It is as though the psychologically weak will become weaker with the passage of time, whereas the strong will become stronger. Because of this, any attempts to improve self-esteem require interventions aimed at the most fundamental and enduring dispositions of the personality.

2. The units of analysis for understanding the dynamics of self-esteem tend to be large. They focus on patterns, styles, dispositions, and traits. This is not meant to imply that discrete units of behavior are unimportant; that is not the case. One of the most important functions of small samples of behavior is to provide a miniature stage on which the enduring styles of the personality can show themselves. Accordingly, understanding the dynamics of self-esteem as we have conceptualized them requires thinking in terms of processes and patterns that endure across time rather than in specific problems and solutions. Certainly both are important, but we are emphasizing broader levels of analysis.

3. The theoretical implications of this model for theories of psychological treatment are fascinating. It follows from this model that:

   a. Psychological anguish induced in treatment is the first sign of personal change in the direction of coping. Thus, pain and discomfort are essential elements in the therapy process so long as they are understood by the client to be the result of increased psychological maturity. The model is based on the assumption that the immediate and long-term benefits of mature psychological responses will negate most of the undesirable consequences of facing up to disturbing problems. Clearly, one of the primary tasks of a therapist is to carefully attend to clients' understanding of the causes and consequences of their coping and avoidance behavior as they occur.

b. Intense personal distress can become a powerful incentive for personal growth and change if clients clearly understand that their distress is a result of their own avoidance patterns, which they have already discussed, defined, and labeled. For this reason, successful therapy requires clients not only to have a clear understanding of their own patterns of avoidance, but also to experience fully the negative self-evaluative thoughts and feelings that accompany these behavior patterns. This is usually the most distressing point in therapy. Ironically, the moment clients do this successfully, they have also engaged in a primary coping response that can be defined, described, and labeled, as can the self-evaluations that will accompany this change. This entire process is based on a high level of emotional arousal and intensity for clients, during which time their thoughts must remain relatively clear and lucid, as they attempt to shift from avoidance to a coping response in the therapy session.

c. Therapists must become more versed in the language and dynamics of psychological processes and patterns that endure across time. The actual treatment of clients requires careful observation and description of behavior and minimal inferences. Descriptive accuracy and labeling are central elements in effective therapy.

4. Finally, we have portrayed self-esteem as both a cause and a consequence of disordered and healthy human behavior. This position recognizes the reciprocal determinism between self-esteem and other crucial considerations in the development of the personality. For this reason, the implications of this model go beyond understanding the origins of high or low levels of self-

esteem. They are extended into other areas, such as (a) understanding some of the underlying dynamics of normal and abnormal behavior, (b) major considerations in the treatment of disordered behavior, and (c) considerations for healthy development for the individual and family. We discuss these considerations in the next chapter.

6

Clinical Applications: Remedial Considerations in Psychotherapy

We have now presented a preliminary model of self-esteem. Its most fundamental elements are the self-evaluative thoughts and feelings that accompany one's tendency to avoid or cope with anxiety-producing conflicts. Our thesis is that these self-evaluations not only accompany coping and avoidance, but also that they are the most fundamental source of intense and enduring feelings of personal approval or disapproval. We have suggested that the act of coping with conflict rather than avoiding it is based on a number of highly desirable psychological attributes, such as insight, reality testing, psychological risk taking, and personal responsibility. Each of these attributes also plays an essential role in the process of healthy psychological growth and development. Psychological avoidance, on the other hand, has emerged as one of the premier considerations in our attempts to understand disordered behavior and its treatment. The act of avoiding personal conflict because of psychological fear and anxiety is probably a staple ingredient in many forms of disordered behavior.

We have also provided a rationale to suggest that favorable self-evaluations are a consequence of a person's tendency to choose coping over avoidance. Our arguments are based on our observation that the very act of realistically facing personal or interpersonal conflict involves psychological responses that are intrinsically pleasing to most individuals and to our larger culture as well. Patterns of avoidance, on the other hand, breed negative self-evaluations. The very act of psychological avoidance, by denial, distortion, and self-deception, precludes the possibility of feeling personal adequacy because of the inadequacies inherent in these responses.

We now wish to turn our attention to the implications and applications of these general concepts in an applied context. This will undoubtedly clarify many facets of the model that we have already introduced as well as illustrate some novel concepts and techniques involved in the remediation of psychopathology and the enhancement of self-esteem. We wish that we had 20 or 30 years of accumulated research evidence available to guide our thinking. Regrettably, that is not the case. What we do have is about 45 years of shared clinical experience to draw on, and that is precisely what we will be doing. There are three areas in which the implications of this model are the most obvious and probably the most useful: (a) remedial considerations in psychotherapy, (b) developmental considerations in psychotherapy, and (c) parenting and marital and family relations. We will focus our attention on remedial considerations in psychotherapy in this chapter, and we will discuss each of the other topics in subsequent chapters.

Psychotherapy: Procedures and Cautions

Our prior clinical experience with the methods that we are discussing has demonstrated them to be influential methods of intervention. At times, they can arouse intense client affective reactions. High levels of emotional intensity and arousal can be good or bad, of course, depending on the therapist's skill and comfort in responding to the affect. It is obvious that high levels of emotional arousal are often frightening or even harmful to some clients. The therapist clearly must use care in dealing with topics about which clients have strong feelings. However, it should be equally obvious that fear and anxiety (intense feelings) are staple ingredients in most types of psychopathology and most forms of psychological treatment. We can hardly expect to make reasonable advances in our understanding and treatment of disordered behavior by charting a course that cautiously steers clear of emotional intensity.

There are four indispensable steps involved in the remediation of psychopathology or in the development of self-esteem that have been derived from our model. Two of these steps are primarily remedial considerations, and the other two are more central in the enhancement of self-esteem. As most clinicians already understand, however, these are seldom mutually exclusive considerations. Because of this, we hope that the reader will master the general principles that we are discussing before making any attempt to apply them. It is our belief that once these general principles are mastered, they can be applied appropriately, in varying degrees and mixtures, to a variety of clinical cases with wisdom and discretion. *However, any attempt to apply the techniques illustrated in our examples without a clear understanding of the underlying principles on which they are based could easily prove to be clinically inappropriate and even harmful to clients.* More often than not, however, we have found that a client's ability to explore honestly the origin and meaning of his or her most intense feelings is an important and, sometimes, even necessary reaffirming psychological experience in the process of psychological treatment. The key to this, of course, is knowing how to handle intense emotions properly. The model that we are proposing provides reasonably clear guidelines and explanations of the role and function of emotional intensity in disordered behavior and its treatment, which we hope the reader will attend to with considerable care. Of particular importance is the nature of the therapeutic relationship, which we will discuss more fully later in this chapter.

We will begin our discussion by identifying the four steps involved in the remediation of psychopathology or the development of self-esteem in general terms. This will be followed by several examples illustrating each of these steps. We will conclude with a more detailed analysis of each of these steps with additional clinical illustrations. The four basic steps are:

1. *Identifying and clearly labeling the dominant avoidance patterns that one uses in anxiety-arousing conflict situations.* This generally requires that clients observe, describe, illustrate, and label their own style of conflict avoidance in specific and concrete terms.

2. *Identifying and clearly labeling the self-evaluative thoughts and feelings associated with these dominant avoidance patterns.* A cognitive understanding of the self-evaluative thoughts is essential but not sufficient. The emotions generated by these thoughts must not only be understood, they must also be fully experienced by the client. Simple recognition of these feelings is not sufficient, for reasons we will explain more fully later in this chapter.

3. *Learning to realistically face negative self-evaluations and avoidance patterns.* This is an important step in the model. It must be understood that the very act of clearly identifying and labeling one's own negative self-evaluative thoughts and feelings is a *coping response* to an anxiety-arousing conflict situation. It is essential that the therapeutic benefits of this response be fully realized. Note that clearly identifying the self-evaluative thoughts and feelings that accompany avoidance patterns creates the possibility for an in vivo corrective learning experience in what must be considered a uniquely penetrating anxiety-arousing conflict situation for the client.

4. *Gradually learning how to cope with personal conflicts.* Clients can then identify and label the ingredients of this new response as well as the self-evaluative thoughts and feelings that accompany it.

Each of these four phases is illustrated in the following clinical interview. Admittedly, it is unusual for all four steps to be covered in a single session. In this particular case, however, it was possible because the client was relatively nondefensive, with a fairly circumscribed problem. She came to the office complaining of excessive fatigue. The interview gradually revealed a woman whose primary means of avoiding rejection and gaining acceptance was by suppressing her own needs while making sure she satisfied the needs of all of those around her. The dynamics of this case, while interesting, are less important than this client's ability to see her role quickly in creating the very problem that she was complaining about. This contributed to her ability to experience fully the emotions that accompanied her coping and avoidance responses as they occurred in the interview. While reading this interview, try to notice what factors seem to account for the client's rapid progress in spite of the fact that this is a first interview.

Introduction and Rapport-Building

Therapist: Tell me, what led you to schedule a meeting for today?

Client: Well, I think that I'm just feeling so worn out and run down—you know, just physically and emotionally washed out.

Therapist: Please tell me more.

Client: Well, maybe if I talk a little about last week, I could describe what my life is like and why I'm feeling this way.

Therapist: Okay.

Client: Well, let's see, as I look back on last week, I see myself wrapped up and so busy with the kids. It's just one thing after another. If it isn't sports, then it's plays and all these extracurricular things that they're in. And I feel like I need to be there to support them. It's just constant, just a steady kind of thing.

Therapist: So, as you see it, your fatigue is the result of the overwhelming amount of activity in your life?

Client: Yes, probably so.

Therapist: Why do you keep it up?

Client: Well, I think it's important for the kids to see that I support them in the things they do. I want to be a supportive person. If I love them, those are the kinds of things I should be willing to do for them. When I do, I think they feel better, and it makes them feel better about our relationship together.

Therapist: It sounds like you take your parental responsibilities very seriously.

Client: Maybe so, but I feel like sometimes I could just scream.

Therapist: A little angry there, huh?

Client: No! I'm not angry. It's just that I can't do any more, but I can't say that to them when I know they want me to be there. When it's important to them, I just feel like I really need to go ahead and do it anyway.

Therapist: Why?
Client: I'm sure they would be disappointed. They might think I wasn't interested in them or I didn't care what they did. It's easy to say you care, but I think it's important to do more than just say it—you have to show it by the way you act. You know, you have to have your behavior match your words.

The form and substance of this dialogue were essentially unchanged for another 15 minutes. The client repeatedly emphasized the "moral" and "socially desirable" reasons for her meticulous adherence to her parental role and responsibilities. She was not inclined to acknowledge that her behavior was motivated by a need for approval from her children or a fear of their rejection. Neither did she seem the least bit interested in exploring her style of developing and maintaining relationships within the family or acknowledging any anger or resentment to those who seemed to have so much control over her life.

As quickly as the therapist judged that the client felt understood enough to tolerate a moderate level of dissonance without becoming too defensive, the focus of the interview was changed so that it became more exploratory and incisive.

Identifying Patterns of Avoidance and Self-Evaluative Thoughts and Feelings

Therapist: Let me see if I can summarize what seems to be bothering you the most. You find yourself in a rather difficult situation. On the one hand, you feel a strong need to be supportive and involved in your children's lives as a way of building a strong relationship. On the other hand, you're tired, you want more time to yourself, and you may even resent others' controlling your life so much. The essential conflict is between what you think you should do for others and what you want to do for yourself. Does that sound like a fair summary of what's bothering you?

Client:	Yeah, I haven't thought of it that way before, but that sounds about right.
Therapist:	What precisely is it you usually do when other people want you to do something you're not really interested in doing?
Client:	What do you mean?
Therapist:	I mean what precisely is it that you usually do when other people want you to do something you're not really interested in doing?
Client:	[Long pause.] I usually do what other people want. I notice that other people do the same thing, though. [Note the defensiveness.]
Therapist:	It sounds like it's hard for you to say no to people.
Client:	It is! When people ask me to do things, I really feel like I should do it for them. But after I say yes, I'm so tight inside. How do you say no to those kinds of things?
Therapist:	What makes it so hard for you?
Client:	I think it's important to have pleasant relationships. You can't say no to people all the time and expect them to like you.
Therapist:	Let's see if we can get an accurate description of what you tend to do in situations where your desires are in conflict with the wishes of others.
Client:	I try to be cooperative and giving, to do my part in relationships even when it's inconvenient. That's my way of trying to be a good friend, or spouse, or mother.
Therapist:	You think of these as very desirable traits, is that right?
Client:	That's right.

The session is now at its first critical juncture. The therapist sees the client's behavior as conflict-avoidant and approval-seeking. The client is describing the same behavior as responsible and desirable. Attempts by the therapist to have the client identify anything negative or avoidant in her behavior patterns have been unsuccessful. The therapist now changes the focus of the interview to the client's actual behavior in the therapy session because it is less abstract, more immediate, and more revealing.

Therapist: What you seem to be saying is that your style of dealing with conflict is to keep things pleasant by doing what others want and expect from you.

Client: Well, yes. Maybe it is.

Therapist: Maybe it is?

Client: Otherwise, I guess I wouldn't have such a hard time saying no. People ask me to do things and I really feel like I should do it for them, but after I say yes, I wish I'd said NO!

Therapist: Are you saying that you give in all the time so people will like and value you?

Client: I have to think about that. I imagine it could be. It's important, I think, to have a pleasantness in relationships.

Therapist: I would like you to determine if this is your way of avoiding unpleasantness and getting people to like you.

Client: I guess that could be true.

Therapist: Tell me about the ways it could be true.

Client: These are hard questions. No one likes to think that they are nice to people just so they will be liked.

Therapist: I agree, they really are hard questions.

Client: Yes, they are. Probably because they are hitting home with me.

Therapist: How does that feel?

Client: Not very good. I didn't realize I was doing that. But I hate people to be disappointed in me. I feel like they can't count on me, that I'm not willing to do things for them. I always thought it was worth the price that I guess I pay to do that. But now I'm not so sure.

Therapist: This way of thinking is kind of new to you?

Client: Yes.

Therapist: Let's try something. What you seem to be saying is that your style for avoiding conflict and gaining approval from others is by doing for others what pleases them the most. At least that's what we're considering so far. Does that sound about right?

Client: Well, yes. I guess I feel like I do that.

Therapist: Do you do that with me as well?

Client: Well, it's important to me, as a client, that you like me.

Therapist:	Please try to describe as accurately as you can how you go about making sure that I will like you.
Client:	I guess by cooperating with you and trying to do and say what you want me to.
Therapist:	So that's what you're doing right now? I ask you these questions and you answer them even though they're unsettling because that's what you think you have to do so I will like you?
Client:	Yes. It's really been hard for me to do, but I thought it was important to do that.
Therapist:	But it's for me you're doing it.
Client:	Yes, I think probably so because I know I trust you a lot, but I feel like maybe if I didn't you wouldn't like me, and maybe. . . .
Therapist:	So, in a sense, you're playing a role or pretending with me right now.
Client:	I guess so.
Therapist:	Do you have a word or a way of describing the way you treat me so I will like you? Do you know what I mean by that?
Client:	The way I behave so you'll like me?
Therapist:	Yes, can you think of a word to summarize the style or pattern of behavior you use to try and make sure I will like you?
Client:	Trying to be positive, pleasant, cooperative. . . .

The client has now started to describe one of her styles for gaining approval from others with a reasonable degree of accuracy, but she continues to cast it in a favorable light by using terms such as "cooperative," "pleasant," and "positive." These terms accurately reflect her overt behavior, but they completely miss the underlying motives that sustain the behavior. These might include fear of rejection or loss of approval. The psychological consequences of her overly compliant interpersonal style are both obvious and consequential. And they are certainly not limited to the fatigue the client described in her initial complaint. They extend into such fundamental areas as (a) a limited sense of personal identity; (b) inability to regulate, balance, or resolve conflict; and (c) a life filled with frustration, guilt, and unhappiness. Because she is a relatively strong woman, the therapist decides to take a more active part in the labeling process to accelerate the movement of the therapy session and to increase the accuracy of the labels attached to the underlying motives of her behavior.

Therapist: How about "selling yourself out"?

Client: That sounds horrible. [Long, long thoughtful pause.] I guess maybe so. I don't really say how I feel inside while I'm doing things for others, and I do feel real tight inside. And, you know, when I say yes to people, that's when the tightness starts.

Therapist: Are the terms "selling yourself out" or "buying approval" accurate descriptions? Is that what we want to call it?

Client: Those are harsh words.

Therapist: Yes, they are both harsh and unflattering, but are they accurate? It is important for you to try and describe your style accurately so we can understand what you do and why.

Client: I guess I see myself pretty much as a "yes" person. It's important that I do that for other people so that I won't disappoint them, so that we'll have a good relationship, so they won't know how I really feel inside. I hide that a lot.

Therapist: When I ask you to describe something, you describe it and then explain and justify it. You don't really need to justify it here. Let's just get a clear understanding of what it is you're doing.

Client: I guess when it gets down to the bottom line, maybe I'm just trying to be somebody I'm not.

Therapist: Okay, and you do that by saying yes when you don't mean it?

Client: Yeah, I do that a lot.

Therapist: Is there anything you want in return for being so nice to people?

Client: I want them to think I'm a good friend. I want my husband to think I'm a good wife. I want my children to think I'm a good mother.

Therapist: I understand. Basically, then, you are trying to gain the approval and acceptance of others by being what they want you to be.

Client: I guess so.

Therapist: Is that too harsh?

Client:	I don't think I really realized that's what I was doing. It's kind of a hard thing to face.
Therapist:	It really is hard, isn't it.
Client:	I think so.
Therapist:	So summarize all that we've said that describes how you are at relating to people. Let's see if we can get to a description that seems accurate to you even though it may be harsh.
Client:	I guess I basically hide myself and that I try to be something I'm not by doing what I think other people would like me to do.
Therapist:	And that description seems accurate to you?
Client:	I hear myself say it. I—yes, I think so.

The client has a reasonably clear description of her behavior, which she seems at least partially willing to own. The next step is to start identifying the self-evaluative thoughts and feelings that accompany this behavior. This is frequently the point at which a great deal of the client's emotion comes to the surface, so the therapist proceeds with caution because it is late in the therapy hour.

Therapist:	We need to go a step further with this, and this is going to be harder than what we just did. Should we wait for another session or should we start now?
Client:	Oh, let's give it a try.
Therapist:	Are you sure? It's going to be harder than what we just did.
Client:	I'll try.
Therapist:	Okay, you have a description of yourself, and at least tentatively it seems accurate to you. Now I want you to tell me how you feel about yourself because you're that way.
Client:	[Long pause, eyes begin to moisten.] I'm disappointed. I'm frustrated because I really would like to be able to say all these things I want to say and still have people not run away from me or push me away because I say how I feel. I'd like to know how to do that.
Therapist:	Know how to do what?
Client:	Be my own person!

Therapist: You mean you want to stop pretending so much?

Client: Yeah, that's a good way to put it.

Therapist: How else do you feel about yourself for pretending so much?

Client: I can't say that I think a whole lot of myself. Sounds kind of like a game. It's a game because I'm trying to fool people so they will like me. It's really disgusting. How can they even like me if they don't know me?

Therapist: And maybe you fooled yourself as well?

Client: I guess I did.

This session is now at a point at which it is *absolutely crucial* that the therapist recognize that the very act of clearly identifying and labeling one's own avoidance patterns and the self-evaluative thoughts and feelings that accompany them is a primary coping response. It is essential that the therapeutic benefits of this response be realized in the session in which it occurs. This is accomplished by having the client identify and describe this more adaptive response and the feeling that accompanies it.

Therapist: You don't seem to be fooling yourself right now. How does that feel to you?

Client: Feels kind of good.

Therapist: Really?

Client: [Tears are now streaming down her cheeks.] Yeah.

Therapist: Even though it hurts that badly?

Client: Yeah.

Therapist: What do the tears mean?

Client: Well, I'm kind of happy that I know this now. I'm hurting, but I think I feel better now that I can say these things to you. I feel better about myself, because you're still sitting here and I don't feel like you hate me for what I've said or you're going to push me away. That feels good.

Therapist: What exactly have you done in this situation that has allowed you to approve of yourself more than usual?

Client: For the first time in a long time, I've been honest with myself and another person about how I really feel.

Therapist: Are you saying that not being honest with your-self and others is the real problem you came here about?

Client: I think so. I didn't know it when I first came in, but I think that has been a big problem for me.

Therapist: An interesting thing has happened here today. You have described yourself as a yes person, as some-one who hides herself from everybody. Then we had what has to be considered a hard conversa-tion, where you presented yourself to me as you really are, and somehow we ended up with you feeling much better than when you walked in the door. Does that make any sense to you?

Client: Just knowing the truth, I guess. Besides, the prob-lem seems more soluble now.

Therapist: Our time is up now, but before we end I would like you to summarize what you learned about yourself today.

Client: I need to learn how to say how I feel more. When I feel like saying no I need to be able to say that, and to tell my kids that I'm just being worn too thin and that even though I'd like to be there, I just can't do everything. And sometimes I will just tell them I still love and support them.

Therapist: So you're really talking about being more honest with yourself and others about your feelings?

Client: Yeah.

Therapist: And how do you feel about the prospect of going through a whole week without buying approval from others by being a servant to them?

Client: Well, if it makes me feel like I do now, I think that would be very important.

Therapist: Our time is just about up, but what we've done today would be worth thinking about and going over next week.

Client: Good, I'll try and see what I can do this week.

In a brief 50-minute session, this client was able to cut all the way through her socially conventional, pleasing interpersonal style and make explicit what she already knew about herself implicitly. She was able to describe accurately major portions of her conflict-avoidant interpersonal style and the negative self-evaluative thoughts and feelings it generated. She experienced moderate levels of her own self-disappointment and, during this very process, started facing some of her personal conflicts with more realism and psychological maturity. As quickly as she did, the therapist started the process of describing and labeling these more adaptive responses and the more favorable self-evaluations they generated. This particular client had two more sessions, which further clarified the materials that were uncovered in the first session. She then terminated therapy but had another session about four months later. She was pleased with the changes that her more self-approving interpersonal style generated.

Although this case is factual, it is unusual because of the obviousness of the client's avoidant style and her willingness and ability to face her personal issues quickly in a single session. Things are seldom this obvious or successful in most clinical cases. That is why we will now discuss, in more detail and with more complex cases, each of the four fundamental considerations involved in the remediation of psychopathology or the development of self-esteem in our model.

Our purpose is to illustrate each of these principles in considerable detail. Prior experience has taught us that the conceptual elements of these principles are easily mastered, whereas recognizing their varied and subtle behavioral manifestations during clinical interviews is far more difficult. Because of this, we will use a case study format for major portions of this chapter. We believe that actual case studies are not only more interesting to read, but also reveal the principles under discussion with greater precision and clarity.

Identifying and Labeling Avoidance Patterns

Rationale

In our earlier discussion of avoidance and psychopathology, we suggested that one's tendency to try to escape from anxiety-arousing conflicts was the quintessential quality of disordered behavior. We reviewed the reasons for believing that the concept of avoidance serves essentially the same function in all of the major theories of disordered behavior: to protect and defend the individual from unpleasant or unwelcome psychological experiences. The specific means by which individuals try to defend themselves from psychological threat are far too ingenious, varied, and numerous to discuss here. They range from the classical defense mechanisms first discussed by Anna Freud (Sandler, 1985) to the interpersonal styles discussed by Satir, Stachowiak, & Taschman (1975) and Millon (1981). Any, or all, of these patterns of avoidance can be used in different combinations by different individuals. It is the job of the astute clinician to assist individual clients with the task of clearly identifying and describing their own basic and enduring patterns of avoidance. The keys to identifying and labeling these patterns successfully include (a) careful and astute observation of patterns of behavior, and (b) skill in discriminating between clients' enduring patterns of avoidance and their situational reactions to conflict. Success in these two areas can pay handsome dividends in the therapeutic process. When both of these tasks are handled successfully, the therapist can reasonably expect the following:

1. Clients are highly motivated for personal growth and change after discovering that their patterns of avoidance are a major cause of their personal pain and unhappiness. This is an important consideration. The psychotherapeutic literature is filled with discussions of resistance, poorly motivated clients, and the powerful role of client motivation in successful psychotherapy (Garfield, 1986).

What we are suggesting is that the very process wherein clients clearly identify and label their own patterns of avoidance explicitly and deliberately accomplishes three important purposes. First, it increases clients' awareness of their own self-defeating behavior patterns. Second, it increases clients' level of subjective distress by making the link between their self-defeating behavior and their unhappiness both explicit and obvious. And third, as clients come to attribute the cause of their psychic unhappiness to their own patterns of avoidance, an increase in client motivation for personal change can be expected. In fact, we suggest that the clarity with which clients see their role in creating their own psychological difficulties will determine their level of personal motivation for psychological change.

2. Far more important, however, is the fact that asking clients to describe their own patterns of avoidance clearly and explicitly calls for a primary coping response from the clients. This task involves at least moderately high levels of risk taking, personal responsibility, and realistically facing an anxiety-arousing personal conflict; clients are immediately required to function at a higher level of psychological adequacy than they may be accustomed to. Although clients may experience distress and embarrassment, this is an absolutely crucial therapeutic maneuver because it creates the possibility that the therapist can call clients' attention to their more adaptive psychological behavior and its consequences in the session in which it occurs. The self-approving thoughts and feelings that can accompany coping over avoidance can be very reassuring to clients even though the reality of many of their problems remains unchanged. Again, this is no small consideration. It can frequently provide clients with renewed hope and a will to persist, which, after all, are central considerations in almost any conception of normality, psychopathology, and cure.

A Case of Sexual Addiction: Mary J.

Introductory information. This young woman, Mary J., was referred by a former client. She arrived for the first interview about 10 minutes early but waited until her appointment time before approaching my office. Mary was in her early thirties, modestly attractive, well-groomed, socially poised, and pleasant to talk with. She conveyed the impression that she was a highly qualified job applicant rather than someone distressed enough to seek the services of a psychotherapist. At my invitation, Mary proceeded to explain why she was seeking psychological help.

She indicated that she had a long-standing sexual problem that her husband now knew about. She had been sexually active outside her marriage since its inception, including male prostitutes, pickups at singles' bars, and chronic masturbation. Mary guessed that there were very few days, if any, in which she had not been sexually active with at least one person other than her spouse. Some days seemed to require more sexual activity than others. Mary also explained in graphic detail how some male images would sexually arouse her to a point of complete distraction. Once she saw someone who fit this description, she could not rest until she was sexually gratified. When this happened, the means of obtaining sexual gratification was of little concern to her. Mary considered it an obsession. She felt guilty about her behavior but said she couldn't seem to help herself no matter how hard she tried. On two prior occasions, she had entered therapy, but these efforts were quickly aborted.

Somehow, Mary had managed to keep her sexual escapades hidden from her husband and four children for over seven years. Her guilt was sufficiently intense that she decided to confess her "sins" to her husband, beg for his forgiveness, and ask for his help in overcoming her problem. Mary indicated that she still loved him and their children dearly. They were now separated, with the understanding that they would try to restore their relationship if she could solve her sexual problems. After talking it over together, Mary and her husband mutually agreed that it would be in the best interest of her children for her to refrain from visiting them until she had reason to believe she could solve her personal sexual problems. She missed them a great deal and was deeply concerned about their not having a mother who would love them as much as she did.

Mary reported feelings of depression, despair, and hopelessness. Suicide had occurred to her on a fairly regular basis for over a year, but she did not meet the traditional criteria of being a high suicide risk at the time of our first meeting. There were no indications of psychosis, multiple personality, or serious dissociative states in which she might not be fully responsible for her behavior. Mary's thoughts and thinking patterns were clear and lucid. The possibility that her excessive sexual escapades were an expression of an underlying characterological disorder was diminished by the absence of other impulse control problems and by her persistence and success in other life pursuits (writing poetry and meaningful participation in civic activities).

Background information. Our second interview focused on Mary's early background. Two distinguishing features quickly emerged. The first was a psychologically ominous father whose behavior was consistent only in its unpredictability. Anger seemed to dominate situations where approval and acceptance would normally occur. Kindness and understanding were more common in situations where rejection would be more typical. Though it was not obvious how this affected Mary, it was clear that it had. It was a topic she could discuss at length and with intense emotions. It was obvious that Mary had few pleasant recollections of father, family, or childhood.

Second, Mary's masturbation habits had an early beginning. Her earliest recollections went back to 7 or 8 years of age. By the time she was 11 or 12, she was masturbating to orgasm with some regularity. By the time she was 15, she had mastered the art of distracting herself from stress with self-induced sexual pleasure, adding a touch of spice to an otherwise boring or stressful existence with an intense orgasm that was enhanced by specific and vivid sexual fantasies. The initial observation that suggested sexual arousal was a way of escaping from stress occurred in the therapy hour. Toward the end of each therapy hour, Mary seemed distracted and more tense. Upon inquiry, she reported that she was thinking more about "cruising" and wanting to stimulate herself than about receiving help with her problem. Although the hypothesis that Mary's sexual activity was primarily a means of distracting herself from psychological unpleasantness was fairly obvious to the therapist, this possibility had clearly escaped Mary's awareness. Her problem might be better defined as anxiety management with sexual excess rather than as sexual addiction. It seemed that the activity took place outside of her marriage because she preferred sexual partners where intimacy was minimal and she could control the relationship.

Identifying patterns of avoidance. Because of Mary's openness and motivation to change, the third session turned into a crucial meeting. It was the first attempt by the therapist and client to explicitly identify her patterns of avoidance. Ironically, the task was made unusually difficult because the client had already provided the therapist with a plausible hypothesis regarding the meaning and function of her excessive sexual behavior. In spite of the fact that her overt behavior was the primary source of this hypothesis, Mary seemed oblivious of what appeared obvious. This made it difficult for the therapist to temporarily suspend his views and listen to the client with unbiased rigor as she attempted to identify and understand her own patterns of avoidance. Because of this, it was particularly important for the therapist to keep two important principles in mind while trying to assist the client.

The first was not selling or talking the client into the validity of any of the therapist's observations. To accomplish this, the primary task of the therapist was to ask the right questions of the client at the right time without being too suggestive. Clients can almost always become more aware of their avoidance patterns when they are asked to observe and describe their own behavior with care and precision. However, they must engage in this process in earnest. For clients to agree with the therapist's perceptions is simply not enough. They must formulate and "try on" their own perceptions. In this situation, a therapist must not do anything for clients that they can do for themselves.

The therapist can ask valuable process questions without suggesting appropriate or even desirable answers to them. These questions are intended to suggest important topics that the client probably should consider, while leaving it up to the client to provide all of the content regarding how they are considered. For example, clients can be asked how they feel about their anger without being given the slightest hint about how they should feel about it.

Second, the client's sense of freedom to answer questions spontaneously has to be scrupulously preserved. This is the only means by which the client can become a contributing member of a therapeutic alliance rather than a dedicated pupil to a skillful teacher. This is an important consideration. Maintaining the client's sense of freedom is the surest means of protecting the client's perceptions and information from being subordinated to the authority of the therapist, *whose perceptions and inferences are frequently wrong.*

More important, however, authentic self-discovery and self-exploration is an essential process in cultivating a disposition for personal risk taking and personal responsibility in the client. The importance of cultivating these two attributes simply cannot be overstated. They are essential ingredients in the coping response. What better way is there to develop risk taking and responsibility in clients than for the therapy process to encourage and reward them in an authentic problem-solving context! We contend that what clients actually experience in the therapy process is one of the best indicators of what they will actually learn.

In the early part of this session (her third), the discussion revolved around Mary's susceptibility and reaction to stress in very general terms. Gradually, the therapist moved the discussion closer to the stress that seemed obvious during the therapy hour. As this happened, the client became more resistant, defensive, and distracted. After about 15 minutes or so, the therapist asked Mary if she noticed what had happened to her during the last 15 minutes. She acted confused by the question. The therapist asked her to close her eyes and recreate vivid images of her behavior, thoughts, and feelings during the last 15 minutes of the session. She was asked to notice her posture, rate of speech, concentration, and personal comfort and discomfort. With no additional coaching, Mary started describing herself as becoming more tense. She was then asked to review the mental images of her behavior, thoughts, and feelings and to identify the best indicators of increasing tension. The important ones revolved around a feeling of subjective distress and anxiety. These were fairly common feelings, particularly in the face of uncertainty or evaluations by others. Mary left the session wondering if she were subject to more stress than she had previously recognized.

The next session was more of the same but with one crucial addition. She was now asked to identify and describe any changes that she noticed in herself once she became overly anxious. The therapist thought it important that Mary become more aware not only of her anxiety and subjective distress but also of the patterns of behavior that accompanied it. Again, she acted confused by the question. Again, she was asked to close her eyes and try to create vivid images of her behavior, thoughts, and feelings once she became anxious. She was asked to pay particular attention to anything that seemed common to different situations. Increased sexual behavior was one of several possibilities mentioned. When Mary was asked which of these possibilities held the most promise for exploration, she indicated her sexual arousal. By the end of the therapy hour, the link between sexual arousal and increased tension was clearly established *in her mind.*

The remaining task was the most important but less difficult. It was for Mary to explore the reasons for increased sexual arousal in the face of psychological pressure. When asked to speculate about the connection between her sexual behavior and tension, she was able to suggest two possibilities with little assistance from the therapist. First, it was a means of temporarily minimizing psychological tension by distraction. Mary called it an obsession with pleasure-seeking. It was fairly obvious that the greater the tension, the greater the obsession. Second, it was a means of avoiding rejection by men by being involved in relationships where she felt indifferent, powerful, and in control. Both of these considerations seemed more than plausible to the therapist because they were crucial, life-long issues for Mary. The therapist summarized this session by saying, "You seem to be saying that you use sex in excess to distract you from your fears and anxiety, and to hide from your fear of men. Does that sound about right?"

The client concurred but in a most dejected mood. It was fairly clear that she felt overwhelmed by the hopelessness of her current situation as well as the growing realization that her most serious problems were the result of her attempts to avoid rather than face the stresses of everyday living. Because she was so upset, the therapist invited Mary to schedule another appointment during the week if she felt it was necessary.

This brings us to an interesting and probably controversial point in the management of this case, and the more general use of the model we are discussing. Some therapists might view their clients' distress as a signal to offer them reassurance or support during a difficult time. Our view is quite different. When clients are actually experiencing stress or engaged in avoidant behavior is the most opportune time to have them try to identify and describe their patterns of behavior and the self-evaluations that accompany them. We believe that there are many important therapeutic benefits to be derived from this process even though clients do not usually find any pleasure in the process at the time it occurs; just the opposite is more likely to be true. This is usually a time of anguish, embarrassment, discouragement, dejection, and sometimes even despair.

Therefore, the therapist must comprehend the therapeutic reasons for exposing a client to such negative thoughts and emotions. More important, the therapist must have a clear understanding of how to manage these feelings so as to maximize their therapeutic benefits while minimizing the risks associated with exposing clients to intense negative feelings.

Earlier, we suggested the following four reasons for having clients clearly and explicitly identify and describe their patterns of avoidance: (a) it increases clients' awareness of their own style of psychological avoidance, (b) it increases clients' level of psychic distress by making the link between their personal unhappiness and their patterns of avoidance more explicit and obvious, (c) it increases clients' intrinsic motivation for psychological change by making it more likely that they will attribute both the cause and consequences of their unhappiness to their own maladaptive behavior, and (d) the very act of clearly identifying and describing one's avoidance patterns is a primary coping response that can be used to generate more favorable self-evaluations.

These principles are illustrated during the next two therapy sessions. While reading them, one must remember that the therapist does not create the intense emotions expressed by the client, but merely helps the client to see the psychological reality that she has created for herself. The intense emotions that Mary expresses are best understood as the inevitable consequence of perceiving this distressing reality with clarity and understanding. Although her distress is obviously unpleasant, it is also a vital signal to the therapist that the client has started realistically facing unpleasant psychological realities that are usually avoided. In many cases, this will be new behavior for a client, and it is vital that the new behavior be clearly labeled, along with the more favorable self-evaluative thoughts that accompany it. As a result of going through this process, Mary achieved a high level of intrinsic motivation for personal change and a surprising amount of hope for the future given the poor prognosis for this case, which was clearly understood by both the client and the therapist.

The next therapy session was far from uneventful. The therapist continually asked the client for examples of how she used sex to (a) distract herself from tension and anxiety or (b) add excitement to an otherwise boring existence. After each example, the therapist would follow up with requests for clarification and details. Although expressed in different forms, the ultimate question was always the same, however. What were you running from? How aware were you that you were using sex to distract yourself? What was it that initially frightened you? What are you learning about your sexual cravings? Each example was followed by a request for another. With each example, Mary's description of her behavior became more exact, as did her understanding of the function that her sexuality played in trying to avoid stress or anxiety or to avoid facing the fact that she was living a life that she considered hollow and meaningless.

The next session was more of the same. When Mary seemed too distressed to go on much longer, the therapist would sympathetically comment on the difficulty of her task and the paramount importance of her being able to clearly recognize and describe her own behavior patterns when she was under stress. With this modest level of support offered, he would then continue with the task of obtaining more descriptions of her behavior. Finally, after three therapy sessions, Mary was asked whether she saw a pattern in her examples. She began to cry uncontrollably as she tried to explain that she now saw herself as a hopeless case. She considered herself a coward, someone who would not tolerate the slightest amount of stress, someone who played with her genitalia when she was upset just like a baby sucking a bottle, and someone who could probably never change because she had been that way so long. Mary was angry with herself for being so immature and angry with the therapist for making explicit what she had known implicitly for a long time. Regrettably, each of her comments was essentially true and insightful. She had now faced the truth about herself and understood the reasons for her self-hatred and low self-esteem, and the difficulty of the task that lay before her.

With this admission, the therapist asked her whether her self-description seemed equally applicable to her behavior during the last three therapy sessions. Mary was stunned by the sudden change in direction by the therapist. She thought about it for a moment before saying no emphatically. Because it was so close to the end of the therapy hour, the therapist closed the session by asking Mary whether she thought she would have such difficult problems to resolve now if she had a history of behaving the way she did during the past two sessions. Again, Mary considered the question thoughtfully before saying, "Probably not." She seemed more angry than pleased over this prospect. Her answer clearly implied that she might be more responsible for her personal problems than she would care to be. The therapist said that she might want to pursue that topic in some detail in a future session. Obviously, the client found the question both interesting and provocative. Mary was now remarkably composed, considering the intensity and difficulty of the session she had just completed.

Summary. One of the first steps in eliminating chronic patterns of psychological avoidance is for clients to be able to clearly recognize, identify, and describe their personal patterns of avoidance. We have described four therapeutic benefits that can be immediately derived from this process. Admittedly, the process can initially be difficult for clients because it requires them to start realistically facing many problems that they usually avoid. However, this process can immediately set the stage for important therapeutic gains many clients desperately need. When clients clearly identify and describe their patterns of avoidance, not only do they become more aware of their self-defeating behavior patterns, they must also engage in a primary coping response during the therapy session. Although self-description is often difficult for clients because of the level of risk taking and personal responsibility involved, it is also essential for therapeutic progress. It is the surest means of exposing clients to the more favorable self-evaluative thoughts and feelings that can accompany coping and the easiest way to teach clients the cognitive, affective, and behavioral components of coping.

Identifying Self-Evaluative
Thoughts and Feelings

Rationale

In an earlier discussion, we suggested that self-evaluative thoughts and feelings are based on a continuous process of noticing, monitoring, thinking about, and evaluating one's behavior. We also noted that these self-evaluations are a psychological reality for most people, and when necessary, such self-evaluative processes can be made reasonably clear and explicit by appropriate methods of observation and inquiry. Finally, we discussed the important differences between our conception of self-evaluative processes and traditional conceptions of self-talk growing out of the cognitive–behavioral models of psychotherapy.

Our analysis suggested that self-talk emphasizes the irrationality of many human emotions and acquired thoughts. Virtually all of these orientations share the assumption that the irrational beliefs contained in self-talk are without foundation. They are simply acquired irrational beliefs with few redeeming qualities and are best disregarded. Self-evaluative processes, on the other hand, are assumed to be based on an entirely different set of assumptions and psychological processes. In the first place, they are not considered to be irrelevant, irrational beliefs. Rather, self-evaluations are assumed to be at least partially valid self-perceptions. As a result, we have suggested that personal disapproval is the inevitable consequence of a personal response style that tends to favor avoidance over coping. The very act of avoidance, by denial, distortion, or self-deception by any means, virtually precludes the possibility of feeling personal adequacy because of the inadequacies inherent in these responses. Conversely, feelings of personal approval are just as inevitable when the personal response style tends to favor coping over avoidance.

The very act of coping involves highly desirable psychological attributes such as risk taking, personal responsibility, and perceptual accuracy. These not only lead to personal development but also reflect on the psychological well-being of the individual.

Contradictory Emotions: A Paradox in Intensity

Increasing clients' awareness of their self-evaluative thoughts and feelings can be one of the most pleasing or distressing aspects of therapy within the confines of our model. We have seldom seen affect as intense, distressing, or long-lasting as that experienced by clients who come to understand unambiguously the role and function of their avoidance behavior and its consequences. Neither have we seen levels of personal approval more enduring than those earned by clients as they gradually learn to face personal issues that they have chronically avoided. We hope that it is obvious that being able to gain access to a client's self-evaluative thoughts and feelings can be a potent therapeutic intervention. Doing so is not difficult. The most important consideration is the consistent and careful differentiation between a direct expression of clients' feelings based on past events and a conditional or contingent expression of their feelings based on current events.

The emotions aroused in clients as they identify and describe their patterns of avoidance are seldom pleasing to them. They are often embarrassed, ashamed, uncomfortable, tense, or agitated. In fact, a well-developed therapeutic relationship is generally considered to be a necessary prerequisite for such revealing self-assessment and self-disclosure. Not surprisingly, then, a generous supply of tissues is usually required whenever a significant portion of a therapy hour is dedicated to an incisive exploration of a client's avoidant behavior. Clients will almost always report extremely negative emotions (pain, remorse, anguish, shame, humiliation, embarrassment, and so forth) if they are asked how they are feeling during this process. It could hardly be expected to be otherwise. They are usually discussing the causes and consequences of what they consider to be their most obvious personal defects and life failures.

An interesting thing happens if the nature of the question about personal feelings is modified slightly. If clients are asked how they feel for being able to face the truth, by being honest with themselves, or not playing games with themselves, their self-evaluative thoughts and feelings will usually be positive. In effect, clients can be feeling horrible about themselves as they recall their past but pleased with themselves as they attempt to cope with these problems in the present. Although these two sets of emotions may seem contradictory, there is no reason to suppose that they cannot coexist at the same time in the same person. Furthermore, they can be equally potent, although that is seldom the case. What is important to note is that the therapist can access either set of emotions. Nonspecific inquiries about how a person is feeling will generally elicit the negative feelings from a person's past. More specific, conditional inquiries (e.g., "How do you feel about yourself for being more honest in this session?") will tend to elicit the more favorable self-evaluative thoughts and feelings generated by their adaptive coping response.

Our contention is that either set of self-evaluations can be elicited from clients most of the time. Obviously, some approximation to a coping response is a prerequisite for favorable self-evaluative thoughts and feelings. However, this seldom presents a problem to therapists working with our model because, as we have said, the very process of having clients realistically identify and describe their patterns of avoidance is a primary coping response. Nevertheless, the negative self-evaluative thoughts and feelings, based on past events, are usually the most obvious and accessible to both the client and the therapist. Because of this, these feelings tend to get more therapeutic attention. This is regrettable in our view for several reasons. First, it encourages clients to repeat stories of personal failure, sometimes endlessly. Aside from the temporary benefits of catharsis and having an attentive listening ear, we see little point in rehearsing and reliving past events in any detail. Besides, most clients have already engaged in a fair amount of personal rumination prior to coming to therapy. Second, and far more important, few therapists appreciate the therapeutic power of having their clients experience a sense of self-approval in the present for having the courage to face the agony of their past. Perhaps an example will help clarify the importance of this most fundamental distinction.

Several years ago, a hardy, robust, middle-aged farmer was referred for psychological treatment by his local physician. His original medical complaint was that he periodically broke out with a severe case of hives. To say that the man found this problem annoying is an obvious injustice to his distress. His doctor found nothing wrong with him and referred him to an allergist. The allergist could not account for the man's symptoms on the basis of sensitivity to pollens. He referred him to a neurologist, who was equally unsuccessful in identifying the cause of the hives. The three physicians decided to refer the man to a therapist in case the hives were part of a stress reaction.

This man was an interesting client. Financially, he was a very successful farmer. He was also a prominent figure in the community and church. He was soft-spoken, slightly detached, but personable. Our first meeting consisted of nothing more than getting acquainted. The second was devoted to talking about his self-consciousness and feelings of inferiority. He seemed to enjoy learning about himself. In the third meeting, we probed his feelings of inferiority and fear of people in more depth and with greater care. As he came to see the personal distress caused by his fear of people, the man expressed considerable regret that he had not learned more about himself sooner. At one point he said, "I am 52 years old and I feel like I have given over half of my life away by being so private." Another time he said, "I feel as though I have cheated my wife and children out of a lot of the happiness we were entitled to." These are sober observations to make about one's life. His regrets were intense and well-founded. His insights were frightening to him.

Yet, when asked by the therapist how he felt now that he was facing the problems he had chronically been avoiding, the man replied, "It gives me a feeling of hope. I don't want to give the other half of my life away." With additional probing by the therapist, the client reluctantly acknowledged feeling proud of himself for being able to face his problems. It is important to notice that these favorable comments were made at precisely the time this man was most distressed about his past.

Favorable and Unfavorable Emotions:
A Paradox in Acceptability

Ironically, the clients with the greatest need for approval from self or others are usually the ones who become the most frightened when they receive it. Yet, this seems to be the case more often than not. A clear understanding of the dynamics that sustain this paradox is crucial if one hopes to work effectively with both positive and negative self-evaluations.

There are three major elements involved in working with this paradox: (a) understanding the dynamics that seem to regulate this phenomenon, (b) developing the ability to recognize this phenomenon accurately when it is actually occurring, and (c) calling clients' attention to this paradox in their behavior as a means of increasing their awareness of the avoidance function that it serves. We will discuss each of these elements briefly.

Most experienced clinicians have watched depressed clients start to feel better, and then, just when it becomes reasonable for both client and therapist to hope for significant client improvement, clients unexpectedly sabotage their therapeutic progress. The sabotage can take many forms, but the result is usually the same. It is seldom fatal to the therapeutic relationship and may not even seriously harm it, nevertheless it will require mostly that future therapy sessions be devoted to reviewing client material that was covered in earlier sessions. Clients seemingly make a strategic retreat to psychological areas to which they are more accustomed, presumably where they feel more comfortable. This happens with enough consistency that one cannot help but wonder whether the prospect of a client's starting to feel better, or having pleasant psychological experiences, or raising expectations for the future is not in some paradoxical way a very threatening experience—so threatening that it almost automatically evokes a massive avoidance response that precludes further therapeutic progress until the avoidance response itself is clearly understood, described, and labeled by the client.

Our understanding of this phenomenon is based on two fundamental considerations. Both of these can be illustrated with our example of a depressed client. However, we have no reason to believe that the underlying principles illustrated in this example are confined to depression. In fact, we suggest that these principles probably have a very broad range of applications when properly understood. The first principle involves what appears to be an almost automatic preference in many clinical populations for the known when compared to the unknown. The second has to do with the inherent fear of failing to meet the new expectations that can accompany improvements in psychological well-being.

As miserable as depressed clients may be, they still experience a moderate level of consistency in their lives. Sometimes, that consistency may be nothing more than lethargy, sleep, or sadness, but still, depressed persons know what to expect from each day, and far more important, hope for little more. On the other hand, there is substantial psychological risk involved in arousing these clients' belief and hope in themselves. There is even greater risk for them in believing in themselves and actually feeling better because it may not last. The depressive state, which was bearable in its consistency, can become unbearable when preceded by delicious moments of hope, happiness, and health. Enduring depression seems to deaden the senses and dilute despair. This somehow makes one's sadness and despair more tolerable. But when hope is reintroduced, the senses are rekindled and the taste of misery is no longer diluted. The same depression that was once tolerable in its constancy now becomes unbearable and in some cases even life-threatening. Clients simply do not want to believe too much in the happiness they desperately seek until it seems less risky and more obtainable.

The primary manifestation of the inherent risks in psychological progress is twofold. First, clients tend to feel safer in endorsing negative emotions rather than positive ones. Second, because it is riskier for them to respond to favorable emotions, they approach these emotions with caution and resistance. Generally speaking, clients can be expected to oversubscribe to their negative self-evaluations and actively resist their more authentic and deeply felt favorable ones.

There are other risks associated with improved psychological well-being. As clients' expectations of themselves increase, the opportunities for failure and disappointment not only increase but also become more obvious. Although heightened expectations for improvement are a favorable signal in many cases, it is important to remember that clients seldom have a history of success in satisfying their own expectations or those of others. Thus, increased expectations for happiness or improvement, no matter how valid, can also resurrect intense fears of failure. It is little wonder, then, that many clients hesitate to believe in themselves or a brighter future, no matter how desperately they yearn for it.

Nevertheless, learning to be relatively comfortable in the presence of these risks is one of the primary reasons for being in therapy in the first place. We have repeatedly suggested that psychological risk taking and personal responsibility are the underlying qualities that mediate one's ability to cope with, rather than avoid, anxiety-arousing conflicts. The therapy hour is the place where these underlying attributes must first be understood and developed if they are to become an integral part of a person's more general psychological character. Generally speaking, the precise fear that the client wants to avoid is the grist the therapeutic mill must grind. Realistically facing what is usually avoided not only helps clients to identify patterns of avoidance and the self-evaluations that accompany them, it also cultivates their capacity for appropriate psychological risk taking at higher levels of personal responsibility. We hope the benefits of these two psychological attributes are now obvious. Without them, a deeply ingrained disposition to cope with personal conflict rather than avoid it is impossible. As we have said earlier, the first place to start developing these attributes is with the person's own patterns of avoidance in the therapeutic session in which they occur.

Recognition of Emotions

Again, we find several paradoxes involved in accurately identifying self-evaluative thoughts and feelings. Our major concern is to differentiate clearly between positive and negative emotions. The origin of a substantial amount of negative affect can be *healthy* psychological behavior, and, conversely, what appear to be pleasant emotions can be the result of *unhealthy* psychological behavior. Although this may seem contradictory at first glance, it really is not. It merely reflects two fundamental propositions about human affairs that are easily observed.

According to our views, coping is a process in which a person is willing to face personal conflict realistically. The more clearly and realistically one faces these conflicts, the more abundant are the reasons for realistic anxiety, sadness, unhappiness, or distress. The natural result of realistically seeing and facing some of the inevitable psychological difficulties everyone must learn to deal with in the course of existence is intense emotion. The precise point at which clients are realistically distressed can be a meaningful signal that they have begun to cope with, rather than avoid, these difficulties. When this happens, the self-evaluative thoughts and feelings about current behavior are likely to be quite favorable even though the most obvious emotions will appear to be negative. An essential element of this treatment method is the therapist's continual and careful differentiation between the self-evaluative thoughts and feelings from past events based on avoidance and the thoughts and feelings about current events based on coping. This distinction is seldom clear to clients initially, and the therapist must assist clients to identify and label their self-evaluative thoughts and feelings under both conditions.

The converse is equally true. What appears to be psychologically pleasing and pleasant is often nothing more than the relief that clients experience temporarily as they skillfully avoid areas of personal or interpersonal conflict. The more intense the conflict, the greater the apparent pleasure derived from avoiding it. These moments of psychological relief and pleasure are as deeply felt and authentic as they are short-lived and self-defeating. At the time in which they occur, the reality of these pleasant feelings cannot be denied. The sense of relief derived from temporarily avoiding difficult personal issues, no matter how intense or deeply felt, should not be confused with the more enduring feelings of personal well-being that reflect genuine self-approval. To illustrate this point, we would like to summarize a case of marital discord seen in our office several years ago.

As a result of an emotional as well as sexual affair by the husband, this marriage was strained well beyond the limits to which most marriages survive. It would be difficult to say whether the wife was more distressed by the affair or by the lack of remorse on the part of the husband. In any event, the wife was devastated, and the husband felt entitled to a sexual fling after years of sexual deprivation and unsatisfying relations in the marriage. However, he had not counted on actually falling in love with another woman. Nevertheless, he did, and, furthermore, he had discovered parts of himself in this new relationship that had remained dormant and stifled in the marriage.

Even though both spouses indicated that they wanted to save their marriage, clearly the marriage would dissolve in the very near future unless some remarkable turnaround occurred. The wife was too hurt and humiliated to be able to respond to her husband's legitimate complaints, and the husband was far too liberated from the marriage to be very deeply concerned about the prospect of a divorce, and his wife knew it.

Fortunately, a short business trip provided the husband with time to carefully consider his past behavior and its implications for his future. He returned home realizing that the problems in the marriage were as much his fault as his wife's and that he was not entitled to an affair because of his frustrations. He was now more than willing to try to do his part in facing and resolving their marital problems. Pride prevented him from saying that he was sorry about the affair, but he could say that it had been wrong of him to cheat on his wife both emotionally and sexually. He seemed sincere in wanting to try to correct the problems in the marriage, which had made a less-than-desirable relationship. His renewed commitment to try to improve the marriage provided the wife with renewed hope for their future. Implicit in his comments was enough of an apology to allow her to face some of her own contributions to their marital difficulties. She tried hard to overlook her husband's past transgressions and work on improving the quality of the marriage relationship on a day-by-day basis.

Regrettably, however, her eagerness to improve the quality of their time spent together gradually pushed her across the line that divides behavior motivated by love, charity, and good will to behavior motivated by fear and anxiety. She started minimizing and avoiding her anger over the entire incident as a means of avoiding unpleasantness in the marriage. She also acted more seductive than she felt and systematically overattended her husband's wants and wishes. Although subtle, her behavior was really a frantic attempt to buy reassurance for the marriage by self-sacrifice and denial. Outwardly, it appeared to be a gallant effort, but it was in fact both fundamentally dishonest and self-deceptive. True, her efforts did improve the general quality of the relationship almost immediately. The husband was so pleased with his wife's new behavior that he had little reason to doubt its authenticity. Furthermore, all these changes provided both partners with favorable experiences that renewed their hope in the future of their marriage. Their sex life improved—again, almost immediately. This was equally pleasing and reassuring. By most external appearances, the marriage had survived the storm and was well along the road to recovery.

In reality, however, this couple had quietly conspired to create an aura of tranquility, hope, and pleasantness as a means of reassuring themselves that the marriage could be saved. While busying themselves with the task of creating pleasantness by avoiding unpleasantness, they failed to make progress on more serious marital issues such as trust, compatibility, consideration, and communication, which were the real cause of their marital difficulties.

The benefits of their sophisticated avoidance strategy were immediate and obvious: it provided reassurance and a sense of relief from imminent disaster. The classic illustration of immediate psychological relief and pleasantness that can result from unhealthy psychological behavior was occurring in their marriage. Its effects are usually short-lived, however. The cost of this avoidance will be equally obvious when the bill comes due.

Not only will this couple have failed to prepare themselves for the next major stressor that hits their marriage, they will also be even less hopeful about their future because the results of their most recent problem-solving efforts have proven to be shallow and unlasting.

Interpreting Client Behavior

There are numerous and varied means by which a therapist can alert clients to the meaning and significance of their behavior. Naturally, different styles are usually based on different assumptions and generally used for different therapeutic purposes. Most therapeutic styles have a loyal professional following that can argue or document the benefits of their approach, or both. Therefore, understanding the similarities and differences between approaches as well as their limitations and benefits is quite important, so we will review them again here.

The analytic approach, for example, is based on the assumption that awareness and insight are the most crucial elements in personality change (Ford & Urban, 1963; Greenson, 1967). Not surprisingly, we find their psychological interpretations and attempts to influence behavior to be heavily loaded with cognitive components designed to promote client insight and understanding into the workings of the personality. Although this is not explicitly stated, it is generally accepted that the positive influence of insight and understanding are not limited to improved understanding alone. Nearly always, the improved understanding of the personality is assumed to have a beneficial influence on other areas of psychological functioning, such as emotions and behavior.

The humanists–existentialists, on the other hand, are interested in increasing their clients' awareness and responsiveness to their own deeply felt human emotions (Rogers, 1961). To this end, we find their interpretations and therapeutic interventions to be aimed at increasing the frequency with which their clients experience their emotions more fully. An essential part of this process is helping the client get past the "blocks" or "resistance" that they have to experiencing their own emotions. Once again, it should be noted that when this task has been successfully accomplished, most of these practitioners assume that the positive benefits of an improved state of emotional harmony are not limited to improved emotional well-being alone. They are more frequently thought of as a catalyst the influence of which naturally extends to the development of more appropriate cognitions and behavior patterns.

The same pattern of thought is found in the cognitive–behavioral orientations. The primary emphasis of these approaches is regulating the reinforcement contingencies that most readily influence and shape observable behavior (Rimm & Masters, 1979). Although the ways and means of accomplishing this task are becoming increasingly more precise and sophisticated in the psychological literature, the cognitive-behavioral approaches continue to assume that newly acquired behavior can shape the form and substance of the emotions and cognitions that accompany it.

Sequential Determinism

In each case, we see that these major approaches to influencing behavior share two common assumptions. The first is the common belief of each that its particular unit of analysis (behavior, thoughts, or feelings) is the most potent entry point into the total system of psychological functioning. Second, each approach assumes that important changes in its primary area of intervention (thoughts, feelings, or behavior) will automatically stimulate changes in the other major areas of psychological functioning in a unidirectional manner. Table 1 summarizes these assumed relationships.

A moment's reflection on the assumptions of these major theoretical orientations reveals the following unsettling points.

1. Each orientation implicitly assumes that all three areas of psychological functioning are interrelated. This is fairly obvious from their common belief that improvement in one area of psychological functioning will affect all the other areas of psychological functioning. This is not an unreasonable assumption or an unlikely reality. However, the rationales that accompany this assumption are highly varied in quality, clarity, and completeness.

Table 1

Units of Analysis and Affected Areas for the Major
Psychotherapeutic Orientations

Major orientation	Primary unit of analysis	Other areas affected
Analytical	Cognitive	Emotional–behavioral
Behavioral	Observable behavior	Thoughts and feelings
Humanistic–existential	Emotional	Cognitive–behavioral
Cognitive–behavioral	Cognitive–behavioral	Emotional

2. Any specific propositions or explanations about how these interrelationships are established or maintained are, for the most part, vague or nonexistent.

3. Each of the major orientations assumes that these areas of psychological functioning are sequentially and unidirectionally related. That is, the behavioral approaches suggest that once observable behavior has successfully been changed, different thoughts and feelings will follow. Similarly, if emotions are the primary target of therapeutic interventions (Gestalt), then the improved emotional state is assumed to influence thoughts and behavior. Finally, a successful cognitive intervention will originally influence patterns of thought and self-talk, but these changed cognitions will then influence feelings and behavior.

In each case, changes in one area of psychological functioning are sequentially related to changes in the other areas of psychological functioning. It is regrettable that these assumptions are offered as declarations with little explanatory power or discussion of the psychological mechanisms that spread this influence. Two considerations have an important bearing on the vitality of this conceptual arrangement.

1. Little justification is provided for the suggestion that these variables are sequentially or unidirectionally related, or both. In

fact, if they were sequentially related, one would expect the same sequence to apply in every case; thus, there would be no possibility for different entry points.

2. Little justification exists for the belief that any of the three primary areas of psychological functioning represents the most potent entry point into the total system of psychological behavior. It seems more reasonable to simply consider all of them as important entry points. All of them can be useful, all of them have been useful, and all of them will probably continue to prove their usefulness in the future.

Reciprocal Determinism

We are interested in trying to develop a system of intervention in which the major domains of psychological functioning are influenced simultaneously instead of sequentially. Our interest in this approach is based on a single assumption. We submit that every psychological event is the product of numerous and varied sources of psychological influence. The more of these sources of influence that are integrated into a conceptual whole, the more complete and useful the conceptual system and its clinical interventions are likely to be. Universally recognized sources of influence include (a) cognitions, (b) behavior, (c) affect, (d) peers and social systems, and (e) biochemical considerations. Bandura (1986) describes his conception of the interactions among behavior, cognitive and other personal factors, and environmental influences as *triadic reciprocality*. Although the temporal relationship remains sequential, the nature of the relationship becomes bidirectional, with each variable affecting the other variables. Although we have no hope of identifying or describing all, or even most, of the factors that go into shaping any specific psychological event, we do want to at least acknowledge and try to integrate some of the most obvious and interactive sources of influence into a unified conceptual system. In other words, we cannot explain the nature of the relationship among determining factors any better than previous theorists, but we believe that a description of this nature must evolve from a more accurate picture of the interaction of these factors, which are reciprocally affecting each other.

To accomplish this, one fundamental conceptual requirement must be satisfied. We must be willing to deal with units and levels of analysis that can accommodate multiple and bidirectional sources of psychological influence. The easiest way to do this is to deal with psychological events as they occur in the "here-and-now," which allows immediate access to the thoughts and feelings that accompany behavior as it occurs. In other words, by accepting as our unit of analysis behavioral products that represent an integrated sample of thoughts, feelings, and behavior, we can include all of these areas of psychological functioning for review and analysis in the context in which they occur and at the time in which they occur. Such an approach is based on the assumption that a person's behavior in the therapeutic setting will ultimately reveal the essence of maladaptive behavior, the function it serves for the individual, and the social conditions under which it tends to appear or disappear.

Experiential learning, then, is the crucial consideration in helping clients come to a fuller realization of their self-defeating patterns of avoidance. We are continually looking for opportunities during the therapy hour to "catch" the client fully engaged in a "Catch-22,"[1] or paradox. Our assumption is that when personal learning takes place simultaneously at a cognitive, behavioral, and affective level, it has more psychological impact than when these domains are insulated from each other.

Summary. Our discussion of self-evaluative thoughts and feelings is one of the most important sections of this book because of the paradoxes and contradictions it contains. Some key issues are summarized below.

1. Whereas most theorists consider self-evaluations to be expressions of irrational beliefs that are best discarded, we consider them to be at least partially valid self-perceptions. There are two major implications that flow from this formulation.

---

[1] This expression comes from Joseph Heller's 1961 novel *Catch-22*, in which the leading character's attempts to be discharged from the army are frustrated by contradictory regulations. The phrase has been widely adopted to mean any situation with contradictory or conflicting demands.

First, a personal response style that favors avoidance over coping cannot completely escape the awareness of most individuals. Because of this, the very act of avoidance—by denial, distortion, or self-deception—virtually precludes the possibility of feeling personal adequacy because of the inadequacies inherent in these responses. Personal disapproval is the inevitable result of a personal response style that tends to favor avoidance over coping. Similarly, feelings of personal approval are just as inevitable when the personal response style tends to favor coping over avoidance.

2. Nonspecific inquiries about how a client is feeling while discussing a specific problem will generally elicit the negative feelings associated with that problem. However, specific conditional inquiries (e.g., "How do you feel about yourself for being more honest with yourself about this problem?") tend to elicit more favorable self-evaluative thoughts and feelings when the client is attempting to cope with the problem rather than avoid it. We see no contradiction in having a client experience an overwhelming sense of personal self-approval in the present for having the courage to face and experience the agony of the past. Neither do we see the value in trying to protect clients from the unfavorable psychological realities they create for themselves when these negative self-evaluative thoughts and feelings can provide the basis for increased motivation for personal change. We submit that these feelings can coexist, and that it is the responsibility of the therapist to judge which set of feelings will best serve the development of the client at any particular point in the therapy process.

3. Generally speaking, clients will find it more threatening to openly acknowledge and experience their basic feelings of self-approval than their enduring feelings of disapproval. This paradox was discussed in terms of underlying dynamic considerations as well as the means by which the therapist can help the client recognize and escape from it.

4. Finally, we suggest the value of having all three major domains of psychological functioning (thoughts, feelings, and behavior) involved in any attempt to work with self-evaluative thoughts and feelings. We suggest this can most easily be accomplished by working with client behavior as it occurs in the

therapy hour. By accepting, as our unit of analysis, behavioral products that represent an integrated sample of thoughts, feelings, and behavior, all of these domains can be subjected to review and analysis by the client and therapist in the context in which they occur, and at the time they occur.

We will now proceed with our case study of Mary J. as a means of more fully illustrating the principles that we have discussed.

The Self-Evaluations of Mary J.

As you may recall from our earlier discussion, Mary has now completed about ten therapy sessions, several of which were rather intense. The focus of each of these sessions was on increasing her awareness of her personal style of avoidance. This process has gradually contributed to the clarity and precision with which shenow understands the meaning and function of her excessive sexual behavior. It is her means of providing some pleasure in an otherwise boring and uneventful life; equally important, it is a means of distracting herself from almost any form of psychological tension, boredom, or pressure. It is now fairly obvious to Mary that her level of sexual activity is clearly related to each of these factors. She has arrived at the point in which she is willing and able to clearly identify and describe the role of her sexual conduct in her style of avoidance. Mary also understands that she has gone to substantial lengths to avoid clearly facing the possibility that she likes and enjoys her sexual behavior and that she has no particular interest in abandoning it, given the important role it plays in her life. She has not found these insights pleasing to face. Naturally, Mary prefers not to talk this way, but this reality is no longer as obscure as it once was. Furthermore, she finds it most unsettling even to consider the possibility that she actually enjoys and uses her sexual behavior to avoid pressure and create pleasure. For obvious reasons, she prefers thinking of herself as a victim of her parents' abuse and an overdeveloped sex drive that she gallantly fought to control.

Although none of this has been easy or pleasant for Mary, it should be noted that she already takes some pride in her accomplishments and is considering increasing her sessions to twice a week. Ironically, her sense of progress is not based on any improvement in her sexual behavior. Her sexual cravings are as intense as ever, as is her willingness to satisfy them at almost any cost.

Up to this point in the therapy process, the client has come to understand two major dimensions about her style of avoidance. As we discuss these patterns of avoidance, the reader should keep two points in mind. First, these patterns cannot possibly be portrayed in the diverse and complete forms in which they present themselves in the therapy room. Our characterizations are, of necessity, oversimplifications. Second, these are deeply ingrained patterns of conflict avoidance that have been refined by over 38 years of functional use—highly polished skills of self-deception that have survived the misery that they have created because they have worked so well. There simply is no substitute for clinical experience in truly grasping the subtle sophistication and psychological influence that these strategies have for self-deception and conflict avoidance. The two components in Mary's style of avoidance are described below.

1. She has developed an effective, highly sophisticated, and subtle "poor-me" story that she regularly uses to legitimize the sexual behavior that she really disapproves of. In essence, the function of Mary's poor-me story is to convince herself that she is entitled to any pleasure she can derive from her sexual conduct because her life is one of misery and deprivation related to the hardship, cruelty, and emotional abuse that her parents imposed on her. In its simplest form, her poor-me story is an attempt to distance herself from the responsibility for her volitional acts of sexual excess. She now clearly recognizes this pattern of conflict avoidance in her personal life and in the therapy sessions as well.

2. Mary has also developed another highly effective strategy: the type of avoidant behavior we call "the dodo routine," a phrase coined during our work with the unwed mother discussed in chapter 5.

In Mary's initial sessions, this style of avoidance became apparent as she would ask her therapist to clarify questions or appear slightly confused about a relevant topic under discussion. Finally, her therapist caught on to the fact that she really understood more about the topic than her questions indicated.

The benefits of this all-too-common style of avoidance are both numerous and obvious. In Mary's case, pretending to know or understand less than was really possible for her allowed her to avoid (a) discussing emotionally laden topics in the therapy hour by keeping the therapist busy explaining terms and their importance to her problem, (b) showing any meaningful initiatives in solving her personal problems because she couldn't understand the meaning of important events without the expert assistance of someone smarter than she, (c) the possibility that others might come to want or expect more from her than could be expected from a struggling dodo, and (d) feeling any significant sense of personal responsibility for her life problems.

Mary is also very aware of the role and function of this avoidance style in her personal life as well as in her therapy sessions. In fact, she now catches herself almost immediately when she starts this routine in the therapy hour, and she now chides her therapist when she catches herself in the act before her therapist does. In good humor, she has asked if the threat of a fee reduction would help keep the therapist more alert! In any event, Mary is able to clearly identify and describe at least two of her main styles of avoiding unpleasant psychological realities.

It is now time to discuss the means by which the self-evaluative processes that accompany avoidance behavior can be integrated into the therapeutic dialogue. Naturally, this takes place at a pace and in a context that is far more gradual than we can present in brief segments from therapy sessions. Our primary interest, however, is to clearly illustrate some of the governing principles of our model, and these segments seem suitable for this purpose.

Two guidelines are useful when the therapist is trying to decide when to start clarifying self-evaluative thoughts and feelings. First, *never* call attention to them before important patterns of avoidance have been clearly identified, described, and owned by the client. Second, *always* call attention to them (a) as quickly as the clients see the role and function that these behavior patterns serve in their current life problems, or (b) in any therapy session in which they present themselves in unmistakable form. Both of these conditions were satisfied after Mary's third session. The client was starting to catch a glimpse of the meaning and significance of her avoidant behavior; additionally, she was actually engaged in the avoidant behavior in the therapy session. It was in the third session that the therapist first started making oblique inquiries about Mary's self-evaluative thoughts and feelings.

The first 30 minutes of the session had been devoted to Mary's exploration and clarification of the role of her poor-me story in her excessive sexual behavior. She was willingly explaining the stupidity of ruining the rest of her life simply because of her parents' personal problems. Mary stated that she had to find some way of getting control of herself before she ended up with AIDS, dead in an alley, or so depressed that she would kill herself out of personal self-disgust. Undoubtedly, Mary meant everything she said, but only her head was participating in her comments. Emotionally, she was already running away from the implications of the cognitive understanding that she was acquiring.

Finally, the therapist stopped her, summarized the essential content that she had been discussing, and asked how she felt about herself for always running to sex when confronted with the everyday hassles of life. Obviously, the therapist already knew the answer to this question, as did the client. So far, the client had only presented these feelings in words. The therapist believed that she needed to experience these emotions in their full intensity if she were ever to combat her sexual problems effectively. It was always assumed by the therapist that emotions as powerful as those that appeared to lie just below the surface of her verbal reports could induce a state of psychological dissonance so powerful that it might actually interfere with her long-standing patterns of avoidance.

Mary briskly responded by saying that she did not understand what her therapist wanted from her. She felt that she had answered the therapist's question before he even asked it. She appeared agitated and angry. The therapist asked whether she recognized what she was doing. After a short pause, she said yes, but not with the cordial tone that usually accompanied her insights. It was obvious she did not want to feel these feelings.

The therapist asked whether she was thinking about stroking herself *now* or about having sex as soon as she could get out of his office, or perhaps was remembering one of her more satisfying encounters. Mary's agitated state visibly melted into the despair of melancholy as she quietly said, "Yes." The confrontation was about over and the client was almost through trying to defend the indefensible. The therapist supportively yet insistently asked, "And how do you feel *about yourself* for wanting to run away from me right now?" There were no words now, only tears. Mary seemed to physically hurt as she cried. It was the kind of emotion that can be frightening, particularly to inexperienced therapists. When the first wave of tears started to subside, the therapist quietly asked her to help him understand the meaning behind all the tears. There were no big surprises. There was self-hatred, despair, dejection, discouragement, disgust for being weak, anger for having thrown in the towel, and hurt because of the loss of love and esteem from her family. Mary's most enduring self-evaluation was self-hatred, at levels of intensity that are usually life-threatening. The truth was now out; she had heard herself say it all. She left the session with all the benefits of a full catharsis and all the burdens of seeing what she was really up against. The session ended with no further discussion of her sexual cravings and an invitation to schedule another appointment if she needed one. She called for another appointment two days later.

After the usual greetings, the eighth session got off to a quick start. She indicated that her anguish was becoming intolerable. She didn't know what to do. The therapist listened attentively as she talked for about 15 minutes before he responded. He needed to see whether she was really starting to face up to these most unpleasant psychological realities or whether avoidance was still the dominating force. If denial, avoidance, or self-deception were still reasonably prominent considerations, then a continued emphasis on identifying and describing avoidance patterns and the self-evaluations that accompany them would have been the most reasonable therapeutic course to follow. Although this may seem strange or even cruel, it is important to remember the two primary objectives of this phase of therapy. The first is to induce an affective level of psychological dissonance so strong that it can be satisfied only by personal change. The second is to create the opportunity for clients to start realistically facing the very problems they usually avoid as a means of teaching them about coping responses and the self-evaluative thoughts and feelings that accompany them. Premature termination of this therapeutic process, once it is started, is seldom in the best interest of the client.

Fortunately, Mary was deeply moved by her last session. She did not know how she could ever stop such deeply ingrained patterns of avoidance, but her disapproval of herself would no longer allow her to continue as she had in the past. Ironically, the client failed to notice that she had been less preoccupied with her sexual "addiction" since the last session than she had been for the past five years. Mary was not particularly confident that she could ever break her long-standing patterns. Although the client offered this as a message of despair, the therapist was pleased to hear it. Clients facing problems of this magnitude realistically should not be sure of themselves: only a fool is certain of things that are not certain.

Mary was already becoming more reality-bound in areas that mattered a great deal to her. Because of this, the therapist asked her whether she had noticed anything new in the way she was now handling her problems. Of course, he would eventually want to know how she felt about herself for her new behavior, but we will say more about that in chapter 7.

An abbreviated case study presentation such as this one can create misunderstandings about the model that we are trying to clarify. Two points strike us as particularly important. First, in actual clinical practice, the event we have just described would probably be repeated many different times and at many different levels of clarity and precision. We are not advocating one-trial learning in the process of psychotherapy. Like most of our colleagues, we see effective therapy as a relatively slow, stable process in which progress is cumulative across time. We are simply illustrating some basic principles that play a crucial role at critical times in the therapy process.

Second, we are using rather difficult and dramatic cases to illustrate these principles for reasons already discussed. Therefore, we want to provide a brief, less dramatic illustration of how to introduce and integrate self-evaluative thoughts and feelings into the therapy dialogue. This time, however, we will use an example that illustrates the development of positive self-evaluations in a marriage relationship. Remember that the underlying therapeutic principles we are discussing do not change because of the type or intensity of self-evaluations involved. Basic styles of coping or defense must first be carefully identified, described, and owned by the client. Then, the self-evaluative thoughts and feelings associated with these behavior patterns can be exposed, explored, and experienced.

This particular marriage had been dying a tedious death for several years. There was nothing dramatic about the decline—just a gradual, insidious loss of interest and good will. Initially, it wasn't clear why the couple had contacted a therapist instead of proceeding with a divorce; this appeared to be a hopeless case. In fact, it was not. This couple's apparent detachment was far too calculated to be taken at face value, and what appeared to be supreme indifference was betrayed by sweaty palms and tapping toes.

Once therapy got started, it did not take long for each partner to unveil a long list of documented complaints against the other. Each complaint brought out a counter-complaint, and each counter-complaint was more heated than the one preceding it. The underlying style of interaction was not unusual for a troubled marriage: "I would take out the garbage if you would iron my shirts like you're supposed to." "Well, if you would just pick up after yourself once in a while, I might have time to iron your shirts." The variations on this theme were endless, but the style remained constant. Both partners blamed the other for their inconsiderate and retaliatory behavior. This type of blaming could have gone on indefinitely, but the therapist quickly made a concerted effort to have the couple try to describe their style of interacting, and they accurately labeled their pattern of reciprocal blaming. With a little additional exploration, both spouses quickly became aware that the other was neither responsible for, nor the cause of, their undesirable behavior. It became embarrassingly clear that both partners were simply using the behavior of the other as a convenient excuse to express their anger and to camouflage their more authentic and tender feelings of personal hurt and disappointment.

The self-evaluations accompanying this behavior pattern became apparent to the husband and wife about as quickly as the pattern of blaming behavior. Simple yet accurate descriptions of the meaning and function of their reciprocal blaming allowed this to occur. They were deeply embarrassed and ashamed. Certainly neither spouse approved of this behavior once it was described with clarity, and each of them started searching for more responsible ways of behaving. Nevertheless, there were frequent slips of the tongue. These were seldom consequential, however. What their individual embarrassment did not stop, the therapist did by simply asking whether they were aware of what they were doing at the time.

Under these conditions, it did not take long before one of the partners started expressing feelings of personal hurt and disappointment. Naturally, the therapist immediately inquired if this type of communication was typical in their marriage. Clearly it was not. "How is it different?" the therapist inquired. They described it as more honest, direct, revealing, and candid. The therapist then asked several questions: "Is this something you approve of? Would it help your marriage if you learned to be more honest about your feelings? How do you feel about yourself when you communicate this way?" The list of potential questions is endless, but they all ask the same thing: *How do you feel about yourself when you act this way?* When self-approval had been clearly established, the therapist focused on clearly identifying and labeling the new behavior, which provided the basis for more favorable self-evaluative thoughts and feelings.

A word of caution: Confusion frequently arises in this process when a client merges the meaning of "self-approving" with that of "self-pleasing." We are not sure why this happens so much, but our experience shows that it does. When this takes place, clients come to think that self-approving means self-pleasing and, in some cases, even doing only what they find pleasing. Our conception of self-approving behavior has little tolerance for such hedonism. Far more often than not, as we have said before, self-approving behavior involves realistically facing difficult personal issues that are typically avoided because of the fear and anxiety associated with them. Certainly, this is not always the case; there are undoubtedly many psychological events that generate authentic and enduring levels of personal approval that do not involve facing issues that are more easily avoided. When problems of chronic low self-esteem are involved, we suggest that overcoming one's disposition to avoid is generally a crucial consideration. Obviously, then, this process will seldom be pleasing in the sense that fun is. The self-approval that we are talking about results from our clients' coming to understand that they can direct their personal affairs in a manner congruent with their most deeply held personal views and values regardless of the difficulty in doing so. Self-approval is a clear sense of personal identity and adequacy, not personal pleasure or indulgence. It is knowing oneself and having a comfortable and realistic belief in the adequacy of the self derived from prior life experiences.

Developmental Considerations in Psychotherapy: Enhancing Coping Responses

We hope it is clear from our earlier discussion that we consider the remediation of deeply ingrained patterns of avoidance to be a vital precondition for personality development. We hope that it is also obvious that the very act of controlling patterns of avoidance constitutes a major therapeutic achievement and is a basic remedial improvement in the structure of the personality. Therefore, we have devoted a full chapter to explaining how to respond therapeutically to long-standing patterns of avoidance. Our intent has been to illustrate how the intense negative self-evaluative thoughts and feelings that are generated by patterns of avoidance can be used to eliminate the behavior that first created them. Obviously, we consider it nearly futile to make any serious attempt at facilitating personality development until pervasive patterns of avoidance are exposed and their debilitating influence at least partially immobilized.

But not everyone is a victim of enduring patterns of avoidance—at least not all the time. Some clients have more patterns of avoidance than others. Still others are inclined to use their patterns of avoidance more extensively and consistently than the rest do. And some clients gradually improve as a result of psychotherapy and abandon their patterns of avoidance. Gradual improvement during psychotherapy usually implies a need for gradual changes in treatment plans, which generally flow from remedial to developmental. In light of these considerations, we suggest that successful psychotherapy calls for continuous and, sometimes, subtle transitions between remedial and developmental considerations. Knowing when to do which is important.

Although the distinction between remedial and developmental considerations can be less obvious than one might hope for at times, there are profound differences in how they are treated. The essence of a remedial approach involves having the client (a) clearly identify and describe patterns of avoidance, and (b) directly experience the self-evaluative thoughts and feelings this response generates. On the other hand, strengthening a coping response involves having the client (a) clearly identify and describe styles of coping, and (b) directly experience the self-evaluative thoughts and feelings that this response generates.

Although the two different types of interventions share many structural similarities, the psychological experience that they provide for the client and, for that matter, the therapist, have little in common. Strengthening a coping response is a rather reaffirming psychological experience that involves progressively higher levels of risk taking and personal responsibility on the client's part. It requires higher and higher levels of client self-direction (autonomy) and the ability to face personal issues squarely. Psychological adequacy is based on personal integrity, authenticity, and accurate self-knowledge more than on practical outcomes or on the responses of others. Inhibiting an avoidance response, however, is similar to stopping a runaway train going downhill. For the client, it is usually scary, involving intense fear and anxiety, but it is an essential step if one hopes to regain control of the train.

Because focusing on developmental or remedial therapeutic processes is such a pivotal choice in the therapy process, we will discuss the primary means for assessing a client's disposition to cope or avoid. The adequacy of this assessment provides the essential information that can guide the therapist's judgment regarding the relative balance between remedial and developmental treatment approaches.

Direct Assessment

This discussion begins with being clear and specific about the assessment question. The question is to determine the degree to which a person is inclined to face realistically or to avoid personal conflict when fear and anxiety are involved. Obviously, this is not a problem in which dichotomous answers are likely. The disposition to cope or avoid exists in varying degrees and mixtures in different people in different circumstances and situations; the assessment problem is highly idiosyncratic. In a literal sense, what we want to know is whether the probability is high, medium, or low that the client will realistically face or avoid personal conflict in general. The key considerations in this problem are threefold: (1) the general disposition of the personality to cope or avoid, (2) the level of fear and anxiety that must be present for the process of avoiding or coping to be present or absent, and (3) the general form, style, and substance of the coping and avoidance response.

When viewed in this light, our assessment problem is substantially simplified. We are now looking for an opportunity to observe directly our clients' response to personal problems involving different levels of fear and anxiety. What better time, place, and circumstance for this to occur than in the first meeting between a therapist and a client? This is seldom a moment of glorious euphoria for most clients. They do not usually know what to expect from the meeting, they are nearly always uneasy during most of the meeting, and, most important, they usually have a limited understanding of the purpose of the meeting. With so much inherent ambiguity, it is hard for the client to manage impressions; equally important, it is hard for the client to know what impressions to try to manage. The first session is, thus, an opportune time for the therapist to observe how a client reacts to stress, fear, and anxiety. Furthermore, the adequacy of this assessment situation can be enhanced by the therapist's level of skill in describing client problems at different levels of clarity and precision, and with word variations that imply different levels of client responsibility for their problems.

Of course, the level of fear and anxiety associated with this conversation can be increased or decreased by the therapist, along with the type and frequency of questions that are asked.

From our point of view, then, the assessment starts as soon as the client enters the room and the therapist asks why the person is there. Although the content of this introductory story is usually fascinating, it should not necessarily command most of the therapist's attention. There is also a client process to be observed carefully. It is the style that the person uses to respond to the stress and fear associated with this intake interview. Are clients embarrassed, awkward, or withdrawn? Are they able to define their problems with reasonable clarity? Are they able to forthrightly provide relevant information? Are they able to say what they want and need? Are their explanations of the causes and consequences of their difficulties realistic or defensive? Are their expectations for help realistic? Do they seem more interested in blaming or improving? Are they already doing what they can to help themselves? In essence, at what level of psychological responsibility (see our discussion in chapter 4) do the clients function in this interview?

These preliminary observations are not all there is to the assessment. The next steps are more revealing. They occur when the therapist starts to discuss openly with the client the validity of these preliminary observations about the client. Of course, a skilled therapist will proceed with this task with extreme sensitivity to the client's tolerance for stress and discomfort. Nevertheless, this is a situational stress assessment. The task of the therapist is to determine two things during the interview: to evaluate client process reactions during the interview, and to focus on client content and substance.

Process Evaluation

Our first task is to determine the clients' capacity for a candid and realistic conversation about the meaning and significance of personal problems with a nonpunitive, reasonably astute professional person. The therapist accomplishes this by patiently but consistently pressing clients for more than they would normally provide voluntarily. Clients who describe their problems with anger in general terms can be asked what it is about them that makes anger a problem in the first place. If they answer evasively, the therapist should ask them whether they are aware of how evasive their answer was. If they answer reluctantly, they can be asked if they are aware of that. If clients eventually take offense at being pressed in this manner, the therapist should ask whether it is customary for them to act indignantly (or however they may act) when they feel offended or mis-understood.

It is equally likely that clients will be questioned about alter-native responses they could have offered. For example, clients can be asked whether they were aware at what point they found themselves annoyed with the questions. Did it occur to them to say that they found the questioning annoying? If they were aware, what stopped them? Do they now wish that they had expressed their feelings more directly? Is it likely they might now be more inclined to speak up under similar circumstances sometime in the future? Are these response tendencies typical outside of this interview?

And so it goes. Each question in the interview leads to an-other. And the style as well as the content, revealed in the an-swer, is carefully observed by the therapist and becomes the basis for the next question. There is a high focus on the here-and-now because it is assumed that behavior within a social microcosm is a reliable guide to the enduring dispositions of the personality. We are much more interested in observing these events directly in our assessment process than we are in having the client tell us about them. At each point in the interview, the therapist is looking for the same thing—what makes this client defensive and avoidant, and when? How deeply ingrained are the patterns of avoidance? Most important, do the patterns of avoidance quickly crumble or evaporate as they are exposed in the process of seeking clarification, or do they tend to become more rigid and entrenched?

When this process is finished, it is our assumption that the client will have been provided with an opportunity to engage in a cordial, nonpunitive, realistic conversation with an unbi-ased professional who is willing and able to have such a con-versation for the purpose of understanding the client's problems. Yet, more important, the therapist has seen at least part of the client's capacity for coping and the pervasiveness of avoidance. If the intake interview has been done properly, these preliminary observations have been made under relatively optimal conditions. This, we suggest, is the essence of the assessment process, which begins with the intake interview and continues throughout the course of the therapy. The information from this continuous assessment process is what should guide the therapist's judgment about the client's need for remedial work, intended to help control or eliminate long-standing patterns of avoidance, or for developmental work, intended to strengthen one's understanding and ability to offer coping responses in the face of personal conflict.

Evaluation of Content and Substance

Our second concern in this assessment process is more substantive. It is to ascertain the specific psychological elements that seem to dominate the client's response patterns, whether they be coping or avoidance. Differences between people are fairly obvious regarding the level of development apparent in their behavioral skills, cognitive capacities, and level of emotional comfort. Not surprisingly, we also find that these same elements usually play a central role in sustaining patterns of avoidance or coping. For some, patterns of avoidance are clearly a function of intense emotional fears that immobilize them; for others, the ability to cope is the result of high levels of emotional well-being that allow them to face with comfort that which is intolerable to others. Similarly, some individuals manifest patterns of avoidance sustained by confusing and unrealistic expectations of personal harm; others, however, are able to cope with extraordinarily difficult situations because they can literally "see" (think about) alternatives and options that virtually guarantee a solution to the most difficult problems. Knowing the psychological domains (thoughts, feelings, behavior) in which individuals are the most adequate and inadequate is an essential prerequisite for understanding their patterns of avoidance and styles of coping. Valid information about how clients use their emotions, thoughts, or feelings in either the process of coping or avoidance can provide a valuable guide for clinical thinking and interventions.

Clinical illustration. The case of Mary J. provides a good illustration of this point. As you may recall, Mary had a history of chronic and almost compulsive sexual activity outside of marriage for a number of years. She finally became so disgusted with her inappropriate sexual conduct that she voluntarily confessed to her husband and asked for his assistance in overcoming her sexual problems. Mary was fully cognizant that her husband might leave her as a result of her confession and, furthermore, that she might lose custody of her children in a divorce. She found these prospects terrifying because of her professed love for her husband and children. In spite of these realities, she was willing and able to "tell all" voluntarily and accept the risks as a necessary step in her rehabilitation.

These few facts provide us with three important pieces of information about Mary's psychological composition. First, she has an extraordinary capacity to endure emotional trauma, at least under some circumstances. Relatively few people have the courage to face consequences as severe as those waiting in the wings for Mary after her voluntary confession. Additionally, her feelings during the intake interview covered a broad spectrum, ranging from despair and disgust to cordial pleasantness. Clearly, this is a woman with relatively easy access to a wide range of emotions, none of which frightens her to the point of avoidance.

Second, we know that Mary has a broad range of behavioral assets at her disposal. She can talk about intense personal problems, she can love and care for her children, she can function effectively in her civic responsibilities, she can manage her personal problems with discretion, and she can function effectively in most of her interpersonal relationships. It is clear that she is not a person plagued with behavioral deficits.

Third, we know that Mary is perfectly able to understand the meaning and consequences of her behavior and be appropriately self-regulating most of the time. This is evident by the clarity of her understanding that her confession could easily lead to a loss of affection by her husband and children. In spite of this, she was able to proceed with her confession because she considered it an essential step in the process of no longer living a life of lies. This observation becomes invalid only when she becomes sexually aroused. Under these conditions, her ability to be self-regulating is seriously impaired. We must wonder why. More important, we must wonder why one who is so psychologically capable in most situations is so inept in others. Our ability to answer these questions will also expose the style and substance of Mary's dominant patterns of avoidance.

Because we know that Mary can respond appropriately to most events in her life, we also know that assessing her when she is sexually aroused is the best way to clearly identify the major components in her avoidance responses. As you may recall from our earlier discussion of Mary's case, she eventually described two dominant patterns of avoidance. The first was a well-developed poor-me story. This was the means by which she would try to convince herself that it was all right for her to break the rules of good conduct—because of her oppressive and impoverished past. It was also her way of trying to justify doing what she really found unjustifiable. Because her sexual behavior was incompatible with her standards of morality, she desperately needed an excuse to blunt the harsh discrepancy between her values and her behavior. Her poor-me story helped provide that excuse and, thereby, allowed her to escape the full force of her own wrath.

Her second pattern of avoidance was her dodo routine, a close relative to her poor-me story. The essence of this response was a philosophical questioning of right and wrong and, on select occasions, wondering whether there was really anything wrong with her own behavior. Its most frequent manifestation, however, was appearing to understand far less about herself and about the meaning and function of her behavior than she actually understood. The type of questions that she asked would suggest her to be an enlightened thinker trying to grapple with issues of personal morality in an objective and detached manner. The fact that these questions were raised by a beleaguered woman in therapy during a major life crisis involving transgressions of her private code of moral conduct reveals them to be impoverished attempts to hide from her own moral condemnation.

Both of these styles of avoidance rely on cognitive distortions. The poor-me story is essentially a system of organized rationalizations intended to distort and excuse the self from what one considers inexcusable. The dodo routine is an attempt to obscure personal accountability by creating ambiguity and confusion in those areas in which personal conduct is inconsistent with deeply held personal beliefs.

The style and function of these avoidance patterns now becomes obvious. It is to allow Mary to escape, or at least minimize, the personal distress and self-recrimination that would inevitably accompany her sexual misconduct if she acknowledged that this was her way of distracting herself from stress and adding an element of pleasure to a tedious existence. The psychological implications of this harsh reality were simply too demeaning and embarrassing to face. The psychological functioning of her behavior is to hide the truth about herself from herself; the style is cognitive distortion, and the pattern is long-standing and effective.

The necessity of having clients clearly identify and describe their patterns of avoidance should now be more obvious than ever. Identification is the means by which clients make explicit the function and style of their avoidance. Description removes the camouflage that hides the processes that clients use to strategically deny, distort, evade, and escape. But, more important, self-identification and description of client patterns instructs the therapist on how to deal with each client. Understanding how a client's system of avoidance works tells us a great deal about how to respond to it when it does occur.

In Mary's case, for example, the function of her cognitive distortions was to minimize the unacceptableness of her behavior in her own eyes, as illustrated by the following example. After one period of prolonged sexual abstinence (3 months), Mary became discouraged and appeared to have lost her will to abstain any longer. In one regard, this was surprising because she had made a herculean effort to get through the first month of abstinence. Additionally, Mary was becoming progressively more aware of the intense self-approval and hope that she was feeling because of her abstinence. Nevertheless, a major argument with her husband that further delayed their reconciliation date, along with two financial setbacks, reinstated her poor-me story in its most spectacular form. The following conversation took place in a crucial session. Note how just a modest understanding of this client's style of cognitive vagueness and distortions guides the clinical intervention.

Mary: I'm not sure what will happen between now and our next session.

Therapist: I'm not sure I understand what you are trying to tell me. [The therapist wants the client to be clear and specific.]

Mary: I just don't know how much longer I can keep this up. It's tough doing this alone. Just at the point I am starting to make real progress, my husband jerks the rug out from under me. His timing couldn't be worse. And the bank isn't going to extend my loan. I'm not sure I see the point of trying as hard as I have. No one is going to give you a break when you really need one.

Therapist: So you are angry and discouraged—and about to do what? [The therapist still wants the client to be clear and specific.]

Mary: Just give up, you know, bag the whole damn thing.

Therapist: It sounds like you are on the verge of doing something, but you don't want to come out and say what it is.

Mary: You know what I mean! What do you want me to do, draw you a picture?

Therapist: Now you sound angry at me.

Mary: Give Wonder Boy a star. He has figured out the obvious. You're no better than the rest of them when I get in a pinch. I was hoping I could get more from you when I needed it the most. The bank has let me down, my husband has let me down, and it looks like you will, too. [Note cognitive distortions.]

Therapist: Do you recognize what you're doing now?

Mary: I know what you want me to say, that this is my poor-me story. But you forgot it's also very true.

Therapist: You're not going to say it, are you?

Mary: [Long pause.] All right, I don't care any more, I want sex, and I'm going to have it tonight.

Therapist: I thought that's what you meant all along, but I wanted you to speak clearly so neither of us would misunderstand what you meant.

Mary: I guess that does make it clear, but that doesn't really change anything, does it?

Therapist: Not unless you want it to.

Mary: It always seems to come to this, and I just can't seem to help myself. I have never been successful before. Why should it be any different now?

The poor-me story is just now starting to go into remission, and the client is becoming slightly less belligerent. The client is still vulnerable and not really able to resist her sexual impulses. This is a crucial point in this therapy session inasmuch as the progress of the last three months now hangs in the balance. The therapeutic task is to intervene in such a way that the full impact of the client's imminent sexual acting out is not diminished by her system of cognitive distortions. This must be done in a way that makes these consequences immediate, concrete, and undeniable. The principle that guides the intervention is to make clear and explicit that which the system of cognitive distortions wants to make vague and obscure.

Therapist: It sounds like you have given up, that there is no point in fighting a losing battle, and the best thing for you to do is to leave now, go get your sex, and schedule another appointment for next week so we can start over again.

Mary: That sounds great, except for the starting over again.

Therapist: Starting over feels like a real setback?

Mary: More than you can imagine, but I don't think I will be able to help myself.

Therapist: How will this affect your reconciliation date with your husband?

Mary: Not very much. I will have a sexual fling, then start abstaining again. We can be reconciled by September 1 instead of June 1.

Therapist: You mean you're not going to tell him about it?
Mary: Absolutely not, he would divorce me immediately.
Therapist: I think it is important that you be honest with your husband. This is important information for him to have while he is deciding if he wants to reconcile or not. Besides, he will probably find out sooner or later, and it is hard to reestablish a trusting relationship when deception is involved. I would like to encourage you to pick up the telephone right now, call your husband, and explain your feelings, what you are about to do, and suggest a postponement of the reconciliation date.

Though this may sound like a form of "reality therapy," it is really much more than that. It is a very specific and limited intervention designed specifically for this client's style of avoidance. The intention of this intervention, as we said before, is to bring the full impact of the meaning and consequences of Mary's sexual behavior into the present discussion. Again, this is being accomplished by making clear and explicit that which Mary's system of cognitive distortions is trying to make vague and obscure.

Mary: I won't do that.
Therapist: Why?
Mary: He would divorce me today.
Therapist: What would you expect?
Mary: I guess I want to have my cake and eat it, too.
Therapist: It sounds like you're in a real bind.

This crisis was over, and the client did abstain from sexually acting out, but there was no reason to suppose this same crisis, or variations of it, would not reappear in future sessions. The next session was devoted to having Mary describe her behavior during this session and the negative self-evaluative thoughts and feelings that accompanied her avoidance behavior. The next several sessions focused more on Mary's coping response when it was present. This stage of her therapy involved numerous transitions between remedial and developmental work. It was

becoming progressively more difficult for Mary's system of cognitive distortions to work or go undetected when they were the
object of such intense interventions.

Please remember that this example and all of the client/ther-
apist dialogue it contains is not an illustration of how to do
outpatient psychotherapy in general terms. Rather, it is an illustration of how to make clinical interventions that are consistent with one's assessment of the style and function of the
client's avoidant behavior. If this case were one in which the
function of the client's avoidant behavior was to avoid intimacy
with her husband because of deep-seated fears of rejection, and
the style of avoidance involved emotional fears and anxiety, it
could not be treated in the same way.

The model that we are proposing is a mechanistic, process-
oriented model of human behavior. It describes the processes
involved in coping and avoidance, but requires the clinician to
make careful observations of these processes in each client.
These observations provide the information to design and direct
clinical interventions. In this sense, the model is both particular
and universal. General principles are described, but they cannot
be applied to the individual without an accurate understanding
of the style and function of the client's avoidance and coping
responses. That is why the direct assessment of client adequacy
and style of coping and avoidance is central to our model.

Coping and Self-Evaluative Processes

Avoidance: The Origins of a Creative Coping Response

From a practical point of view, the ability to quickly differentiate patterns of avoidance from styles of coping is as important
to successful psychotherapy as any other single consideration.
We would hasten to add that failure to make this distinction
regularly could not only neutralize therapeutic progress, it
could also be hazardous to client well-being. Remember that
the first phase of psychotherapy can be a tense and tortuous
time for clients. This is the time when they are asked to do what
they usually avoid—to realistically start facing intense personal

conflict by clearly identifying and describing their own patterns of avoidance. This can be difficult for clients. It requires them to function at higher levels of personal risk and responsibility than they are generally accustomed to. This involves candid self-disclosure, realistic self-examination, and a willingness to try to face unpleasant psychological realities that are usually at the very heart of their avoidance tendencies. Fortunately, accomplishing this task successfully can be spread over as much time as the client requires, and the therapist can provide a supportive therapeutic relationship as well as professional assistance in managing the discomfort and anxiety that will inevitably accompany this difficult task. Gradually, clients will complete the assigned task and honestly, candidly, and explicitly identify and describe their own patterns of avoidance. There are many important client benefits to be derived from this process that have been discussed in an earlier chapter. The most important is that the client cannot possibly accomplish this task without successfully engaging in a series of high-level coping responses, usually in a content area saturated with intense affect, fear, and anxiety. Although the immediate goal of this task is to sensitize clients to some of their undesirable psychological attributes by having them repeatedly ponder the power of their chronic patterns of avoidance, the long-term objective is to create a primary coping response for tutorial purposes within the therapeutic relationship.

However, the intense negative emotions that usually accompany a client's explicit labeling of patterns of avoidance are so dominant that clients seldom, if ever, even notice the more mature psychological behavior that this process involves unless the therapist calls attention to it. Of course, the therapist must see through the intensity of the moment and respond to the higher levels of personal risk and responsibility inherent in this level of psychological inquiry and activity. That is why it is essential that the therapist be able to clearly recognize and differentiate coping from avoidance at their most fundamental levels and at the time in which these responses actually occur.

Inability to make this distinction regularly and accurately can compromise the entire therapeutic program. Every time this happens, clients will be left submerged in a quagmire of intense, negative self-evaluations at the precise moment in which their behavior is the most adaptive and likely to lead to successful conflict resolution. We cannot think of a therapeutic failure more consequential than this one. Each time it happens, clients are not only left to needlessly relive intense negative feelings from the past, they are also denied the opportunity to explore the meaning, significance, and immediate psychological benefits that accompany realistic coping responses in the face of intense personal conflict.

Because of the importance of identifying the coping response inherent in realistically facing one's patterns of avoidance and their consequences, it seems appropriate to review the reasons for having clients identify their patterns of avoidance in the first place. There are three primary reasons. First, clients must make explicit the style and function of their avoidant behavior. Second, clients are introduced to the scope and intensity of the negative self-evaluations that accompany their avoidant behavior. Third, clients are engaged in a therapeutic task that can be accomplished only with a series of high-level coping responses.

Creating the opportunity for the client to engage in high-level coping responses is crucial for three additional reasons. First, it provides an experiential basis for clients to (a) identify and describe the most influential elements involved in their own coping responses, (b) understand the consequences that generally accompany coping as opposed to avoiding, and (c) understand the scope and significance of the favorable self-evaluative thoughts and feelings that can accompany a primary coping response.

Obviously, none of this can be accomplished if the therapist is unclear about the most fundamental differences between psychological coping and avoidance. This can be difficult to do at times. We have not defined either coping or avoidance in behavioral terms that are easily recognized; rather, we have defined them with regard to the underlying psychological attributes that are assumed to drive them. Coping is based on psychological risk-taking and personal responsibility. In our view, these are the psychological attributes that seem essential to the process of realistically facing personal conflict and productively learning from it. This is the path of personal insight, reality testing, self-exploration, and personal growth through conflict resolution. Each of these responses involves relatively high levels of psychological risk taking as well as personal responsibility.

One of the first and most obvious manifestations of coping, as we have defined it, is a willingness to accept the self as one of the primary causal agents in creating its own psychological difficulties. It is a willingness to see and accept imperfections in the self, and as a result of these perceptions, to try to improve by self-examination and the acquisition of a more accurate understanding of the self and of the world that surrounds it.

We are not suggesting that identifying the negative self-evaluations that accompany patterns of avoidance are the only relevant coping responses that we can work with. Actually, any will do. This particular response just happens to be one that will appear regularly because of the way we have structured the therapy process. However, any significant coping response can serve the same tutorial purposes for the client so long as the self-evaluations that accompany it are still fresh. What is most central to this entire process is the skill and ability of the therapist to react quickly and accurately to authentic coping responses when they occur. The fact that the transition from avoidance to coping can be both gradual and subtle only suggests the need for the therapist to review this judgment regularly, and with considerable care.

Remember, in both coping and avoidance, it is the underlying function that the behavior serves for the personality that defines coping or avoidance. Avoidance is based on denial and distortions of various kinds, but the result is always the same. It is to flee from the fear and anxiety associated with the conflict. The inadequacies inherent in these responses virtually preclude the possibility of psychological growth and development. Coping, on the other hand, is a process in which the short-term discomfort of facing imperfections in the self is tolerated as a means of cultivating psychological enrichment for the future. The ultimate reward is the development of a life-style in which the quality and integrity of one's psychological experiences are every bit as important, and perhaps even more important, than other, practical considerations, such as acceptance by others, appearance, and achievements. In the long run, we suggest that a firmly rooted sense of personal well-being is the source of a great deal of human happiness and personal success.

Perhaps the best way to illustrate how a primary coping response can have its origin in one's attempt to describe patterns of avoidance is with a clinical illustration. Note how the therapist capitalizes on the appearance of this coping response once it is clearly established and how oblivious the client was of its existence right up to the time the therapist called her attention to it.

Clinical illustration. Mary J. has now completed over six months of intensive therapy. During this time, she has made more progress than had originally been anticipated. Nevertheless, she is still far from reaching an enduring resolution to her most pressing sexual problems and personal concerns. Some may wonder why we consider her progress so satisfactory while she is still plagued with so many of her original complaints. We have several reasons for suggesting this.

First, Mary is now able to clearly and consistently identify and describe her patterns of avoidance any time she really wants to. They are simply no longer a mystery to her. She is equally aware of the contempt that she feels for herself when she engages in her poor-me story or dodo routine. More than anything else, Mary seems to despise the personal weakness that the use of these avoidance strategies implies about her. Nevertheless, she still uses these routines occasionally, more often outside her therapy sessions than during them. Yet, she seldom fools herself about the meaning and purpose of her avoidant behavior, and she now clearly understands the origins of much of her self-contempt. Her avoidance patterns are gradually becoming psychologically useless and, because of this, Mary is continually confronted with the unpleasant reality that she is the author and architect of most of the personal problems she complained about that brought her to therapy. Additionally, Mary is starting to develop an idea of what it might be like to be truly different. This conception is far from clear or explicit, but she does understand that it would involve substantial increases in personal honesty with herself and others. Translating this abstract idea into the practice of living on a daily basis is

consistently problematic because of the immediate consequences that it always seems to involve, but the idea is starting
to take shape. Finally, her relationship with her therapist is
nearly fully developed. She talks openly and honestly about her
concerns. She feels a full range of emotions in many therapy
hours. Relationship issues between Mary and her therapist are
discussed openly, frequently at Mary's insistence. The therapist's exaggerated power base has become more realistic in
Mary's eyes, and he is now accepted in the relationship as both
a person and professional therapist eager to help her change
and grow. Most important, however, Mary likes and approves
of the way in which she acts while she is with her therapist.
She describes herself as open, spontaneous, and more alive than
usual. Feeling her personal distress is part of what she calls
being alive. Paradoxically, she is finding most of her therapy
hours to be intensely enjoyable even though they usually involve tears, uncertainty, and facing the very life issues that she
has usually avoided.

At this time, Mary had successfully abstained from sexual
intercourse with anyone for more than 23 weeks. Remember
that she and her husband had temporarily separated until her
sexual problems were resolved. She masturbated on several occasions but that was the full extent of her sexual activity. Several
factors played a role in her abstinence. Certainly, her therapy
helped by immobilizing her ability to deny and distort the real
meaning and consequences of her inappropriate sexual behavior, but her wish to save her marriage was even more influential. She was simply afraid that any inappropriate sexual activity on her part would not be accepted by her husband; he
would divorce her immediately. Her abstinence proved to be a
daily struggle and, finally the inevitable happened. She spent
some time alone with a friend one evening and they ended up
in bed. Even though she was racked with guilt the next morning, her sexual activity persisted through the next several days.
Finally, in a state of near desperation and panic, she called her
therapist and they met immediately.

The therapeutic issues involved in this meeting were both
consequential and emotional but not terribly complex. The first
concern of the therapist was to determine the effects of this most
recent incident on Mary's well-being. Even though such a re-

lapse was predictable, it could be perceived by Mary as a major blow to her therapeutic progress. These effects had to be carefully assessed. The therapist's second concern was to ascertain the degree to which she was going to attempt to avoid or cope with the issues raised by her most recent sexual behavior. Divorce was now a clear possibility, as was a loss of hope for future improvement. For the first 45 minutes of the session, the therapist patiently and attentively listened to Mary explain all of her views and feelings about her sexual episode. She was clear in her expression and offered few excuses. Her sexual cravings and the tension associated with them simply became more than she could tolerate. Her decision to have sex was quite deliberate.

Mary was facing this problem with far more honesty than usual. She became avoidant only when she started considering the potential consequences if her spouse knew what had happened. The prospect of a divorce was now more imminent and terrifying than ever before. This made it very difficult for Mary to not avoid the obvious issues she was now faced with. Even though her massive system of avoidance was not operative, she was not inclined to tell her husband what had happened. Mary was ready to be honest with herself about the meaning and significance of her behavior in the privacy of her therapist's office, but she was not at all sure she wanted to extend that candor to her husband. The session ended at this point and another meeting was scheduled for the next day.

Early in the next meeting, Mary's major concern was the prospect of divorce if she let her husband know about her most recent sexual incident. She knew she should tell him about it, that he was entitled to know about it, and, actually, she wanted to tell him about it; but she was sure he would divorce her if she did. The therapist focused on letting Mary talk about her ambivalent feelings and occasionally paraphrased her dilemma. Finally, she decided that she could not and would not tell her husband. The therapist had been waiting for her decision, and now he simply asked for her description of the means by which she was trying to save her marriage.

"I'm a liar!" she snapped back. "You know it, I know it, but my husband isn't sure about it, and this marriage has to be saved. I can't stand the thought of losing my children. And I love my husband. He's the kind of person I've always wanted, and I'm not going to give him up. I can tell him about this later, maybe in six months or so. This won't happen again, and by then it will be easier for him to understand and accept what I've done." The therapist indicated that there were many good reasons for her not to tell her husband and that he was particularly pleased about her ability to accurately call herself a liar at appropriate and limited times. For obvious reasons, she did not like his comment. She was now caught in the classic struggle of feeling compelled to do something she disapproves of because it seems to be the only means available of accomplishing what she does approve of.

The heart of this conflict was quickly exposed in its completeness in the following session. Mary could no longer lie to herself or her spouse without feeling a great deal of self-recrimination, nor could she willingly submit herself to the prospect of a divorce by being honest. In the past, Mary easily avoided such a dilemma by hiding the truth about the meaning and consequences of her behavior from herself and others. This allowed her to postpone negative consequences almost indefinitely. However, now there was an immediate price to be paid for avoidance or coping. Avoidance was now explicitly associated with feelings of personal weakness and a relatively clear understanding of its self-defeating nature. Coping required realistically facing the possibility of losing the family she loved. Her past had now caught up with her on all counts.

The therapeutic issue was now becoming clear. Mary had to decide what kind of a person she wanted to be in these intensely difficult conflict situations, and that is what the therapist focused on for the next two sessions. The client was repeatedly confronted with the same difficult question in a variety of forms and formats: What do you need to do in this situation so you can approve of yourself whether your husband files for a divorce or not? Mary sought reassurance from the therapist that honesty was the best policy, but the therapist kept asking what she needed to do to have her own approval! This was hard for Mary. She was accustomed to thinking in strategic terms—of how to get what she wanted from other people. She had virtually no experience in thinking about what she needed to do to earn her own approval.

Mary struggled with this problem without even noticing her self-candor and courage in facing what was probably the most difficult and conflicted choice in her life. At this point, the therapist started asking her if she had noticed how she was handling this problem. Although this type of questioning can be developed in different ways, it always involves the same underlying issues: What do you notice about the way in which you are trying to deal with this problem? What are you doing differently? Is it typical of you to try to face problems as realistically as you are now? If you had tried to deal with other problems in the past in the same way in which you are dealing with this one, would your life be different? What specifically are you doing differently now? What do you think of yourself when you act this way? How does it feel to be the person you have been for the last 30 minutes? If you could be like this more often, would you be happier with yourself?

These questions are all reducible to the same two essential points. The first is a simple description of how clients actually behave while they are in the middle of the conflict and how this is different from the past. The second is how clients feel about themselves for their honesty, courage, lack of deception, or willingness to face problems rather than avoiding them, or whatever they do when they actually start facing problems instead of avoiding them.

Mary was so caught up in her dilemma that she had difficulty even understanding the therapist's new set of questions. She was deeply concerned about how much she would tell her husband, and the prospect of looking at the underlying processes involved in her own problem solving did not arouse much interest or enthusiasm in her. Nevertheless, Mary's therapist explained that it could be valuable to understand clearly what she was doing that was different from her past behavior. With this encouragement, she discussed what she considered to be the new ingredients in her current problem solving. She started by describing herself as comfortable in her relationship with her therapist. This was the first time that she had really been known by another person. It seemed to Mary that anything was all right with the therapist so long as she stayed "straight" with herself about what she was doing and why. This made it easier for her to face things that she usually avoided and not play games with herself. This resulted in her being more honest and open about her real thoughts and feelings. She also indicated that she liked herself when she acted this way and hoped that she could learn to be like this without the assistance of her therapist.

The therapist then paraphrased this message back to Mary and asked if his understanding was accurate. She indicated that it was. He then asked what turned out to be a poignant question: What would she do in her current dilemma if she were to act just like the kind of person she wanted to be? Mary's answer was disarming in its simplicity. She would tell her husband simply because he was entitled to know. She would also face up to whatever consequences followed because it was more important to be honest with her husband than to live a lie with him. Mary quickly added that she did not believe she had the courage to actually do what she had just described, however. The therapist asked how it felt to be clear in her own mind about what she wanted to do even if she was not sure she could actually do it. She was glad that she understood, but was afraid of the whole situation.

When she returned for her next session, Mary reported that she had gone ahead and told her husband everything. A divorce now seemed unavoidable. She indicated that she had been crying all week, felt seriously depressed about what she had done to her life, and did not know if she could go on. Interestingly, Mary did not regret having been honest with her husband. She still felt that she had done the right thing but deeply regretted the consequences that were sure to follow. She wished this were all a bad dream that would end. It seemed to her that her whole life was about to fall apart.

Commentary

In spite of the intensity of these meetings and the serious consequences that they involved, two points are clearly illustrated in this example. The first is how the process of clearly describing patterns of avoidance can be turned into a primary coping response. The second is the high level of personal risk and responsibility that can be involved in coping as opposed to avoiding. Both of these points could have been illustrated with examples that would be far less controversial than this one. Additionally, other examples could have been selected that would not involve such negative real consequences as a result of coping at high levels of personal risk and responsibility. We thought it best, however, to use an illustration that contained complex issues involving serious life consequences at the outset and to save the less drastic and more typical examples for later. This is our way of trying to flush out the conceptual and practical issues involved in clinical interventions that can be as potent as those described. Once these basic issues have been given the thoughtful consideration they deserve, the reader can judge the merits of these interventions on principle and merit rather than on carefully selected clinical examples that would have almost universal appeal.

There are several points about the way in which this case was managed that should be discussed. A severe critic could point out that the management of this case was seriously flawed for the following reasons:

1. The therapist played a major role in causing a divorce needlessly by showing too much allegiance to preconceived theoretical assumptions on how to manage a case without enough regard for client welfare.

2. The therapist was guilty of overinfluencing the client in the direction of personal values and patterns of behavior that were not of the client's choosing.

3. The therapist had too much control over the client's behavior without the client's full understanding of the nature and extent of that control.

As a result, the critic could say, the client's autonomy and ability to be self-directing were fundamentally compromised because of the therapist's influence.

Each of these criticisms should command the attention of any serious professional. We are, in fact, trying to describe incisive methods of intervention that are intended to influence client behavior. Additionally, we view the task of the therapist, at least partially, as being able to intervene in client behavior in such a way that it will make a difference. The issue we face is not one of therapist influence but of the appropriateness of that influence. From our point of view, therapeutic influence should improve a client's willingness and ability to cope with personal conflict rather than to avoid it. This involves realistically facing problems and oneself, improved perceptions of reality, high levels of personal risk and responsibility, and an increased capacity for self-direction. Note that we do not suggest that the job of the therapist is to protect the client from any of the unpleasant realities or consequences that accompany their self-defeating behavior patterns. Neither have we suggested that coping will automatically lead immediately to outcomes that the client will find pleasant or enjoyable. What we have suggested is that clients can gain their own approval by coping instead of avoiding, and that this self-approval can be an enduring and helpful element in personal growth and self-direction. We suggest that this is true whether the immediate external consequences of coping are favorable or unfavorable. Our view is that the long-term consequences of coping will *always* be more favorable than those of avoiding, and a major responsibility in case management is to assist clients in overcoming their disposition to accept the short-term benefits of avoidance at the cost of the long-term benefits of coping. As difficult as this task may appear to be, we suggest that one of the therapist's greatest tools in this process is the immediate feelings of client self-approval that can be generated by coping with difficult real life situations. In this light, we ask the reader to consider the following observations about the interaction between client and therapist in our previous example:

1. The therapist did not create the client's avoidance tendencies or the intense negative self-evaluations that accompanied them. His role was to help the client remove the camouflage that she had carefully put in place to protect herself from having to face her conflict avoidance tendency and the problems that it created.

2. The client's own clear identification and description of herself as a liar in the crisis situation was a psychological reality, and once this was clearly perceived by the client, it served as a catalyst for much of her subsequent behavior.

3. The negative self-evaluative thoughts and feelings that the client associated with being a liar were also a psychological

reality, and once these feelings were clearly perceived and understood by the client, they became a primary source of her motivation for change during the crisis situation. The client came to believe that lying was not an appropriate means of saving an important relationship, and the act of accepting the consequences of telling the truth constitutes a primary coping response of the highest order. The spouse's response (seeking a divorce) to Mary's truthfulness does not diminish the psychological maturity inherent in her response, nor is it likely to diminish the client's sense of self-approval for behavior that she considers appropriate.

4. Mary clearly understood the possible consequences of being honest with her husband, and she took this step voluntarily and deliberately. She did not report any regrets about the act of being more honest; in fact, she felt proud of this achievement. She did, however, have solemn regrets about the sexual activities she had engaged in which led her husband to initiate a divorce.

Taking these observations into consideration, we suggest that this client was functioning at an extraordinarily high level of personal self-direction under the most difficult circumstances imaginable. We also suggest that if she continues to function at this same level, her prognosis for the future is outstanding even though she is now confronted with several major adjustment problems because of the imminence of a divorce. Finally, and perhaps paradoxically, we suggest that the behavior that precipitated this crisis in Mary's life (candor with her husband) is also the basis for her rapidly improving prognosis for the future. Mary's disposition to avoid is gradually being replaced by her ability to cope with conflict. This ability will gradually become more obvious as she cultivates the two underlying psychological attributes essential to coping. These are psychological risk taking and personal responsibility, both of which are now becoming apparent in Mary's style of coping.

Strengthening the Disposition to Cope

For a variety of reasons, it is not always necessary to create a coping response during the therapy hour for the benefit of the client. As we said earlier, not all clients are complete victims of chronic and pervasive patterns of avoidance. Still others can move more freely between patterns of coping and avoidance, depending on the situations in which they find themselves. Some clients gradually improve in psychotherapy and start to abandon volitionally their patterns of avoidance. For any of these reasons, the major therapeutic task can shift from creating new coping responses to strengthening already existing ones. Of course, the disposition to cope must be strengthened in those areas in which the client is most inclined to be defensive and avoidant. Even though this process can be similar to that which we have already described (identifying patterns of behavior and the self-evaluations they generate), several important differences should be noted.

In the first place, strengthening a coping response does not generally involve the high levels of emotional intensity portrayed in our last example. This is not meant to imply that this type of intervention is less important or that it should be undertaken casually. In fact, strengthening the disposition to cope is the "harvest" of the entire therapeutic process, and the point with which client gains will be the most obvious and profound. The therapist cannot catch a quick nap just because the client is not immersed in the chaos of filing emotional bankruptcy during emotionally depressed times.

Strengthening the disposition to cope is different from and more pleasant for the client than describing avoidance patterns because it does not involve attempts to alter the personality in such fundamental ways. It does not call for the acquisition of brand-new behavior patterns or profound increases in the client's level of personal risk and responsibility. These interventions are more comfortable for clients simply because so much less is asked of them. Equally important, however, is the obvious fact that this stage of therapy asks clients to focus their attention on the patterns of behavior that they most approve of. It is a time to learn how to think well of one's self; to identify and describe one's favorable patterns of behavior and the self-evaluations that they generate; to learn how to accept self-compliments graciously and appreciatively; and to explore the significance and risks involved in being a self-approving, self-directing human being who cares deeply about the self and others.

Certainly, some psychological tensions will be associated with these tasks. It is not easy for clients to accept the burdens of personal self-direction and personal approval. Also, in our culture, there are many negative associations with these terms, which may require therapeutic discussion. Nevertheless, it should be obvious that this can be a pleasant and rewarding experience for clients. It is certainly an essential one, and one that does not feel remotely similar to the grueling experience of describing one's patterns of avoidance.

Second, strengthening the tendency to cope is perceived by most clients as being more relevant to their reasons for being in therapy. It has an immediate and obvious problem-solving orientation that seems to be welcomed by many clients. More than client perception is involved in this difference, however. The therapist's primary role in this phase of therapy is to help clients identify and describe the main elements involved in their best coping responses and the self-evaluative thoughts and feelings that accompany them. When clients complain of mild depression or of a series of unsatisfying interpersonal relationships, for example, they can be asked quite early how they feel about themselves for the way in which they conduct their lives within the problem area that they have identified. The source of disapproval can be quickly identified, and, more important, clients' attention can then be focused on what they need to do so that they can approve of themselves in the problem area.

When a therapist is attempting to strengthen coping responses, a major portion of each therapy hour should be devoted to (a) understanding the conditions that tend to increase the tendency to avoid, (b) careful exploration of the sources of anxiety in that situation that seem to be the source of the avoidance, (c) careful exploration of what clients need to do in the conflict situation to approve of their behavior in that situation, and (d) careful exploration of the self-evaluative thoughts and feelings that accompany clients' coping responses in general and in this specific problem situation.

A good example of the entire process is contained in our earlier example of a housewife who tried to avoid the possibility of being rejected by those she valued and respected. She did this by continually placing herself in the service of those whose approval she valued the most as a means of obtaining their appreciation and approval. This case study is presented in chapter 6.

As you may recall, this housewife started her first therapy hour by complaining of fatigue and depression and ended it with a relatively clear understanding that

1. She attempted to buy approval from others by being conflict avoidant and denying her own wants and wishes,

2. She was basically dishonest with herself and others about her true feelings regarding many important topics and events in her personal life,

3. She considered herself weak and inadequate because of her attempts to buy approval rather than present herself as the person she really was,

4. It felt very pleasing to her to be honest with herself and the therapist during her first meeting (coping response),

5. A major portion of her future happiness depended on her being as honest with herself and others as she was during this first therapy hour, and

6. It was well within her psychological capabilities to be more honest with herself and others immediately.

Those who are interested may wish to reread this case study in its entirety (see chapter 6) because it contains much of the original therapist–client dialogue, which focuses basically on strengthening an already-existing coping response.

Returning to the case study of Mary J., one of the best examples we have seen of strengthening a coping response occurred two weeks after Mary told her husband about her most recent sexual encounters. Mary had accepted the prospect of a divorce and was now struggling with her own emotions of anger, loneliness, and fear for her future. By sheer coincidence, Mary received a letter that week from a sibling. It was an open letter to the family in which he confessed to all that his life was falling apart, that he had had serious sexual problems, that a divorce was imminent because of these sexual problems, and that he desperately needed support from the family. Mary called all of the siblings and found out that many of the children had serious sexual problems, that all of them were in therapy at the present time, and that the origins of these problems went back to sexual abuse they had suffered as children. Even though everybody knew something about the abuse, none of them had spoken to each other or their parents about them.

Mary arranged a family meeting for a weekend in which the children flew home from all over the country to confront their parents. It was a meeting intended to be helpful by bringing all their problems out into the open where they could be dealt with, including confronting the parents with their inappropriate sexual behavior. When Mary returned from this meeting, she spent an entire hour talking about her behavior while at home. She had confronted a highly manipulative mother and refused to accept the burden of her emotional problems any longer. She had confronted her father with things that should have been dealt with years ago. Also, she expressed love and appreciation to her parents and siblings for all the good things that had been done for her. Mary declared herself fully and openly to her entire family and no longer had anything to hide from any of them. She also indicated that she wanted close relationships with all of them, but that she would no longer act in ways she disapproved of for their benefit. She won the respect and admiration of her family for bringing them together.

When Mary finished telling her story, the therapist simply asked how she felt about herself for all she had done. "Proud," she replied. "What is it that you are most proud of?" the therapist asked. She described the elements in her behavior that she was pleased with. "Brave" and "courageous" were among the first words she used. When she had exhausted her description, the therapist then focused on how she felt about herself for being able to do all she had done. She consistently reported feelings of personal pleasure and integrity that she had never felt before. At one point, the therapist asked if she considered herself to be "healthy" while she was at home over the weekend.

At first, she said yes but then reconsidered her answer. She talked about all of the problems that she still had to solve. The implication seemed to be that until all of these problems were resolved, it would be unwise to consider herself healthy, even on a temporary basis. It appeared to the therapist that she was starting to experience the risk of considering herself an adequate person who could trust herself to run her life in ways she approved of. This is always a critical point in the therapy process, and she seemed afraid to believe in herself in spite of the overwhelming evidence that it was starting to be true. Having noticed this slight digression, the therapist asked whether she was being as honest with herself right this minute as she was while at home. She said no, adding that she considered herself to have been extremely healthy while she was at home and that she had actually fulfilled all of her fondest expectations of herself. Her greatest concern was her ability to keep it up. The therapist considered that a valid concern but not one that negated the maturity of some of her emerging behavior patterns.

It is doubtful that Mary will now encounter many conflict situations in which she can engage in her avoidance routines oblivious of their meaning or not have some clear ideas about how she can be different in conflict situations so that she will approve of herself both at the time and when the conflict has been resolved. Whether she will consistently be different in these situations is still an open question, but it should be obvious that Mary has experientially learned a great deal about coping in the last month, and that this learning has taken place at different levels of psychological functioning (cognitive, behavioral, and affective).

Some Important Questions

Because this model and the treatment methods that it generates have been demonstrated and discussed in a number of professional forums prior to this publication, we are aware of some of the most common questions and concerns it raises. The three questions that appear most frequently are

1. Are not these treatment techniques unnecessarily confrontational and hard on clients?

2. Why is it necessary to be so confrontational with clients?

3. A client's presenting complaints seem to play a minimal role in the actual therapy process. Instead, you seem to assume that decreasing the tendency to be conflict avoidant and increasing the disposition to cope will benefit most clients. How do you actually judge therapeutic progress?

We find the first two questions on confrontation puzzling, and, frankly, we have spent a considerable amount of time trying to understand them. We have concluded that each of these two questions is probably best understood at two different levels of meaning. The first is substantive and is a literal request for additional explanation and information. The second is more emotional and is an expression of the personal discomfort frequently associated with emotional intensity and with the unpleasant experiences it is assumed to generate in the self and others. We would like to try and answer both of these questions at both levels of meaning. This will be followed by a discussion of how to judge therapeutic progress.

Substantive commentary. The first two questions focus on confrontation. Obviously, how these questions are answered depends on how one defines confrontation. We think the term has two general meanings. The first and most common conception is that of one person confronting another, usually with unpleasant feedback, though this is not always the case. The other is when people confront themselves or face something about themselves they had previously been unaware of. Again, it is most generally assumed that what one faces is unpleasant or undesirable. We would amend these popular conceptions by altering their preoccupation with negative attributes. Confrontation can and usually does involve both positive and negative considerations. Frankly, we have come to consider the immediate and direct expression of meaningful regard or affection to be more frightening to most clients than facing a list of well-documented personal faults. In our view, then, confrontation can be both interpersonal and intrapsychic, and it involves both positive and negative attributes or feelings.

With this definition in mind, we suggest that our model is not unnecessarily confrontational or hard on clients! Certainly clients are asked to face themselves (self-confrontation) by identifying and describing their patterns of avoidance and coping. The therapist is clearly an adjunct to this process when necessary (interpersonal feedback), but all forms of psychotherapy ask clients to face themselves in one form or another. Increased self-awareness is a staple item in most treatment forms. What distinguishes this treatment format from others is not that it is more confrontational or unnecessarily confrontational, but the relevance of what clients are confronted with. Asking clients to identify and describe their patterns of avoidance and the self-evaluative thoughts and feelings associated with them is serious psychological business because it is so revealing and relevant. The same is true of the coping response. We consider the relevance of the psychological material that this model has selected to focus on to be one of the major strengths of the model.

This brings us to the question of how hard this relevance (as opposed to confrontation) is on clients and why it is necessary. Two points seem obvious to us.

First, we cannot imagine any theory proposing to focus on psychological material that is considered irrelevant! The real issue, then, is not relevance, but the intensity of client reactions to such relevant material. This we consider to be a vital and valid concern. We have no wish to see clients overwhelmed by emotional reactions that they find frightening, unhelpful, or distressing. This makes therapeutic timing as crucial a consideration in this model as in all other treatment forms. Clients must be ready to deal with material that would be rated high on psychological immediacy and intensity. That is also why we always ask clients to identify and describe their own patterns of avoidance and the self-evaluations that accompany them. Although it may not appear to be so at first glance, we are proposing a treatment model in which the client controls the pace of therapeutic movement far more than the therapist. One of the primary responsibilities of the therapist is to keep the therapeutic process and content focused on highly relevant materials. Certainly a nudge here and there can be helpful to the client, but having clients identify and describe their patterns of avoidance during the therapy session is far more important than pushing them through these experiences. This is our way of helping clients recognize and respond to the anxiety associated with problem areas before these problems are the focus of therapy. We are basically describing a therapeutic process in which the therapist keeps clients focused on relevant material, and the rate at which clients move forward is determined by their own progress with each therapeutic task. We suggest, then, that the therapist interventions we are proposing are no more intrusive than those of most other treatment techniques. They are more relevant and incisive, and that is why it is important to allow clients a great deal of latitude in the rate at which they move through the developmental tasks in this model.

Emotional considerations. We cannot help wondering whether some of the concern expressed about client discomfort is not partially an expression of therapist discomfort as well. In the treatment format that we are describing, emotions can be intense at times, and much of the conversation is both relevant and consequential. Yet, these are not conditions commonly associated with fun and relaxation; neither should they be. Certainly, some of the emotionally intense, and cognitively poignant, therapy sessions we have already described are not the place for a therapist who has many unresolved emotional issues that need to be kept under control. In our view, a good therapist is one who has a reasonably high tolerance for the emotional distress of others without becoming overly protective or nurturing.

In our view, one of the most important underlying principles in effective psychotherapy is never to do something for clients that they can do for themselves. Equally important is remembering that the therapist's emotional comfort and stability when a client reports emotional confusion can be a source of immense reassurance to the client. Probably, one of the most unfortunate events that can take place in therapy is for a client to try to protect the therapist from emotional discomfort by not talking about the emotionally laden issues that are most in need of therapeutic discussion. Regrettably, our experience as clinical supervisors suggests that this happens more than most of us would guess.

In brief, we are asking therapists to be sure they can tolerate the emotional discomfort of their clients reasonably well before they make any attempt to protect them from the distress that is frequently a consequence of a radically improved awareness of their own self-defeating behavior patterns. Although most therapists abhor client suffering just as we do, the intensely negative feelings that are a result of more accurate client perceptions are an important source of motivation for the client to change. Furthermore, facing these negative feelings realistically can become an immediate and primary coping response that generates high levels of client self-approval, which can more than offset the distress of facing problems that are usually avoided.

Therapeutic progress. If low self-esteem is a major consideration in the development of dysfunctional behavior, as we believe it is, and if human development is based on the development of progressively higher levels of personal self-esteem, then client improvement is a multidimensional phenomenon based on the following assumptions:

1. Disruption of chronic or pervasive patterns of avoidance must generally precede any serious attempt to enhance the development of the personality. The very act of successfully controlling patterns of avoidance is a major therapeutic achievement and constitutes a basic remedial improvement in the structure of the personality.

2. Developmental progress is assessed most readily by observing the relationship among (a) internally directed behavior patterns, (b) levels of appropriate risk taking, (c) improved human functioning, and (d) improved feelings of self-worth and personal approval.

The interrelationships among these variables are sequentially summarized as:

1. Internally directed behavior is necessary for responsible risk taking. The appearance of appropriate psychological risk taking is one of the first developmental signs of client improvement.

2. Responsible risk taking is a necessary condition to correct patterns of self-defeating behavior.

3. The sense of self-efficacy that generally accompanies correcting self-defeating behavior is intrinsically rewarding and enhances self-esteem. This is the second developmental sign of client improvement.

4. A secure sense of self-esteem is the underlying basis for self-directing behavior.

5. Responsible risk taking can be initially promoted in the therapeutic relationship even when it has been totally absent in the client's prior psychological experiences.

The circular relationships among these variables are portrayed in Figure 2.

Inspection of the figure reveals that each of these variables can sequentially enrich the other variables in a continuous cycle that gradually leads to progressively higher levels of appropriate client risk taking, personal responsibility, internally directed behavior, and improved levels of self-esteem. The psychologically healthy individual is one who has a sufficient amount of self-esteem to support internally directed behavior. These people are aware of, but not entirely controlled by, the demands, pressures, and constraints of their social environments. As a result, they can take appropriate psychological risks (both interpersonal and intrapsychic), which provides them with a continuous source of learning about themselves and their social relationships. The willingness to engage in responsible risk taking enables them to correct self-defeating behavior when it does occur, which in turn demonstrates self-efficacy and improves self-esteem.

One of the major goals of psychological treatment is for the therapist to help the client initiate this process of personal growth if it is not operative or to enhance its effectiveness if it is only partially operative. We ask the reader to note that we are not attempting to discuss client improvement in more generic terms. We are restricting our comments to the evaluation of self-esteem and its antecedents, which are the focal considerations of the model we are discussing.

Summary

We started this chapter by differentiating remedial and developmental considerations in the therapeutic process. The major therapeutic task in a developmental framework is increasing the client's understanding and ability to face personal conflict realistically and forthrightly. We suggested that the more ade-

Figure 2

The Development and Maintenance of High or Low Levels of Self-Esteem

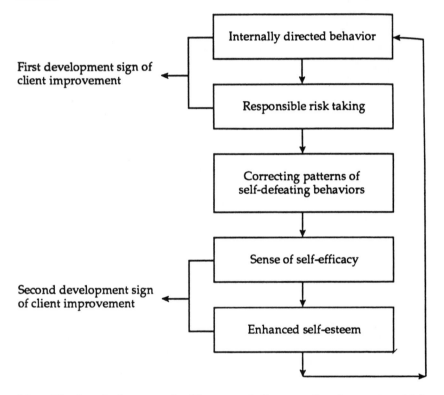

Note. The level of personal self-esteem influences the degree to which life events can be stressful. This in turn affects the personal response that is most likely to appear. If coping prevails, the individual faces problems honestly, realistically, and nondefensively. This produces favorable self-evaluative thoughts, which provide the self-generated approval that raises self-esteem, and so forth. The converse is true if low self-esteem, high personal stress, and a defensive response style prevail. Unfavorable self-evaluations trigger denial, deception, and avoidance in an attempt to disavow that which has already been glimpsed to be true. This process provides self-generated disapproval as a form of feedback to the self about personal inadequacy.

quate the adjustment of the client, the less time and attention should remedial considerations require. We also indicated that it makes little sense to attempt facilitating personality development seriously until deeply ingrained patterns of avoidance are at least exposed and their debilitating influence at least partially immobilized.

Even though the distinction between remedial and developmental considerations may be less obvious than we might hope for, we suggest that successful psychotherapy is likely to consist of a series of balanced transitions between remedial and developmental considerations. That is why we devoted a substantial amount of space to discussing how a therapist can assess a client's disposition to cope or avoid during the therapy session. Judgments about a client's disposition to cope or avoid at any given moment are the basis for a therapist's choosing between remedial and developmental therapeutic work. Our view is that a therapist's choice to focus on remedial or developmental considerations is one of the most important choice points in the entire therapy process.

We discussed the therapeutic means of actually creating a coping response by the client during the therapy hour. This was proposed as one of the most reliable means of experientially teaching clients about the elements and consequences of this more mature psychological behavior. This was followed by a discussion of how to strengthen the disposition to cope in clients who are not the victims of chronic and pervasive longstanding patterns of avoidance. Creating new coping responses or strengthening existing dispositions to cope was considered essential to a developmental approach to psychotherapy. This is the means by which clients can experientially identify and describe the elements most central to their own coping responses, and the self-evaluative thoughts and feelings that accompany them.

8

Unique Qualities of the Therapeutic Relationship

Types of Therapeutic Relationships

There can be little doubt that the quality of the client–therapist relationship is a primary component of the therapeutic process. Its importance seems to be universally understood and accepted among all therapeutic orientations (Orlinsky & Howard, 1986). Although some radical behavior therapists argue that the therapeutic relationship is an irrelevant consideration in client improvement, most orientations consider it to be at least a prerequisite to positive change and possibly a primary curative factor in and of itself (Frank, 1973; Prochaska, 1984).

There are serious differences of opinion about the most essential ingredients of a healthy therapeutic relationship. Discussions about helping relationships regularly include such diverse qualities as the carefully calculated neutrality of the analyst (Greenson, 1967) to the transparent involvement and authenticity of the humanistic and existential approaches (Rogers, 1957). In spite of this diversity, any discussion of the therapeutic relationship cannot lose sight of the complexity of this phenomenon or its centrality in the therapeutic process. In our discussion, we will emphasize what we consider to be the two cardinal considerations in any therapeutic relationship. The first is the relationship characteristics that are essential to the treatment model we have proposed. The second is the role that these attributes are assumed to play in the therapy process.

Before discussing these two considerations in detail, however, we will outline some of the most important dimensions along which therapeutic relationships regularly differ. It will quickly become obvious that what one considers a good therapeutic relationship is usually an extension of other, more basic views such as (a) the underlying causes of disordered behavior, (b) the nature of human beings and their potential for perfectibility, (c) the optimal conditions for human growth and development, (d) the degree to which humans are considered to be unique creatures or simply another of nature's creations bound by natural laws, and (e) the practitioner's guiding theory of psychotherapy and the treatment techniques that it emphasizes.

We have selected five bipolar dimensions[1] that seem to represent the major views and values out of which different types of therapeutic relationships grow in the mental health professions. As you might expect, there are serious and substantive disagreements about the relative merits of each of these dimensions as well as what the optimal mixture of ingredients might be for an ideal therapeutic relationship. These disagreements make it interesting and useful to note the similarities and differences among the types of therapeutic relationships that can be created.

We understand that the descriptive dimensions that we are proposing are not exhaustive; neither are they mutually exclusive of each other. In some cases, they may not even be applicable to all systems of psychotherapy. We consider them to be useful descriptive tools that can help clarify some of the important ways in which therapeutic relationships can differ. The five dimensions include (a) therapist involvement—high to low, (b) therapist time orientation—past or present, (c) therapist

---

[1] Much of the material included in this section was developed by Dr. Richard L. Bednar and Dr. Theodore J. Kaul in an unpublished manuscript entitled "Group Psychotherapy: A Comparative Review and Analysis."

role—teacher or facilitator, (d) emphasis on client content or personality style, and (e) individual autonomy—high to low.

Therapist Involvement

One of the most obvious ways in which therapeutic relationships differ is the degree to which therapists retain a detached neutrality in their dealings with clients or become personally involved and allow their own primary thoughts and feelings to become part of the therapeutic process. The end points of this continuum can be represented by the later views of Carl Rogers (1980), when he was emphasizing the importance of experiencing and encountering clients, and the early writings of Freud (1912/1957), in which the therapist's carefully calculated neutrality was essential if client projections and transference were to be complete and uninterpreted.

Therapists who remain technically neutral avoid direct personal involvement with their clients for a variety of reasons. It can be the means of avoiding countertransference problems, retaining the objectivity necessary for dispassionate diagnosis, or a recognition of the power and status ascribed to a therapist in any therapeutic relationship. These therapists may appear ambiguous, unapproachable, or even invulnerable to their clients. However, they assume this orientation as a consequence of some important beliefs about the origins of abnormality and its cure.

In contrast is the therapist who defines an ideal relationship as one in which both the client and the therapist are open, congruent, and authentic in their respective expressions of thoughts and feelings. These therapists are likely to deal directly with their clients and expect to be dealt with as individuals of equal worth and power in the therapy relationship. These therapists may offer direct feedback, interpret the here-and-now, and be as open in their expression of negative reactions as of positive ones. Some may even go so far as to suggest that the very process of encountering another individual in the here-and-now is the essence of the therapeutic process, although many would disagree with this view. These therapists tend to be anything but passive, and they do not view themselves as a mirror for improving client self-perceptions.

Time Orientation: Past or Present

Therapists who assume that the past is the dominant determinant of psychological distress create a different type of therapeutic relationship from those who view the present as a microcosm representing all the important psychological elements from the past. These differences are apparent in most therapy sessions. They are reflected by the degree to which clients are systematically encouraged to experience and express psychological events as they occur, or recall and reconstruct them from the past. The level of cognitive or affective arousal closely parallels this continuum, with experiential learning in the here-and-now being associated with the highest levels of affective arousal.

The dominant tool of a therapeutic approach that emphasizes historical considerations is the interpretation of the meaning of present behavior in terms of historical conflicts. This mode of psychological activity is generally cognitive and takes place at low levels of immediacy, intensity, and affective arousal. However, this is not always the case. High levels of emotional expression are common in moments of intense catharsis or accompanying particularly poignant insights. These events are less common than continuous attempts to understand the present by acquiring more penetrating insight into the past. The ideal relationship for this type of psychological activity would appear to be one that is *calm, patient, stable, reassuring, analytical,* and *accepting.*

In contrast, therapists who emphasize the importance of the here-and-now tend to ignore historical interpretations of behavior. They recognize the existence of the past, of course, but they try to deal with it as it manifests itself in the present. When they interpret, they stress the immediacy and intensity of the experience in the moment. Because these therapists assume that historical conflicts can find full expression in the here-and-now, these conflicts need not be intellectually reconstructed to be understood; they can be reexperienced in their fullness and resolved in the present. Accordingly, these therapists work in an intense and volatile relationship because of the intensity that can accompany their evocative and, at times, provocative interventions, designed to bring the psychological traumas of the past right into the consulting room. Terms that could be used to describe this therapeutic relationship include *confrontational, probing,* and *experiential.*

Therapist Role: Teacher or Facilitator

This is an interesting dimension because the two end points of this continuum represent two distinct philosophical orientations toward psychological treatment. Other terms have been used to describe this continuum. Two common ones are (a) structured versus unstructured, and (b) directive versus nondirective. No matter what terms are used to describe this continuum, however, the underlying dimension and its most fundamental attributes remain essentially unchanged; so do the relationship characteristics that they breed.

One end of this continuum is represented by proponents who argue that treatment technologies exist. Because they exist, and because we have good evidence that they work, they should be used. Naturally, it is therapists who understand how to apply these technologies to the problems of their clients. According to this view, it is both efficient and responsible for therapists to plan the activities of their clients, much as teachers plan the learning activities of their pupils. They go into the therapy hour with the intention of creating situations designed to provide clients with the type of learning experiences that will maximize their growth. This point of view is most clearly represented by the behavioral and cognitive–behavioral approaches, in which clients are taught new patterns of thinking or behaving (Beck, Rush, Shaw, & Emery, 1979; Ellis, 1973). Although, the relationship between the client and therapist during this process can be both warm and nurturing, few clients will fail to recognize or respond to therapists as the informed expert. Therapeutic relationships of this type tend to be *task centered, cordial, focused, hierarchical,* and *problem centered.*

Other approaches champion a more idiographic and democratic attitude toward their clients. Denouncing the role of the therapist as a teacher as too proscriptive and prescriptive, they argue that what is important is the uniqueness of the individual and each therapy hour. In this context, the therapist is a facilitator of experiential learning. What is valued is that clients increase their awareness of themselves and others and learn to present themselves more congruently. According to this view, this uniqueness cannot be elicited or commanded; it must be allowed to evolve and appear naturally. The most effective means of eliciting that uniqueness is to leave the therapy hour unstructured by having the therapist abandon the role of expert teacher and assist clients to express their most deeply felt needs and problems. With few exceptions, therapists of this persuasion see attempts to structure the therapy process as controlling and intrusive. This type of therapeutic relationship is usually described as *client centered, supportive, expressive, democratic, exploratory,* and *genuine.*

Client Content or Personality Style

At first glance, this dimension may appear to represent a therapeutic focus factor rather than a relationship characteristic. In a sense, that is entirely true. But, as we have already noted, the way in which therapy is conducted virtually defines the therapeutic relationship. A therapist closely aligned with the content end of this continuum assumes that it is the literal content of the client'scomplaints that warrants the therapist's interventions. These therapists orient their treatment activities toward clarifying the meaning and consequences of the clients' concerns and then developing problem-solving strategies to alleviate them. These relationships are generally seen as *collaborative, cooperative, problem centered,* generally *more cognitive than affective,* and *reality bound.*

Therapists who emphasize client styles, or patterns of behavior, assume that content is important only in its revelation of the client's enduring styles of functioning. Styles are presumed to be based on trait-like dispositions about which people may have limited awareness. These styles are generally considered to be deeply ingrained patterns that produce consistent and wide-ranging effects. Examples of some frequently discussed psychological styles include (a) approval seekers, (b) conflict avoiders, (c) noncompliers, (d) nurturers, and (e) pleasers and placaters. The therapist's primary task is to increase clients' understanding of the underlying psychological dispositions central to their recurring problems. Insight alone, however, is not enough. Therapists' efforts are also directed toward influencing clients' general style of behavior, though not necessarily any specific problem situation revealed by the client. These relationships usually have high levels of trust and warmth to support the depth of self-exploration involved. They also have relatively high levels of psychological immediacy and intensity because many of the clients' trait dispositions find expression during the therapeutic hour and become the grist for the therapeutic mill.

Individual Autonomy: High to Low

The final relationship dimension we have elected to discuss is the role of individual autonomy in the therapeutic relationship. This continuum closely resembles that of the therapist as an expert teacher or facilitator of experiential learning, but it differs in several important respects and deserves additional comment in its own right.

Therapeutic relationships that are high on individual autonomy (for both the therapist and client) place a heavy emphasis on personal responsibility, individual accountability, personal freedom, and an absence of client caretaking. Client problems, no matter how serious, tend to be viewed by the therapist as opportunities for the clients to learn more about themselves. These therapists are not very inclined to do for the client what clients could do for themselves. Although therapists who create this kind of relationship can be warm, supportive, nurturing, and caring, they are more likely to require that clients explore the meaning and significance of their dependency than they are to provide the approval and reassurance that these clients seem to need.

These relationships appear to have some of the same attributes associated with the concept of "tough love" (York, York,

& Wachtel, 1982), which has emerged in recent years. Individuals are cared for, but in a context in which they are expected to exercise their individual freedom and assume the responsibilities that go with it. Of course, these therapists also expect the same thing of themselves and tend to avoid symbiotic involvements or dialogues with their clients.

Other therapeutic approaches minimize the client's sense of individual autonomy, at least in early sessions, as when the therapist assumes the responsibility for teaching the client new ways of thinking or behaving. Understanding that the client must learn techniques of behavior change, the therapist takes complete responsibility for directing the therapy process. Clients are literally dependent on the counsel and expertise of the therapist and must learn to be good students. It is important to notice that we are not suggesting that this type of dependence is bad or undesirable. In the restricted way we are using this term, all of us are dependent on the expertise of others as we learn throughout our life span. This, of course, does not alter the fact that these relationships would still be rated low on individual autonomy.

Summary. In this section, we have described some of the dimensions along which therapeutic relationships can differ. Even though these dimensions are not all-encompassing or mutually exclusive, each one provides different descriptive information about the ways in which therapeutic relationships can differ. These nine dimensions and their most important relationship characteristics are summarized below:

1. Therapist involvement—The degree to which the therapist's personal presence, thoughts, and feelings are part of the therapeutic process is measured on this dimension.

2. Therapist neutrality—The therapist is reactive primarily to client verbalizations and is a consistent, careful, and objective observer of the client and the therapeutic process.

3. Historical orientation—The meaning of present behavior tends to be interpreted in terms of historical, unresolved conflicts. Therapy sessions tend to be more cognitive than affective, with interpretation being a primary treatment technique.

4. Here-and-now orientation—Clients are encouraged to experience and express their feelings about psychological events as they occur. Therapy sessions tend to be more affective than cognitive, with experiential learning being a central consideration.

5. *Therapist as an expert teacher*—The therapist teaches clients new ways of thinking and behaving based on expert knowledge. The teaching process is relatively explicit rather than implicit in the orienting theory.

6. *Therapist as a facilitator*—These relationships tend to be client-centered, supportive, and democratic as a means of increasing client sensitivity to self and others and more congruent expressions of the authentic self.

7. *Client content*—The literal content of client complaints becomes a central consideration in the therapy process. The therapist tries to help clarify and interpret the meaning and significance of the client's concerns, and then explores the means for solving these problems in a collaborative, cooperative, problem-solving relationship.

8. *Client personality style*—High levels of trust and support are required to sustain the depth of self-exploration required for clients to obtain a greater understanding of their underlying trait-like disposition, which seems to be the cause of a variety of their recurring psychological problems.

9. *Individual autonomy*—High levels of individual autonomy are most apparent in relationships in which individuals can be cared for, but are still expected to exercise their individual will and accept the responsibility of making their needs known and finding acceptable ways to satisfy these needs.

Inspection of Table 2 reveals that a variety of different therapeutic relationships can be described with reasonable accuracy using these dimensions.

Even though there may be some disagreement about the way in which we have applied these descriptors to the treatment systems in Table 2, there can be little doubt that therapeutic relationships do differ based on the philosophical underpinnings of the orienting theory. Also, notice that these relationship dimensions tend to cluster in patterns or profiles. For example, high ratings on the therapist-as-expert-teacher category appear to be systematically related to other categories, such as therapist

Table 2

Descriptive Characteristics of Four Therapy Orientations

Dimension	Psycho-dynamic	Humanistic–existential	Strict behaviorist	Cognitive–behavioral
Personal involvement	L	H	L	L
Therapist neutrality	H	L	H	H
Historical orientation	H	L	L	L
Here-and-now orientation	L	H	L	M
Expert teacher	M	L	H	H
Experiential learning	M	H	L	M
Content-centered	L	L	H	H
Personality styles	M	M	L	L
Individual autonomy	L	H	L	L

Note. H = high, M = moderate, L = low.

neutrality, involvement, and autonomy. Similarly, high ratings on therapist involvement seem to vary with other categories such as facilitator, experiential learning, and time orientation. This interdependence should not be surprising, however. Most new therapy orientations are created as a reaction to the deficiencies in existing treatment approaches, and new theories tend to emphasize new and opposite elements. The development of behaviorism, for example, was a reaction (at least in part) to the psychoanalytic influence of the time. Over the years, each changing philosophy has added new dimensions to what can be considered a therapeutic relationship.

Relationship Characteristics

In this section, we will describe what we consider to be the optimal combination of relationship characteristics for the therapeutic relationship we are proposing. To illustrate the type and level of these relationship attributes, we will use the clinical example we first used to illustrate the major elements in our model. This was the example in which a young housewife chronically tried to avoid rejection and gain acceptance by suppressing her own needs and meticulously attending to the wishes of others. She originally came to therapy complaining of fatigue, but the definition of her problem was altered dramatically in her first session as her therapist had her focus on her style of gaining approval.

We reproduce this session in its entirety to illustrate each of the relationship dimensions we will be discussing. Brief explanatory notes have also been inserted in the text to help clarify important relationship considerations in this session. All of this material is intended to help illustrate and clarify the role and function of the relationship characteristics that will be discussed after this clinical case illustration.

Introduction and Rapport-Building

Therapist: Tell me, what led you to schedule a meeting for today?

Client: Well, I think that I'm just feeling so worn out and run down and—you know, just physically and emotionally washed out.

Therapist: Please tell me more.

Client: Well, maybe if I talk a little about last week, I could describe what my life is like and why I'm feeling this way.

Therapist: Okay.

Client: Well, let's see, as I look back on last week, I see myself wrapped up and so busy with the kids. It's just one thing after another. If it isn't sports, then it's plays and all these extracurricular things that they're in. And I feel like I need to be there to support them. It's just constant, just a steady kind of thing.

Therapist: So, as you see it, your fatigue is the result of the overwhelming amount of activity in your life?

Client: Yes, probably so.

Therapist: Why do you keep it up?

Client: Well, I think it's important for the kids to see that I support them in the things they do. I want to be a supportive person. If I love them, those are the kinds of things I should be willing to do for them. When I do, I think they feel better, and it makes them feel better about our relationship together.

Therapist: It sounds like you take your parental responsibilities very seriously.

Client: Maybe so, but I feel like sometimes I could just scream.

Therapist: A little angry there, huh?

Client: No! I'm not angry. It's just that I can't do any more, but I can't say that to them when I know they want me to be there. When it's important to them, I just feel like I really need to go ahead and do it anyway.

Therapist: Why?

Client: I'm sure they would be disappointed. They might think I wasn't interested in them or I didn't care what they did. It's easy to say you care, but I think it's important to do more than just say it—you have to show it by the way you act. You know, you have to have your behavior match your words.

The form and substance of this dialogue was essentially unchanged for another 15 minutes. The client repeatedly emphasized the "moral" and "socially desirable" reasons for her meticulous adherence to her parental role and responsibilities. She was not inclined to acknowledge that her behavior was motivated by a need for approval from her children or a fear of their rejection. Neither did she seem the least bit interested in exploring her "style" of developing and maintaining relationships within the family or acknowledging any anger or resentment toward those who seemed to have so much control over her life.

As quickly as the therapist judged that the client felt understood enough to tolerate a moderate level of dissonance without becoming too defensive, the focus of the interview was changed so that it became more exploratory and incisive.

Identifying Patterns of Avoidance and Self-Evaluative Thoughts and Feelings

Therapist: Let me see if I can summarize what seems to be bothering you the most. You find yourself in a rather difficult situation. On the one hand, you feel a strong need to be supportive and involved in your children's lives as a way of building a strong relationship. On the other hand, you're tired, you want more time to yourself, and you may even resent others' controlling your life so much. The essential conflict is between what you think you should do for others and what you want to do for yourself. Does that sound like a fair summary of what's bothering you?

The therapist has now taken the role of expert teacher and will begin to shape the session in such a way that the client can become aware of her self-defeating style. Notice how the succession of questions leads the client to more and more specific descriptions of her behavior and the purpose it serves. In spite of client content concerning her physical symptoms, the discussion is centered around her personality style.

Client: Yeah, I haven't thought of it that way before, but that sounds about right.
Therapist: What precisely is it you usually do when other people want you to do something you're not really interested in doing?
Client: What do you mean?
Therapist: I mean what precisely is it that you usually do when other people want you to do something you're not really interested in doing?
Client: [Long pause.] I usually do what other people want. I notice that other people do the same thing, though. [Note the defensiveness.]
Therapist: It sounds like it's hard for you to say no to people.

> Client: It is! When people ask me to do things, I really feel like I should do it for them. But after I say yes, I'm so tight inside. How do you say no to those kinds of things?
>
> Therapist: What makes it so hard for you?
>
> Client: I think it's important to have pleasant relationships. You can't say no to people all the time and expect them to like you.
>
> Therapist: Let's see if we can get an accurate description of what you tend to do in situations where your desires are in conflict with the wishes of others.
>
> Client: I try to be cooperative and giving, to do my part in relationships even when it's inconvenient. That's my way of trying to be a good friend, or spouse, or mother.
>
> Therapist: You think of these as very desirable traits, is that right?
>
> Client: That's right.

The session is now at its first critical juncture. The therapist sees the client's behavior as conflict-avoidant and approval-seeking. The client is describing the same behavior as responsible and desirable. Attempts by the therapist to have the client identify anything negative or avoidant in her behavior patterns have been unsuccessful. The therapist now changes the focus of the interview to the client's actual behavior in the therapy session because it is less abstract, more immediate, and more revealing.

> Therapist: What you seem to be saying is that your style of dealing with conflict is to keep things pleasant by doing what others want and expect from you.
>
> Client: Well, yes. Maybe it is.
>
> Therapist: Maybe it is?
>
> Client: Otherwise, I guess I wouldn't have such a hard time saying no. People ask me to do things and I really feel like I should do it for them, but after I say yes, I wish I'd said NO!

Therapist: Are you saying that you give in all the time so people will like and value you?

Client: I have to think about that. I imagine it could be. It's important, I think, to have a pleasantness in relationships.

Therapist: I would like you to determine if this is your way of avoiding unpleasantness and getting people to like you.

Client: I guess that could be true.

Therapist: Tell me about the ways it could be true.

Client: These are hard questions. No one likes to think that they are nice to people just so they will be liked.

Therapist: I agree, they really are hard questions. [Therapist involvement through support.]

Client: Yes, they are. Probably because they are hitting home with me.

Therapist: How does that feel?

Client: Not very good. I didn't realize I was doing that. But I hate people to be disappointed in me. I feel like they can't count on me, that I'm not willing to do things for them. I always thought it was worth the price that I guess I pay to do that. But now I'm not so sure.

Therapist: This way of thinking is kind of new to you?

Client: Yes.

Therapist: Let's try something. What you seem to be saying is that your style for avoiding conflict and gaining approval from others is by doing for others what pleases them the most. At least that's what we're considering so far. Does that sound about right?

Client: Well, yes. I guess I feel like I do that.

Therapist: Do you do that with me as well?

Client: Well, it's important to me, as a client, that you like me.

With this intervention, the therapist has become intensely involved in the therapeutic process in the here-and-now. The following interventions highlight the here-and-now experiential learning nature of the treatment.

Therapist:	Please try to describe as accurately as you can how you go about making sure that I will like you.
Client:	I guess by cooperating with you and trying to do and say what you want me to.
Therapist:	So that's what you're doing right now? I ask you these questions and you answer them even though they're unsettling because that's what you think you have to do so I will like you?
Client:	Yes. It's really been hard for me to do, but I thought it was important to do that.
Therapist:	But it's for me you're doing it?
Client:	Yes, I think probably so because I know I trust you a lot, but I feel like maybe if I didn't you wouldn't like me, and maybe....
Therapist:	So, in a sense, you're playing a role or pretending with me right now?
Client:	I guess so.
Therapist:	Do you have a word or a way of describing the way you treat me so I will like you? Do you know what I mean by that?
Client:	The way I behave so you'll like me?
Therapist:	Yes, can you think of a word to summarize the style or pattern of behavior you use to try and make sure I will like you?
Client:	Trying to be positive, pleasant, cooperative....

The client has now started to describe one of her styles for gaining approval from others with a reasonable degree of accuracy, but she continues to cast it in a favorable light by using terms such as cooperative, pleasant, and positive. These terms accurately reflect her overt behavior, but they completely miss the underlying motives that sustain the behavior. These might include fear of rejection or loss of approval. The psychological consequences of her overly compliant interpersonal style are both obvious and consequential. They are certainly not limited to the fatigue that the client described in her initial complaint. They extend into such fundamental areas as (a) a limited sense of personal identity, (b) inability to regulate, balance, or resolve conflict, and (c) a life filled with frustration, guilt, and unhappiness. Because she is a relatively strong woman, the therapist decides to take a more active part in the labeling process to accelerate the movement of the therapy session and to increase the accuracy of the labels attached to the underlying motives of her behavior.

Therapist: How about "selling yourself out"? [Therapist involvement through nonneutrality.]

Client: That sounds horrible. [Long, thoughtful pause.] I guess maybe so. I don't really say how I feel inside while I'm doing things for others, and I do feel real tight inside. And, you know, when I say yes to people, that's when the tightness starts.

Therapist: Are the terms "selling yourself out" or "buying approval" accurate descriptions? Is that what we want to call it?

Notice how the therapist explicitly maintains client autonomy throughout this next section by always asking the client to improve or validate the descriptors used to describe her style.

Client: Those are harsh words.

Therapist: Yes, they are both harsh and unflattering, but are they accurate? It is important for you to try and describe your style accurately so we can understand what you do and why. [Therapist involvement through support.]

Client: I guess I see myself pretty much as a "yes" person. It's important that I do that for other people so that I won't disappoint them, so that we'll have a good relationship, so they won't know how I really feel inside. I hide that a lot.

Therapist: When I ask you to describe something, you describe it, then explain and justify it. You don't really need to justify it here. Let's just get a clear understanding of what it is you're doing.

Client: I guess when it gets down to the bottom line, maybe I'm just trying to be somebody I'm not.

Therapist: Okay, and you do that by saying yes when you don't mean it?

Client: Yeah, I do that a lot.

Therapist: Is there anything you want in return for being so nice to people?

Client: I want them to think I'm a good friend. I want my husband to think I'm a good wife. I want my children to think I'm a good mother.

Therapist: I understand. Basically, then, you are trying to gain the approval and acceptance of others by being what they want you to be.

Client: I guess so.

Therapist: Is that too harsh? [Therapist maintains client autonomy.]

Client: I don't think I really realized that's what I was doing. It's kind of a hard thing to face.

Therapist: It really is hard, isn't it? [Support and involvement.]

Client: I think so.

Therapist: So summarize all that we've said that describes how you are at relating to people. Let's see if we can get to a description that seems accurate to you even though it may be harsh.

Client: I guess I basically hide myself and that I try to be something I'm not by doing what I think other people would like me to do.

Therapist: And that description seems accurate to you? [Note again the emphasis on client autonomy.]

Client: I hear myself say it. I—yes, I think so.

The client has a reasonably clear description of her behavior, which she seems partially willing to accept. The next step is to start identifying the self-evaluative thoughts and feelings that accompany this behavior. This is frequently the point at which a great deal of the client's emotion comes to the surface, so the therapist proceeds with caution because it is late in the therapy hour.

Therapist: We need to go a step further with this, and this is going to be harder than what we just did. Should we wait for another session or should we start now? [Again, the explicit expectation of client autonomy and decision making.]

Client: Oh, let's give it a try.

Therapist: Are you sure? It's going to be harder than what we just did.

Client: I'll try.

Therapist: Okay, you have a description of yourself, and at least tentatively it seems accurate to you. Now I want you to tell me how you feel about yourself because you're that way.

Client: [Long pause, eyes begin to moisten.] I'm disappointed. I'm frustrated because I really would like to be able to say all these things I want to say and still have people not run away from me or push me away because I say how I feel. I'd like to know how to do that.

Therapist: Know how to do what?

Client: Be my own person!

Therapist: You mean you want to stop pretending so much?

Client: Yeah, that's a good way to put it.

Therapist: How else do you feel about yourself for pretending so much?

Client: I can't say that I think a whole lot of myself. Sounds kind of like a game. It's a game because I'm trying to fool people so they will like me. It's really disgusting. How can they even like me if they don't know me?

Therapist: And maybe you fooled yourself as well?

Client: I guess I did.

Strengthening the Coping Response

This session is now to the point at which it is *absolutely crucial* that the therapist recognize that the very act of clearly identifying and labeling one's own avoidance patterns and the self-evaluative thoughts and feelings that accompany them is a primary coping response. It is essential that the therapeutic benefits of this response be realized in the session in which it occurs. This is accomplished by having the client identify and describe this adaptive response and the feeling that accompanies it.

Therapist: You don't seem to be fooling yourself right now. How does that feel to you?

The therapist has now shifted from describing the client's avoidance to describing the client's coping in the session. Notice how the method of learning still emphasizes here-and-now experiential learning, with the expert teacher helping the client to see the immediate change in her typical style of behaving.

Client: Feels kind of good.

Therapist: Really?

Client: [Tears are now streaming down her cheeks.] Yeah!

Therapist: Even though it hurts that badly?

Client: Yeah.

Therapist: What do the tears mean?

Client: Well, I'm kind of happy that I know this now. I'm hurting, but I think I feel better now that I can say these things to you. I feel better about myself, because you're still sitting here and I don't feel like you hate me for what I've said or you're going to push me away. That feels good.

Therapist: What exactly have you done in this situation that has allowed you to approve of yourself more than usual?

Client: For the first time in a long time, I've been honest with myself and another person about how I really feel.

Therapist: Are you saying that not being honest with yourself and others is the real problem you came here about?

Client: I think so. I didn't know it when I first came in, but I think that has been a big problem for me.

Therapist: An interesting thing has happened here today. You have described yourself as a "yes" person, as someone who hides herself from everybody. Then we had what has to be considered a hard conversation, where you presented yourself to me as you really are, and somehow we ended up with you feeling much better than when you walked in the door. Does that make any sense to you?

Client: Yes, just knowing the truth, I guess. Besides, the problem seems more soluble now.

Therapist: Our time is up now, but before we end I would like you to summarize what you learned about yourself today.

Client: I need to learn how to say how I feel more. When I feel like saying no, I need to be able to say that, and to tell my kids that I'm just being worn too thin and that even though I'd like to be there, I just can't do everything. And sometimes I will just tell them I still love and support them.

Therapist: So you're really talking about being more honest with yourself and others about your feelings?

Client: Yeah.

Therapist: And how do you feel about the prospect of going through a whole week without buying approval from others by being a servant to them?

Client: Well, if it makes me feel like I do now, I think that would be very important.

Therapist: Our time is just about up, but what we've done today would be worth thinking about and going over next week.

Client: Good, I'll try and see what I can do this week.

Therapist Involvement

Therapist involvement can take many forms. It can vary from session to session, or minute by minute, within a session. Its manifestations can be subtle or obvious, as can be its effects. However, high involvement generally involves unambiguous personal expression by the therapist, and minimal levels of congruence between important therapist feelings and behavior. This is not to say that this is all therapists do, or that they even do it a lot. Rather, on selected occasions, therapists are willing to make some of their feelings and values known to the client. Expressions of personal support and encouragement for the client are probably the most common form but not necessarily the most important. Openly challenging and confronting clients with their incongruities is an expression of involvement in which therapist observations directly influence the course of therapy. No matter what specific form the therapist's involvement takes, its cardinal feature is always the same—the introduction of the therapist's views in such a way that the client can react to them. In this process, the therapist generally becomes a less ambiguous person to the client.

There are two noteworthy observations about therapist involvement in our case illustration. First, the therapist's observations and thoughts about the client's behavior play an obvious and influential role in the therapy process. There is very little about the therapist's comments that is neutral or reactive. The therapist is far more proactive and provocative than neutral. The most obvious example takes place as the client describes her behavior. The client's description was socially appropriate and emphasized terms such as cooperative, pleasant, and positive. The therapist suggested another label (selling yourself out), which was psychologically more relevant and designed to capture the avoidant nature of her behavior. This new label represented a dramatic shift in the explicit and implied meaning of her behavior that could hardly be ignored. It was a form of confrontation, dissonance induction, and reality testing in one sentence. And the increased level of client distress that followed this comment suggests the value and validity of the new label. The client's tears, depth of self-exploration, and self-disclosure, all increased after this comment; so did the value of the therapy session.

It is important to notice the timing and style of this confrontation. The confrontation itself was delivered as a question, not a statement. It was a nonhostile, matter-of-fact invitation to consider an alternative. Implicitly, such statements demean the value of the client's socially appropriate and conventional behavior. Explicitly, they suggest the value of candor and realism, even when it is painful. But once the confrontation was delivered, the client was asked if the label was too harsh, which, of course, creates the opportunity to modify or disown it. The value of these confrontations resides in their ultimate validity and usefulness to the client, not the persuasive power of the therapist. They are occasions in which therapists openly share their perceptions and then create opportunities for clients to examine them to determine their value and accuracy.

But our second point is equally important. What about the client's level of comfort or distress during this process? Lieberman, Yalom, and Miles (1973) made it quite clear that the charismatic therapist can be quite dangerous, at least in group work. Their data indicated that therapists who were overly provocative, confronting, or demanding were associated with the highest frequency of client casualties. We believe that the essential dynamics of this process (overwhelming the client) are equally applicable and destructive in individual therapy. That is why it is absolutely essential that therapist involvement also convey a high level of support, encouragement, patience, humanness, and commitment to the client. The therapist's most benevolent motives are critical here, and they must be clearly perceived and understood by the client. They must also be authentic. Our assumption is that even the most revealing information, interpretations, or confrontations can be helpful as long as the therapist is perceived as offering them for the benefit of the client. In this particular example we have a limited but relevant number of examples of therapist support. Notice the frequency of statements such as (a) "Are you ready to go further now, or should we wait until the next session?" (b) "Yes, these are really hard questions," (c) "Is that too harsh?" and (d) "Does that description sound accurate to you?"

We want the humanness of the therapist to show for other reasons as well. In our view, it is easier for a client to have a meaningful relationship with a therapist who is comfortable showing his or her human qualities some of the time. We see nothing wrong with it if the client and therapist exchange an occasional joke or the therapist self-discloses a bit about a bad day. These brief retreats from the core business of therapy are enlightening to the client. They personalize the therapist and make it easier for the client to feel comfortable in the relationship. Sometimes, it makes the relationship more comfortable for the therapist as well.

Summary. A high level of therapist involvement has two major components and purposes in our view. First, it is a personal tool for relationship development. It allows the therapist to be seen, at least partially, for the type of person he or she is. It brings an element of informality, casualness, and humanness to the relationship. This can improve the basic nature of the relationship, which can be developed by increasing candor, trust, psychological risk taking, and interpersonal comfort.

Second, it is the quality of the therapeutic relationship that allows the therapist to introduce the client productively to levels of psychological dissonance that would normally be intolerable and unproductive. Highly dissonant materials cannot profitably be introduced into the therapy process by a therapist whose personal qualities are essentially unknown and whose response to intense client distress is uncertain. High levels of therapist involvement are essential for those times in which the therapist's interpretations, confrontations, or opinions are offered as a means of inducing high levels of client dissonance or "unfreezing."

Time Orientation: Past or Present

It is probably obvious to the reader by now that we consider the most potent treatment interventions to be those that take place in the psychological present, or the here-and-now. Naturally, we have no rule against discussing historical events with clients; these are excellent opportunities for rapport-building. They also provide the therapist with valuable information that can help clarify the origins of the client's current patterns of thinking and behaving. However, when it is time for the serious business of therapy to begin, we offer the following guidelines for the therapeutic use of the here-and-now for your consideration:

1. The units of analysis involved in our model are rather complex. As you recall, they are deeply ingrained patterns of behavior that are assumed to transcend time, place, and circumstances. They also involve cognition, emotion, and behavior. Because of this, we have suggested that when a client is continually encouraged to experience and express thoughts and feelings as they occur; sooner or later, these enduring patterns of behavior are certain to make their appearance in the therapy.

2. Once these patterns of behavior emerge in the therapy session, the astute therapist may have the client (a) describe them in their completeness as they occur, (b) identify the psychological function the behavior patterns were serving when they first appeared in the therapy session, (c) attach summary labels to

the patterns of behavior, and (d) inquire about the self-evalua-tive thoughts and feelings that accompany these behavior pat-terns. Our belief is that this entire process takes place at high levels of precision, clarity, and intensity when the behavior in question is taking place in the therapy room rather than simply being recalled from past events.

3. We have also suggested that human thoughts, feelings, and behavior are best considered as integrated rather than separate systems. Each of these components (thoughts, feelings, and be-havior) affects, and is affected by, every other component in a continuous cycle of reciprocal influence.

Although we have no guiding theory to lead us through this complex maze of interacting human elements, we still consider it important to try to deal with them (cognitions, feelings, and behavior) as though they were interrelated systems. This is a difficult task, but one that is simplified when the client's be-havior in the consulting room is the topic of the therapy session. Asking clients to observe and describe clearly their behavior patterns as they occur (behavioral focus), label the meaning and function of the behavior (cognitive activity), and then identify and experience the self-evaluative thoughts and feelings that accompany that behavior (affective experiential activity) is an important step in responding to client behavior as a unified system. The alternative, of course, is to continue developing treatment approaches that emphasize primarily one of the three: behavior, thoughts, or feelings.

If we return to the example of the young housewife, we find another useful illustration of bringing client issues into the here-and-now. A critical phase of this interview occured as the ther-apist helped the client describe her style of avoiding rejection (being a pleaser and placater of others), and the self-evaluative thoughts and feelings accompanying that pattern of behavior (self-recrimination and embarrassment). To help the client deal with this problem once it had been made explicit, the therapist asked the client if she were also trying to please him in the same way during the therapy session. In this segment, the therapist asked her how she tried to gain his approval, and more impor-tantly, how she felt about herself for pretending during her ther-apy hour. This intervention was pivotal in the process of diminishing this client's inclination to be a pleaser and placater in the therapy sessions. It also created the opportunity, and an implicit demand, for the client to be more honest in her self-presentation and to experience the benefits of a more authentic self-presentation. All of this took place at high levels of cognitive, emotional, and behavioral immediacy and intensity because the topic of discussion during the therapy hour was the psychological events taking place in the consulting room.

Summary. We suggest three important points from this example. First, clients do have a tendency to bring their enduring patterns of behavior into the therapy room with them. This is hardly a startling revelation to most of us. Second, these patterns of behavior can become the primary grist for the therapeutic mill. They can be identified, labeled, and experienced in the fullness in the consulting room. At the precise moment in which the client becomes the most disheartened, the therapist can ask how the client needs to act in the relationship *right now* to be the type of person he or she has always wanted to be. These new behaviors can also be identified, labeled, and experienced by the client to enhance learning. Third, cognitions, affect, and behavior are all the focus of therapy during this process. It is our assumption that the more psychological domains are involved in the change process, the more durable the changes will be. Finally, the relationship between the client and therapist provides a format for all of these events in the here-and-now that can facilitate learning at three levels simultaneously (cognitive, affective, and behavioral). We suggest that this will result in therapeutic outcomes in which people understand more, feel better, and act differently.

Therapist Role: Teacher or Facilitator

There is a bit of a problem here. On each of the relationship dimensions already discussed, we have consistently suggested the merits of one side of each relationship characteristic over its opposite. We have opted for high involvement and low neutrality, and for more emphasis on the here-and-now compared to the there-and-then. However, on this relationship dimension, we are going to straddle a fine line. We will suggest that the therapist is both an expert teacher and a facilitator of experiential learning. Our discussion will strive to clarify the fundamental differences between these two roles and the conditions under which each is called for. This is a therapeutic relationship that attempts to preserve the role of the therapist as an expert teacher, but what the client understands is more experiential than cognitive, and what the client learns is more personal than universal.

Therapeutic process. When we talk about the therapist as an expert teacher, we are referring to someone who understands the general principles of self-approving behavior and teaches them to the client. In our mechanistic model, the treatment format is an expression of general conceptual principles that are applied in such a way that the client ultimately acquires a clear understanding of them. This is accomplished by having clients identify and describe clearly their patterns of coping and avoidance and the self-evaluative thoughts and feelings that accompany them. As a result of this process, clients may be expected to learn such generalizable statements as

1. "My personal approval depends a great deal on how I react to situations I have a tendency to fear."

2. "Realistically coping with situations I have had a tendency to avoid adds to my perception of myself as capable, strong, and brave."

3. "Avoiding difficult situations adds to my perception of myself as weak, inadequate, and spineless."

4. "Realistically and candidly determining what I can and should expect of myself in conflict situations is my responsibility."

5. "Responding to conflict situations in ways that I thoughtfully approve of is in my long-term best interests."

Other examples could be listed, but these will suffice for now. That clients learn these general principles is central to the treatment. It is the means by which clients can convert their therapy experiences into more abstract and generalizable principles. When these principles are clearly and properly understood, they can also be applied to new conflict situations. One of the primary roles of the therapist is to arrange events in therapy so that the client will actually experience the value of each principle being taught. This is the sense in which we consider the therapist to be an expert teacher. In other words, expert therapists should have such a clear understanding of the theoretical issues that they can plan for and make happen experiential learning moments for the client.

Therapeutic content. Even though the overall therapeutic process is shaped by the expert therapist, as we have already discussed, the content of every case is peculiar to that client. Admittedly, clients will eventually be asked to discuss their unique style of avoidance or the feelings they have about themselves because of their avoidance. Similarly, clients will ultimately be asked what they can do in conflict situations so they will be more approving of their own behavior. However, this is where the similarity ends. Theory does not provide answers to these questions; only the client can. This is where general therapeutic skills are important. Before clients can provide meaningful descriptions of their own behavior patterns, the therapist will usually have to help clarify, probe, observe, interpret, and provoke; and when this is done well, clients will describe themselves and their unique feelings and reaction patterns in considerable depth. Many insights occur along the way. Most important, clients actually (a) experience the depth of despair that is associated with their patterns of avoidance, and (b) feel renewed hope as they cope with difficulties that they usually avoid, first during the therapy hour, and later in their larger social environment. This is the point at which the renewed, vital sense of self is fashioned by clients and their particular concerns, not by the force of the verbally persuasive therapist.

Our clinical illustrations are saturated with examples of the therapist functioning as an expert teacher. These include (a) teaching clients the value of being able to describe their behavior and its underlying meaning accurately, (b) teaching clients that self-evaluative thoughts and feelings accompany their patterns of behavior, (c) teaching clients that avoidance is associated with self-disapproval, whereas coping tends to breed self-approval, and (d) teaching clients that personal approval and disapproval are more a function of coping and avoidance than of favorable or unfavorable outcomes, the ease or difficulty of the task, or almost any other set of external considerations.

Notice, however, that these principles are not taught didactically. The therapist does not explain them to the client or, for that matter, even suggest them. The client actually experiences them, and then the therapist intervenes so that these events are labeled accurately to facilitate understanding and long-term retention. The continuous interchange between the therapist as an expert teacher and facilitator of experiential learning becomes more frequent in the second half of the session.

Summary. In this section, we have suggested that the therapist is both an expert teacher and a facilitator of experiential learning. The therapist is a teacher because the therapy process is structured in such a way that clients are taught generalizable principles regarding the management of their psychic lives. What clients actually understand as these principles are taught is more experiential than cognitive, and what clients learn is more particular than general. The therapist's role as an expert teacher is most obvious when he or she applies general principles in the treatment sessions in such a way that clients both experience and understand the value of the principle being taught. The therapist's role as a facilitator of experiential learning is most obvious when the therapist helps clients understand the particular meaning of, and the consequences that attend, their particular style of coping and avoidance.

Client Content or Personality Style

We clearly emphasize personality style over client content. Even a casual reading of our earlier case illustration reveals the therapist's reluctance to attend to the literal meaning of the content used by the client to define her problems. Instead, the therapist postponed any significant interventions until some of her more enduring personality patterns started to appear. Eventually, these patterns were described and labeled and became the core considerations throughout the session. To illustrate the influence of this focus on the form and substance of this session, simply try to imagine what this session would have been like if the therapist had pursued the literal meaning of the content presented by the client with equivalent focus and intensity. Without getting into value-laden arguments about which is better, it is probably clear that the different emphases of these two approaches would yield quite different types of therapy hours. Because our emphasis consistently favors dealing with styles of coping and defense over the literal meaning of client content, we offer the following guidelines for your consideration.

1. Asking clients to identify clearly and describe accurately their styles of avoidance is an inherently difficult and anxiety-arousing task. The results of this process may have many beneficial results, but the threat that can accompany the level of insight and self-disclosure required to complete this task should never be underestimated by the therapist. The general quality and rapport of the therapeutic relationship is obviously important. Engaging in this process can also help create a therapeutic relationship that is high in candor, trust, and intimacy.

2. Paradoxically, we do not believe that therapist reassurance, encouragement, coaching, or sympathy is useful in helping clients through the difficult task of identifying their own patterns of avoidance. If clients resist or avoid this task, no matter what the reason, they should be allowed to do so—maybe even encouraged at times. Even the most subtle forms of therapeutic pressure should be scrupulously avoided by the therapist. Instead, the focus should be on having clients describe how they are going about avoiding the task while the avoidance is taking place. Implicitly, the therapeutic message is that avoidance is really OK, maybe even necessary so long as the client is willing to own up to it and understand it. Note that we did not suggest that clients be asked *why* they are avoiding, only *how* they are avoiding in the moment.

3. The therapist's own feelings about the necessity of this process are important considerations. Watching clients experience intense and negative self-evaluative thoughts and feelings can be very difficult. Many therapists instinctively want to rescue clients from intense suffering. In the model we have proposed, however, suffering is the raw material from which coping responses are experientially forged by the client and, because of this, we have every expectation that significant suffering precedes significant improvement. Our comfort with client suffering is seldom misperceived by clients, and we have come to believe that our comfort is a source of unspoken reassurance to

them at their periods of greatest vulnerability. We would add that therapist comfort in the face of client suffering needs to be an expression of conviction and confidence to help clients through difficult phases of therapy, not a role-playing technique.

In the clinical case illustration that we have been using, it is fairly clear that (a) the therapist was responsible for getting the client to eventually identify, describe, and label her enduring patterns of avoidance, (b) this process was both difficult and upsetting to the client, (c) the therapist was clearly task oriented, reasonably understanding, but seldom reassuring, (d) the absence of reassurance and encouragement by the therapist did not hinder client progress, and (e) the client's rapid improvement was a direct result of facing, experiencing, and then resolving her own feelings of personal disapproval.

Summary. Enduring patterns of client coping and defense are the staple ingredient in our treatment model. This approach requires a therapeutic relationship that is high in (a) task-centeredness; (b) trust, candor, and risk taking; and (c) therapist comfort in the face of client distress.

Individual Autonomy: High to Low

Generally speaking, client autonomy is fostered in most therapeutic relationships by minimizing the structure of the treatment approach, minimizing the demands on client behavior, and working in a treatment format that is either (a) client centered or (b) intentionally ambiguous. It is generally assumed that in either of these two conditions, the client is more likely to provide or make a major contribution to finding a personally relevant and psychologically meaningful direction for the therapy process. One of the frequently accepted indicators of clients' autonomy is their ability to be self-directing within the therapeutic relationship. We agree with this view.

The intervention strategies described in this book have high as well as explicit demand characteristics for client behavior. These are not the psychological conditions typically associated with high levels of client autonomy. Paradoxically, our ideal therapeutic relationship is one that is intended to foster and, certainly, require high levels of autonomy. Obviously, we have a bit of explaining to do. We will focus our discussion on the assumptions that are at the heart of this apparent contradiction.

Our conceptualization of the means by which client autonomy can be created, maintained, or both in a therapeutic relationship departs from the traditional views on this topic. A careful analysis of the assumptions of these traditional views reveals the basis for our disagreement with them. It also clarifies the origin of our own views. Essentially, therapeutic structure and high demand characteristics are usually assumed to be incompatible with the development of client autonomy. The logic of this assumption is simple and straightforward. It is believed that clients will be more self-directing in a less structured therapeutic environment simply because there are fewer external cues to respond to. This view is based on the assumption that systems of psychological treatment differ substantially with regard to levels of treatment structure. Many describe treatment approaches based on their inherent levels of structure and ambiguity. Treatment systems with high levels of structure typically refer to the behavioral and cognitive–behavioral approaches. Client-centered and analytical orientations are generally considered to be less structured and more ambiguous.

The assumption that treatment orientations differ substantially with regard to levels of treatment structure is flawed both semantically and conceptually. Structure literally refers to an "organized entity" or an "organization of interrelated events." The opposite of structure is not ambiguity; it is chaos and disorganization. It is a lack of conceptual orderliness and consensual meaning. In our view, theories of therapy do not simply vary on a continuum of structure–ambiguity; all approaches to psychological treatment are highly structured intellectual products. The intellectual structure inherent in these theories is always conveyed to clients, sometimes implicitly and inefficiently, other times explicitly and efficiently. Nevertheless, any approach to psychological treatment that warrants the title of "theory" (in the most casual meaning of the term) has rather clear expectations of how clients should behave during the therapy process if they are to improve. We suggest that systems of psychological treatment do not vary on levels of structure nearly as much as they do on the clarity and explicitness with which they make their expectations known.

For example, it is clear with even a modest understanding of classical psychoanalytic theory that client insight is a staple element in the cure, and that client introspection and self-exploration are essential ingredients in the process. The treatment process is also highly structured, so that clients are encouraged to respond to internal cues and stimuli as a means of enhancing insight, introspection, and self-exploration. During treatment sessions, the therapist maintains a neutral posture because neutrality is assumed to be the optimal condition for encouraging material to come bubbling up from the client's unconscious for review. Note that all of these conditions are structured for the client. Actually, this treatment orientation is highly structured, with the appropriate behavior of the client and therapist well defined. It is misleading and unfortunate that this treatment has mistakenly been referred to as "unstructured" and, by implication, a treatment with low demand characteristics for client behavior. Rather, its demand characteristics are high, as is its level of imposed structure.

The same analysis applies to client-centered approaches. Again, we find that theory sets the expectations for client and therapist behavior in a series of highly organized and interrelated psychological events. Therapists are expected to listen attentively, nod reassuringly, be responsive to client initiatives, and be open and candid with their enduring feelings about the client. Clients are expected to self-disclose, express feelings as they occur, and select the topics for discussion that are most important to them. This treatment, as are all others, is theory centered, not client centered; and because of this, it is a highly structured treatment system with unique demand characteristics for client behavior.

In essence, we are suggesting that any intellectually respectable system of psychological treatment cannot vary on a continuum of structure–ambiguity. Ambiguity, as we have stated, is not the opposite of structure. Besides, all treatment systems are highly structured patterns of thought and behavior, and vary mostly with regard to their completeness and the clarity with which they make their behavioral demands explicit. Ambiguity probably refers to treatment systems with vague rather than explicit demand characteristics and, gradually and unintentionally becomes a descriptor of the treatment itself.

These are consequential arguments. If they are accepted, they redefine the appropriate role of treatment structure and client demand characteristics in the development of client autonomy. Originally, client autonomy was assumed to be served best in a treatment format with minimal structure, minimal demand characteristics on client behavior, and high client-centeredness. We suggest that the development of client autonomy can best be served in a therapeutic relationship that is highly structured for the precise purpose of increasing client autonomy and that uses influential and explicit demand characteristics for client behavior designed specifically for that purpose. Client-centeredness is an irrelevant consideration and ambiguity is a major distraction. In this context, the therapeutic relationship we consider ideal rates extraordinarily high on client autonomy. The expectation of high levels of client autonomy is in evidence throughout the clinical illustrations that we have been using. Clients are continually asked to decide such important matters as (a) the accuracy of descriptive labels, (b) the amounts and levels of emotional intensity that they can tolerate during the session, (c) the types of behavior that they most disapprove of in themselves, (d) the ways they would need to change so that they could approve of themselves, (e) their willingness to move on to new tasks clearly defined as difficult, and, most important, (f) their acceptance of appropriate levels of personal responsibility for problem solving within the therapeutic framework provided.

Summary

We have challenged the traditional view, which suggests that client autonomy is enhanced in a therapeutic environment that is unstructured and has low demand characteristics for specific types of client behavior. Generally, it has been assumed that clients will be more autonomous and self-directing in this type of environment simply because there are fewer external cues to guide their behavior. This point of view seems seriously flawed for several reasons. First, all systems of psychotherapy are highly organized (highly structured) systems of thought, with clear expectations for both client and therapist behavior. Some of these expectations may be more vague than explicit, but that does not alter either their existence or influence. Second, because of this, we suggest that calling any system of psychological treatment unstructured with low demand characteristics for client behavior is inaccurate and misleading. And, third, we propose that client autonomy is enhanced most effectively by using a treatment format explicitly structured with obvious demand characteristics designed expressly for the purpose of increasing client autonomy.

Uniqueness of the Therapeutic Relationship

Seemingly, each of our bipolar dimensions for describing different types of therapeutic relationships is technically relevant, but collectively, they omit important considerations. Some of the most important events that take place within a therapeutic relationship occur only because of a special feeling of trust and confidence that exists between the client and therapist. This trust must be earned by both parties, and it is usually the result of intense levels of intimacy and conflict resolution. It is this feeling, which is so difficult to describe but which clearly exists, that allows clients to say out loud what they are terrified to even think, or for the therapist to push and have clients respond to what they have always avoided. Most remarkable, however, is for the client and therapist to laugh spontaneously when others would cry, and cry together when others could not understand why. This is a relationship quality that transcends our technical relationship dimensions and reflects the feelings and attitudes that bond a client and therapist together in trust as they walk together in the client's psychic mine field.

Orlinsky and Howard (1986) have suggested three principal components derived from an extensive analysis of research data that seem to be essential to the type of therapeutic bonding we are discussing. These three components are role investment, empathic resonance, and mutual affirmation. These principles are described below:

1. Role investment. There is an intense and affective investment of energy in relationship roles, evident in the patient's self-expressive emotional attachment to the therapist and in the therapist's active collaboration through whichever technique he or she feels most capable of and confident in using.

2. Empathic resonance. A second element associated with cohesiveness of the social bond in beneficial psychotherapy is the good personal contact and the solid grounding in one another that is made by the participants. This personal contact is characterized by mutual comfortableness and trust, a lack of defensiveness on both sides (seen in the patient's spontaneity and the therapist's genuineness), and also by a strong and sensitive rapport, a sense of being on the same wavelength, that arises through empathic resonance and reciprocal understanding.

3. Mutual affirmation. There is, finally, an expansive mutual goodwill mobilized between participants in beneficial psychotherapy, a strong sense of affirmation that is not merely acceptance, but acceptance and encouragement of independence, that can be challenging as well as supportive out of concern and respect for the other person's basic interests and autonomy.

It is only within a relationship framework such as the one just described that our specific relationship attributes can be properly understood. Confrontations that take place in this context may not feel very confrontational to the participants, and the exchange of emotionally charged feedback can occur graciously, appreciatively, and comfortably.

Paradoxically, it must be noted that the so-called high-risk behaviors that are so central to our treatment methods are both a cause and a consequence of the developing therapeutic relationship. Gradually, increasing levels of authenticity, congruence, and general risk taking in the relationship usually breed higher levels of interpersonal trust, and higher levels of trust gradually reduce the perceived risk of authenticity and congruence (Bednar, Melnick, & Kaul, 1974). In our view, a healthy therapeutic relationship is one in which moderate levels of risk taking gradually improve the therapeutic bonding, and the improved therapeutic bonding gradually decreases the perceived risk for even the highest levels of psychological risk taking. The therapeutic relationship, then, is both served and serviced by the ever-increasing levels of psychological risk taking that we consider essential to effective treatment.

Eventually, clients come to feel sufficiently safe in the therapeutic relationship to deliberately and, at times, even eagerly expose the patterns of thinking and behaving that are the source of their recurring psychological difficulties. This is precisely the context in which client learning becomes optimal. The therapeutic relationship allows clients to face themselves candidly, and in this process, the therapist teaches clients the value of self-approving behavior and its consequences at the precise moment it occurs. This is a therapeutic relationship that preserves the role of the therapist as an expert teacher, but what is taught is far more experiential than cognitive and tailored precisely to enhance the client's disposition to cope rather than avoid.

Marital and Family Therapy: Primary and Unique Considerations

What Is Marital and Family Therapy?

Marital and family therapies have unique features that warrant consideration before continuing with applications of our self–esteem model. However, the essential therapeutic strategy is still to replace avoidant behavior with coping responses in a way that vividly exposes clients to the affective experiences that accompany their coping and avoidance.

The marital and family therapies made their debut 30 or 40 years after the advent of individual psychotherapy. Practitioners began to recognize the growing need for a unique form of treatment for couples and families, and the practice of family therapy started to emerge as an entirely separate treatment modality.

At their very conception, the marital and family therapies were intended to be different from the accepted treatment approaches of the day. These changes would ultimately prove themselves to be as radical as they were important. The prevailing emphasis on intrapsychic conflict would be minimized and, in its place, a new conceptual star would appear: the power and influence of social systems and interpersonal relations. The conceptual seeds of these unique considerations were to be found in cybernetics, general systems theory, and social-learning paradigms. Although these models are widely accepted today, they were based on a common assumption that was quite different in its day, that is, the essence of maladaptive behavior patterns, the function that they serve, and the conditions under which they are most likely to appear or disappear can be observed best in a social context. This assumption marked the end of a preoccupation with intrapsychic conflicts and individual behavior and the beginning of a movement that would emphasize the influence of interpersonal relations and the social environment.

Doing family therapy requires the therapist to look at individuals in terms of their role, influence, and effects within the larger social system. This is not to say that marital therapy does not acknowledge the power of individual pathology, but that these disturbances are most important as they manifest themselves in family relations. With sufficient skill and experience, the marital–family therapist can access several unique and powerful sources of psychological learning that are simply not available in treatments designed exclusively for individuals. These include:

1. enabling meaningful dialogues directly among family members when conflict arises;

2. having family members participate in new roles with which they may be unfamiliar or resistant to try, such as providing and receiving healthy emotional support; and

3. identifying and clarifying various patterns of dysfunctional behavior in the relationship in which they occur at the time they occur.

Because of such considerations, the therapeutic environment of marital and family therapy is seldom as insulated from the frustrating realities of everyday life as is individual therapy. Clients have to interact with those with whom they share significant relationships and, more often than not, intense anger and frustration. This type of interaction leads to high levels of immediacy and intensity as clients discuss personal problems and conflicts with each other, often in front of other family members. When high levels of emotion are responded to with equally high levels of professional skill, it can result in insights and understanding that may not be obtainable in more neutral psychological environments.

Primary and Unique Sources of Learning

While the aforementioned features are not exclusive to marital and family therapy, the frequency with which they occur in these settings certainly exceeds those found in individual approaches. This frequency contributes to a prime therapeutic milieu through which the therapist can tap into four sources of psychological learning. They are

1. the family as a social microcosm,
2. the role and availability of interpersonal feedback,
3. the role and availability of consensual validation, and
4. the reciprocity of client roles,

We will discuss each of these primary and unique sources of learning. In our discussion, it is important to remember continually that the benefits to be gained from each source of learning are seldom the result of the behavior or dialogues that they create. Rather, each source of learning is a medium through which the underlying psychological attributes that mediate healthy behavior are shaped, strengthened, and refined. For example, the unique information that becomes available as a result of exchanging interpersonal feedback can be of unquestionable therapeutic value. However, developing the underlying psychological attributes that allow one to provide credible interpersonal feedback is infinitely more important. These attributes include personal risk, personal responsibility, and self-direction, all of which are direct correlates of self-esteem. Because there are such robust considerations influencing a broad spectrum of psychological functioning across a variety of settings, we also consider them to be the core mediating variables of healthy behavior generally.

Accordingly, the four primary and unique sources of psychological learning that will be discussed are not only valuable in helping couples or families to resolve their immediate presenting problems, they can also strengthen the underlying psychological processes and attributes required to maintain those gains. Because many of the concepts and propositions that we use to access and fully activate these underlying processes are drawn from small-group theory, we will frequently use the terms family, marital couple, and couples interchangeably inasmuch as they all deal with multiple clients in a small-group setting.

Social Microcosm

According to Goldenberg and Goldenberg (1985),

> A family is far more than a collection of individuals sharing a specific physical and psychological space. A family is a natural social system, with properties all its own, one that has evolved a set of rules, is replete with assigned and ascribed roles for its members, has an organized power structure, has developed intricate overt and covert forms of communication, and has elaborate ways of negotiating and problem solving that permit various tasks to be performed effectively. The relationship between members of this microculture is deep and multilayered, and is based largely on shared history, shared internalized perceptions and assumptions about the world, and a shared sense of purpose. Within such a system, individuals are tied to one another by powerful, durable, reciprocal emotional attachments and loyalties that may fluctuate in intensity over time but nevertheless persist over the lifetime of the family. (p. 3)

Several factors contribute to the potency of therapy when the family is viewed as a social microcosm. The most obvious is the opportunity that the therapist has to enter this preexisting complex system and view the family's maladaptive behavior patterns in vivo. For example, comments well received and understood by one family member may be a source of irritation and contention to another. Unavoidably, each client must learn to deal with all other family members under the watchful tutelage of the therapist. Given these circumstances, the pathology of the family, couple, or individual do not have to be described to be understood; one must only carefully observe the personal styles and coping patterns that recapitulate the social problems and processes that brought each client to therapy in the first place.

When couples and families are viewed as a miniature social system in which pervasive problems are reenacted, it provides unlimited opportunities for each client to participate actively in dysfunctional behavior, identify it, and then address it directly, as opposed to merely speculating on causes and effects based on self-reports of past events. An example may be useful in illustrating precisely how a social microcosm directs clinical observations and interventions. Keep in mind that the essence of the concept is that therapy within small groups is a stage on which family members portray their individual coping–avoidance styles with different people and situations. Also, because personal problems generally find direct expression in the marriage or family, these problems and the pathological processes that sustain them are available for direct observation. As a result, assessment and interventions tend to be based on experiences as they occur. This allows maladaptive behavior patterns to be clearly identified, described, and labeled. The result is a dramatic increase in the relevance and the immediacy and intensity of the therapeutic process.

In a social microcosm there are both personal and interpersonal influences that affect individuals and their behavior in the family. Although these two levels of influence are by far the most common, they are not necessarily the most important. Psychological functioning in a small group (family) is regularly influenced not only by individuals, but by the prevailing roles and norms of the larger social system. A small group is required for one to explore the reciprocal influences between themselves and the social system to which they belong. Other forms of psychological treatment are seldom presented with equivalent real life opportunities for individuals to learn how and why they respond to group pressures as they do. Probably, more important are the rare opportunities for clients to experience and explore how their individual behavior affects the functioning of a small group.

Assessments and interventions based on experiences as they occur tend to involve higher levels of psychological immediacy and intensity as well. They also tend to involve the simultaneous and correlated expression of thoughts, feelings, and behavior inasmuch as each of these variables is a natural antecedent or concomitant of behavior. In a small group setting, the opportunities for corrective emotional experiences, clear identification, description and labeling of inappropriate behavior, and immediate reinforcement of new coping patterns are substantially greater compared to other forms of treatment.

Figure 1 graphically illustrates the most essential therapeutic elements of the family when viewed as a social microcosm.

All of the previous considerations converge to define a final characteristic of the family as a social microcosm that is seldom recognized. More than any other treatment approach, a small group setting can naturally short–circuit some of the fundamental elements common to many forms of maladaptive and self–defeating behavior. If, as we have previously postulated, avoidance of feared situations is one of the fundamental dimensions common to disordered behavior, then circumstances that interfere with this avoidance can be of immense therapeutic assistance. Spouses and families can provide this type of unique assistance.

Many fears are involved in the disposition of clients to avoid further rejection, hurt feelings, and negative social experiences. We have earlier described this avoidant behavior in terms of approval-seeking and impression management, that is, presenting oneself to others in a way that is congruent with the expectations, values, and dominant interests of others. Because most people are aware of their impression management tendencies, they are also aware that much of the feedback they receive is in response to the facades they have presented. The effects of such feedback is, therefore, minimal inasmuch as the limitations on the credibility of the feedback are clearly understood by the impression manager.

The undesirable effects of impression management are not limited to invalidating the credibility of feedback. Another more basic self-defeating process is also involved. Also, the more one acts in ways governed by external influences, the less responsive and aware one becomes of one's own primary thoughts and feelings. These are hardly the conditions for fostering a clear sense of identity and the personal values required for meaningful self-direction. Both of these characteristics (identity and internal control) have long been associated with effective

Figure 1

The Family as a Social Microcosm

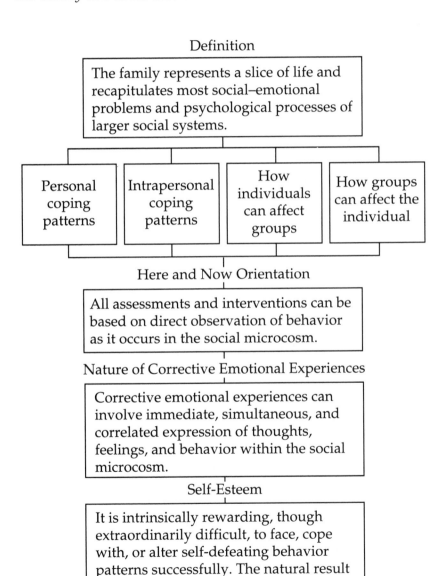

Definition

> The family represents a slice of life and recapitulates most social–emotional problems and psychological processes of larger social systems.

| Personal coping patterns | Intrapersonal coping patterns | How individuals can affect groups | How groups can affect the individual |

Here and Now Orientation

> All assessments and interventions can be based on direct observation of behavior as it occurs in the social microcosm.

Nature of Corrective Emotional Experiences

> Corrective emotional experiences can involve immediate, simultaneous, and correlated expression of thoughts, feelings, and behavior within the social microcosm.

Self-Esteem

> It is intrinsically rewarding, though extraordinarily difficult, to face, cope with, or alter self-defeating behavior patterns successfully. The natural result of facing problems successfully is increased self-esteem.

human functioning. In brief, impression management undermines the vitality of both personal and interpersonal learning.

In a marriage or family, both of these processes can be effectively short circuited. The reasons are simple. Impression management in one-on-one relationships is not particularly difficult. It only requires sustained practice and minimal levels of sensitivity to the wants and wishes of others. However, as the number of people in the social matrix increases, the complexity and feasibility of impression management declines. Family members learn quickly that comments meant to gain favor in the eyes of some family members may arouse the wrath of others. Impression management in a marriage or family becomes even less effective when a skilled therapist is introduced into the dysfunctional system.

Being in a social setting that denies the traditional benefits of effective impression management has two important effects. First, family members can be systematically denied the dubious benefits of external approval that they have learned to skillfully acquire in the past. This sets the stage for learning new methods of relating that are based on more authentic expressions of the self. These are much more favorable conditions for the development of trust, intimacy, candor, shared risk taking, and personal responsibility in interpersonal transactions. In many cases, the ability of a client to acknowledge a problem openly in front of other group members represents the highest level of psychological risk and responsibility that they have experienced in years. Although such an experience may be uncomfortable, it is generally recognized by all to require personal courage and represents a moderate level of adequacy that signifies the beginning attempts to cope with personal problems rather than to avoid them. Taking appropriate psychological risks and behaving in ways that reflect higher levels of personal responsibility are frequently followed by well-earned increases in self-esteem.

Additional therapeutic significance of the social microcosm can be summarized in terms of some very fundamental assumptions regarding the interference of pathological behavior and the development of healthier behavior. These assumptions are:

1. Internally controlled behavior is necessary for responsible risk taking.

2. Responsible risk taking is necessary to correct self-defeating behavior.

3. The sense of self-efficacy that accompanies correcting self-defeating behavior is intrinsically rewarding and enhances self-esteem.

4. A secure sense of self-esteem is the basis for internally directed behavior.

5. Responsible risk taking can be promoted even in the relative absence of internally directed behavior through the appropriate use of the therapeutic social microcosm.

The psychologically healthy individual is one who has a sufficient amount of self-esteem to support internally directed behavior. Such persons are aware of, but not entirely subject to, the demands, pressures, and constraints of their social milieu. As a result, such persons can take appropriate risks in social situations that provide them with continuous sources of learning about themselves and their social relationships. The willingness to engage in responsible risk-taking enables them to correct self-defeating behavior quickly, which in turn demonstrates self-efficacy and improves self-esteem. One of the goals of marital or family treatments is to replicate this process of personal growth, but within the confines of a therapeutic social microcosm with the assistance of a skilled therapist. This process is portrayed in Figure 2.

Interpersonal Feedback

Dyads and small groups provide two of the few places where multiple sources of feedback from different perspectives can be made available to individuals. More important, though seldom acknowledged, the small group is probably the only place where clients can come to increase their understanding of why it is so difficult to express openly their thoughts and feelings about the nature of the relationships they share with others. Interpersonal feedback is a complex process that occupies a central role in several major theoretical approaches to personality development, psychotherapy, and psychopathology.

Our discussion of interpersonal feedback must necessarily be limited in scope. We will address only those issues and processes most central to small-group theory and practice. These

Figure 2

Processes Mediating Personal Growth in Social Settings

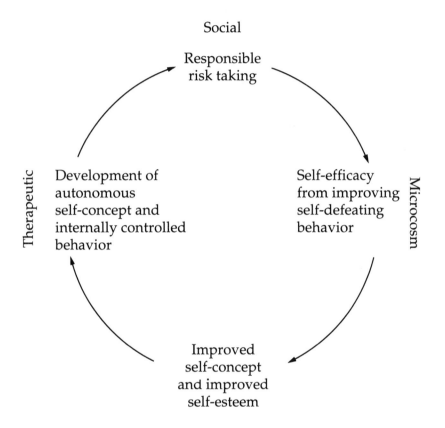

are (a) feedback as a source of information, and (b) feedback as a process mediated by more basic psychological attributes.

Feedback as a Source of Information

Interpersonal feedback is a communication process that emphasizes the description and evaluation of the behavior of one person by others. We have intentionally used the terms "description" and "evaluation" to separate the affective and cognitive components of the feedback processes. *Descriptive feedback* is a factual description of a person's behavior in any variety of situations. Its presumed benefits provide a mirror for persons to increase their understanding of how they are perceived by others. In many cases, clients are simply unaware of how they are perceived by others. Appropriate assertiveness may be viewed as aggressiveness and hostility. Intended friendliness may often be seen as seductive behavior. Quiet solitude may be seen as arrogance. For obvious reasons, factual descriptions of behavior and how they are labeled by others can be an important source of psychological learning for those clients whose self-descriptions do not correspond closely to that of their peers.

Evaluative feedback goes beyond description and labeling. It includes preferences, value judgments, and tends to explain and clarify emotional reactions between people. Evaluative feedback often takes the form of self-disclosure by the speaker, but the thrust of the message is basically that the speaker is attracted to, angry at, or avoidant of the target person. It is feedback that is not affectively neutral. In fact, the contrary is true. Interpersonal feedback that is affectively loaded initially tends to elicit affectively loaded responses. This makes the exchange of evaluative feedback an extraordinarily potent psychological experience that has been shown to be as harmful in some cases as it is helpful in others. It is a form of psychological intervention that should be used cautiously by inexperienced therapists, particularly in a small-group setting.

Given that interpersonal feedback is basically an exchange of cognitive and affective information among people, it is important to have an elementary understanding of the communication processes that influence the potency, receptivity, and effects of feedback exchanges. Table 1 summarizes some of the variables that influence the quality of interpersonal feedback as well as their presumed effects.

Contained in Figure 3 is a series of descriptive dimensions along which the delivery of interpersonal feedback can vary.

On each of these dimensions, we have indicated the qualities most likely to enhance the quality of feedback as a source of psychological learning in a small-group setting. The meaning of most of these dimensions is relatively clear, and we will elaborate on them only briefly, mostly by example.

Directness. A *direct communication* is one that is clear and to the point, and requires minimal interpretation to be understood

Table 1

Dimensions Along Which Interpersonal Feedback Can Vary

Dimension	Least Potent	Most Potent
Directness	Unclear	Clear
	Indirect	Direct
Content	Informational	Interpersonal
Immediacy	Past, future, out-of-group events	Here-and-now
Person Focus	Feedback without self-disclosure	Self-disclosure accompanies feedback

accurately. An example of a clear and direct communication in response to a request for feedback from a spouse or family member would be: "I do not like your boasting about your achievements all the time. I wish you would stop. I usually tune you out as soon as you start boasting." An example of an indirect communication in the same situation would be: "I guess you have your quirks just like everybody. We all have our problems." The levels of specificity and directness are major ingredients affecting the clarity of these two messages.

Immediacy. *Immediacy* refers to the degree to which the feedback is about events that are currently taking place. For example, the statement: "I am getting a headache from your smoking, would you please go outside to finish," is different from "I frequently get headaches when people smoke around me." The former statement involves both the people and the events relevant to the social situation and, therefore, has greater impact. It is generally recognized that the psychological risk involved in the delivery of feedback increases as the feedback focuses on events as they occur.

Content. The content focus of feedback can vary from the most socially appropriate statements such as, "I like your new dress," to highly personal exchanges that clarify the meaning and nature of the relationships between the discussants: "I have found myself feeling very attracted to you and would like to spend more time together with you. How do you feel about me?" Feedback typically becomes a more potent source of interpersonal learning as it focuses on the significance and quality of the relationships between the discussants. Although topical conversations may be the bread and butter of daily social intercourse, they are far less relevant as aids to personal growth. Once again, we will call the reader's attention to the fact that the communication processes that are most conducive to interpersonal learning also involve higher levels of psychological risk taking.

Self-disclosure. Feedback that contains elements of self-disclosure can enhance the quality of the message. Examples would be, "I am sexually turned on by you and it frightens me," or "I trust you enough to make myself vulnerable to you." When feedback messages contain self-disclosures of this type, the receptivity to the message may be increased because of the shared risk taking implicit in the message. Openness demonstrated by one party may more easily be reciprocated by another. However, it should also be evident that premature self-disclosure can have a negative effect because of the personal nature of such messages. As is the case with all psychological risk taking, self-disclosure can reap significant benefits, but it contains significant inherent risks as well.

One additional point needs to be clarified. It is important to perceive interpersonal feedback as a continuous process rather than as a singular event. The communication theorists posit that we cannot not communicate. A similar proposition can be made about the therapeutic environment. Communication takes place constantly among members of a family. It is only a matter of the degree to which these interpersonal messages are integrated into the treatment process or viewed as distracting elements that interfere with other theoretical considerations deemed to be more important.

Psychological Benefits of Feedback

So far, we have emphasized the traditional role of feedback in problem solving: the exchange of psychologically relevant information. It would be misleading to conclude, however, that the exchange of information is the only, or the most important, therapeutic function served by feedback. The actual process of exchanging feedback is mediated by other more basic psychological attributes, many of which are central elements in a broad range of effective human behavior. In many cases, the use of interpersonal feedback is merely the means of gaining access to these other, more basic psychological attributes for the purpose of exercising, developing, refining, and shaping these psychological mediators of improved human functioning.

We can best illustrate our point with an example. One of the most common and puzzling experiences occurs regularly the first time family group members attempt to discuss how they really see each other. This generally occurs early in the therapy process and the request for feedback tends to be simple and straight forward. Usually, such a request can be taken at face value; someone is curious about the type of impression they make. Seldom is the request made in such a way that would suggest the need for carefully reasoned and documented character analysis or sweeping value judgments regarding the worth of the individual. It tends to be simply a request for information about perceptions: the type of information that people privately gossip about all the time.

Nevertheless, such a request usually generates an inordinate level of anxiety, avoidance, and a misunderstanding of the literal meaning of the request. Seldom do clients show a willingness to share their thoughts and perceptions of others, although such impressions are clearly present. Put simply, adults tend to be very apprehensive about the prospects of telling others how they really see them, particularly in the face of conflict. Certainly, the avoidance is far out of proportion to any real risks associated with the task. Furthermore, this phenomenon tends to occur regardless of the client population (professors of psychology, clergymen, outpatient clientele, or students) or treatment orientation of the therapist. One way of trying to understand why this phenomenon occurs so consistently is by looking at the psychological properties involved in the ability to give personal, relevant, and effective feedback to another person.

We submit that personal risk, responsibility, and the ability to be internally directed are among the primary psychological attributes required in the delivery of interpersonal feedback. This process is important for two primary reasons. First, many of the fictitious and exaggerated fears assumed to be associated with the delivery of feedback can be reality tested. Some of these fears include:

1. Giving negative feedback may prove to be hurtful to the person requesting the feedback.

2. If the feedback is hurtful (no matter how valid), the hurt will be the responsibility of the messenger, not of the message.

3. Expressions of intimacy, caring, or affection leave the speaker open for rejection or misunderstanding after they have clearly declared their feelings.

4. Others may retaliate if critical feedback is given, or others may judge the type of person one is because of the nature of the feedback that the person provides.

5. The process of delivering interpersonal feedback is also a process of self-declaration in that one's thoughts, feelings, and values become known (at least in a limited way), which then provides a basis for interpersonal acceptance or rejection by others.

Such reality testing can involve new learning of the most profound type. Old beliefs may be discarded because new social experiences and exaggerated social fears can acquire a more realistic perspective. Second and most important, the actual process of delivering interpersonal feedback can produce a unique psychological experience of self-efficacy that allows one to experience one's own adequacy as evidenced by one's ability to confront a difficult situation authentically (absence of impression management) and find that both internal and external approval are more dependent on authenticity than impression management. The relationships among these variables are summarized in Figure 3.

Consensual Validation

Consensual validation reflects shared social perceptions. Coming from multiple sources that are at least in partial agreement, it

Figure 3

Interpersonal Feedback

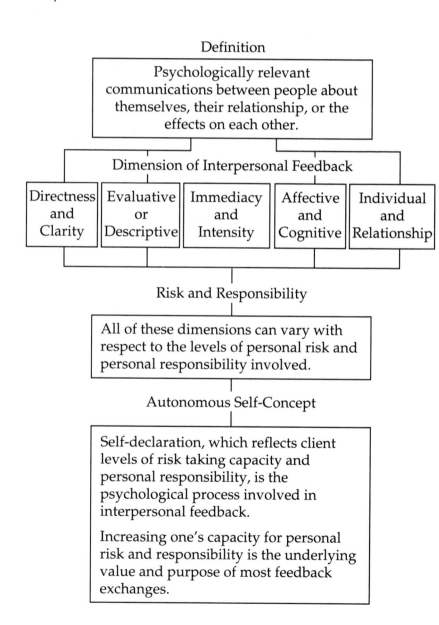

Definition

Psychologically relevant
communications between people about
themselves, their relationship, or the
effects on each other.

Dimension of Interpersonal Feedback

| Directness and Clarity | Evaluative or Descriptive | Immediacy and Intensity | Affective and Cognitive | Individual and Relationship |

Risk and Responsibility

All of these dimensions can vary with
respect to the levels of personal risk and
personal responsibility involved.

Autonomous Self-Concept

Self-declaration, which reflects client
levels of risk taking capacity and
personal responsibility, is the
psychological process involved in
interpersonal feedback.

Increasing one's capacity for personal
risk and responsibility is the underlying
value and purpose of most feedback
exchanges.

has the ability to confirm or disconfirm self-perceptions and interpersonal perceptions. Dissonance-inducing feedback from one person is much easier to disregard. One can merely attribute the unfavorable feedback to some "quirk" or "personality conflict." However, with consensually validated feedback from multiple sources, the individual is confronted with the undeniable fact that numerous people are affected by their behavior in the same way. Dismissing interpersonal feedback of this caliber requires a person to rise to extraordinary defensive heights or start processing the discrepant information in a healthier fashion. Obviously, skilled judgment is involved in the use of consensually validated feedback inasmuch as it would appear to be as potentially harmful if used inappropriately as it could be helpful when orchestrated appropriately.

That feedback from multiple sources is consensual does not necessarily imply that the feedback is therefore valid. Although this may seem somewhat surprising, it should be made clear that a number of group processes can contaminate the accuracy of consensually validated feedback. Examples of these unhealthy processes could include (a) scapegoating, (b) thoughtless conformity to, or rebellion from, authority figures, (c) methods of administering punishment to group deviants or noncompliant individuals, and (d) expressions of personal pathology by family members. Clearly then, caution must be exercised in the use of consensually validated feedback within therapy inasmuch as the content of that feedback cannot automatically be assumed to be valid. However, all of these patterns that may surface in the process of formulating and delivering such feedback are important sources of learning. In fact, such processes as scapegoating, rebellion, and compliance can be examined only in a family or small group where these processes are allowed to occur.

The utility and potency of consensual validation is affected by several factors. The most important is the level of trust and cohesion in the family. The more cohesive a family, for example, the more likely members will be to take each other seriously and exchange feedback freely, openly, and honestly. These conditions are precisely the ones that guarantee that the feedback will not be contaminated by other less healthy group processes.

As a matter of fact, one of the primary criteria for judging the accuracy and authenticity of consensually validated feedback is the degree to which it arises freely, spontaneously, and independently from multiple sources. The optimal conditions for the delivery of consensually validated feedback is a cohesive feeling among family members that are viewed as credible sources of information.

If one accepts the premise that internally directed behavior, responsible risk taking, and personal responsibilities are all major elements in healthy psychic functioning, it is easy to understand the value of consensual validation as a curative process. Consensual validation creates a variety of situations in which couples, families, or members of other groups are either (a) forced to consider information discrepant from their self-perceptions, (b) compelled to use defensive maneuvers as a means of evading the feedback, (c) allowed to experience public confirmation of self-concepts and interpersonal perceptions, and (d) stand independently, but nondefensively in rejecting the views of others. By using the family setting as a vehicle to stimulate the risk taking, responsibility, and independence involved in a healthy process of consensual validation, a family therapist has at his disposal a powerful treatment strategy for interrupting self-defeating behavior patterns and stimulating a healthier pattern of coping that is usually related to the development of a healthier social system.

Reciprocity of Helping Relations

One of the most unique opportunities for social learning in marital or family therapy is the degree to which family members are encouraged to function in the role of both receivers of help (dependence) and givers of help (independence). The issue of psychological independence and dependence are well recognized in the literature as one of those developmental processes that cuts across the life span and generally requires continuous personal balancing and adjustment.

In dyads and families, individuals can be continually confronted with the psychological task of learning how to ask for what they want and need from others; and conversely, learning how to set limits on relationships that seem to demand more than can be given freely. These issues come into clear focus as family members are encouraged to participate in helping other members of the family. Examples of helping relationships can range from one family member agreeing to weather a crisis with another who is suicidal to the less dramatic, but no less important, sharing of "tough" feedback in supportive ways. In such cases, family members must learn appropriate methods of helping and being helped by each other. This reciprocative interaction provides the opportunity to then experience a sense of appreciation for and from others.

This type of social learning can be effective only as family members overcome their resistance to poignant and, therefore, threatening social involvement. This resistance can be as varied as the family members themselves. It includes feeling inadequate to help others when many others find it difficult to help themselves. Additionally, when family members overvalue the role of the therapist (and undervalue their own), they may feel presumptuous in offering suggestions not previously considered. On the opposite end of the spectrum, seeking help from others is avoided for fear that such requests may be rejected or ignored. Some may feel that to disclose personal concerns would burden their associates and contribute to stress or tension within the family.

The greatest therapeutic benefit is derived through the process of working out these issues of dependence and independence, establishing appropriate interpersonal boundaries that can accommodate both receiving and providing help, and establishing relationships that are consistent with the wants and wishes of the participants.

Theoretical Linkage

Because the principles of the avoidance–coping model must now be applied to a more complete and complex social environment, some modifications in our procedures are necessary. Sequentially, the most important steps in this therapeutic process remain unchanged. They include

1. carefully managed exposure to increased risk taking and coping responses, which

2. facilitates immediate feelings of self-efficacy as a result of eliminating self-defeating behavior, which

3. gradually but consistently contributes to improved self-esteem, which

4. contributes to a more autonomous and durable sense of self, which

5. increases one's capacity for appropriate risk taking and coping responses.

This cycle can easily become self-perpetuating as each new phase of the cycle digs deeper and uncovers more critical concerns to be addressed in therapy. Each of the primary and unique sources of learning can be made into a highly individualized catalyst to activate and maintain this therapeutic process. Clinically speaking, each of these unique sources provides the means by which clients are carefully exposed to increasing levels of personal risk and responsibility in areas of individual concern. Diagnostically, each source can alert couples or families to the dynamics of the social microcosm they have created, the roles they play in it, and the patterns of coping and avoidance that are reinforced by it. Each of these activities is in the service of the same overarching objective—boot-strapping more adaptive behavior and the more favorable self-evaluations that accompany them in the moment-by-moment transactions of therapy. We will discuss and illustrate these diagnostic and therapeutic activities more fully.

Clinical Illustration: Couples and Families as Social Microcosms

In individual psychotherapy, clients are expected to talk about pressing personal issues. This usually takes place in a consulting room far removed from the people and problems of concern to them. Clients do talk about what they fear, hope for, want, and feel, but they talk only to the therapist. The medium is essentially verbal, and the mode is mostly cognitive, although this is clearly not always the case. It is a highly specialized form of psychological recall, emotional massage, introspection, analysis, and in some cases, behavioral preparation and rehearsal.

However, the marital or family therapy consulting room is not nearly as havened because client dialogues are seldom as private. Here, conflicted parties come together to talk directly with each other about the difficulties that they share. Like individual therapy, the medium is mostly verbal, but the mode is far more experiential because divergent thoughts, feelings, and behavior collide as clients demonstrate what "ails them" right in the consulting room. It is a living demonstration of dysfunctional behavior and personal strengths that words alone seldom capture with such vivid clarity.

There are important differences between talking about doing something and actually doing it. One of the more important differences is the level and intensity of the personal risk involved. Generally speaking, "doing" is riskier than "talking" about doing. In a social microcosm, doing is far more common than merely talking. By viewing the marriage or family as a social microcosm in which enduring personality patterns play themselves out, the most essential ingredients for the therapeutic mill (styles of coping, avoidance and self-evaluative feelings) become apparent at varying levels of personal risk. Such a variety of events is seldom available to a therapist in a more neutral psychological environment. Two points are particularly noteworthy:

1. The level of personal risk required to engage one's own spouse or family with revealing candor is conspicuously higher than merely talking with one's therapist.

2. Not only are varying levels of personal risk and responsibility more apparent and accessible in a social microcosm, there is also a more complete spectrum of psychic functioning to observe.

We all understand that behavior is regularly and concomitantly influenced by intrapsychic, interpersonal, and systemic considerations. Yet, we seldom see clients in a setting that allows us to evaluate the importance of these different influences more vividly than in an ongoing social system. In brief, a social microcosm provides the optimal conditions necessary for the full utilization of the therapeutic principles contained in our orientating theory. Opportunities for managed risk taking are abundant; topics for discussion are naturally relevant; and a complete spectrum of social, intrapsychic, and interpersonal influences is obvious. Because of this psychologically fertile context, interpersonal feedback, consensual validation, and reciprocal role functions regularly display the styles of coping and avoidance that are at the heart of client difficulties.

The following clinical situations demonstrate the phenomenon of clients replicating their dysfunctional behavior in the social microcosm of therapy. A brief background will be given after which the role of interpersonal feedback, consensual validation, and reciprocal role functions will be highlighted.

There you go getting relevant again! To say that this was an unusual case would be an understatement. It was the most demanding marital case I had seen in 25 years of practice. Both Sheila and Ron were extremely intelligent, emotionally alive, and financially successful. In many important regards, they were both rather healthy people, particularly Sheila. It is doubtful that she would have ever had occasion to see a therapist had she not been married to Ron, although she would have thoroughly enjoyed individual therapy if she had. She was that open and comfortable with herself.

However, living with Ron had its problems. For the most part, he was industrious, affectionate, responsible, and appropriate. Few of their friends would have ever guessed that he was capable of inflicting verbal or physical abuse on Sheila, but he was. The first time it happened two decades earlier, she immediately left him and took the children with her. Ron utterly panicked. He was sorry, repentant, apologetic, humble, frightened, and willing to do anything to make amends to the woman he reported loving deeply and completely. For an entire month, he lived alone and for the entire month, he prayed continuously that he would not lose his family. He did not. Sheila went back, but only because she eventually started believing this was just an isolated event—a freak incident that would not happen again.

But it did happen again, four years later. True, four years was a long time between episodes, but it had happened again, and then again, and then again. Each time the same pattern repeated itself. An unexpected explosion, then deeply felt tears and re-morse from Ron until Sheila returned. Another period of time would pass and then there would be another explosion. Grad-ually, Sheila became afraid of Ron. Her anger at herself for not leaving was becoming more obvious as she started showing symptoms of depression. For her, it was like riding a train with a perfect knowledge that the tracks were defective and that a crash was inevitable before the end of the trip. She hated it.

For Ron, it was a continuous effort to be on his best behavior, particularly when things got tense. He knew that Sheila was close to leaving him if things did not improve quickly. Yet, in spite of his best efforts, he always failed at stopping his explo-sive impulses. His fear of losing his family was well founded and growing.

Diagnostically, he was what Millon (1969) has described as an *active ambivalent* personality. This type of person has not yet resolved the tension between their needs for affection and af-filiation and their deeply ingrained fear and distrust of those who could provide it. It is not uncommon for these people to vacillate between desperately seeking the approval of others like dependent personalities and fleeing from it once it is ob-tained to the interpersonal detachment and angry self-center-edness that can be so characteristic of the narcissistic, passive-aggressive, and paranoid type disorders.

I first saw them after Ron's most recent abusive episode. Sheila had reached the point at which she was simply unwilling to accept any more abuse, yet she did not want to end a 20-year marriage that had a lot of redeeming qualities and tender memories. They are now in their 38th session and deeply in-volved in facing their core conflicts. In the preceding sessions, Sheila has gradually come to see that she had a style of subtly avoiding conflict with Ron because she saw him as more fragile and less capable than she. Her perceptions were essentially ac-curate. Her protectiveness was part of her way of trying to be a caring and supportive wife.

Ron recognized but was far from resolving the painful reality of his dependency needs, the depth and intensity of which felt humiliating to him. He seemed to understand that his periods of verbal and physical outbursts were usually preceded by intense, and usually unrecognized, feelings of inadequacy, hurt, and rejection. He was gradually coming to the realization that his abusive tendencies were intimately linked to his need to not be as vulnerable as he sometimes felt. This dysfunctional pattern became a central issue as Ron engaged in it during therapy.

When they entered the consulting room, it was obvious that Sheila had something on her mind. She was usually transparent when she was distressed. It was equally obvious that Ron was not going to ask what was bothering her. The therapist waited for several minutes while the two evasively used small talk to fill the time. When it was clear that neither was prepared to introduce the dreaded topic, the therapist asked each to explain what was being avoided. Sheila indicated that she was afraid because she knew that, if she spoke honestly, it would hurt Ron's feelings and that could make things worse. Ron was afraid that Sheila was waiting to give him bad news.

Therapist:	Ron, your wife has something important to talk with you about, but is withdrawing from you because she is afraid you can't handle it without getting ugly. This seems to be happening quite often. Do you want to know more about why she is so afraid of you?
Ron:	(looks over at Sheila) I really would like to know what it is I do that bothers you so much. Will you tell me?
Sheila:	I'm not sure that's a good idea. We started talking openly in our last session, but an hour after we left you clammed up and haven't been the same since. You slept on the sofa three nights and I still have no idea what's bothering you. I'm afraid of what will happen if you don't like what I say. Besides, I'm not sure it's worth the trouble it creates to try and talk to you, and then pay for it all week.
Ron:	Keep it to yourself then!
Therapist:	Are you acting angry now because you feel hurt again?
Ron:	(Long pause, then quietly says) Probably.
Therapist:	You are being evasive. Is that what you mean to do?

Ron: (Very angry) No, but I get tired of being accused of causing all the trouble all the time. It would be nice for her to accept some blame once in a while.

Therapist: If you were to be honest with your deepest feelings right now, what would you be saying instead of sounding so angry?

Ron: (Very long pause) I don't know!

Therapist: Apparently, something has been bothering you since our last session and you have been avoiding it ever since. You seem to be acting now the same way Sheila described your behavior all week. We can talk about it if you want to, but it looks like it may be a tough session. I'm not going to encourage Sheila to talk to you openly about this until you're willing to be equally open with your feelings with her. If today isn't the time to do that, we can do it another time.

Commentary. At this point, there is no need for further description by either Ron or Sheila regarding Ron's use of anger as a way to avoid his feelings of dependency, vulnerability, and emotional inadequacy. He has "done it" in front of his wife and the therapist. The social microcosm in which Ron and Sheila live and suffer is being replicated and, therefore, immediately available for therapeutic intervention. With the use of interpersonal feedback, the avoidant behavior is then made explicit and now becomes the topic of discussion.

Clinical Illustration: Interpersonal Feedback

In our view, the exchange of interpersonal feedback involves varying degrees and mixtures of psychological risk (unknown consequences), personal responsibility (owning up), and the ability to be internally directed (maintain views independent of environmental support or rejection). Each of these ingredients is a major underlying element of coping responses. Although the content contained in feedback is always important, it is seldom as important as cultivating the underlying attributes involved in its delivery. Feedback can regularly be used to therapeutically develop, shape, and strengthen the underlying mediators of effective human functioning. Returning to our case with Ron and Sheila, the following dialogue illustrates how feedback was used to activate the basic curative processes from our orientating theory. Please notice the degree to which the content contained in the feedback is of vital importance to the relationship, but still secondary to the favorable self and other evaluations that were generated by them while actually coping with this most difficult dilemma.

(There is a long pause. Ron looks up with tears in his eyes and starts talking. He reports in emotional detail how much he loves his wife and how afraid he is that he has lost her. He realizes he has made huge mistakes in the past and is sorry for them.)

Therapist: It sounds like you want to be more open with your feelings.

Ron: (More authentic demeanor) Yes. At least I want to try.

Therapist: You realize that this could be a difficult session, that Sheila is probably going to say things that will be difficult to listen to. This is when you seem most likely to get angry and abusive. Are you ready to take the risk involved in talking about this?

Ron: (He looks at Sheila, pauses to collect his thoughts, then speaks.) Would you tell me why it's so hard to talk with me?

Sheila spent the next 30 minutes telling Ron that she is about ready to give up on their marriage. She indicated that she has lost respect for him, that she no longer trusts him, that she looks forward to being away, and that she is seeing a lawyer and considering a divorce. Through the entire 30 minutes Sheila's voice was shaking from nervousness, and her eyes were moist. Her style of delivery was sincere, not hostile, and her attitude was frank, not protective. The feedback was harsh and poignant, probably because it was also truthful and sincere. It was one of the few times that Sheila had been so completely honest and nonprotective about her real views and feelings.

While Sheila was talking, Ron listened carefully, sometimes because the therapist insisted that he do so. When Sheila finished, the therapist asked Ron to summarize the most important things that he had heard. He was remarkably accurate in his summary. His devastation was far more obvious than any anger he felt. The therapist asked him whether he was aware of how he felt and whether he could describe his thoughts and feelings without retaliating or denying what he was experiencing. Essentially, he reported remorse for what he had done in the past and understood why she felt as she did. Then he cried. Sheila was touched by the sincerity and depth of his feelings.

Therapist:	You have both been very honest with each other, and it's obvious how bad you both feel because of it. Has this session been good for you and you need more just like it, or is this something that should have been avoided?
Sheila:	It was good for me. I finally said what I have needed to say for a long time. And it gives me hope when we talk like this without it turning ugly. I like Ron when he shows his tenderness. I feel very forgiving right now. I just don't believe this will last.
Therapist:	In other words, there is something about this conversation that feels good to you in spite of its intensity and the fact that nothing has been resolved?
Sheila:	That's right. I feel like we have talked, and that doesn't happen very much in our lives.
Therapist:	(To Ron) Sheila says she liked this session. You listened to some pretty hard things today. How do you feel about Sheila for being so honest with you?
Ron:	I can't help admiring her honesty. I can't do what she just did. I just don't have what it takes to do that, but I wish I did.
Therapist:	Tell me, how do you feel right now and how do you feel about yourself for listening so carefully to what Sheila had to say, before reacting?

Ron: I feel scared for our marriage. I feel sick inside.

Therapist: And how do you feel about yourself for listening, feeling, and being truthful instead of exploding?

Ron: I just don't know why it's so hard sometimes. But I know in my heart if I were like this more often we wouldn't even be in this office right now.

Therapist: So what is it you are feeling about yourself right now?

Ron: I don't know exactly what I'm feeling, part of it is regret for what I have done, but part of me feels hopeful. It's hard to explain. I feel good. I'm relaxed. I'm comfortable with myself. I don't think I could even act abusive when I feel like this.

Therapist: It's probably called self-approval—something you may not have felt very often. What do you suppose you did that you approve of so much?

Ron: I listened. I talked about my feelings. I was more honest with myself and Sheila. I acted more like the person I want to be. (Long pause) But the only time I seem able to do that is when I am here!

Therapist: So you feel your own approval for the way you have handled this difficult hour?

Ron: Yes, a lot more than I usually do.

Finding the positive through sincerity. The therapist continued to process the self-evaluative thoughts and feelings that Sheila and Ron had as a result of their behavior during this session. Essentially, both reported far more approval for themselves and each other than disapproval. They were asked specifically which things they did that seemed to be the most important in earning their own approval. As usual, the therapist focused far more on what was required for self-approval than for the spouse's approval, and as usual, there was a conspicuously high level of agreement on what earned self-approval and what earned spouse approval. It appears that when persons express themselves with sincerity, congruence, modesty, and integrity, the benefits to the relationships are not only obvious, but their influence usually overpowers the negative feelings and differences that typically divide couples and families.

Therapist: We have been together for about an hour. During this time you have shared a lot of thoughts and feelings. Most of the discussion has been painful and upsetting. We have identified many problems, but resolved none. Yet, you both seem more comfortable with yourselves and each other now than when the session started. How do you suppose that happened?

Ron: I feel drained. Why don't you just tell us instead of making us figure out what you probably already know?

Therapist: That would be easier wouldn't it. Sheila, what do you think?

Sheila: I don't know what it is. I know I do feel a lot better about myself and toward Ron. Maybe it's because I don't feel so hopeless.

Therapist: That's interesting. Thirty minutes ago you seemed to feel utterly hopeless. Nothing has really changed since then—no problems have been resolved. What do you suppose has happened in this room that would have lifted your hopes? What changed inside of you and what changed it?

Ron: I think the way we have treated each other has made the difference. I think I just acted better and Sheila appreciates it.

Therapist: Is that what made the difference for you Sheila?

Sheila: I don't think so. It's a lot more than that. Ron can act reasonable when he is really angry. He does it all the time. I think I trust him more right now because what he is saying seems to be coming from his heart. I think it's his attitude and feelings that are making the difference to me.

Therapist: Are you saying that you trust him when he is like this?

Sheila: I don't know if it's that I trust him or that I'm just not afraid of him.

Therapist: What ever it is seems to make a big difference doesn't it?

Sheila: It really does. I can't help wondering what our marriage would be like if we could be like this more often.

Therapist: One thing seems fairly clear, the way you handled today's session seems important to your happiness and the survival of your marriage. Somehow you have created a little good will in your relationship today. You need to think about how you two did that while talking about the very issues that usually divide you and lead to the problems that got your marriage in trouble in the first place.

Commentary. The levels of personal risk, responsibility, and self-direction in this session were fairly high and entirely appropriate. So were the feelings of self- and other approval that were generated by them. Sheila approved of herself for finally leveling with Ron about her deepest feelings of despair about their deteriorating relationship. It was a hard thing for her to do, but also one that she believed she should have done much earlier. In the process of making herself known, she again demonstrated the very qualities of strength and character that Ron had always admired in her.

Ron's escape routes from his tender feelings were largely blocked by the therapist. Additionally, he was asked regularly to speak openly and honestly about his thoughts and feelings. Fortunately, he was able to do so. In these, more mature, coping responses, he not only found greater favor in his own eyes, but in Sheila's eyes as well. It is important to notice that this hope-instilling process was largely mediated by the psychological ingredients involved in this exchange, not its content. In fact, the literal content that was discussed contributed little by way of solutions, hope, or mutual understanding. So why did this couple come to feel hopeful when the nature and seriousness of their dilemma appeared to be even more hopeless as a result of their discussion? Our theoretical answer is remarkably simple. The psychological attributes inherent in this discussion (coping rather than avoidance) were more powerful and influential than the hopelessness of the content that they were discussing. Words and content were simply less important than the more fundamental psychological processes that give rise to them.

Clinical Illustration: Consensual Validation

As mentioned earlier, consensual validation creates a variety of interpersonal situations in which couples or families are

1. forced to consider information discrepant from their self-perceptions,

2. compelled to rise to new defensive heights in the presence of other family members and the therapist as a means of evading the feedback,

3. allowed and encouraged to experience public confirmation of self-concepts and interpersonal perceptions, and

4. stand independently, but nondefensively in rejecting the views of others.

By using family members or spouses in a healthy process of consensual validation, therapists have at their disposal a powerful treatment strategy for interrupting self-defeating behavior patterns and stimulating a healthier pattern of coping that is usually related to the development of a healthier social system as illustrated by the following example.

The death of a suicidal wish. Denise had a long history of depression, but it had never led to an actual suicide attempt until three years earlier. One afternoon, she was found unconscious as a result of a drug overdose. It was difficult to tell exactly how many pills she had taken, but her vital signs did not suggest that she was close to death. Since then, her bouts with depression have continued, but she has never been rehospitalized because of it; neither has she reported the kinds of suicidal thoughts that require professional attention. For the most part, the family took these difficulties in stride and tried to be supportive and understanding.

Recently, however, it seemed to Jeff, her husband, that Denise's depressions were starting to occur more frequently. Although he had not said so publicly, he wondered whether his wife's new cycle of depression were related to the children getting older. They were now more independent of her and less responsive to her depressive moods. After one particularly difficult period, Jeff decided to consult a therapist. After expressing his concern about his wife and what he perceived to be the growing tensions between her and the children, the therapist asked him to bring in the entire family to talk it over. That started a series of meetings in which the family attempted to discuss the relationships that they shared, the dynamics of family life together, and Denise's depression and previous suicide attempt. As one might expect, many hidden thoughts and feelings quickly started bubbling to the surface with only the slightest encouragement. It all started slowly, but as the family gained more experience in talking openly about topics that they usually avoided, a strange thing started to happen. People came to understand that they all seemed to share a common, but largely unspoken, resentment of Denise. Needless to say, most of these hidden feelings were not very flattering. Neither was Denise flattered as the pressure mounted for her to face some of her manipulative tendencies.

It was about the 15th session when the emotional log jam started to break up. Family members now seemed to understand implicitly that everybody had agreed to a vague, but clearly understood rule to protect Denise from family conflict so as not to get her "depressed" again. The therapist knew this topic would have to be dealt with, but was less clear as to how or when to do it. Then, unexpectedly, an unusual opportunity presented itself. Denise got inappropriately angry over a minor matter and proceeded to act rather badly toward the children. She was angry and entirely unreasonable in both word and deed, yet no one made any attempt to explain or defend oneself from her obvious unreasonableness. Jeff also remained silent. Everybody seemed more than willing to let Denise's outburst pass, apparently in the hope that the incident would quickly end.

The therapist understood that asking the family to deal with this situation was as dangerous as it was important. He started by asking the family to describe how they were reacting to Denise's anger. It took a long time before they could even start to acknowledge that they felt uneasy expressing their real thoughts and feelings. Naturally, these views were expressed with considerable caution and gentleness that was as obvious as it was phony. It was not difficult for the therapist to decide that Denise would have to bear a substantial burden in opening up the channels of communication that she had so skillfully closed.

The therapist started the following dialogue with Denise:

Therapist: Let me summarize what I think just happened. You got angry and the family basically decided to swallow their thoughts and feelings rather than try to be more honest with you. They have said in the most gentle way possible that they withhold their real thoughts and feelings from you to help prevent another depression. In essence, your family has decided not to be honest with you as a way of protecting you. Is that OK with you?

Denise: Not at all.

Therapist: If you want to know how they really feel about you for getting so angry, this might be a good time to ask. This situation would be a good one to work with.

(The therapist understood full well that Denise has been using her depressive episodes to manipulate and control the family members' responses to her. He also understood that it was unlikely that family members would level with her without her at least appearing to want to know how they really felt. Theoretically, the critical issue was not what might be said, but helping all family members to start learning how to cope with the realities of a situation that they have chronically avoided.)

Denise: (Speaking to the family.) I don't think it's fair of you to deceive me this way. I have enough troubles without this. (Notice the poor me story and the mixed message which seems characteristic of her in these situations.)

(Long pause before the therapist finally speaks.)

Therapist: My guess is that everybody had a fairly strong personal reaction to what you (Denise) just said. The problem we face is seeing if everybody is truly willing to talk about this situation openly

and learn from it. I would like you as a family to
talk it over and then let me know if you think it
is important for the family to learn how to handle
this situation and others that are similar to it. I will
stay out of the discussion until you decide.

(At this point, the therapist has asked the family to do what it
usually could not do—to talk openly about a topic that it usually avoided. Instead of dealing with Denise directly, however,
the therapist reduced the amount of risk and responsibility involved by backing away from the core issue and merely asking
them to decide if the family needs to try to talk about the issue.
The therapist's job now was to watch for styles of coping and
avoidance individually and collectively as they responded to
this challenge.)

It took the remainder of this session and two others for them
to make their decision. Sequentially, it started out with a lot of
awkward silences. The therapist did not participate in the dialogue, but did help the family to process the meaning and function of their silences. Nobody had any trouble understanding
that it was a style of avoidance—a style that was all too common when Denise was involved. It was motivated by fear and
uncertainty about how Denise would react. The fear of precip-
itating an otherwise unnecessary depression was usually on
their minds, a fact that Denise traded on subtly and with considerable skill.

With that fact experientially established, the therapist repeatedly asked the same three question, but in slightly different
ways. They were:

1. Do you approve of yourselves and the way your family
avoids difficult issues that involve your wife and mother?

2. Why are you so afraid to be more open with each other?

3. How would you like your family to be able to handle this
situation that could be upsetting to Denise?

By the time they had discussed these questions for two and
a half sessions, they were all cognizant of their dominant style
of avoidance, moderately uncomfortable because of it, and
hopeful that they could become more open with each other.
With this background work completed, it appeared that the
time had come to deal with Denise.

The therapist understood that what was to follow would be difficult for Denise, the family, and himself. He decided that the best route to follow would be to provide Denise with feedback, but only the feedback that she directly requested from specific family members. She was going to have to initiate the dismantling of the processes that she had so successfully devised.

Therapist: We have spent a lot of time talking about the reasons family members are reluctant to be open with you about their real thoughts and feelings. Essentially, they are afraid to be honest because of the threat of another depression if they upset you. We saw that happen the other day when you got so angry, and nobody would respond to you. If you want to try and deal with this problem, now would be a good time to take as much time as you want and talk to family members as long as you want to find out everything you ever wanted to know about how people are responding to you and what feelings they most frequently withhold from you.

The therapist wanted to put Denise completely in charge of how much feedback she received and from whom. For several reasons, he wanted to create a situation in which her style of avoidance became completely transparent or started to function at higher than usual levels of personal risk and responsibility. First, her directly requesting feedback from others improved the chances of family members responding to her truthfully and nondefensively. Second, this is a form of behavioral rehearsal, which when successful, can create powerful internal and external rewards for her and the family. And third, putting Denise in charge was a way of helping her cultivate the underlying attributes and skills required for more effective human functioning.

It was slow getting started, but gradually people in the family started talking with her more openly. It was upsetting to be sure, but not nearly as upsetting as they had feared. The entire family told Denise in their own way that they were angry at her for using her depression to manipulate and control them.

They said it with care and concern, but they also said it plainly. The message was so consensual and so powerful that Denise had no place to hide. It was true and she knew it. She cried often; and when she did, other family members cried with her because they loved her and let it show. The truth was out now, and Denise would have to change, but she would have the love and support of her family which she had not experienced for a long time. The therapist carefully asked Denise whether she really wanted to have a different kind of relationship with her family and what that would be like. He thought that it was important for the family to hear what she really wanted. That proved to be a tender and moving dialogue for the entire family. Until the therapist mentioned it, hardly anyone even noticed that the very conversation that they were having was exactly what they had hoped to achieve sometime in the future. Naturally, he also asked how they felt about themselves for what they were now doing and experiencing. They all thought it had been difficult and painful, but they clearly approved of themselves for finally facing a difficult issue and, now, treating mother as a regular family member in spite of her depressions. They reported greater hope for the family because they believed that handling future problems in much the same way would save everybody a lot of grief.

Commentary. A number of subsequent sessions were devoted to processing all that had happened in these sessions. And that is precisely the point. Lewin called it "unfreezing" and Festinger called it "dissonance" induction. The name is not nearly so important as understanding its therapeutic power. The success of these sessions was due in large measure to the power of consensual validation to disrupt gradually that which had been well accepted. Each family member came face to face with the personal risks involved in making oneself known to Denise more authentically, Denise had to face the risks involved in facing herself, and the social system that they had all created was now less likely to tolerate or encourage such massive levels of deception and avoidance. The issue that was faced was well ingrained in the fabric of this family, and it is doubtful whether anything less than a massive and consensual dose of authentic feedback from multiple sources would have disrupted these well established family patterns.

Although this was a problem in which consensual validation played a vital role in creating an immediate solution, it was also a powerful vehicle for gaining access to the self-evaluative thoughts and feelings that the individuals had about themselves and the larger social system to which they belonged. It is a good illustration of the simple reality that when patterns of avoidance are understood and described explicitly, they can hardly ever be approved of implicitly or explicitly. This seems to be true regardless of whether the avoidance takes place intrapsychically, interpersonally, or systemically. The converse is equally true. Feelings of self-approval regularly accompany attempts to deal with that which people have a tendency to avoid on the same levels.

In this particular case, the transition from avoidance to coping was enhanced by the inherent rewards of coping and by the family setting in which coping responses were quickly imitated by others once they started appearing. Additionally, as people were asked to attend to the self-evaluative thoughts and feelings about themselves and the social system that they were creating at various stages in this processes, they were reshaping themselves, their behavioral dispositions, and their family.

Clinical Illustration: Reciprocal Relations

Marital and family participants all share a common dilemma: learning how to ask for what they want and need from each other and, conversely, learning how to limit what others demand to what can be freely given. This process involves coming to grips with the basic issues involved in psychological independence, dependence, and interdependence. In our view, a *healthy relationship* is one in which self-approval and the approval of significant others are based on respect and authentic self-representation, not on conformity or compliance with the wishes of others.

Therapeutically, the cardinal therapeutic consideration involving reciprocal relations is not interpersonal learning, the outcome of such dialogues, or the issues that they raise, although all these considerations are important. Rather, it is the high level of personal and interpersonal honesty required to sustain these conversations and the levels of self-approval and the genuine approval of others they can generate that are paramount. Talking openly and directly about basic wants and needs with others is seldom easy, particularly when one wants or needs more attention or love than another. Setting appropriate limits and expectations to what can be freely given is equally difficult, but the benefits of such dialogues can be profound indeed and the results can be extended far beyond the immediate problem being discussed. These benefits are easily understood in the context of increasing levels of personal risk, responsibility, and internal control in a social setting that is a close approximation to the social realities that we all live with. Our underlying assumption remains the same: As these issues are explored in a coping style, they will generate respect and understanding regardless of the outcome so long as authentic coping is the custom rather than the subtleties of avoidance.

I need help, but can't ask! It was the worst crisis yet. Ron and Sheila seemed to be near the end of their rope even though there had been no new abuse of any kind. It all started innocently enough. Sheila went to visit Janet, one of their daughters. It was a good reunion, but something was different about Janet. She wanted to talk to her mother about things that she never wanted to talk about before. She wanted to know why her dad had hit her, why her mother had not defended her, and why mother stayed married to him. It was gut-wrenching, poignant, straight talk between mother and daughter. There was neither room nor need for anything less than absolute frankness between them. It lasted two and a half days. For the entire time, they talked, laughed, and cried together, usually until the wee hours of the morning. When the visit was over, they felt as close to each other as they ever had, but the experience was not all positive. Sheila had seen and heard first hand what she had managed not to comprehend before—the emotional damage that Ron had inflicted on their daughter. It was worse than she had imagined. She was angry at Ron for doing it. She was angry at herself for allowing it to happen.

Naturally, the homecoming was not what Ron was expecting or hoping for. He had missed Sheila and wanted to show his genuine affection for her no matter how unusual or awkward it might be for him; but that was not going to happen. As soon as Sheila stepped off the plane, Ron knew he was not meeting a happy wife eager to see him. He did not know what was wrong, but he did know that it was serious. Sheila started talking as soon as they got in the car. She wanted Ron to hear and understand how their daughter felt about him, and how she felt because of the emotional suffering that he had caused her. Once again, her attitude was one of forthrightness rather than of vindictive hostility, and courageous self–declaration rather than protectiveness. She clearly understood the risks of talking with her husband this openly and reported being frightened about what might happen. However, she had already resolved in her mind never again to shrink from these situations no matter what the risk to herself, not ever. So, they talked even though she was scared, and he was mortified. He had learned enough in therapy to recognize and fight his reflexive instincts to be defensive. So, he tried hard to listen carefully instead of reacting angrily. It cost him though. He hurt deeply and profoundly because he did not hide. There were no excuses or hollow apologies. The truth was the truth, and he was guilty. He saw no hope of ever being able to make up for what he was or what he had done. All seemed utterly hopeless to him and, to a lesser degree, to Sheila.

The first part of their session was devoted to Sheila reporting in detail all that had happened since their session the week before. As she talked, one could see Ron's fuse starting to burn slowly as the vivid accounts of his humiliating behavior proceeded. He hated having the therapist hear such detailed accounts of how he had acted years earlier. He managed to keep the appearance of composure on the outside, but on the inside, one could sense his anger grow as his feelings of personal devastation and hurt grew, and then systematically converted to anger. When he did speak, his words were reasonable, but his style was cold and crisp. Gradually, he started lashing out at Sheila verbally, talking about her inability to love or care for him, her lack of appreciation for all that he provided, her unresponsiveness to his improvements in therapy, and the futility of even trying to work things out with her. He said that he knew that he had acted like a swine in the past, and that she would never forgive him. It sounded like a strange thing to say unless one understood that it was all projection, pure and simple. He was really talking about his own inability to forgive himself.

At this point, the therapist became more involved. It was clear that this dialogue was deteriorating rapidly. He first got Ron's attention and reviewed his primary style of avoidance with him, which had been discussed many times in the past. It went something like this: (a) Ron feeling vulnerable, personally inadequate, and self contemptuous; (b) then projecting these feelings on others (usually Sheila) so that he could talk about their feelings toward him accusatively rather than face his own feelings about himself, (c) pushing others away with his hostility and then justifying his anger with their uncaring attitude toward him, and finally, (d) blaming others, or at least sharing the blame with others, for his bad behavior. The therapist asked Ron what the chances were that he was engaged in that avoidance process right now. The following dialogue then ensued:

Ron:	Probably. I know it's something we have talked about before. But it doesn't feel like I am. I'm trying hard not to be defensive. But I feel like I need to be real careful about what I say to you. It feels like you two may be my enemies, even though I know better. I can't tell what I'm doing.
Therapist:	It sounds like you may be having a lot of confused thoughts and feelings right now.
Ron:	This is really hard. I never thought I would feel like this. I want to get up and leave, but I know I can't. I have to stay here and face this. And even if I face it, I think its all too late. Nobody could ever forgive me for what I have done, not Sheila, not Janet, not you.
Therapist:	This is hard isn't it? You must feel terribly alone right now.
Ron:	I've never felt so alone before. I don't know what to do because I have brought all this on myself.
Therapist:	It sounds like you are suffering alone, partly because you don't feel like you deserve anybody's kindness or help.
Ron:	I have brought all this on myself. I'm so sorry for what I have done, but what is done is done and I can't change that now. I don't have anybody to blame but myself.

Therapist: It sounds like you feel angry with yourself.
     Ron: That's an understatement. I hate what I have done and I don't blame anyone for how they feel about me. I don't deserve any better.

Up to this point the therapist had restricted himself to paraphrasing and reflecting Ron's most basic thoughts and feelings because he was far too defensive to process more than this. His anxiety and fear needed to be reduced before moving on to the more serious work of this session. The therapist continued this type of dialogue for a time to improve his rapport with Ron, to reduce his imagined fear of being attacked by Sheila or the therapist, and to convey a sense of understanding and support for his efforts in trying to face a very difficult situation more responsibly. As Ron gradually became less guarded and more relaxed with himself, the therapist gradually started making a critical transition in the therapy process.

Therapist: It sounds like even in your suffering you don't expect or want any help from others because you don't deserve any help or support.
     Ron: That's right, I don't feel worthy of help or kindness.
Therapist: So here you are in a difficult situation in your marriage that you are prepared to endure alone because you won't ask or accept help from others.
     Ron: What are you saying?
Therapist: What are you afraid I might be saying?
     Ron: Are you saying that others may be more willing to care about me if I would let them? Why should they care about me after what I have done to them?

This is the critical transition point in the therapy process. Stylistically, Ron has been extremely self-punitive, but avoidant of the real issue. Historically, his self-punitive behavior has been a means of skillful gaining of support and sympathy from others rather than truly coping with difficult issues. This should not be taken to mean that his self-punitive thoughts and feelings were fake or entirely manipulative. These feelings were real and intense. It is equally true that Ron was extraordinarily skillful in using these feelings in the interpersonal equation that controls others in short-sighted and self-serving ways. The therapist wanted to move him past his subtle sympathy seeking and face the vital issue that he had yet to deal with, that is, to ask directly for the emotional support that he had always sought indirectly, and face the potential or actual rejection in a more open and responsible way. This was the core of a long-established pattern of avoidance and the basis for some of his most intense negative self evaluative feelings. The appearance of a coping response in this difficult situation could not only help with the immediate problem at hand, but could also provide him with equally intense feelings of self-approval and hope as he started to resolve the underlying cause of his personal and marital problems.

Therapist:	This is an important part of this session. It may be the most important part of any session we have ever had. You may not mean to do it, but you are actually pushing Sheila farther away from you right now by acting tough and independent when you really seem to be feeling vulnerable and afraid. You feel alone, yet you are unwilling to ask your wife to be a companion to you in this time of difficulty. You are moving in a direction of "going it alone" again which almost always leads you into more difficulties. You don't have to react to this situation the way you usually do, you can try and change how you respond to this problem right now if you want to!
Ron:	I have no idea what to do differently!
Therapist:	What would you do or say with Sheila right now if you stopped trying to act so independent and expressed your deepest feelings to her so she could truly understand how you feel and what you are going through? I want you to invite Sheila into your life instead of pushing her away.

(Ron proceeds with a long, deeply emotional and highly detailed apology for all of his bad conduct over the years. It was far too eloquent to reproduce in its entirety. Suffice it to say that it was touching, emotional, and sincere. His voice quivered the entire time and tears ran down his checks. It lasted four or five minutes. As soon as he was finished, he immediately looked over at the therapist as though he was looking for a sign of approval for his efforts.)

Therapist: You left the most important part out!

Ron: What do you mean?

Therapist: You apologized with depth and sincerity, but you didn't really invite her into your life!

Ron: I can't do that.

Therapist: It sounds like you are at a tough choice point, doesn't it.

Ron: You don't cut any slack at all do you! (His demeanor is now noticeably more comfortable and relaxed, though he is clearly uncomfortable with where this is headed. This comment was offered with a touch of humor as well as discomfort.)

Therapist: What is it you didn't say?

Ron: (Long pause, then he starts to speak, stops again for another long pause and then says,) I can't do this. I don't know how to do this.

Therapist: What are you having trouble with?

Ron: How can I ask someone to help me—to stand by me when I have let them down so much?

Therapist: There, you said it to me. Now you need to say it to your wife.

Ron: (Another long pause, then a deep sigh.) Will you help me get through this? Will you stay with me even after all that I have done?

Therapist: (To Sheila) Don't answer his question too quickly and only answer with your most trustworthy feelings. His question is too important for you to be polite, sympathetic, or temporarily supportive. Tell him if you really have anything left for him.

Sheila: (After a very long pause) Yes, I will stay with you. I want to help you. I don't enjoy seeing you suffer. I feel bad that you have to go through all of this. But you have to understand one thing. I won't stay with you or even try to help you when you start pushing me away again. The therapist was right when he said you try to act tough and independent when you feel weak and vulnerable.

And when you do, it feels hopeless to me. You're kidding yourself and you're trying to kid me. I know better. You're not fooling anybody. When you first started talking, I was thinking we're not going to make it. But when you invited me into your life the way you just did, I still want to come. I like that part of you. I knew it was there when we got married and that is the reason I married you. The only hope I have for us is when I see you like this. You inviting me into your life makes me feel wanted and important. I don't feel that from you very much.

Commentary. This was an illustration that involved a complete role reversal for the spouses. The husband abandoned his role as the dominant provider and learned to express his need to be cared for and supported by another. In doing so, he excused himself from the requirement of trying to maintain a level of pseudo-independence and adequacy that he was unable to sustain. He also found out that he was still acceptable to his wife even when he felt to be the most unacceptable to himself. It was a brief, but poignant moment.

More important, as this session was processed more carefully, Ron expressed great pleasure about having not only expressed his vulnerability and remorse under difficult circumstances but also for having had the courage to do so. It was this courage that not only aroused his wife's faltering hopes, but his own as well. The underlying qualities of character ingredient in the act is what led both of them to believe that they might yet be able to overcome the difficulty that had plagued them for so long. The paradox, of course, is that the strength required to own up to his weaknesses was an unusual demonstration of adequacy that was never present in his pathological attempts to be strong, controlling, reassuring, or appropriate. It was the strength inherent in this act of coping that both of them saw and approved of so fundamentally.

Sheila, on the other hand, stopped acting as if she were less capable than she really was. She abandoned her naive view of denying her feelings so as to appear supportive and so she could consider herself a dutiful wife. Instead, she spoke with the emotional and analytical clarity that she was always capable of. She could provide authentic support for Ron, but not unconditionally. Her conditions were eminently fair and healthy. Ron would have to invite her into his life and treat her as a partner and companion in the relationship, not someone to be supervised and criticized. She had love to give and would share it with Ron, but only so long as he worked at truly sharing his inner life with her. Again, the paradox is obvious. Ron experienced more favorable regard from her in her brutal clarity than he ever had in her role playing attempts to appear more caring than she really felt.

This was a case in which the couple moved from an adversarial relationship to an alliance of mutual help and support, at least during this session, and the nature of the self-evaluative thoughts and feelings were noticeably higher because of it. Naturally, these feelings were processed more carefully and in greater depth at the next session. The purpose was for these clients to learn from their own experience what they had done to earn such high levels of approval from themselves and each other. This couple is acquiring the capacity to ask for what is needed and to provide what is available in ways that are intrinsically more satisfying to them. This is a form of therapy that emphasizes underlying patterns and processes over situations and content and the self evaluative thoughts and feelings that accompany basic processes.

A Complete Clinical Illustration

The simplified summaries that we have used to illustrate the complex role of feedback, consensual validation, and reciprocal role function are necessarily incomplete and, therefore, misleading in varying degrees and mixtures. They say little and only touch on the most critical segments of a limited number of therapy sessions. They omit the ground work and preparation that give rise to these more consequential moments and ignore the careful but tedious work of processing and clarifying what follows.

Before proceeding with a more complete clinical illustration, several comments are in order that should give more balance and perspective to our presentation. First, we understand that there is more to marital and family therapy than the four primary and unique considerations that we have been discussing. In fact, these considerations are important only because they allow the therapist to incisively gain access to the patterns of coping and avoidance inherent in those activities. It is the awareness of these patterns of avoidance and coping and of the evaluative thoughts and feelings of both self and others that is the backbone of our therapeutic concerns. Any dialogue or activity that provides equivalent clarity about these patterns and the self-evaluative thoughts and feelings that they create is equally important. This may include a wide range of activities.

It is understood that there is substantially more to marital and family therapy than just patterns of coping, avoidance, and self-evaluative feelings. Therapist credibility has to be established, client therapist relationships developed, role expectations clarified, and clients listened to attentively. All of these considerations and others like them serve vital therapeutic functions that should not be overlooked or taken lightly. In our view, all successful clinical cases ultimately come face to face with core considerations and dilemmas. We suggest that a clear understanding of styles of avoidance and coping and the self-evaluative feelings that these patterns create can be extraordinary useful tools for incisively identifying, clarifying, and working through these core dilemmas. We will illustrate what we consider to be the most essential steps in this process with an example of a successful middle-aged couple who denied the reality of their failing marriage as long as possible before seeking professional help.

I was surprised when I received their call for an appointment. They were the pillars of the community. I was not surprised, however, when they asked for an appointment time when nobody else would be in the office. It is not unusual for clients to not tell others that they are seeing a therapist, but it is unusual for them to make an appointment after regular office hours to assure not being seen by others.

Building Rapport and Defining Issues: Sessions 1 and 2

The first two sessions were not particularly eventful. There were the usual concerns and nervous questions about confidentiality, expectations, and prior family problems that were discussed, but only briefly. The only thing unusual about these sessions was the high level of discomfort that accompanied these routine topics for most other couples. It was easy to notice and to wonder why they were so on edge.

Harry was in his mid-forties, generally well-poised, and a successful and well-known professional in the community. Sally was about the same age, equally poised in most situations, and well-known and successful in her own right. Ironically, however, they both gave the impression that they would have been more comfortable accepting an award for the outstanding couple of the decade on national television than talking about their personal lives privately.

Nevertheless, with the preliminaries out of the way, the process of discussing the reasons and goals for therapy began in earnest. It was slow going. Both Harry and Sally had difficulty expressing how they saw themselves, their spouse, or the problems in their marriage. It seemed as though each was preoccupied with appearances and impressions to such a degree that they were unaccustomed to expressing their thoughts and feelings with any degree of candor. The therapist listened attentively, but initially confined his role to rapport and relationship building by paraphrasing or clarifying when it seemed appropriate.

By the end of the second session, the couple was decidedly more relaxed, but still cautious. They had defined their marital problem as a breakdown in communication even though they had little understanding of what that might mean or what they expected from each other. It was a problem statement that reflected the same cosmetic platitudes as the couple presenting it. They did report a vague, but consistent feeling of discontent that each could describe, but attribute to nothing in particular. In spite of the lack of urgency and distress that they reported verbally, the fact remained that they were seeking the services of a professional therapist with a level of discomfort that might more reasonably be associated with open heart surgery.

Styles of Avoidance and Self-Evaluative Feelings: Sessions 3 to 6

The third session was more eventful and productive. The therapist started the session by asking the couple to describe the way in which they saw themselves interact with each other as they talked about their marital problems during the last two sessions. It was slow going again. It did not take long before it was obvious that they did not want to describe themselves. That is not unusual, however. It is an incisive question, particularly for those who are more concerned about impressions than problem solving. There are many reasons why a couple might feel resistant to such a request, but the most likely was also the most obvious in this case. The nature of their avoidance patterns was as obvious to them as it was to the therapist. Talking about them would be embarrassing. It would make explicit that which had always remained implicit. The process of real therapeutic work was about to begin, and their discomfort and resistance was a natural and inevitable consequence of that reality. The following dialogue illustrates how that resistance was used to further explore the style of avoidance that seemed to dominate this couple's style of self presentation and problem solving.

Therapist:	Would you try and describe the way you see yourselves and each other as you have talked about your marital problems during the last two sessions.
Sally:	What do you mean? I don't know what you are asking for when you say to describe the way we see ourselves talking to each other?
Therapist:	Do you find my request confusing, or does it make you nervous and your questions are just a way of avoiding it?

Sally:	It's probably both. We're not used to talking so openly about ourselves, but we don't understand what you mean either.
Therapist:	Pretend that you are simply observers watching another couple talk over their marital problems. Your job is to describe how each of the spouses acts and interacts with the other. Forget about what is being said and focus your attention on the most common styles and patterns you see while talking with each other. Examples might include who is being dominant or submissive and when, who gets angry and how does the other react, how each of you acts when you get defensive. Do you get the idea? I want you to describe what you see when you look at the way you act and interact with each other.

By explaining and illustrating what is wanted from the clients so clearly, they are put in a position of having to actively and obviously resist the request or simply get started. If they resist, they will be demonstrating another type or level of avoidance that they can be asked to describe as soon as it becomes appropriate. If they get started, the demand characteristics of the situation and the request itself automatically move them in the direction of therapeutic work.

It is important to notice that in the process of explaining and clarifying what the clients are to do, the therapist does not excuse them from any of the risk or responsibility inherent in the task. Instead, he merely focuses it more clearly. The therapist structures and controls the process and task that the clients are to engage in, but does not provide any structure or direction for actually doing the task. The clients are free to respond as they will, provided that it is within the general arena of describing how they see themselves act and interact with each other.

Harry:	Why do you want us to do this? We have all been here for these sessions. Why would we go back and describe them again?
Therapist:	Take a minute before you answer, then try and describe what you are doing with me right now?

Harry: I don't know what it is you want me to say!

Therapist: Sally, what is it that you see going on between Harry and me? Would you try and describe it to us the way you would if you were talking with your best friend right after this session.

This is the first use of feedback in this session. It should be noted that it was solicited by the therapist, not Harry. This would be atypical. Generally speaking, it is better for clients to ask for feedback that they are interested in receiving to reduce resistance. In this case, it is being used to benefit the development of the session and Sally more than Harry. Also notice the possibility that the stage is being set for Harry to be confronted with consensually validated feedback in a few minutes from both Sally and the therapist if it seems necessary and appropriate.

Sally: I'll try, but I am not that sure of how to do this.

Therapist: Just sit back in the chair, close your eyes and describe what you saw just as you would try to describe a car, or the behavior of any other person.

Sally: He is trying to change the topic by asking questions.

Therapist: That's very good, but don't stop yet. Talk about everything you saw going on.

Sally: He is trying to find a polite way to get out of doing what you asked. He doesn't want to just come out and say that he doesn't want to do it, so he is evading you. He does the same thing to me all the time. He does it by changing the topic, pretending he doesn't understand, or by asking questions.

Therapist: Bingo! That was excellent. That's also what I want both of you to do—to talk openly and candidly about the way you have acted and interacted with each other for the last two sessions.

It took time to further process this short exchange, but what followed was a fairly long and detailed account (three full sessions) of how and why this couple had been acting during the first two sessions. Naturally, how they presented themselves in the sessions was an extension of their more general styles which was also discussed. Their ability to describe accurately was impressive. Essentially, they described themselves as (a) being polite and appropriate no matter how they felt inside, (b) evasive in the face of conflict, and (c) distrustful of each other. When asked to select a name that most accurately described their personal and interpersonal styles they choose "chameleon" because of its ability to fit in and adapt to its surroundings. It is unusual to have such an obvious avoidance pattern adopted by both spouses in a marriage, but the process of identifying and labeling them stays essentially the same no matter how complex or subtle they may be.

Naturally, many other things were discussed in these sessions, but thematically the therapist kept the focus on their most dominant patterns of avoidance. On a number of occasions, the couple wanted to talk more about what was being avoided than how it was avoided. In each instance, the therapist patiently, but persistently moved the focus back to style in favor of content and speculations. This process continued until the couple seemed to reach a level of self-consciousness about their dominant pattern of avoidance that they spontaneously started recognizing or correcting their chameleon-like dialogues right in the sessions.

Needless to say, none of these activities was a source of pleasure to them. It was hard to own up to what they were saying about themselves; and making things explicit added both clarity and additional discomfort to the conversation, as it usually does. The therapist had them talk a good deal about the precise elements in their behavior that caused their embarrassment. By the end of the seventh session, Harry and Sally had little remaining tolerance for their emotional and verbal duplicity and the disapproval and embarrassment that it generated. Because of the clarity with which these core sources of marital difficulty had now been exposed to all, it was time for a shift in therapeutic emphasis. During this entire process, the therapist conscientiously attended to their personal discomfort by first acknowledging it, and then asking them to explain precisely what they had been doing that caused the discomfort.

Coping and Self-Evaluative Feelings: Session 7

In most cases like this, there is a paradox that inevitably starts to unfold. As clients face their personal weaknesses with increasing candor and integrity, there is a corresponding increase in their level of psychological comfort and self-approval. It is seldom noticed, however, because of the degree to which clients are absorbed in the more immediate and obvious feelings associated with the problem that they are trying to face or discuss. So, just as the clients are facing themselves more openly than usual, the therapist shifts the focus from their feelings about the problem at hand to their feelings about themselves for trying to face the problem at hand. It is a shift away from content to the more important ingredients supporting the process. These attributes and the self-evaluative feelings that they engender became the focal points of the therapy. This process is illustrated in the following abbreviated segment:

Therapist: This would be a good time to pull everything together you have said about yourselves and your relationship during the last few sessions. Let's see if we can get a summary of what you consider the most important points.

Harry: The most important thing is that neither one of us is very honest with our feelings. We act more like puppets than real people. We try to make things look better than they are to keep up impressions. We both play the game, and that's why we don't trust each other very much.

Therapist: The word you picked to describe this was "chameleon". Does that still seem accurate to you?

Sally: Fits like a glove.

Therapist: And tell me about the core feelings you have about yourself for acting like a chameleon.

Harry: It's a hard thing to face about yourself. It's embarrassing. When you actually say the words out loud, it feels even worse. It's some combination of childishness, foolishness, and stupidity. I hate the fact we have done it so much.

Therapist:	In other words, you have a lot of bad feelings about yourselves for hiding and pretending with your feelings instead of being more honest and forthright with them.
Sally:	I hate to say so, but that's right.
Therapist:	And what are the most frequent feelings about yourself you experience.
Harry:	Weakness, cowardice, disappointment, self-hate, a resolve to stop doing it.
Therapist:	Sounds ugly!
Harry:	It's not nice.
Therapist:	And how would you describe the way you have dealt with your feelings right now and during the last few sessions?

The critical transition has begun. The task now is to call the clients' attention to their new behavior (being more self-disclosing, congruent, declarative, and honest with self and others) and the feelings that they have about themselves for acting this way. The clear labeling of the new behavior is critical. So is the identification of the self-evaluative thoughts and feelings that accompany them. The essential steps in identifying a coping response are the same as those involved in avoidance. Clear description comes first, then comes succinct labeling, and finally, the full affective exploration of the self-evaluative thoughts and feelings that accompany the response. The fact that this case involves relatively healthy people with patterns of avoidance that are relatively obvious may make the job easier, but it does not alter the underlying process.

Harry and Sally quickly recognized their improving candor with each other, both emotionally and intellectually. Even though they reported it to be more uncomfortable most times, they both felt that it was a more appropriate way to behave with each other. Neither of them wanted to be deceived or protected any more, and both agreed to work at being more revealing with their deeper thoughts and feelings. They were quick to add, however, that they feared what this might lead to as they talked about their lives together. The therapist noted the paradox that their self-approval seemed to require them to talk about things that they found difficult to discuss and wanted to avoid. The implications of this observation were not lost on Sally and Harry.

Clarifying the Core Conflict: Session 8

With the first phase of the therapy now completed (an introduction to identifying and extinguishing avoidance, enhancing coping, and clarifying self-evaluative feelings), the couple was better prepared to enter into direct dialogue with each other about the problems that they shared. The therapist's primary concern at this stage was to help create a dialogue in which coping, regardless of the content being discussed, was more prevalent than avoidance. Again, it was a matter of favoring style over substance. Our assumption is that in any dyad or family, one must learn to behave in ways that one approves of and respects before one can expect the approval and respect of others. What is needed is love and respect freely given because it is based on enduring authenticity, not impression management or manipulation. This requires each spouse to know oneself first, and then to make oneself known to the other. In this case, a frank discussion of what they usually avoided was used as a primary vehicle to facilitate this process as illustrated in the following segment:

Therapist: Both of you seem to find it difficult, yet more rewarding to be more honest in your dealings with each other. Do you think it's time to start talking to each other more honestly about the things you have been working so hard to avoid before therapy?

Harry: I think we're going to have to try sometime.

Therapist: Where would you like to start.

Sally: (Long silence.) This is hard. I want to be more honest with my feelings with you, but I'm afraid of what I have to say.

Therapist: Can you talk about your fear with Harry?

Sally: You have done things in the past that I know about. We have never talked about them because I didn't think our marriage could survive it. Maybe it won't now. I know about Helen. I've known about it all the time. I just learned to live with it. But no more.

(Long, long silence as Sally cries, Harry stares into the floor and the therapist waits. After a silence that lasted at least four or five minutes, the therapist speaks because it appears Harry is immobilized by the confrontation. Notice how the therapist emphasizes process instead of content).

Therapist: (to Harry) It looks like you are in a difficult spot right now of the kind you used to avoid at all cost. What is it you need to say right now that you normally wouldn't say. I want you to try and represent yourself to Sally so that you can approve of yourself in this situation no matter how she reacts to you.

Harry: (looking at therapist) I don't know what to. . .

Therapist: (cuts him off) You need to be talking with Sally.

Harry: I don't know what to say. I keep trying to think of what I need to do or say that I can approve of. I don't approve of what I did. I have no justification. I cheated. I have hurt our marriage. I'm sorry. I'm truly sorry. The words sound hollow and don't change anything, but that's what I am really thinking and feeling.

Sally: That's not the worst of it! You just lied to my face about it all the time. I can't even imagine what you must think of me to have treated me with such utter disregard.

The secret is out. Sally is devastated by what Harry has done. She seems to be equally angry at herself for playing the role of a "dummy" during the process (which may represent a secondary style of avoidance). Harry's capacity for duplicity is now in full view. Whether or not his remorse transcends merely getting caught remains to be seen. Harry and Sally are about to fully experience the psychic suffering that is ingredient in the violation of the trusts involved in an ongoing relationship. The suffering is unavoidable, but the way in which the suffering is done is not. Coping, or fully expressing thoughts and feelings as they occur, is vital to dealing with emotions and conflict in our approach. For Sally this will include:

1. Her underlying feelings of betrayal by Harry.
2. Her feelings of self-betrayal for not speaking up.
3. Her willingness and ability to forgive.

Harry will be brought face to face with:

1. His willingness to be secretly self-indulgent.
2. His capacity for loyalty to and trust with another.
3. His willingness to seek forgiveness.

Working Through the Core Conflict: Sessions 9 to 20

Maintaining the vital balance between coping and avoidance is the primary responsibility of the therapist once the core issues are clearly identified and understood. Naturally, other therapeutic adjuncts such as clarification, interpretation, catharsis, modeling, and empathy are also important, but they are secondary to maintaining a pattern of coping as the core issues are addressed by clients. This requires the therapist to continually monitor and be alert to the self-evaluative thoughts and feelings accompanying the way in which each spouse is dealing with the other. Avoidant responses need to be processed immediately, preferably by merely asking the clients to describe what they are doing and why, as a gentle reminder of what has already been learned. Some examples of this process follow.

Self Evaluative Processes: Avoiding Avoidance

It has been one session since Harry and Sally started facing their core dilemma—interpersonal distrust and personal duplicity. Harry has steadfastly remained apologetic and has tried to accept Sally's hostility, probably because he could not see what else he could do. Sally has become progressively more open with her hostility and aggression. It has been cathartic for her, but of little therapeutic significance in a larger sense.

The therapist views Sally's attitude and behavior as a way of avoiding the expression of her deeper feelings of hurt, betrayal, and personal foolishness. Although her behavior gives the appearance of being more open and congruent, it is in reality a more subtle reenactment of her enduring tendency to avoid the expression of her deeper feelings and the discomfort associated with them. Additionally, the therapist sees Harry's passive and apologetic attitude as a way of avoiding deeper conflict with Sally. Essentially then, both spouses are continuing in their basic pattern of avoidance, but in a way that is more subtle and difficult to deal with because it gives the appearance of being healthier than it really is. It is crucial for therapists to learn to recognize and respond to the function that any behavior serves (in this case, avoidance and further impression management) rather than the behavior itself. After allowing Sally to fully express her more obvious feelings, the following dialogue ensued:

Therapist:	Your anger toward Harry seems perfectly natural and understandable. I can't help wondering if you are expressing all of your feelings, or avoiding the more tender ones?
Sally:	The only thing I feel is anger. The more I think about what he did to me, the more anger I feel.
Therapist:	You said that you might be angry at me for asking. Do you feel anger or annoyance at me?
Sally:	No, not really. I suppose I'm just worked up over everything that has happened.
Therapist:	You did sound angry though. Maybe anger is all you want to feel right now.
Sally:	Maybe.
Therapist:	Would you like to talk about your anger?
Sally:	If you think it would be a good idea!
Therapist:	It's your anger, do you want to try and understand it better?
Sally:	I'm sorry . . . yes, let's talk about it.
Therapist:	What do you suppose you would say about yourself if you tried to express the feelings behind your anger with the same intensity and clarity with which you are expressing the anger?

The therapist wants to shift the dialogue from a hostile interpersonal confrontation between Sally and Harry to an intrapsychic exploration by Sally. Only after she understands the meaning of her anger more completely can she talk with Harry more congruently. This step is a way of short circuiting the needless aggression that is sure to follow if their avoidance is not interrupted and replaced with a more authentic exchange between Sally and Harry.

> Sally: What do you mean?
> Therapist: Let's try something. I want you to lean back, close your eyes, and forget about Harry and what he has done. Review in your mind the details of the way you have been acting. Then, decide if you approve of what you see. Remember, you don't have to justify or explain any of your feelings or behavior. I just want you to focus your attention on you feelings towards yourself . . . if you approve of what you have been doing and why.

This is a situation in which the therapist believes that he can trust Sally to report her self-evaluative feelings accurately. In earlier sessions, she had demonstrated the ability to report both self approval and disapproval even when it was difficult to do so. The therapist wanted to see whether Sally could interrupt her avoidance using her own self-evaluative feelings rather than go through the more laborious task of describing the behavior first. Our assumption in these situations is always the same: Clients rarely approve of their avoidant behavior no matter what form it takes, particularly if they are given time and encouragement to reflect and become more aware of what they are doing and why. All of this is being done because the therapist wants to facilitate a discussion between Sally and Harry that seems more timely than amplify a situational style of avoidance.

> Sally: (talking directly to the therapist after a full five minute delay) I'm beating Harry up. I want to hurt him back because he hurt me so much for so long.

And no, I don't approve. But that doesn't change
how I feel though. I really do want to hurt him
back.

Therapist: Revenge is your motive, and hostility is your
weapon!

Sally: That's what it is. I wish it wasn't, but that's what
it is.

Therapist: And what are you avoiding by being so angry?

Sally: (Long pause.) Deep inside I am hurt—really, really
hurt. I didn't think I could ever get hurt so bad.

Therapist: Are you willing to express those hurt feeling directly to Harry just the way you feel them? Can
you do it so he will understand what it would be
like to be in your shoes right now?

Sally began a long, emotional self-disclosure that left little
room for imagination about her suffering through this entire
ordeal. She explained what it felt like to be cheated on, lied to,
and to suffer alone while she pretended to not know what was
going on behind her back. Her contempt of self was as obvious
as was her contempt for Harry. But what was most obvious was
the depth and intensity of her pain and suffering. It was all
expressed honestly and congruently. It moved Harry to tears as
he came face to face with the full emotional consequences of
what he had done.

Therapist: (To Harry) You need to respond to Sally with the
same honesty she has shared with you.

(Harry tenderly takes Sally in his arms, holds her while she
cries and says nothing. After about 15 minutes and Sally's sobbing stops, he tells her how he feels about himself for what he
has done in agonizing detail. He also expresses his feelings
about her. He apologizes with sincerity.)

Paradoxically, this intervention clarified the extent of their alienation from each other and, at the same time, provided them
with an important shared emotional experience that was more

authentic than anything that they had shared in years. Even though such experiences are the very basis for reconstructing damaged relationships, they can also be threatening. In this case, their feelings were ambivalent as one would expect them to be. The dialogue was emotionally satisfying because of the concern for each other that it contained, but distressing because of the intimacy that it created when trust was still in doubt. It was a step in the direction of healing, but a step that had been approached and taken with caution.

As is customary in these situations, their feelings about the dilemma were unpleasant and negative, yet their feelings about themselves for their conduct and motives in the dilemma were most favorable. The differentiation between the general feelings about a problem and specific feelings for the way in which the problem is being handled is seldom more apparent or important than in these critical situations. These feelings, when properly noted and explored, selectively reinforce and shape the very behavior that the clients themselves consider most appropriate.

More important, however, is the reality that the last level of avoidance had now been exposed and successfully interrupted for both Sally and Harry. Not only was coping replacing avoidance, but some of the core reasons for the avoidance were expressed openly and congruently. The risk of knowing themselves, and then making themselves known to the other was in full progress. This knowledge and these experiences are the substance that gives relationships endurance if there is to be any.

Such an intense episode provides an enormous amount of material for consideration, most of which cannot be discussed in detail here. In this case, it included

1. Sally's self-evaluative feelings for shifting from avoidance (expressing anger and hostility) to coping (expressing the hurt and anguish that she felt). She clearly recognized and approved of the ingredients required for the change, but described the experience as fatiguing, draining, and not one that she was eager to repeat. The implications of that statement had to be processed as well.

2. Harry's clear labeling of the most essential traits about himself that allowed him to have an affair and to lie to Sally. The full affective exploration of the self-evaluative thoughts and feelings tied to these traits was equally critical.

3. The full exploration of how Sally and Harry saw each other while each was engaged in behavior that they themselves approved of while dealing with the problems they shared more openly and congruently.

4. The full exploration of the type of life that Harry and Sally would have together if they had a history of dealing with each other and with life's problems in the same manner as that used in dealing with the issues in the consulting room.

Clarifying Cognitively What Has Been Learned Experientially

Some therapeutic events are more emotionally charged than others, but all such events contain the seeds of important psychological lessons to be harvested by the therapy process. One essential step in this process is helping clients to understand cognitively that which they have felt and learned experientially. The clarity with which emotionally charged events are clearly understood is a form of future response facilitation. The accuracy with which poignant events are understood in a single therapuetic moment is what allows them to be generalized, transferred, and applied to new situations.

The first phases of therapy tend to be more experiential than cognitive, although this is not always the case. This is when clients are usually reexposed to the emotions as well as to the events that have been inhibiting and frightening them. Even though these feelings and the experiences that they generate are of paramount importance, the style of avoidance (traits and patterns) is even more important. Feelings of anxiety or fear are needed to activate the avoidance patterns in which we are initially so interested. Capitalizing fully on the intimate and robust relationship between experiential and cognitive learning in this process is vital if clients are to escape their habits of avoidance fully and replace them with enduring patterns of coping. The overall importance of cognitive and experiential learning in our model is illustrated by the emphasis placed on precise description and labeling on the one hand, and fully experiencing self-evaluative feelings on the other.

Harry and Sally are now in the 19th session. They are trying to determine whether they have a future together. Sally is still more cautious than Harry, but she is pleased with the changes in their relationship. She still has unresolved feelings that these changes might not last. Harry is eager for the relationship to continue, but not willing to push his views because he still considers himself as the cause of their difficulties. They are approaching an intellectual reconciliation for a future together, but a feeling of trust is still missing. What follows is the description of Harry and Sally sharing a poignant event together, then having it clarified cognitively in such a way that it alters their definition of themselves, their problem, and their future together. Notice the fluidity with which intrapsychic, interpersonal, and systemic considerations are all included in the processing of this event.

Sally and Harry are talking about their distrust of each other. Each is blaming the other for the distrust, and each has ample evidence to support the contention that the other is not trustworthy. Neither of them is the least bit inclined to accept the other's point of view or to consider the distrust as a form of projection, which is certainly the case to some extent. Harry and Sally are stuck because they do not yet recognize their own intrapsychic discomfort about their prior duplicity and impression management, the effects this defensiveness is currently having on their relationship, or the way in which the relationship they have created actually encourages this process. It is an important therapeutic hurdle that has yet to be faced and mastered.

The therapist asked them to explain to each other the basis for their distrust. The feedback they exchanged was crisp and essentially valid, but based on historical events that were as common as they were duplicitous. More recent events that were far more trustworthy were not mentioned at all. Both clients had changed substantially in recent weeks, but those changes were simply ignored in the feedback. The therapist called their attention to this observation and asked what that might mean.

They struggled with the question only briefly before coming to the realization that each was actively defending against new levels of intimacy because of fear and feelings of blame for their marital difficulties. The therapist suggested that it might be useful for them to express their deeper feelings rather than to hide them by blaming. What followed was a series of candid and emotional self-disclosures about self-punitive feelings and fear of commitment. In this process, a growing respect and affection for each other was expressed openly because of the recent changes, but this happened only after their fears were shared more openly. It was a remarkably authentic experience and a welcomed break from the sophisticated blaming and bickering that preceded it. It was another highly intimate emotional experience that was providing a basis for a new and growing trust.

After the experience had reached its emotional peak, the therapist asked them to notice and describe how they were feeling at that moment compared to when the session started. The answer was both easy and obvious once the question was asked— more comfortable, less anxious, more trusting, less guarded, warmer, less angry. The therapeutic movement from avoidance to coping had been completed with the usual emotional results. Now it was time to process this event cognitively for the future benefit of the clients. Central questions in this process included:

1. Why did your feelings change so much within the session? What happened to make such a difference?

2. What did each of you do to preserve the stalemate and blaming that was going on?

3. What did each of you do to interrupt the stalemate and blaming that was going on?

4. When did you approve of your own behavior the most and when the least? When did you approve of your spouse's behavior the most and when the least?

5. Could you deal with this type of impasse in the future? What would you do to accomplish the same improvement without a therapist? What stopped you from doing that right in this session?

A good deal of additional therapy time was devoted to processing these questions and others like them. There were many different forms to the questions, but the guiding principle of all of them was the same: "What are the key ingredients of what just happened here and how well do you understand them?" It is to be noted, however, that none of these questions would be considered appropriate in the absence of the experiential events and learning that preceded them.

These were vital sessions for this couple. They provided a foundation for (a) understanding the style and purpose of their blaming, (b) expressing and experiencing the tenderness they felt for each other that was being masked by the fear-motivated blaming, (c) cognitively rehearsing how they could respond to future situations more productively, (d) clarifying once again the nature of their own and others' feelings toward them for coping rather than avoiding, and (e) reinstilling a sense of hope and personal control over what happens to them. These sessions were devoted almost exclusively to strengthening the coping responses of this couple as they were in the final stages of therapy.

A less dramatic but equally useful variation of the same process can be used to end any session that has included important experiential learning. For example:

Therapist: Before we end the session I would like to ask each of you to take a few minutes and think about the session, the role you played in its development, and the feelings you have about yourself and your partner during the session.

Harry: It was a good session. Sally is expressing her reservation in a way that I can't disagree with. I know right where I stand with her. I think I have been patient, not so much to please her, but because I don't think I have the right to ask for more. I hope we can work this out. We have both been foolish, but me far more than her. At least, I feel like I am now able to be honest with myself and her. That's what most of this session felt like to me.

Sally:	I like what we are doing. I just don't know what to do about my fear of getting deeply involved with Harry again. In many ways, I think I feel closer to him than I ever have before—that's probably what I am afraid of.
Therapist:	In other words, you both like what you are doing and feeling in the session even though problems you face are yet to be resolved. You both seem to be regretful of Sally's cautiousness, but accepting of those feelings.
Harry and Sally:	That's how I see things.
Therapist:	Can you be more specific about what you see yourself or your spouse doing that pleases you?

Although this intervention is short, near the end of a session, and completely lacking in drama, it is a powerful summary. It is a way for the couple to describe and take inventory of their progress. It is also a way for them to describe and shape their own patterns and style of interaction by selectively reinforcing that which they find most satisfying. And finally, it is a way of highlighting the elements in their own therapeutic process that seem to be working.

Approaching Termination

The roles of the therapist and client change as the time for termination approaches. Before termination is even considered, clients should have acquired a good functional understanding of the role of avoidance, coping, and self-evaluative feelings in the development and remedation of their personal and interpersonal difficulties. Additionally, the therapist will have been gradually increasing the responsibility of the clients within the therapy sessions to govern their own experiential and cognitive learning with the use of these concepts. The final phases of therapy begin when the therapist has the clients schedule home sessions to talk over their relationship without the therapist present. The remaining therapy sessions are used exclusively to review these home sessions and the progress or difficulties that grow out of them.

This transition went smoothly with Harry and Sally because they were such capable clients, and their progress had been so steady. This is not always the case. Nevertheless, Harry and Sally complained briefly about the therapist not being present, but then quickly accepted the additional burdens of facing their relationship issues honestly and on their own. They continued seeing the therapist twice a month for two additional months and then once a month for three more months before terminating.

Summary

We have described a therapeutic process for couples and families that emphasizes the development of healthy psychological processes far more than any other values, content, or conflict. Our approach is based on different assumptions, but four of the more important ones are

1. Individual feelings of personal approval and personal well-being play a vital role in the dynamics of all family relationships.

2. Each member of a family or marriage must learn to behave in ways that they themselves approve of and respect before they can expect or accept the approval and respect of others.

3. The psychological process required to participate in feedback exchanges, consensual validation process, and reciprocal helping roles can produce a unique psychological experience of self-efficacy; one that allows a person to experience their own adequacy as evidenced by their ability to confront difficult situations authentically (absence of impression management) and find that both internal and external approval are more dependent on authenticity than impression management.

4. The underlying attributes involved in each of the processes named above include personal risk, personal responsibility, and self-direction. Theoretically, each of these attributes is considered a core mediating variable of healthy behavior more generally because they influence a broad spectrum of psychological functioning across a variety of settings.

Accordingly, we have described a therapeutic process that places self-evaluative thoughts and feelings at the heart of the therapeutic process. We have also described how to use the primary and unique sources of interpersonal learning in marital and family therapy as catalysts for improving not only personal self-esteem, but the underlying attributes of healthy behavior more generally.

10

Family Relations and the Development of Self-Esteem in Children

The impact of parents' behavior upon a child's self-esteem is undeniable; given the immaturity of children, however, parents' expression of their own resolution of the self-esteem question is far more influential than what they teach verbally. Evidence suggests that children are unable to conceptualize a self until the age 8 years or older (Harter, 1983). Moreover, it is not until a child reaches adolescence that he or she can truly use such cognitive material to produce behavior-influencing understanding (Selman, 1980). Thus, whereas parents may understand and attempt to teach valuable concepts of self-esteem, for the child, these concepts must be translated into experiences and feelings rather than described verbally.

The Therapeutic Task

Because this is a book about self-esteem and psychotherapy, the task for the therapist treating self-esteem difficulties in children or in the family becomes even more complex than treating individual adults. First, where in the family structure does the therapist intervene—with the child individually, with the family as a group, or with the parents as a consultant? Second, inherent in the choice is another question: What is the nature of the therapist's influence in each grouping?

There are, of course, major philosophical schools of thought that address these questions, so we will not attempt to answer them here. However, inasmuch as the positioning of the therapist in the relationship is a critical consideration in this book, we will examine very briefly one conceptualization of the factors involved in treating children.

We suggest that there are three components: the knowledge component, the insight component, and the intervention component. The *knowledge* component considers this question: What do the therapist or the parents need to know about the psychology of children and adolescents or the particular child? By definition, children are immature organisms whose phenomenological world differs from that of adults. The component assumes that expert understanding fosters effective intervention as well as emotional acceptance and patience. Through family therapy or consultation, parents respect the child's immaturity, recognize the relevant psychological issues in the child's developmental stage, and discern how they are being viewed by the child. They can then match their teaching or their actions to the child's needs.

The *insight* component is a question directed primarily at the parents: What do parents need to learn, recognize, or change about themselves that will affect their influence efforts? As will be discussed in greater detail later in the chapter, parents bring their own history to the interaction process. By virtue of their early experiences, they will be differentially sensitive to particular issues in the child's life. As they understand themselves better through the therapeutic process, parents experience greater freedom to modify their approach to again match the child's need.

The *intervention* component poses the most complex question for treatment of children, indeed, perhaps for the entire field of psychotherapy: How do therapists structure their interventions to maximize the opportunity for beneficial change? By choosing to see children individually, therapists focus both the knowledge and insight component upon themselves, reparenting the children, as it were. Therapists emphasize their impact upon the affective qualities of the relationship, as models to be imitated or as counselors to children.

If therapists choose to see the family, they spread their influence, affecting the interactions of the family. Here they are likely to use both the knowledge and insight components in the immediacy of communication. The therapist's personality and demonstration of interactive processes continue to serve as a model but more distantly than in individual therapy. Intervention in the family presumes to develop skills, entailing an active, often directly or indirectly instructional stance for the therapist.

As consultants, therapists assume that their focused influence upon the parents will affect the child or children indirectly but powerfully, because of the intensity of the parental relationship as well as the sheer number of hours of interaction. In effect, the therapist assumes that change in the parents will have a reverberating effect in the family.

Finally, a secondary prong of the intervention component entails this question: What form of communication produces behavior change most effectively? Many years of discussion and debate have been devoted to this issue, particularly as regards children. Again, although we will not attempt to describe the polemic, we suggest that a fundamental error is committed by many parents and some therapists: They assume that accurate dispensing of the knowledge component *ought to* provide the necessary and sufficient conditions for change. In other words, they believe that telling equals teaching and that teaching equals behavioral change. However, it does not because a part of anything learned entails an affective element as well as a cognitive one.

An example would be a father "teaching" his child to swim. When the child is frightened of the water, he tells him to relax. However, instructions to relax are generally insufficient modifiers of something as primitive as anxiety about water. When the child continues to be afraid in spite of the father's instruction, he becomes irritated, increasing the volume of his "solution" and the anxiety of the situation for the child. Soon, the child is more afraid of the father than of the water, looking for any avenue of escape from the situation, or dissolving into tears. The child probably will *not* learn to swim, at least not in that session.

In other words, the problem for the therapist and parents is the affective "packaging" of the knowledge or insight. Because behavior change always entails both affective and cognitive parts, influence attempts must consider both in the communication. In the example above, the father correctly recognized that the child needed to relax in order to learn to swim, but doing nothing more than saying so was useless and even counterproductive. The father's real task was to create a learning situation calculated to help the child relax, perhaps by play or initially letting the child ride his back while he swam. The therapist's task is analogous: Whether working directly with the child or consulting with the parents, the therapist must construct interventions that will be "heard" both cognitively and affectively.

In this chapter, we discuss primarily the therapist as a consultant to parents. The therapist's interaction with the child will be in the role of an assessment expert, gathering information about the child's development and personality that will help the parents in their influence attempts. Using that knowledge component, the therapist can then help the parents use more effective parenting strategies. In addition, the therapist addresses the insight component, working directly to treat the parents' self-esteem difficulties, knowing that their influence will be greatest as models of self-esteem. Finally, the therapist can assist the parents to fashion their communications in ways that will match the child's maturity and personality to increase their influence effectiveness.

The structure of the chapter roughly follows the knowledge, insight, and intervention components for the therapist. First, we consider more general issues of developmental processes and common parental practices. The second section focuses on the relevance of parental self-esteem and its consequences for the child. Next, we describe a conceptualization of the changing roles of acceptance, power, and autonomy. The concluding section deals with strategies for implementing particular elements of the self-esteem model with children.

The immediate question is, of course: What are the implications for the parent-child relationship, derived from the self-esteem model presented? Although some of our suggestions coincide with those of earlier writers, it will be seen that the propositions of the model yield concepts that are substantially different from those of Coopersmith and others. We began this book posing a paradox: How is it that so many people who ostensibly have reason to feel a strong sense of self-esteem confess privately to such grave self-doubts and personal beliefs in their own inadequacy? The thematic thrust of our argument has been that the pivotal element in positive self-esteem (in adults, thus far), even the expression of healthy emotional behavior, is the moment-to-moment decision to confront and cope with difficulties rather than avoid them. Our question must be, then, *What can parents do to provide the best possible opportunity for children to develop a stable sense of self-esteem, which ultimately includes the predilection to cope with difficult situations rather than avoid them?*

Assumptions and Caveats

Several assumptions must be mentioned that are integral to our propositions. First, the entire process of developing self-esteem assumes a caring relationship. The qualities of affection and concern for the welfare of the child are so fundamental that we have little to say to parents who are not so emotionally invested. Similarly, therapists' care for their clients is axiomatic. No ethical therapist would presume to treat parents or families without at least a modicum of regard for their well-being.

Next, the development of self-esteem must be considered within the larger developmental process of the child. The nature of the parent-child relationship as well as the tasks of healthy development must change over time. An effective relationship at one time will not necessarily be so worthwhile an influence at a later stage of development. Also, general principles may be functional, yet their expression may need to take a different form. Although we suggest, for example, that acceptance is always important, its communication changes dramatically. (The 2-year-old boy may thrive on a direct "I love you," while the strapping 16-year-old may prefer "Hey, big fella, how's it going today?") The acceptance is identical, but the language has changed. Other relationships, such as the control dimension, shift in both expression and substance to match the child's developmental needs.

A corollary to the developmental assumption is this: Parents all too frequently choose their parenting styles not from a consideration of the child's present need but from the unexamined reservoir of their own experiences in being parented. Having been learned at a more primitive level, their initial, "reflexive" response to exigencies of the moment will be either to repeat their analogous experience or, if they had a strong negative reaction to the event, to react in an opposite fashion, equally without planning. Because parents draw from their affective summary of what it was like for them as children, then, what the child usually receives over time is a thematic and somewhat homogeneous experience. Thus, even caring parents are apt to be more effective at some stages of the child's development and less so at others.

Another assumption is illustrated in this truism: To treat your children in the same way, you have to treat them differently. Children vary considerably, even within families. A parenting strategy used with good effect on one child at age three may be inappropriate for a sibling at that age. Excellent longitudinal studies (Thomas, Chess, & Birch, 1968; Thomas & Chess, 1977) clearly indicate temperamental differences that must be taken into account. In the adolescent years, what is coping for one child may be avoiding for another. Dependent, anxious children will fear challenging or disagreeing with others; whereas the oppositional child, whose interpersonal strategy may be that the-best-defense-is-a-good-offence (misspelling intended), may be most fearful of a warm, cooperative relationship.

A final assumption is that we freely admit that we have been describing an agentive theory in this book. Children, although influenced greatly by parents, are not caused. In spite of their best efforts, some children will not choose the outcomes that parents have prepared for them or interpret the parents' persuasions as they intended them to be perceived. Other significant people (i.e., teachers, peers, even strangers) affect the lives of children in both beneficial and harmful ways, and, in the case of hurtful experiences, children's interpretations may not be

completely countermanded by the efforts of parents or therapists. Such is particularly the case in adolescence, when, for
most, there is a dramatic resurgence of the need to be accepted.
Issues relevant to self-esteem, resolved successfully in childhood, resurface in the search for identity at a time when parental influence may be seen as a threat to self-definition.

Thus, the most expert counsel does not produce inevitable
results, but it may increase understanding, foster planning by
parents, and emphasize critical learning experiences at the appropriate developmental stage, thereby increasing the chances
for fostering self-esteem.

Common Assumptions About Parenting and Self-Esteem

Most of the commonsense approaches to developing self-esteem
are based on the expectation that children gradually internalize
beliefs about themselves that are communicated to them by
their social environment. The reader already knows that the
model presented emphasizes the internal nature of self-esteem
in the adult. However, the tasks of parenting are particularly
complex because children are initially developmentally incapable of responding to an internal set of expectations. Parents
cannot simply determine to teach children to cope and confront
issues as they themselves are doing because the child's balance
between the control of emotions and the control of thinking is
so much different. Fostering a general sense of positive self-
feeling requires an overarching strategy, a *Weltanschauung* or
worldview, that takes into account developmental immaturity
as discussed earlier and planning for parental activities, *which
strategically change as the child matures.*

The importance of the parents' viewpoint and its predicating
influence may be illustrated by the humorous experience of a
colleague and friend. He had just finished his PhD in child psychology. As sometimes happens, he found that his training was
looked at with some suspicion by his relatives, particularly his
in-laws. (Perhaps it is an occupational hazard that, using Cooley's looking-glass self-concept, one's extended family members

expect dentist in-laws to be looking at their children's teeth and psychologist in-laws to be "analyzing" their children's behavior.) At the conclusion of a visit from one such in-law, the mother observed her 3-year-old son riding his cousin's tricycle with great enthusiasm. With some delight at the opportunity for a challenge of my friend's skill (now that he was so smart that he had a PhD in the subject), she said, "Since you are the expert, let's see how you get Johnny to give up the tricycle and come with me." My friend responded, "I'll do what I know how to do." He walked over to Johnny, told him it was time for him to go home now, to please come again some time, and lifted him, screaming, into his mother's car. Johnny's mother drove away, nonplussed, with Johnny still crying mightily. In retelling the story, my friend remarked that it seemed that the goal of many parents was to have their child grow up without crying. His relative may have assumed that the "expert" parent can and should somehow manipulate the child into accepting unpleasant experiences without protest, a goal devoutly desired by most parents by late afternoon.

This story is symbolic of several child-rearing styles of parents, who, though certainly caring, raise children at risk for the chronic difficulties of low self-esteem discussed in this book. Let us consider several parenting theories.

Unconditional love theory. First is the belief that children with high self-esteem are those who have been raised with so much love and praise that they are somehow failure-safe, embarrassment-proof, and humiliation-protected. This unconditional love theory of building self-esteem sometimes uses a metaphor: the love bucket. If parents keep this love bucket full to overflowing, nothing can go wrong. Disappointments must be assuaged and smoothed over quickly, as though they were dangerously infectious. Parents must work overtime to construe reality so the child will never question the self or its abilities. They, therefore, must singlehandedly compete against the possible ego bumps and bruises outside of the family.

The error, of course, is that complex problems, especially human ones, are seldom solved by simply lavishing more praise, or more love, or more money on them. It is, in its nucleus, a defensive, avoidant decision that fears coping with what may be a child's very real shortcomings. This parenting style, therefore, contains the very ingredients that we have suggested foster low self-esteem.

No parent can successfully hover close enough to protect a child from those less caring and less admiring; nor is it helpful. Self-esteem must be of a more robust construction than a child's dependence upon parental praise. Indeed, Adler (Ansbacher & Ansbacher, 1956) wrote eloquently of both the dangers of indulging a child and the beneficial psychological stance inherent in accepting imperfection in oneself. Baumrind (Baumrind, 1963, 1966, 1971, 1975) found preschool children of indulgent parents to be the most unhappy and insecure of the groups she studied. Parents must not teach the child to avoid the honest need for self-appraisal and change.

We have suggested earlier that accurate, negative feedback is a reality for most people. It can be a healthy, if unpleasant, part of the self-evaluation process. Furthermore, parents who unfailingly pursue a course of attempting to contradict external negative feedback will find that the child considers them a less and less credible source of evaluation. Adolescents frequently do anyway, indicating their suspicion of parents' feedback with something like, "Oh, you always say I look good. That's just because you're my mom."

Self-esteem-equals-success theory. A second erroneous theory for developing self-esteem is that parents must see that children have so many training opportunities—dancing, music lessons, athletics, or preschool—that they will be guaranteed some arena in which they are more successful than age-mates. They must be winners in order to feel good about themselves. The self-esteem-equals-success theory assumes that positive self-feeling is in short supply and is available only to the victorious. (Philosophically, William James may be blamed to some extent for the theory, e.g., his successes/pretensions ratio. Our self-esteem depends upon what we back ourselves to be. If we are successful, we have a right to feel self-love.) Parents subscribing to this theory have the oppressive responsibility of assessing the child's gifts and providing the all-important head start in training that will save the child from the dangers of competing without an advantage. Children of average or less than average endowment are doomed either to the tension-ridden effort to become more than they are or to the resignation of inferiority.

The error in this theory is a fundamental and critical one, we believe, one that pervades much of the adult business world. It entails a mistaken focus on *outcome,* that is, on the belief that self-esteem is constructed by the result, the end point, or so-called bottom line of an endeavor. Self-esteem is thought to be a by-product of winning or achieving some goal, a competitive process in which trust and cooperation are irrelevant goals. Although some portion of the assumption is true, in that success brings a sense of accomplishment, we have again suggested that it is neither necessary nor sufficient to produce lasting self-esteem. If children must always win to continue to feel good about themselves, they and their parents must constantly experience the stress of having to do as well or better each time they compete. (Again, we are reminded of one of James's solutions to problems of self-esteem: Abandon some of our pretensions.)

We have asserted, instead, that the *process* is the essential element, that is choosing to cope and to face the difficult challenges. Children can take pride in the effort and the desire committed to an activity without being dependent on external judges declaring them the winners. (When the judge is another child or set of peers, a positive evaluation is risky, at best.) Indeed, we have suggested that positive, self-affirming thoughts and feelings occur when we confront issues, regardless of the outcome. The experiment described in chapter 3 noted that people viewed themselves positively for coping in spite of the anticipation that their coping response might have no effect on the outcome. As T. S. Eliot has said, "For us, there is only the trying. The rest is not our business" (Eliot, 1940).

The social invulnerability theory. A third parenting theory, somewhat similar to the preceding one, assumes that self-esteem equals socialization, that is, if children can be trained so carefully and so well that their behavior is unassailable, they will be safe from the pangs of low self-esteem. This social invulnerability theory negates the possibility of a positive, confident sense of self in favor of protection from criticism. Like the earlier theory, it implies that the evaluation of the self resides in others' judgment, not in one's own. The emotional goal that these parents project onto their children is the absence of dread that one is vulnerable to attack. (The work of George Herbert Mead [1934] bears some distant but recognizable philosophical relationship to this theory and the one following. He suggested that we internalize the voices of significant others; therefore, to feel good about ourselves we must adapt ourselves sufficiently to persuade the voices to approve of us. By that mechanism we can come to say approving things of ourselves.)

Here, the error seems to be more obvious. Striving for invulnerability generates the very anxiety that intensifies the likelihood of avoidance, which we have suggested is the seedbed of pathological behavior. The commitment to impression management as a style of life is evident, as are its deleterious consequences, so amply described by Rogers (1950). By contrast, attempts at definition of the concept of self-esteem in the psychological literature usually have described self-esteem positively, as a confidence-building, "freeing" experience, attended by feelings of competence and self-control. The essential choice to face difficulties requires a willingness to view criticism as an acceptable, even integral (albeit not sought-after), part of the decision. Doing things less than perfectly is "part of the territory."

Self-esteem-equals-belonging theory. A final mistaken child-rearing theory, following the description of Mead's theory above, suggests that because the source of self-esteem is positive affirmation from others, children with high self-esteem are those who are successful at winning approbation. Abandoning the goal of invulnerability as impossible to reach, this self-esteem-equals-belonging theory emphasizes "fitting in," teaching children that they can feel good about themselves when they can get others to accept them. Emphasizing obedience and conformity, these parents teach great sensitivity to social nuance and custom. Children are trained to consider offending someone as the source of greatest social danger; they will experience anxiety or a sense of threatening obligation until the breach of acceptance is healed. The family ethic, spoken or unspoken, is, "What will people think?"

This style of seeking positive self-feeling is as futile as the effort to be invulnerable because it also depends totally upon the appraisals of others. Impression management is ingredient in the life-style because children must mold and adapt themselves to meet the perceived demands of those from whom they have chosen to seek approval.

Referring to our earlier discussion, genuine positive feedback is apt to be received with disbelief because children may conclude that the praise is due only to their skill at presenting themselves. Individuals cannot experience more than a fleeting sense of self-confidence when they are aware that their position depends upon pleasing an audience. By definition, they have created a position in which they are inferior. They cannot rely upon their own internal feedback because others are always the final judges of their performance. Constantly seeking feedback from others, therefore, they can never be sure of its veracity when they are so certain of their own dissembling.

Parenthetically, as clinicians we have frequently observed that clients who in therapy describe themselves as pleasers have a deeply felt wish to be accepted just as they are. They express their fatigue and resentment at "having to put on a show" for everyone. Yet, when asked to describe who they really are, they seldom can express a definition, having devoted themselves so exclusively to impression management. Although initially they seem unacquainted with their own self-evaluative thoughts, some practice produces a realization of intense self-disapproval.

We do not wish to denigrate the importance of belonging. Choosing to listen only to one's own feelings or fearing intimate, and therefore binding, relationships is not an answer, representing instead a different form of insecurity. We assume that positive self-esteem includes belonging, but that it is accompanied by the feeling of being equal to others, not dependent. If one's essential definition is that of being equal to others, one can listen to both inside and outside voices.

Although there certainly are other, similar theories regarding the development of self-esteem, we consider the four listed as being the most common. Note that our focus was on strategies of caring parents who want happiness for their children. We have not considered the effects of destructive styles, for example, when parents are indifferent or even hostile to the child's welfare. We do so now briefly.

Indifferent and hostile parenting styles. It goes without saying that parental attitudes of neglect and cruelty do *not* enhance self-esteem (either in the child or the parents). We earlier noted evidence that children before the age of 8 years are incapable of articulating a separate sense of self (Harter, 1983), and they are hence unable to define themselves otherwise than that which is communicated by parents. Thus, indifferent or rejecting parents variously teach children that they are intrusive burdens to be borne, or incompetent competitors for the scarce resources of the family, or somehow even that they are enemies within the family, deserving of the parents' vituperation. Inside the cognitive immaturity of the young child, the interpretation of events requires causes, usually one-dimensional, sequential explanations. Therefore, being hurt, chastised, or pointedly ignored is equivalent to being punished, and being punished means to children they must have done something wrong. Unable to recognize the possibility that their parents' responses to them may be coming from the parents' own unresolved difficulties, the children blame themselves, coming to believe that they are somehow defective, unable to be good enough to be loved.

It is interesting to note that, in spite of such difficult beginnings, some children from neglecting or abusive backgrounds emerge from childhood surprisingly intact. We suggest that there are two crucial, related elements that may explain such survivors of deleterious child-rearing environments: consistency and a distorted form of non-impression-management parenting. Parents who are consistently harsh provide at least a predictable environment from which children can learn skills and *must* learn self-reliance if they are to survive. They may indeed develop a certain resilience from being forced to cope with their nonsupportive surroundings. (The damage to their emotional-affectional lives as adults is often serious, however.)

Also, parents who make no pretense of their hostility toward their children are similarly predictable. In that sense, these parents do not attempt to manage impressions of themselves to the children, and, for their part, the children may learn to cope with their parents' response to them. On the other hand, parents who insist verbally on their love and concern while betraying their hostility in other subtle ways present the child with a much more complex and threatening task. Indeed, early research in psychopathology suggests that a totally unpredictable environment may be the circumstance of most harm to psychological development (Bateson, Jackson, Haley, & Weakland, 1956). Johnson, Giffin, Watson, and Beckett (1956) observed, with regard to 27 schizophrenic child patients and their families, that:

> When these children perceived the anger and hostility of a parent, as they did on many occasions, immediately the parent would deny that he was angry and would insist that the child deny it too, so that the child was faced with the dilemma of whether to believe the parent or his own senses. If he believed his senses, he maintained a firm grip on reality; if he believed the parent, he maintained the relationship but distorted his perception of reality. Repeated parental denial resulted in the child's failure to develop adequate reality testing. (p. 143)

Thus, in an extreme and backward fashion, these observations illustrate the fundamental error in choosing impression management as a means of pursuing self-esteem, either personally or as a parent.

Discussion

Except for the indifferent and hostile parenting styles just described, there is an underlying theme for each strategy considered that harks back to the summary of early writers on self-esteem in chapter 2: Rejection and the fear of rejection are twin sides of *the* malevolent force that destroys positive self-feeling. Simply put, people fear being pushed away and alone. (Recall William James's [1890/1981] comment quoted earlier: "No more fiendish punishment could be devised, were such a thing physically possible, than that one should be turned into society and remain absolutely unnoticed by all the members thereof.") The experience of self-esteem is assumed to be ultimately social, therefore, referenced and calibrated by the response from other people or in comparison to them.

We do not question the fundamental importance of acceptance and nurturance, but the assumptions have not gone far enough. Greenwald and Breckler (1985) described the development of the self proceeding through four stages: the *diffuse* self, or a self that has not been differentiated; the *public* self, which derives its definition from the feedback of others; the *private* self, wherein true self-definition commences and an identity is established; and the *collective* self, in which the self becomes egoless, identifying with concerns of larger groups. We have suggested earlier that the child grows up needing acceptance, but that the balance between acceptance and individuality shifts gradually toward individuality and a greater need for acceptance from oneself. It is the internal decision of what one must do to approve of oneself that is the touchstone for self-esteem in the adult. *Thus, the critical mistake in the common parenting styles is that parents oriented toward avoiding rejection train only for the development of the public self. The question of fostering the child's development of a private self may remain unasked and unanswered.*

Of course, some of the blame for parents' focusing exclusively on the development of the public self rests with the fact that they have not been focusing at all. They want the children to be happy and successful, but they also do not want them to be a source of trouble or concern. Like the mother of the child on his cousin's bicycle, a parent's de facto goal may be to raise the children with as little difficulty as possible, preferring pleasing, obedient children to ones who, in their adolescence, become responsive to their own approval. It is disconcerting even to democratic parents to have their children reach conclusions that are different from the ones they themselves have reached. Solipsism, the problem of assuming that one's conclusions are the only correct ones, is not limited to the young.

Parenthetically, an important, usually overlooked consequence of this generic "pleasing-us-is-best-for-you" expectation is an interesting incongruity: parents expect their sons or daughters never to disagree with them, *yet to be noncompliant* when pressured by peers to use drugs or violate other family values. Although these children may in fact refuse to participate in such situations, they are simply unprepared by experience to know how to disagree amicably. Later in the chapter, we will discuss the proposition that parents must foster the opportunity for the child to learn to say "No" to significant others, on the basis of merit and rationality.

Here, then, is one of the fundamental elements in the answer to our question of developing self-esteem: *Parents must planfully attend to the process of fostering the development of the internal component, the private self, which enjoys acceptance but is prepared to prefer self-approval to that of others when necessary.*

Concept Summary

Having considered a number of general issues relevant to the process of parents' fostering self-esteem in their children, we summarize concepts that the therapist can use in the treatment of families with self-esteem difficulties:

1. Child-rearing strategies of parents must accommodate the developmental stage and the individual personality of the child. The therapist can assist parents in assessing the unique position of each child in the family to develop a conceptualization of his or her present needs. As in our earlier discussion of intervention, the therapist can coach parents in the language of its presentation, especially when the language must be long-term, nonverbal, or even nonconceptual.

2. Through the interview process, the therapist can help parents evaluate their own "childhood-constructed" expectations about parenting, assisting them to become more aware of their communication style and planful in modifying it to meet their child's needs. Frequently, the therapist can do much to help the child by helping the parents work through unresolved issues in their own lives. Through consultation with the therapist, parents can learn to be more consistent and predictable, providing a collateral benefit for the child.

3. For the sake of both the child and the parents, the therapist must stress the value of focusing on process, not on outcome. Parents must accept the agency of the child, recognizing that their best efforts may not be immediately or even ultimately successful in enhancing the child's self-esteem. However, they

will foster their own self-esteem by remembering that they also must focus on process, not outcome, coping with what the child may need as well as the possible frustration attendant upon the child's not using the experiences for growth. In addition, the therapist can teach parents both to encourage the child to focus on trying and to learn themselves to take pride in the process of the child's activities rather than the end-point achievements.

4. The therapist must model as well as teach the positive, robust nature of self-esteem, in which negative as well as positive feedback is an accepted ingredient, shortcomings are essential parts of being human, and displeasure, even rejection, of some people is to be expected and accepted.

5. The therapist can help parents become aware of the importance of the child's developing the private self as adolescence approaches. They must anticipate that the child does not always have to please them. When parents respect the child's need to develop individuality, the child becomes more aware of and responsive to inner direction. A particular strategy, illustrated in greater detail later in the chapter, may be to encourage deliberately that the child disagree on merit.

6. The therapist's most important task with parents is to attend to the parents' authenticity, emphasizing the fundamental bankruptcy of impression management, a recurrent theme of this book.

Parental Self-Esteem

We propose that the degree to which parents have resolved their own questions of personal self-esteem will have more influence on their children than anything they might attempt to teach them verbally. In considering the proposition and its implications for treatment of self-esteem difficulties in the family, we address in a broad context the insight component described earlier in the chapter.

Several lines of evidence in psychology converge to underscore the importance of the parents' example in teaching self-esteem. We noted earlier Harter's (1983) conclusion that children before the age of 8 years are generally maturationally unable to recognize a separate sense of self. In other words, the formation of an "I" who observes and influences the "me" does not occur until at least middle childhood. Even then, developmental theories of both cognition (Flavell, 1985) and personality (Erikson, 1968) suggest that it is not until adolescence that children become truly self-conscious, using the capacity of self-reflection to study themselves and thereby choose to alter behavior. This is not, of course, to suggest that children are not learning about the self. Hardly! The major proportion of the self-definition upon which the adolescent and adult reflect is formed in the early years. It is simply that the learning comes primarily from observing parents and significant others and receiving messages about oneself through their actions. When adolescents are prepared to use the skills of self-reflection, it is as though they found much of the basic structure of the self already in place, as though their self-beliefs were unquestioned givens.

A related conceptual track emphasizes the power of modeling in influencing behavior (see Bandura, 1986, for a review). The role of observation and imitation is amply demonstrated to be one of the fundamental sources of learning for the child. Moreover, the elements that increase the model's influence—warmth, identification, and prestige—are all present in the healthy parent-child relationship.

Therefore, parents must recognize that their children will learn more from their example than from anything they may tell them. The parents' actions, their problem-solving approaches, and their responses to stress represent a one- or two-person seminar on life. For the young child, whose self-esteem so fundamentally pivots on being accepted, parents' attitudes toward themselves—whether prizing or indifference or rejection—are unavoidably communicated.

The most central aspect of the modeling process, therefore, focuses on the parents' congruence, their personal demonstration of authenticity, or, on the other hand, their dissimulation and pretense in avoiding issues. So many parents assume that they must pretend to be what they are not *for the sake of the child*. We suggest that what children will learn, then, is *to pretend to be what they are not*, with all the consequences that the choice of impression management entails. Contrary to expectation, we propose that, for the sake of the child, parents permit the child to observe their struggles, their difficulties, and their conflicts *because struggling is a primary coping response.*

Thus, the parent's authenticity—the willingness to face difficulties, to recognize methods of avoidance and seek congruence—is critical. In that sense, all the apparently adult concepts of this book are indirectly but clearly influential in developing self-esteem in children. Children may not be able to describe how they feel about themselves for choosing to avoid problems, but they will most surely observe its effect.

It is ironic that some parents see healthy self-esteem for themselves as a wishful dream but are most anxious to do anything they can to protect their children from similar pain. They may view a search for their own positive self-feeling as being egoistic, detracting from the needs of their children. Their message is masked as self-sacrifice, but ultimately is perceived by the child as evidence that the world's demands are threatening. Worse still, the client is asked to learn to cope with those demands while observing a most intimate model who does not.

Self-Esteem *Weltanschauung*

In discussing the elements of parenting that form the self-esteem-enhancing worldview, or *Weltanschauung*, one must note that the worldview is equally important for the therapist, if not more so. Focusing on the knowledge component of therapy, in this section we construct a template that the therapist can use to assess the particular family's need for change. Although we present our findings as numbered conclusions, they are not mutually exclusive. Several are closely related to earlier conclusions or are extensions of them.

1. Optimism, either in therapy or parenting, is therapeutic.

Parenting can be complex; there are too many ideas or principles to think about and too little time to do them all. Any book about psychology or parenting runs the risk of suggesting so many considerations that the parent becomes paralyzed, unable to decisively act as a parent. Thus, in the midst of the complexity of consulting with parents, it is vital that parents see the therapist's optimism about the challenge of the task. Because one of the corresponding attitudes of esteem is confidence, to approach solving self-esteem problems with children anxiously is ironically futile. Therapists, demonstrating their own enjoyment of the issues, can encourage parents to accept parenting as the challenging, rigorous, frustrating, sometimes disappointing, but rewarding task that it is. As they develop their skills, particularly experiencing their own authenticity, parents can be encouraged to trust their instincts more, corroborating the growth of their competence.

Naturally, the parents' optimism is important to the child. During the early years, children look out at the outside world through their parents' eyes. When children see their parents approach difficulties with energy and a willingness to cope, they will be more likely to define the world as an exciting and challenging place to be, not a place to be approached apprehensively. Similarly, children will see themselves in their parents' eyes. The parents' expression of confidence in dealing with and helping children solve problems will significantly reassure them that difficulties can be temporary.

2. The three dimensions of parenting are acceptance, expectations, and autonomy.

The earlier review of research in parental characteristics associated with the development of self-esteem highlighted three dimensions: parental warmth, expectations for performance, and respect for the child's individuality (which we abbreviated above to acceptance, expectations, and autonomy). The findings suggest that parents of high-self-esteem children are seen as being relatively higher on each parenting dimension than are parents of low-self-esteem children; that is, the parents combine high warmth with high expectations and high respect for individuality. The therapist can evaluate parental values along the dimensions and plan interventions to assist parents to adjust toward a healthier balance.

Once again, however, we suggest that most models of self-esteem have not gone far enough. The findings provided by Coopersmith (1967, 1969) and Baumrind (1963, 1966, 1971) in their separate research describe a static picture of parental characteristics. We have proposed that, although the values remain constant, their form must change to match the child's readiness for movement from external acceptance to internal acceptance, from external expectations to internal expectations, and from parental granting of latitude for individuality to internal autonomy. Each of these dimensions will be considered briefly.

Acceptance

To young children, nothing looms so large in their psychological world as their perception of being important in their parents' lives. The ubiquity of children's need to be loved, to feel that they occupy a central place in their parents' eyes, and to know that they belong in the family is evident in many aspects of child-rearing, from sibling rivalry to the negative dependence of an adolescent.

The child's experience of being accepted inside the family is vital throughout development, but it is critical in the formative years before adolescence. When children doubt their place, the otherwise normal stresses outside the family are exacerbated. We recall a client in her mid-thirties, struggling still to overcome the residual effects of a childhood of abuse. A devastating moment in her childhood came when she realized that she was different from the other children in the third grade. Most of the girls were climbing on the jungle gyms in the playground when she noticed with shock that none of the other girls had holes in their panties. She knew with shame that she had no underpants without holes, nor were they ever as clean as those she glimpsed on the bars above her. She never played on the bars again, for fear of others' recognition of her differentness.

Now, as an adult, this woman viewed the event as pivotal in her belief of not belonging and of being inferior. Yet, as she allowed herself to remember the experiences of her childhood, she recognized that the playground and her panties represented the humiliating secret of feeling unsafe in her home, which she was terrified to have anyone discover.

In the example, the client did not recall that she was not accepted at school; her sense of not belonging in the family undermined her self-esteem anywhere else. Most clinicians have encountered clients as adults whose most deeply felt hurt is of not being good enough to feel truly loved by their parents. As one might expect, their presenting complaints are those of trying vainly to please others and *not feeling accepted.* It is, therefore, the undeniable sense of belonging in the family that frees the child to leave to seek other attachments. The primary reason for the child's confidence is that the parents' external acceptance, so critical in childhood, has become internal. Children carry it with them, and they enjoy, but are not vulnerably dependent upon, acceptance from others.

Expectations

We hasten to add expectations or the power dimension to acceptance because it indicates both a more active process than might be connoted by acceptance and an awareness of the need to look beyond nurturing to the development of competence. The concept of unconditional love seems to be particularly misdirecting. Diana Baumrind (1975), preferring the idea of commitment, expresses the comparison articulately:

> The parent who expresses love unconditionally is encouraging the child to be selfish and demanding while she herself is not. Thus she reinforces exactly the behavior which she does not approve of—greedy, demanding, inconsiderate behavior. . . . On the other hand, I do believe that to the extent possible, a parent's *commitment* to the child should be unconditional. That is, the parent should stay contained *in* the experience with the child, no matter what the child does. . . . The parent continues to care for the child because it is her child and not because of the child's merits. Since she is human, the quality of her feeling for him depends upon the child's actions, but her interest in his welfare does not depend upon his actions and is abiding. This abiding interest is expressed not in gratifying the child's whims, nor in being gentle and kind with him, nor in approval of his actions, nor even in approving of what he is as a person. Unconditional *commitment* means that the child's interests are perceived among the parent's most important interests. . . . (p. 278)

Thus, acceptance exists side by side with expectations for age-appropriate performance. Parents know they must look beyond the pull of current desires or fears of the child—as well as their own impulses to indulge—to the concern for developing maturity.

Consistent, reasonable demands for working hard are the prime mover for the sense of self-confidence so integral to self-esteem. Because performance requires skills, parents must accept their responsibility as trainers. They must model, teach, and assist their children until they determine that the children know how to do what is expected of them. Beyond that, as a general rule, parents must then expect children to do what they can for themselves. In that way, children's sense of efficacy in the family and the larger world grows. Their sense of belonging in the family is enhanced by contribution to family maintenance tasks, such as household chores or yard care.

Again, we suggest that parental demand for performance, an external expectation, leads developmentally to internal expectations *and* confidence in meeting those expectations. Reasonable discipline from parents through middle childhood puts into place the structure from which the child experiences confidence in his or her self-discipline as an adolescent.

Autonomy

Coopersmith, Baumrind, and other theorists of parental antecedents of self-esteem agree that competent, high-self-esteem children experienced parental respect for their individuality. Thus, juxtaposed with the bonding and controlling elements that, left unmitigated, would foster the pathologically enmeshed family, parents' active willingness to encourage differentiation adds the vital dimension of autonomy. Carl Rogers (1950) premised much of his theory of psychotherapy on the need of individuals to respect their personal uniqueness.

Earlier in the chapter, we described the unfortunate sequelae to persons who, having tried hard to meet others' definitions of worth, had never developed their own. Parents must encourage, not just passively allow, differences to foster children's skill in hearing their own voice, recognizing what they themselves feel and desire. What initially may appear to be willful egocentricity in young children gives way to an interactive process between parents and children by which they learn to know themselves. The interaction of learning to differentiate self from others continues with peers and finally becomes the internal dialogue that builds the self-definition known as identity.

Given the overall thrust of the book, it is not surprising that we see this element of parenting as fundamental to the development of self-esteem. Indeed, we have even suggested and will elaborate in the next section the importance of the child's learning to disagree in the family. Moreover, we have proposed that the amelioration of self-esteem difficulties requires that the therapist assist the client in recognizing the self-evaluative processes. Any person must be reasonably sensitive to his or her own feelings and values to ask, "What must I do in this situation to approve of myself?"

3. The control relationship between parent and child shifts gradually to match developmental needs.

It is within the control dimension that parents are required to be most alert to the child's maturing; more strategic alterations in their parenting are dictated here than in the other dimensions. Parents, whose goal it is to prepare the child to be an adult with good self-esteem, must planfully modify their control of the child's life to match his or her readiness for responsibility and decision making. It is a complex task for several reasons. First, the learning residue of the parents' history is particularly germane to the issue of control. The amalgam of childhood memories is apt to foster a homogeneous, even rigid, response to the task of disciplining one's children. Much of a family therapist's work, where adolescents are involved, focuses on the issue of control—parental domination or abdication of control, and the child's rebellion or anxieties created by parental control.

Second, parents apply their experience with older siblings to the younger ones even though it may not be appropriate. Unfortunately, the trauma of an older brother's or sister's mistakes sometimes impels parents to knee-jerk, unwarranted attempts at control, which may provoke (in the younger siblings) the very situation the parents are seeking to avoid.

Finally, almost by definition, the maturation process dictates that children will test limits. Parents must be sensitive to the children's development, discerning between the children's desire for power and their readiness for the attendant responsibility.

With those complexities in mind, we suggest, in broad outlines, a declining power curve in which parental control shifts gradually from total control (vertical) to influence by permission (lateral).

Infants. Schematically, the parent–child relationship during infancy is vertical, or nearly so, as shown in the diagram below:

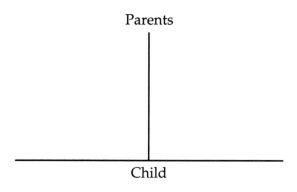

At this stage, the child is completely dependent upon the parents for nurturance and protection. We have suggested that the major component, at this age, for later self-esteem is the child's sense of being loved and belonging within the family. Erikson's (1963) theory of developmental stages emphasized the essential need for the child to reach out for acceptance and have the parents reach back. The child's latitude for expressing individuality at this stage may be limited to that which is already present by virtue of biological temperament.

Yet, even in such immaturity, the thrill of growing and doing for oneself is clear. Anyone who has observed the total delight of a child taking his or her first steps can see the power of functionally autonomous reinforcement. In those moments, the child may appreciate praise but does not need it. Indeed, research on intrinsic versus extrinsic reinforcement (Lepper, 1983) suggests that children feel more motivation to continue to achieve if they experience their own reward rather than being rewarded by parents. It is certainly true that many a parent, thinking to encourage a child who is singing in solitary play, offers praise, only to find that the child stops upon recognizing that he or she was being observed.

Preschoolers. As children grow, emerging abilities provide opportunities for developing age-appropriate competencies and learning socialization, such as sharing and cooperative play. Their cognitive immaturity still dictates that most of the control for their lives must be external, residing in parents, older siblings, or teachers. As mentioned, Baumrind (1975) found that preschool children were already the beneficiaries of parental styles that combined warmth with high expectations for maturity and respect for individuality. In the preschool period, the power relationship might be visualized as shown in the diagram below:

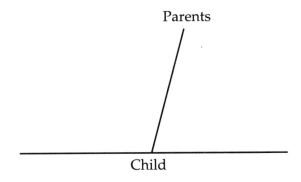

The parents' focus for the child, at this age, begins to combine acceptance with expectations for performance, even though performance may be somewhat limited, such as to self-help, obedience, and basic socialization skills. Autonomy issues also have their beginnings. Parents must decide how to deal with the child's dislike of certain foods. Particularly important is the confusion between feelings and actions. Although it may be several years before the discrimination is well learned, the child can hear that it may be acceptable to experience anger, but that it is unacceptable to act out those feelings in certain ways.

The continuing parenting principle is to balance control, which provides clear expectations and boundaries, with appropriate latitude to match the child's readiness for expression of responsibility and individuality. Thus, parents discuss and agree upon what the child can be expected to do, and they provide the training necessary for the child to meet those expectations. They designate activities in which the child may choose without interference. They continue to respect age-appropriate immaturity, recognizing that growth is saltatory, not continuous. In other words, parents accept that the child will occasionally disappoint them; however, those lapses in maturity do not cause them to rescind opportunities immediately.

Midchildhood. Midchildhood, or the latency period, is a time in which the development of skills is essential in the establishment of self-esteem. Children are now in school, comparing themselves daily to peers. Total acceptance by parents without regard to accomplishment becomes suspect as the demand increases for the child to accept his or her place in a larger group. Harter's (1982, 1983) research evidenced the emergence of the importance of competence for feelings of self-worth. Praise or expressions of affection can be tied more effectively to actual activities by which the child can acquire a sense of efficacy. Parental time with the child also shifts somewhat from entertainment time together to learning and skill-building time. Participation in household and personal maintenance increases the child's sense of belonging as a contributing member. Presumably, the child's sense of self emerges during this time; in Greenwald's and Breckler's (1985) terms, the public self is the focus of development.

Individual differences continue to gradually set the trajectory for the child's later definition of self as a unique personality. Although the potential for rebellion is still relatively small, parental respect for the child's expression of preferences, within limits, can "put money in the bank" for the relationship when the feelings of need for latitude intensify, that is, the parents' willingness to understand and respond respectfully to their children's choices gives the parents leverage when they must ask the children to do things that they do not want to do. The power relationship may look something like this:

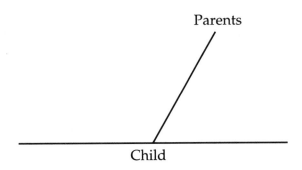

Parents

Child

Preadolescence. As the latency period of a child wanes, there are important value issues that are nonnegotiable, but the parents realize that the child's growing cognitive abilities permit generalization. Parents can now expect children to recognize the general principles of the family's values; they can give up reciting rules in favor of asking children to judge their own behavior. Belongingness in the family is assumed, and the parents' nurturance has shifted somewhat to create an image for the child of a "safe place" to discuss the challenges and disappointments of the outside world. That does not mean that the child is protected from negative feedback; it is, instead, an integral part of the atmosphere of the home. The high levels of trust ensure that feedback is seen as task-oriented requests for change, not hurtful personal criticism.

At this age, a critical element for the establishment of the private self emerges. Up to this point, the parents' agenda for the child has been the process of teaching skills, teaching rules and then principles, and teaching the self-discipline that accompanies obedience. The child will have learned the confidence that attends knowing what is appropriate in given social circumstances.

Now the child enters the time in which the parents allow enough latitude to learn the essential skill of *disagreeing* amicably. As one of the distinguishing features of our model, we suggest that a fundamental way of fostering self-esteem overlooked by most parents is the skill of expressing differences with others rationally. Beginning at a time when the child's desire to please is still strong and authority is accepted, parents can agree that, in some arenas of behavior, the child can choose *and win* an argument in spite of their objections. This process assumes that parents are communicating their willingness to respect the child's individuality.

It is not only important that children learn to disagree reasonably, but that they experience making a choice that is at variance with their parents' counsel, yet still maintaining as strong a caring relationship with them. Children learn that differences can exist without endangering their sense of belonging to the family, that sometimes they have to (and have the right to) make decisions at variance with those they would like to please. Thus, children begin to learn the complex, important skill of recognizing internally how they feel and of arguing rationally for respect for their choices, and by the time peers attempt to persuade them to take drugs, children can be comfortable in refusing. They will already have had the experience of being noncompliant with people whose acceptance is much more important than that of peers. As the diagram shows below, the power relationship continues to become more lateral:

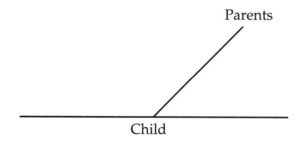

Parents

Child

Parents' choices of appropriate arenas for disagreement are important, of course. They must not give children latitude to make choices where they are not willing to let them experience the results of an ill-advised choice; nor is it helpful for children to experience more power than responsibility. If parents accede to children's irrational, emotional demands, later hurt is guaranteed when they encounter authorities such as schoolteachers, coaches, or police. The opportunities that the parents choose as appropriate for disagreement may seem trivial to the onlooker, but it is in exactly those small issues that the child can enjoy developing confidence in being different without threatening fundamental family values. For example, the child may want to buy shoes that the parents think are too expensive or that might not be appropriate for their intended use. In that arena, they can ask the child to justify buying the shoes and to deal with their objections. Then, they may respond with, "Although we don't agree with you, if that is what you want, we will buy the shoes and you can earn the money for the extra amount." Children thus experience their parents' trust in making their own decisions (in certain arenas), and they experience the accomplishment of listening to and representing the self when it would be safer to acquiesce.

Adolescence. During adolescence, when the child may be in the throes of self-questioning, it is important that the power relationship be shifted laterally enough so that differentiation from parents is an accepted process and that it is not being confused with the turmoil of other value choices. When adolescents believe that the parental control / respect-for-individuality ratio is unfair, they may come to define parents' love in terms of, "Don't you trust me?" Adolescents are by now well aware of their parents' values. If adolescents decide to force a more lateral relationship in a power conflict, they are well prepared to hurt the parents, violating the parents' most important values as a weapon in the conflict, even though the adolescents may hold the same values themselves. The schematic of the relationship may look like this:

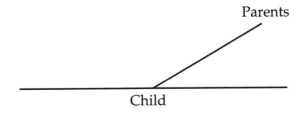

Also, if parents have accepted the differentiation process, they are in a position to be confidantes to their children because the children will know that discussing concerns with their parents will not limit their latitude to choose. Thus, as mentioned, parents may be of considerably more influence than they would be if they had continued to intrude into the children's lives. They do not abdicate being parents and retaining the responsibility to demand respect for critical family ethics (there are still some nonnegotiable values) nor do they attempt to be laissez-faire buddies who do not disagree or who hope to wield influence by passive unconditional acceptance.

Recent research regarding the development of the self (Harter, 1983) suggested a resurgence of the child's concern for acceptance during adolescence, with the significant difference being that the judges of acceptability now are the child's peers. The parents' control of the child's sense of self via their nurturance wanes and may even become suspect during the most turbulent times of striving for identity. It is hoped, however, that the necessary tools for the continued construction of self-esteem are in place.

A second theme relevant for self-esteem that is proposed to emerge during adolescence is that of the development of self-control. Several theoretical concepts converge here: the individual's striving for identity, the quest for self-consistency, and, presumably, the development of the private self. Although we will suggest that it begin earlier, it is at this stage that parents can most effectively use the verbal procedures of the self-esteem model, assisting the adolescent to recognize self-evaluative processes and their consequences for self-esteem.

Toward the end of adolescence, the parental power relationship will be complete, and it will look something like the diagram below:

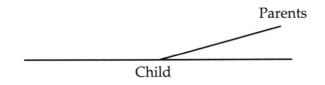

Parents

Child

The parents will still be viewed as parents, but their role will be approximately that of beloved advisors or mentors. The relationship will never be completely lateral because of the child's respect for the history of the parents' commitment. Children know that they are free to ask for their parents' counsel and equally free to choose their own direction. They know that the parents' commitment is abiding. Again, they recognize that commitment comes with expectations. The violation of particularly deeply held family values cannot be tolerated, and children know that. Although they are free to choose, those violations would, out of mutual understanding, require that children live out of the home. For the parents, relinquishing the need to control is their best assurance that the children's choices will be rational, not reactive.

Intervention Component Issues

In therapy as in life, there is always too much information being communicated from moment to moment to use it all. The therapist must deliberately choose the point of entry, the strategic portions of the event flow on which to apply change techniques. We have already suggested that the most important task for the therapist in treating self-esteem difficulties in the family is to assist the parents in resolving their personal self-esteem problems. Two final considerations are discussed, one in which the task is little more than helping parents recognize the implications of the choices in the parenting dimensions, and another that transposes some of the verbal concepts of the model for parents.

1. If parents must choose among parenting dimensions, the acceptance/bonding dimension is the most important.

Given that therapists will be working with families because something has gone wrong, they must frequently assist the family to restore or, perhaps, create for the first time the balance of the parenting dimensions discussed. We suggest that many parents come to therapy agitated because their control techniques are not working. Their predictable response to problems with children is to intensify their efforts and in effect, to try harder to do *what is already not working*. Therapists must frequently assist parents to choose a more adaptive ordering of priorities among the dimensions, "picking their fights," as it were. While it is certainly true that occasionally parents may need to intensify their control of the child, we propose that most often the primary dimension to restore is the sense of acceptance and belonging, which provides leverage for parental control.

Parents certainly have had more experience than the child with the exigencies of life, and their relatively broader purview provides perspective that the child does not possess. Their influence on the child as guides in developing self-esteem, strengthens as they continue to be accepted as credible authorities. Yet, the time comes in all children's lives when the only reason for continuing to value their parents' counsel or direction is that they cannot deny their parents' commitment to them. Other parental means of exercising control, such as intimidation or guilt, diminish with the child's developing maturity and frequently even become the sources of unreasoning opposition. Adolescents are especially sensitive to disingenuousness, reacting immediately to the perception of being manipulated, even when they know that it may be in their best interests. (Ironically, a son may express the effectiveness of Dad's modeling by being as stubborn and willful as he is; Dad's determination to control is vitiated by his very demand.) Manipulation is anathema to a person engaged in defining the self as an individual. Thus, even parents who perceive themselves as desiring their child's success may find themselves shut out by dint of their overweening attempts to control. Again, the importance of the personal authenticity of parents looms large.

Children who enjoy a strong sense of identification with and respect toward their parents will feel the pull of reciprocity in being considerate of their parents' wishes, because the children recognize the parents' desire to be responsive to legitimate concerns. Children can trust their parents' motives for them, knowing that they are prized but acknowledged as separate entities. Children will feel free to express concerns, doubts, or hopes when they know that their parents will not attempt to force their solutions to problems on the children. Parents will find that their counsel, although it must compete with other sources as the child grows, maintains its favored position of trust. Just as important, they will find the child apt to forgive parental mistakes, recognizing their abiding concern in spite of occasional lapses.

2. As the child matures, parents can use the verbal concepts of the model.

Herein, the therapist can act somewhat like a behavioral coach. Earlier, we discussed how important it is that the parents be authentic themselves. The degree of their congruence and self-esteem will do much to encourage the child's own efforts. The child, observing and identifying with the parents' determination to face conflict situations, will be more apt to accept the anxiety inherent in such circumstances as unwanted but also as unavoidable and, therefore, acceptable.

Parents must use their experiences and those of the child as they observe them to talk about the events, their feelings, and their perception of the outcome. Without preaching, they can use activities as they occur as in vivo experiments in self-esteem enhancement. Knowing that they serve as models for imitative learning, parents can augment the learning effect by verbalizing the process as it takes place.

An example might be: The parent verbalizes a conflict situation, "I think there is a misunderstanding between me and Mrs. Jones, our neighbor. I need to talk to her about [situation]." Next, the parent verbalizes the anxieties attendant on coping with the conflict, "But I don't want to say anything about it. I might get mad and say something I would regret, or she might misunderstand me and the situation would get even worse. I wish she would just realize [solution]. I get nervous when I think about having to say something difficult to someone I don't know well." Now, the parent verbalizes the consequences of avoiding the conflict and models the decision to confront instead, "But I know if I don't say anything, probably nothing will improve. And I won't feel good about myself, because I never feel good about me when I feel as though I've been too afraid to do what needs to be done. So I'm going to do my best to work this out with Mrs. Jones. It still may not work, but I'll feel better for having tried." Of course, it is essential that the parent then proceed to confront the situation and report its consequences, emphasizing self-evaluative thoughts. "Well, I'm really glad I did that. [Describe the resolution.] You know, whenever I face these situations instead of avoiding them, I feel good about myself. I feel as though I can handle the problems that occur."

Thus, children will become familiar with the concepts as well as their own self-evaluations, moving toward the quintessential question for the model: "What must I do in this circumstance in order to approve of myself?"

Recognizing the importance of facing and coping with difficult situations, parents will also watch for situations in which children feel anxiety and unwillingness to face something; the parents then support them as they face it anyway. It is most important that parents gently and judiciously insist that children face their conflict circumstances. The parents can then discuss the process of coping, helping the child to learn the difference between having to do something that isn't easy or is unpleasant and having to do something that is "awful." Then, as they see the child facing issues, parents can ask, "How do you feel about yourself for [doing what needed to be done]?" They can help children to recognize and notice self-approving feelings, and emphasize their consequences. Parents can help children realize that they will feel stronger, more courageous, more in control, and that they won't need parents or anyone else at those times to tell them.

Similarly, when the child is struggling with decisions, parents can ask, "What do you have to do to approve of yourself in this situation?" When the child is clearly avoiding an issue, they can increase the child's accountability to the self by asking, "How do you feel about what you are doing right now?" Although this process requires a relatively high level of cognitive and emotional maturity, the children will "teach" their parents their readiness for such reflection by their response to the process. There are times, of course, when the child knows well enough that repeating the probing questions may be not only unnecessary but provocative. The parents' knowing smile and continued insistence on coping will convey the message without occasioning resentment.

Summary and Conclusion

The therapist's tasks in treating self-esteem difficulties in the family are diverse—as an assessment expert, teacher, model of attitudes, behavioral coach, and therapist to parents. The most important therapeutic goal, we have suggested, is that parents recognize *and cope with* the fundamental importance of their own authenticity, in the presence of their children. In addition but subsidiary to the parents' self-esteem, we have described parenting dimensions and a developmentally paced process for inculcating relevant attitudes about self-esteem in the child or adolescent. Assuming the parents' genuine desire for the child's welfare, the therapist can use the concepts presented as a template by which to prepare a treatment plan for the family.

Finally, a note to the therapist. To the degree to which a therapist acts as a substitute parent (*in loco parentis*) to a client, we believe it to be important that he or she follow the principles of parenting set forth in this chapter. The therapist's behavior, like that of the parents, serves as a model for the child. If the therapist is to be a good model, that behavior ought to be similar to that of parents of high-self-esteem children—that is, it should combine warmth with high expectations and high respect for individuality. We further suggest that it is incumbent on the therapist to be authentic and to shun impression management. It is vital that the therapist achieve congruence in the therapeutic relationship: actions must match words and the therapist must embody the behavior that he or she wishes to teach. Only then will the therapist be truly able to assist in the client's struggle toward identity, self-consistency, and self-esteem.

11

Treatment Caveats
and Conundrums

We are acutely aware of a fundamental problem that attends the development of any theoretical framework: that a theory's defining terms, processes, and prescriptions themselves can be problematic, which were described by Hofstadter (1985) as, "rules 'frozen' into a machine's design." He stated, "Doesn't the very fact of being frozen make any foreordained system / program / machine / organism vulnerable in some way that actually follows from the rules themselves?" (p. 546).

Once any system is established, whether it be cybernetic or psychological, its components can be recognized by both their function and dysfunction. Using a simple household analogy, the function of bleach in the wash is to enhance cleaning. Yet, when used with only slight impropriety, its dysfunctional use will ruin the fabric that it was intended to clean. Similarly, in psychotherapy, the function of transference is to create a relationship through which the therapist can gain an understanding of the client's fundamental methods of interacting with significant others, which in turn can provide a catalyst for change in the patient. One of the potential dysfunctions in this process is for the therapist to misuse it in ways that are self-serving, that is, deflecting well-earned patient criticism or resentment or exploiting the client in a variety of ways (Lidz, 1983). Our purpose in the current discussion is to alert the reader to the most likely dysfunctional uses that can accompany our model.

There are predictable problems that a therapist is likely to encounter when he or she starts using our treatment model, particularly if his or her understanding of why we do what we do is less than incisive and clear. These problems and the major considerations associated with them are the focus of this chapter. We will limit our discussion to the four fundamental levels of intervention contained within our model, namely (a) identifying and labeling the client's dominant avoidance patterns, (b) identifying and labeling the self-evaluative thoughts and feelings associated with these dominant avoidant styles, (c) assisting the client in facing negative self-evaluations and avoidance patterns realistically, and (d) assisting the client to gradually learn to cope with personal conflicts.

As each of the principal four steps in our model is discussed, we will provide case examples that will illustrate the dysfunctions or clinical conundrums that can attend our model and offer caveats and suggestions as a means of forecasting potential problems and dealing with existing ones as they occur.

When Labeling Is Tainted by Psychopathology

Given the theoretical premise that avoidance of threatening, fearful situations induces negative self-evaluations, one of the crucial steps in providing treatment is the identification of a client's avoidance patterns. As discussed in Chapter 6, the role of the therapist in identifying the client's avoidant style consists of accurately interpreting the client's self-reports of when they demonstrated avoidant behavior and, more important, carefully observing, within the therapy setting, those moments in which the client manifests avoidant behavior in the "here and now."

The labeling of the avoidant style can be a powerful therapeutic moment. It is not unlike the naming process of which M. Scott Peck (1983) spoke when finally recognizing the nature of his clients' malady:

> To name something correctly gives us a certain amount of power over it. . . . Today I am afraid of it still, but it is not a

blind fear. Knowing its name, I know something of the dimensions of that force. Because I have that much of safe ground on which to stand, I can afford to be curious as to its nature. I can afford to move toward it. I would proceed to work with them, . . . not because I would have significant confidence in my power to heal them—but simply because, knowing the name, I have grown strong enough to do the learning and attempt the work. And it is our task to work the fields that we know." (p. 68).

As the client is able to label avoidant behavior, there is a sense of empowerment that accompanies giving a potent source of negative self-evaluations a name. What was heretofore avoided is now confronted—a coping behavior in and of itself. Additionally, the client's chosen name for the avoidant behavior becomes a label full of meaning and significance to which both therapist and client can refer with a minimal amount of words. As avoidant behavior is repeated during a therapy session, the therapist can simply say, "What are you doing right this minute?" The client will typically respond by using the label of the previously identified avoidant behavior. This creates a critical cognitive and affective link between the actual avoidant behavior and the feelings that it generates. It also increases the client's ability to recognize when he or she is using avoidant behavior and subsequently to respond with a coping behavior instead.

These critical functions of labeling also bring with them some unique potential dysfunctions. We have consistently noted two in our clinical work and while training graduate students and workshop participants:

1. when the labeling process becomes contaminated by the clients' pathology and becomes an extension of thoughts and behavior that are themselves avoidant, and

2. when clients choose to minimize and understate their avoidant behavior.

When Labeling Is Part of the Avoidance

Although the function of labeling a client's avoidant style is to make explicit the manner in which psychic discomfort is created through abdicating personal responsibility and shying away from personal risk taking, there are clinical cases in which the labeling process itself can actually become an extended, sophisticated form of avoidance. In such cases, it is absolutely essential for the therapist to understand the theoretical purpose of the labeling process. It is not simply a technique or clinical procedure. Such restricted meaning can lead the therapist to create an iatrogenic condition wherein the treatment contributes to the problem that is being treated.

The nature and severity of a client's problem as well as the client's fundamental ego strength and coping abilities, must all be considered. Otherwise, techniques will be applied indiscriminately regardless of the problem presented (Beutler & Clarkin, 1990). The therapist must be particularly astute in ascertaining what function labeling may serve relative to the intrapsychic processes of the client. In other words, how is the client processing the labeling? What affective response does it generate? What cognitive distortions could be occurring? In many instances, the client may already have been using a pathological form of labeling that is simply self-punitive. The therapist as well as the client must be able to recognize the fundamental difference between nonproductive self-deprecation and honest and clear acknowledgment of one's own avoidant style. The former may consist of old and inaccurate labels that are reflective of deeply entrenched self-defeating attitudes and behavior. The latter are fresh insights that represent honestly facing and coping with problems heretofore obscured by generalized self-flagellation.

A classic example of such a client is the adult who has been sexually abused as a child. The following case study illustrates how the shame-based personality may distort the labeling process if the therapist is not sufficiently astute in identifying the client's propensity toward self-punitive statements.

Maggie. Maggie is a 28-year-old attorney who entered therapy after one failed marriage and was now facing the prospect of separating from her current husband. She considered her marital stress as the cause of her inability to sleep and of an increasing difficulty in concentrating while on the job. As the therapist inquired further about her sleeplessness, Maggie recounted having dreadful nightmares of monsters with huge jaws and jagged teeth eating her or of men without faces sawing her into little pieces. She also described periods of time at work during which she "fuzzes out" and "doesn't feel like herself." These complaints and other mild dissociative symptoms lead the therapist to explore the possibility of sexual abuse or similar trauma in the client's life. A stringent psychosocial–sexual history revealed that Maggie's first husband beat her and raped her on several occasions. Her current husband has verbally abused her and has told her that he found her physically revolting and disgusting—terms that she had used to describe her own physical appearance.

After several sessions, Maggie recounted the first time in which she was sexually abused when she was eight years old. She described it in an emotionally detached manner, one that typified her generally low range of affect. When any emotion was shown, it was usually of self-loathing for not having screamed out or run away while she was being abused.

By the sixth session, it was evident through her self-descriptions that Maggie considered herself fundamentally flawed, that her life was "poison," and that she was undeserving of being a part of any relationship in which she could be loved or cared for. Consequently, she constantly validated her own sense of being disgusting by engaging in relationships in which she will be treated as such. In some regrettable, destructive way, Maggie would rather become involved with someone whom she could readily identify as being abusive and remain emotionally detached (which, in essence, is a reenactment of what she did as a child when she was abused) than to enter a relationship in which she would be required to become emotionally open and, therefore, vulnerable to true rejection once her flaw is exposed.

This pattern of entering self-defeating relationships could be perceived as avoidance of emotional intimacy and as sabotaging any opportunity to receive the caring and nurturing that Maggie so desperately wanted but was afraid to risk. So long as she remained in abusive relationships, she could deflect any responsibility that she may have in contributing to her misery by keeping the focus on her abusive partner. With such a perception, a therapist could begin the labeling process by having Maggie describe in detail her tendency to enter into abusive relationships and her rejection of emotional intimacy with anyone who is caring and reasonably stable, therefore, denying herself of what she wants the most: love and acceptance.

We enter the therapy session at the point in which the therapist asks Maggie to label this avoidant pattern. While reading the following dialogue, it is important to understand that all the aforementioned assumptions are, in fact, an accurate description of Maggie's intrapsychic processes. However, as discussed further, in the absence of accounting for a history of sexual abuse and understanding the psychodynamics of the shame-based personality, the labeling process, regardless of how accurate it is, could simply be another shaming experience.

Therapist: How would you describe yourself when you reject those who are capable of giving you the nurturing you say you want and instead run to a relationship where you are sure to be abused?

Maggie: That's sick, isn't it. I can't stand it! That is so screwed up!

Therapist: Sick? Is that how you would describe yourself?

Maggie: Well that's right, isn't it? I mean, what kind of a person would keep subjecting herself to that kind of abuse? Yeah, sick. Twisted. Off the wall.

At this point, it is evident that Maggie has entered into a shaming mode. The label "sick" has simply become validation of what she has always considered herself—flawed. Furthermore, this validation has taken place with the assistance of her therapist! In Maggie's mind, now the therapist knows, explicitly, just how mentally disturbed she is. Maggie has been shamed once again. Shame-prone individuals experience their shame as more than just a transient emotion. Shame confirms the negative nature of their identity. Persons who have been severely abused feel that it is better to be bad than to be nothing, which, in the absence of having a flawed identity, is exactly what they feel they would be—a cipher—nothing. These are critical considerations that must be discerned by the therapist before any effective intervention can take place.

According to Harper and Hoopes (1990), the beliefs of shame-prone individuals include, "If others discover how bad I am, they will abandon me," "Others will eventually victimize me," and, "When others offer positive feedback, I believe they do not know me well enough. If they really knew me, they would see me as bad." The social behavior, the way these persons establish interpersonal relationships, leans toward their establishing a context in which others will do things "to them." Revictimization is common because of this tendency. Additionally, the therapist must be aware that the client will also be waiting to see whether he or she will be abusive. In the eyes of the client, engaging in the labeling process without this awareness may put the therapist in the position of inflicting further abuse.

These are the very processes that have kept Maggie psychologically stuck in believing that she is only worthy of abuse. This is a cardinal characteristic of abuse victims. As early as 1971, Hallie indicated that the perpetrator will ascribe blame of the abuse to the victims who, "after blame is convincingly ascribed, victims may then even come to believe the degrading characterizations that have been attributed to them."

The therapist is in a very precarious position. The label "sick" will not allow Maggie to provide herself with accurate self-evaluative thoughts and feelings. Any self-evaluation will simply be a resonating of past shame and self-loathing—neither of which will promote any therapeutic gain. The therapist must absolutely recognize that her use of the word "sick" is part of her pathology, the self-deprecation that she has used throughout her life. This is an illustration of labeling as an expression of the pathology rather than an insightful and illuminating recognition of it. What Maggie did when the therapist asked her to face her avoidance by labeling it was in fact to *avoid* the process by labeling it. The therapist must make this explicit.

Another paramount consideration is the fact that the client–therapist relationship must be such that the client understands that the therapist will not be abusive, and the client must be sufficiently comfortable within the relationship to "expose" to the therapist what she considers to be the flaws that, if uncovered, would cause the therapist to reject her. This is all necessary groundwork in order for the labeling process to be beneficial.

The following dialogue demonstrates how the therapist brought to Maggie's attention her self-abuse when he asked her to label her dominant avoidant style.

Therapist: What are you doing right now? Right this very moment?

Client: I'm hating myself. That's what I'm doing.

Therapist: (Softly.) It sounds really abusive to me. Like your abusing yourself.

Client: What do you mean?

Therapist: I mean you're not waiting for anyone else to hurt you. You're doing it yourself. Doesn't your husband call you sick and crazy? Didn't your previous husband treat you like you were sick and crazy? Didn't your uncle who abused you blame you for it? You were wrong? You were bad? What—maybe even sick? And now you're just doing it to yourself. Abusing yourself. Let's just give you a baseball bat and you can beat yourself to death once and for all.

Client: (Sobbing.) But I am sick. I, . . . I must be crazy.

Therapist: Who's that talking right now. Is that really you or the people that abused you?

Client: (She cries for a few moments before responding.) All my life it was always me. I was seeing things wrong. I must be out of my mind. I couldn't trust what I saw or heard. Bill was a master at twisting everything around so that things were my fault. And, and when Elaine's boy friend . . . I had to keep quiet. I couldn't tell anyone what happened. I was supposed to act like it didn't happen. And if it didn't happen then I must have made it up! I must have been crazy!

Therapist: Maggie. Do you really want to know if you are crazy? If you are sick?

Client: (Hesitantly.) Yes.

Therapist: Well then go ahead. Ask yourself. Are you the one who is sick? Are you really the one who is crazy. And don't be so ready to answer. Take your time. Answer for yourself. Don't let the abusers do it for you.

Client: (Thoughtful pause.) No, damnit. I'm not sick. They're the ones who are sick. They're the ones who are crazy!

Therapist: (Nods.) How are you right now?

Client: How do you mean?

Therapist: I mean . . . are you acting crazy or sick right now?
Client: No way. My stomach's tied up in knots, but I've
              never felt healthier.
Therapist: You don't sound very sick to me.

Had the therapist taken at face value the label offered by the client—sick—in all likelihood the client would have used the experience as a reminder of just how sick she already knew she was and now she had to acknowledge it in front of her therapist as well. The labeling process would, therefore, serve only to continue the client's self-abusive style, which, distilled to its most fundamental level, is a way of avoiding ever getting better. We have learned the hard way that using labeling prematurely can be damaging. One client whom we have seen dissociated when she was asked to label her avoidance before the depth of her negative self-perception was properly understood by the therapist.

In our clinical dialogue, however, the therapist recognized the client labeling herself as being self-victimized and anchored it to the abuse that she had suffered in her marriages and as a child. Making this process explicit, naming it for what it was, was a necessary prerequisite to using our model effectively. In the absence of identifying a client's defense mechanisms, cognitive distortions, and thoroughly understanding the client's avoidant style before beginning the labeling process, the filter through which the client processes all perceptions can distort any therapeutic process as well.

Now that the therapist has identified and made explicit Maggie's self-shaming that, in effect, is a psychological reenactment of the abuse that she suffered as a child, it can now be used as a label for how she reinjures herself and potentially sabotages any possible gains that might take place during a session. Examination of self-evaluative thoughts and feelings can now follow. However, this must be done carefully. Although we will be addressing possible pitfalls of the self-evaluative process later, it may be helpful to follow our client–therapist dialogue at least partially into the self-evaluation phase.

Therapist:	What is it like for you to realize you may be doing to yourself something very similar to what your abusers have done to you?
Client:	It seems so utterly stupid.
Therapist:	Say more.
Client:	I get angry to think that because of what happened to me I wind up beating myself up like this. It's just one more little goodie that those bastards left me. How does my mind do this? It is so warped. *I* am so warped. I could just....
Therapist:	What a minute. What are you doing to yourself right now?
Client:	(Pause.) I'm ... abusing myself.
Therapist:	Yes. What do you feel about that? That you do that to yourself?
Client:	I hate it! I want to stop doing it. But it's like this thick, ugly voice keeps telling me that I'm disgusting.
Therapist:	OK. If you were the person you wanted to be. If you were strong, clear thinking and whole, what would you want to say back to it? How would you want to answer that voice?
Client:	I'd tell it it was lying. I'd tell it to get out of my head. I'd tell it to leave me alone.
Therapist:	Go ahead. Say it. Say it out loud if you have to. Try for just one second to answer it back the way you want to.
Client:	(Pause. She looks down at her lap and then whispers.) You're a damn liar. I'm not going to listen to you anymore. Get the hell out of my head! (She starts to cry.)
Therapist:	That must have been really difficult for you to do.
Client:	It's, it's almost impossible. It's too big, too loud.
Therapist:	But just for a moment you talked back to it. I want you to relax now. Take some deep breaths. Don't answer right away, but tell me, how do you feel about yourself for doing what you just did.
Client:	It almost physically hurt inside my head while I was doing it.
Therapist:	I'm not surprised. But you did it anyway. Tell me what you feel about yourself for being able to do it in spite of the pain?

Client: It's like I'm more in control . . . the real me. It was hard and I did do it anyway. That's all right. That's good.

Therapist: You approve of yourself.

Client: Yes. When I can do that sort of thing I do approve of myself.

Therapist: Then it seems to me that your job in here, when we meet, is to be aware of when the negative voices, the abusive ones, are telling you how sick you are. Do you know what I mean? If we are in the middle of a session and you start thinking self-abusive thoughts, you have to let me know. You have to say out loud that that is what's going on inside of your head. OK?

Client: I get it. But then what?

Therapist: Then you have to decide if you're going to listen to them.

You will notice that when the therapist asked Maggie to think about how she psychologically punished herself, she immediately entered her self-punitive mode. At this juncture, the therapist asked her to identify what she was doing—using an avoidant response—when asked to evaluate herself. This is the fundamental avoidant style that had to be uncovered. Now that it was made explicit as Maggie was in the process of doing it, the therapist could then again turn Maggie inward and have her look at herself. Although the therapist required Maggie to look at herself, he intentionally used words that were nonpunitive and possibly one step removed from actually saying, "How do you feel about yourself for doing that." Instead, his question, "What do you feel about that," still pushed Maggie inward but in a less threatening manner; one that would not necessarily precipitate her self-abuse. The therapist must be able to adapt the labeling and self-evaluative process to accommodate the client's level of ego strength and ability to be self-reflective. Furthermore, once Maggie described her shaming as, "thick, ugly voices," the therapist picked up on this important revelation rather than pushing for a direct answer from Maggie regarding her feelings about being self-abusive. The therapist provided an opportunity for Maggie to begin entertaining the idea that she could counter the negative voices, which in turn created an opportunity for Maggie to be self-approving. The step involved in identifying negative self-evaluative thoughts and feelings associated with avoidance was momentarily set aside to allow the client to experience a coping response and explore how she felt about herself for coping with the negative voices inside of her head rather than avoiding them by accepting them as true and, ultimately, incorporating them into a shaming core identity.

Flexibility based on client need, ability, and therapeutic opportunity are essential when using the four basic steps of our model. These three considerations are described by Beutler and Clarkin (1990) as, "Selecting the level of intervention to fit the patient's method of coping, altering treatment menus to fit the mediating tasks and goals that define the phases through which treatment progresses and, adapting specific in-therapy procedures to the moment-by-moment treatment states the occur between a patient and therapist" (p. 223). The restricted therapist will simply look at the four steps of labeling avoidance, identifying self-evaluative thoughts and feelings, facing negative self-evaluations, and learning to cope, as procedures to apply to a client rather than processes to offer and adapt to the client.

Narcissism: Minimizing Labeling

Additional challenges that can attend the labeling of avoidance can be described best in the context of therapy with the narcissistic client. Although a true narcissistic personality rarely enters therapy of his or her own volition, the characteristics that attend this disorder will allow us to explore in extremes the tendency to want to avoid the labeling process by minimizing self-defeating behavior or using euphemistic descriptors— something that many clients do to a greater or lesser degree.

We have found Lorna Smith Benjamin's (1993) interpersonal summary of Narcissistic Personality Disorder to be the most cogent as a foundation on which to build a discussion of how the characteristics of such individuals must be accounted for when applying the labeling process. She stated,

There is extreme vulnerability to criticism or being ignored, together with a strong wish for love, support, and admiring deference from others. The baseline position involves non-contingent love of self and presumptive control of others. If the support is withdrawn, or if there is any evidence of lack of perfection, the self-concept degrades to self-criticism. Totally lacking in empathy, these persons treat others with contempt, and the self above and beyond the fray. (p. 147)

Our experience has been that individuals with this personality disorder usually seek therapy as a result of bouts of depression attending the phase during which self-criticism is at its strongest or, more frequently, when a marriage is at a critical point and the spouse insists on therapy. We will describe a marital therapy case excerpt to illustrate the challenge of applying the labeling process with a narcissistic individual. As with our previous case of an adult who was sexually abused as a child, the therapist must be keenly aware of how such a client is going to defend against making his avoidant style explicit, labeling it, and then describing self-evaluative thoughts and feelings. Without this foreknowledge, the narcissistic client can be adept at deflecting the therapeutic process and use it to further avoid responsibility for contributing to the marital discord that brought him and his spouse into therapy in the first place. One should note the client's initial need to seek approval from the therapist; then, as the discussion focuses on his behavior, how he euphemistically describes how he treats his wife to deflect any semblance of criticism and, when that does not work, how he becomes angry and then uses harsh labels to describe himself—not as a way of accurately describing his behavior, but once again to avoid realistically looking at his behavior.

Therapist: What I'd like you to do, Sheri, is describe in precise detail the last time you and Kevin fought. Try to describe the incident like you were watching a video of you two. It's very important not to leave anything important out.

Sheri: OK. But it's going to be hard to do.

Therapist:	How come?
Sheri:	Because Kevin is going to get angry with me. He'll interrupt and tell me I'm not seeing it the way it really happened.
Therapist:	That's OK with me. But we should know if that's what you're going to do Kevin. It sounds like Sheri is feeling pretty threatened.
Kevin:	(With good-natured concern.) No, I am not going to interrupt. Go ahead, Sheri. Tell it like you see it. There's no reason to be threatened. (To the therapist.) But I have to ask. Can I let you know if I disagree or would like to add something?
Therapist:	Why don't we let Sheri describe what she remembers and when she's finished I think it's important that you tell us how you saw things happening. Kind of take turns. Does that sound all right with you two?
Kevin:	Fine.
Sheri:	Yeah. That's fine.
Therapist:	So why don't you go ahead, Sheri.

(Sheri recounts how Kevin came home and thought that the house was not as clean as he wanted it. Kevin reprimands Sheri as if she were a little girl. When Sheri protests, Kevin calls her ungrateful for all the things he provides the family. He then becomes verbally abusive. He walks over to the stereo cabinet, looks at it and commands Sheri to dust it again. When she becomes angry, he grabs her by the arm and starts pushing her toward their bedroom. He pushes her into the bedroom and tells her to stay there until she can be reasonable. Sheri describes how powerless she feels at this point and winds up lying on the bed crying.)

Therapist:	What do you think, Kevin?
Kevin:	(Patronizingly.) I'm not surprised that she perceived what happened like that. But you have to understand some things.
Therapist:	OK.
Kevin:	(Leaning toward the therapist.) You understand how tough it is to bust your head all day at work, try to buy nice things for the family, all the stress and garbage you have to put up with just to try and get ahead a little bit. (Therapist looks intently at Kevin, but gives no response, only an indication that he is listening.) Anyway, when you come

	home and see that nothing has been done to keep the house nice, you just start wondering if it is worth it all.
Therapist:	Could I ask you a question?
Kevin:	Sure.
Therapist:	When you felt that the house wasn't clean, did you call Sheri an "ungrateful bitch"?
Kevin:	(Pauses.) Don't you get angry sometimes? I mean, just every once in a while you get just a little inappropriate?
Therapist:	I don't call my wife a bitch, if that's what you're asking.
Kevin:	OK. OK. That was out of line. But I'd been working since seven that morning. I was tired, and fact of the matter is the place looked like a dump.
Therapist:	So when you've been working hard and you're tired, you are more inclined to call your wife names, become physically abusive, and treat her as if she were a little child. How would you describe yourself when you behave like that?
Kevin:	I don't buy that at all.
Therapist:	Tell me how you see it.
Kevin:	There are times when someone has to take charge, especially when Sheri falls short of what I would expect any responsible wife to do. And I wasn't abusive. I hardly touched her at all when I suggested she go into the bedroom and cool off so we could talk about things in a rational manner. I was simply being direct and trying to short circuit a problem that could get much bigger than it did.
Sheri:	(Angry and frustrated.) That's not it at all. You degrade me and treat me like I was a two-year old. You always do this—make me look like I'm an idiot and you're in the right!

At this point, two important processes have been uncovered: Kevin's abusive behavior toward his wife as revealed in Sheri's description of their last blow-up, and his tendency to minimize the gravity of his behavior and need to shift the blame to Sheri. He is attempting to avoid labeling his treatment of Sheri as anything but reasonable and even helpful. The less experienced therapist might be tempted to apply a problem-solving process to this past conflict and focus on how Kevin could improve his treatment toward Sheri. Although this certainly will need to be examined, the more critical task at hand is to identify how, right in the midst of therapy, Kevin's avoidant behavior manifests itself in the form of minimization. Before Kevin can do anything different, he must recognize his need to place himself in a positive light—particularly when he feels threatened, as he is at this juncture. This is an extremely sensitive moment for the therapist. Based on Benjamin's profile of the narcissist, if he feels a withdrawal of support, his self-concept could decompensate to self-degradation, which, in effect, is another avoidant behavior. The therapist, therefore, has the onerous task of identifying any and all avoidant processes as they happen, all of which can distort the labeling process and negate any benefit that can be derived from this step. In the next dialogue, the therapist will acknowledge Kevin's minimizations while attempting to maintain support—a difficult thing to do now that Kevin is perceiving the therapist as a threat and as being nonsupportive. To complicate things even more, Sheri has now found the courage to express the anger that she feels when Kevin patronizes and abuses her. (We have purposely made things easier for the therapist so as to facilitate the illustrations of the concepts we are presenting. Would that therapy were as simple as textbook examples make it look!)

Therapist:	Is this the first time you've told Kevin that that's how you feel when he abuses you? Like a child that has been unjustly chastised?
Sheri:	Well, not like I just did. Not as clear. I'm afraid I usually freak out or just break down and cry.
Therapist:	Sounds to me then, that this is the first time you've risked telling Kevin just exactly how you feel. It must have been very difficult to say such an important thing; something that we need to address. But can I ask you a favor? I don't want you to think that we are ignoring you, but could we keep on taking a look at Kevin for just a few more minutes and then get back to what you just said?
Sheri:	You bet.

Therapist: Kevin. Look back at what you just said a moment ago. There seems to be a great big discrepancy between Sheri's description of how you treated her and how you perceived it. Let me try to summarize what could be the most damaging things that Sheri remembers you doing and you tell me how you would describe someone who does those sorts of things.

Kevin: (Impatiently and curtly.) Fine.

(Although it may be helpful for the therapist at this point to acknowledge Kevin's impatience and discuss what he is feeling, the therapist will choose to continue in his current direction to maintain focus on Kevin's minimizing the problem and using that as a way of avoiding responsibility for his part in this most recent blow-up. Additionally, by not acknowledging Kevin's displeasure, the therapist may also precipitate an outburst from Kevin which would provide excellent material for discussion. We would assume that Sheri would typically attempt to assuage Kevin's building anger and thus "buy into" Kevin's need for control—something the therapist must not do.)

Therapist: OK. You come home tired. The house isn't clean. You become angry and call your wife a bitch. You order her to dust the stereo cabinet for a second time. When she protests you physically force her into the bedroom, slam the door and tell her not to come out until she can be reasonable. How would you describe yourself for doing that?

Kevin: You're taking things out of context.

Therapist: (Apologetically.) I know. And it really makes things sound bad saying it that way, but I'm wondering if there is a context in which it's appropriate to call your wife names and use physical force on her?

Kevin: My hell, it's ... it wasn't that bad, and I resent you for making me look like a real SOB.

Therapist: I don't mean to, Kevin. And this might be a good place to stop for a minute and take a look at what's going on between us. How would you describe yourself in the last couple of seconds. How

	would you describe how you've been talking to me?
Kevin:	I've disagreed with what you've said but I've kept my cool. I've been honest.
Therapist:	How have you seen it, Sheri?
Sheri:	He's trying to make how he treats me look better than it is. And he's doing the same thing to you that he does to me.
Kevin:	Don't give me that. . .
Therapist:	I know this is hard, Kevin, but what Sheri has to say could really be important for us to hear. Would you be willing to let her finish?
Kevin:	(Visibly angry.) Yeah, yeah.
Therapist:	Say more, Sheri.
Sheri:	He started getting huffy with you just like he does with me. Then, when you try to call him on it, he either gets this patronizing attitude and starts twisting things around or he gets mad and starts to throw things. Then, he turns around and tries to blame it on you.
Therapist:	So what has just happened here between Kevin and me is what happens to you and Kevin at home.
Sheri:	That's right.
Kevin:	(To therapist). Wait a minute. What has "just happened here" between you and me?
Therapist:	Do you really want to know?
Kevin:	(Somewhat sarcastically.) Yeah, I really want to know.
Therapist:	OK. But I need to ask you a question. How would you describe the tone of voice you've been using talking to me for the past few minutes?
Kevin:	What? What has that got to do with anything?
Therapist:	What are you doing right now?
Kevin:	What am I doing?
Sheri:	(Interrupting.) You're answering his questions with a question. So you're not answering his questions.
Therapist:	That's what it looks like to me. It's almost like we're playing a game of tennis—I ask you a question and you hit it right back at me. I wonder what you're thinking and feeling that stops you from having a meaningful discussion with me?

Such defensiveness in narcissistic clients is not uncommon. To discuss with Kevin his minimization of the labels he uses to describe his abusive behavior toward Sheri, the therapist must recognize and then attend to the other avoidant tactics that Kevin will use to divert attention away from his tendency to minimize. The tendency of many therapists would be to become involved in answering Kevin's questions and consequently become side-tracked and unwittingly allow him to avoid answering the questions he has been asked. It is extremely critical for the therapist to look beyond the content of the comments that the client makes and to focus on the function that they serve. Then, that is what must be made explicit. In this particular case, Kevin would answer the therapist's questions with a question of his own; and, much like the tennis match that the therapist alluded to, the therapeutic ball must be returned to the client. In other words, as each new attempt is made to avoid, the therapist must bring it to the client's attention and, then, turn the client inward to ask himself whether that is what he really wants to do. Such instances require the client to face his own defensiveness and acknowledge how it contributes to the problem at hand, or continue in a defensive fashion that is obvious to therapist, client, and anyone else in the room.

The paramount principle governing the narcissist's use of avoidance is to avoid taking responsibility for the fact that he *is* being avoidant. It is essential for the therapist to pay particular attention to the process behind the interpersonal exchange between client and therapist. Much like a mutating virus, the narcissistic personality will alter his behavior when the therapist makes explicit what the client is currently doing. The therapist must be able to identify each mutation and bring it to the client's attention.

Clients who verbally minimize their avoidant behavior and offer weak labels typically feel more self-disapproving than their initial labeling would indicate. The therapist's task, therefore, is to help the client to verbalize more accurately what he actually feels, and to make explicit what is already implicit. The most powerful labels are those that accurately reflect the client's most fundamental thoughts and feelings regarding their avoidant behavior. Consequently, when a client labels how he ignores his wife when he comes home from work every night by retrieving a beer out of the fridge and parking himself on the couch to read the sports section of the newspaper, as "being tired," the therapist must challenge the label. This can be done by questioning substantively the accuracy of the statement ("Do you mean that all men who are tired after they come home from work handle their fatigue by not speaking to their wives?"), or the therapist can evaluate the label based on the impact that the behavior has on the client's marriage ("If you would describe your behavior simply as being tired, I wonder why it has caused so much trouble between you and your wife?").

At this stage of the labeling process, the therapist can require the client to be more accurate and self-revealing. This can be done by asking the client to be as honest as he can with himself; not to be fearful of appearing foolish and bad, and not to be so nice to himself, which can be done with a hint of humor. As the typical defensive maneuvers of new clients give way to more openness and a willingness to participate in the therapeutic process, the more candid they become as they offer their own unique labels for their avoidant and dysfunctional behavior. The therapist's responsibility, as previously stated, is to assure that the label is accurate and sufficiently descriptive.

Impoverished Capacity For Self-Evaluative Thoughts and Feelings

In this next section we will combine steps two and three of our model: identifying and labeling the self-evaluative thoughts and feelings associated with dominant styles of avoidance and assisting the client realistically to face negative self-evaluations and avoidance patterns. Clearly identifying the self-evaluative thoughts and feelings that are associated with avoidance is a process of experience as well as understanding. Simply having an intellectual recognition of what a client thinks and feels is not enough. The client must know, through immediate trial, what it is like to *experience* his own disapproval. This must be done under the observation and direction of the astute therapist so that it will be part of a coping response during therapy.

Our model presupposes the ability to be self-evaluative as an ubiquitous human characteristic. Theoretically, at some level, most individuals have at least a rudimentary ability to examine how they think and feel about themselves. However, on a pragmatic level, we have found clients whose stunted ability to be self-evaluative has posed considerable challenges in the application of our model. We will discuss some of these challenges through two case studies.

Angela. During a therapy session, Angela was asked to evaluate how she thought and felt about herself for being so susceptible to her mother's manipulations. There seemed to be little difference in how Angela reacted to her mother's stinging accusations as a child and how she now reacted as an adult when her mother came to pay her a rare visit: Angela's head would droop, eyes on her feet, and she would withdraw so deeply that she had described herself as so minute she was undetectable even to herself. When asked how she saw herself, she could only reply, "There is nothing to see."

Angela's severe absence of identity and ego strength were manifested routinely in every facet of her life. She was an "easy mark" for men, and had several affairs, all of which ended in her being abandoned. She had lost several jobs because of her uncanny knack at being a scapegoat. Easily dismissed, she never argued when she was overcharged for something or when someone would cut in line in front of her. She was literally a cipher—to herself and to others. Needless to say, it was not surprising that after a severe bout with depression, she was referred to her current therapist.

Angela was not "borderline," below "normal mental functioning," or "schizoid." She simply had little opportunity in her 32 years to exercise an identity. In the absence of a sense of self, there was very little self that she could evaluate. At this point, what does the therapist do? This is a conundrum to which the following caveat must be attached before it can be answered sufficiently: Models are made for clients and not the other way around. Therefore, one must consider the client first and then determine whether the model is applicable. Furthermore, modification of the model may be in order for therapeutic progress to take place; both of these may warrant consideration in Angela's case.

Considering the background from which Angela has come (punitive, deprecating mother) and the negative experiences that she has had thus far in her adult life (negative interpersonal experiences, little chance for personal development), it may be well to consider the meaning of her cryptic statement, "There is nothing to see," when asked how she saw herself as part of the self-evaluative process. This could be easily misinterpreted as simply that Angela perceives herself as "a nothing" when, in fact, it is a manifestation of her inability to see herself at all. Again, although this would be a complete impossibility for any sentient being, in Angela's case, when she was asked to get in touch with what she thought and felt about herself, it was almost as if the therapist where speaking to her in a foreign language. She had, for all intents and purposes, never really been asked what she thought or felt and, therefore, had very little understanding of what that meant. The therapist must therefore put aside the notion that Angela's past psychological weakness can be the impetus for negative self-evaluative thoughts and feelings and engage in more rudimentary work. This process may take considerable time and entail creating opportunities in and out of therapy that would enable Angela to become psychologically hearty enough to acknowledge herself as a meaningful, entitled human being, before enduring the rigors of self-evaluation.

An ancillary note of caution should be considered: Those individuals who suffer from severe personality disorders such as borderline personality disorder are always difficult and pose challenges even to the most seasoned therapist, regardless of what modality is used. When dealing with the misinterpretations and confusions of the words and actions of those present at the time of borderline disorganization (Kroll, 1988), the cognitive distortions will inevitably get in the way of each of the four steps in our model. Again, much more rudimentary groundwork must be laid before our model can yield therapeutic benefit.

In addition to individuals whose identities are so impoverished that the self-evaluative process becomes impeded, there are patients who generally avoid feelings of any kind as a dominant style of avoidance. In other words, they are able to clearly describe and label inappropriate or self-defeating behavior, but they are unable to view it except in a detached fashion. For those who defend in this manner, we must frankly acknowledge the possibility that they may not be able to participate fully in an affectively beneficial experience.

Warren. Warren was a dutiful provider for his wife and three children. He was conscientious at work and was reliable in any community or civic activities in which he participated. For five years, he had suffered from chronic fatigue syndrome (CFS). Ever since his wife could remember, she and the children had suffered from the strict, authoritarian way in which he handled things at home.

Warren had enough self-awareness and psychological savvy that he was able to describe, with his wife's colorful commentary, how he imposed unreasonable demands on the family. He also appropriately listened to his wife's tentative and careful descriptions of his behavior that led to their 16-year-old daughter running away from home: The reason for which they had entered therapy in the first place. When the therapist asked him to label his inflexibility and often harsh treatment of his family, he offered words such as, "Sometimes draconian," "I'm the son of an alcoholic and I act that way," and, nodding his head, "A real SOB, I guess." Although these words were uttered with a minimal amount of emotion, they were not without hesitation and thoughtfulness. Warren's responses seemed genuine.

However, when asked to take a look at what he thought and felt about himself when viewed in such negative terms, initially he could only reply, "I don't know. I've never thought about it that way before." When the therapist asked him to add more to his statement, Warren gave a very intelligent, convincing argument for discipline in the home, ways of curtailing the rising tide of gang-related crime, and how, "this was the only way he knew how to do things."

The obvious use of intellectualization as a means of avoidance was not lost to the therapist. Yet, the problem, particularly as it related to self-evaluative thoughts and feelings, was a bit more complex than just trying to punch through a client's defense mechanisms. It not only required guiding Warren out of his emotional cocoon, but the therapist also had to assist Warren in experiencing the self-approval that could arise from taking such a risk. Warren had essentially learned early in life that emotion, either negative or positive, was unacceptable. One was not to show anger and fear when Dad came home drunk and beat up Mom, and one was not to show excitement and happiness at other times because if one did, one would get beaten up. It was a much more effective self-survival tool to feel as little as possible or at least not to show it.

Under such circumstances, Warren learned that the more he was able to control his environment, external events, and his own reactions to both, the better off he would be. This evolved into an obsessive–compulsive personality disorder (OCPD) that, when Warren married, made life difficult for his wife and the children that eventually came along.

Therefore, it was the therapist's task not only to elicit self-evaluative thoughts and feelings but also to assist Warren in legitimizing the emotion that attended them. As is the case with many who develop OCPD, Warren had a lot of unresolved anger. This was extremely difficult to acknowledge. To let it show, particularly in front of the therapist, was almost impossible; but both had to happen before the efficacy of self-evaluation could be realized.

An additional element contributed to the unique problems of this case. Warren's family protected him from any possibility that he would turn inward and experience any negative self-evaluations that might provide the motivation for change. His eldest daughter remained silent when Warren would forbid her to date, wear trendy clothes, etc. Eventually, she ran away. Because Warren intimidated his family and he legitimately suffered from CFS, his wife and younger children would use his illness as an excuse to protect him from any of the therapist's interpretations that they thought might threaten or hurt Warren. So when Warren's wife described how he insisted that even his 14-year-old son go to bed at nine o'clock, even on week-ends, she prefaced her remark with, "But you know how loud teenagers can be, and with Warren's CFS, he needs all the rest he can get or he just won't make it to work on Monday." As we stated in our previous chapter, perceiving the family or marriage as a social microcosm and treating it as such allows these variables to be more closely controlled and, hopefully, treated as the family comes to realize the role it plays in maintaining client pathology.

One final point needs to be made with regard to Warren's inability to be self-evaluative: not only had he learned to suppress negative feelings, he was also required to dismiss any positive feelings as well. It was, therefore, absolutely essential that, at the moment, Warren be able to express his anger toward his father, for example, and that the therapist make explicit what Warren was doing and to have Warren now focus on what it felt like to acknowledge and release anger. This process had to precede Warren's ability to become appropriately angry with himself if that is part of his self-evaluations. Feelings must be cultivated before they can be applied to the in-vivo experience that is essential to negative self-evaluative thoughts and feelings.

When the appropriate time comes and clients' are asked how they think and feel about themselves, the therapist must make sure that what is being asked is understood. Many clients tearfully say that they feel horrible, but that is not what is being asked. When this happens, the therapist needs to acknowledge their pain but must again ask how the clients feel for facing things about themselves that they most likely never have before. It is at this point that clients' are introduced to the paradoxical relationship between the pain of the self-evaluation and the hope that seems to be inherent in the act of coping. This point must not be lost to the clients. Some therapists rush through this step and, in the process, lose an important therapeutic moment. The therapists should ask the clients how they would describe their behavior during the time spent in facing negative self-evaluations and avoidant styles. Clients need to be as explicit in this description of coping as they are in describing past avoidant behavior. If necessary, the therapist should tell the clients to slow down, close their eyes, and replay in their head how they had behaved. Then, the therapist must ask the clients to dig deep down inside and find words that express how they feel about themselves for such behavior. At this point, if there are any vestiges of sabotage still lurking inside the clients' head, they will emerge. The therapist should be on the look out for vague responses, "I don't knows," minimizing the coping response, and so forth. If any of these arise, they need to be made explicit and discussed.

Finally, flexibility of our model and of the therapist are paramount. In many instances, it may be more therapeutic to allow the session to end early with the client feeling the full effect of negative self-evaluations. This is particularly true of clients who have "stuffed" their feelings for a long time. In one instance, a session was ended 20 minutes early with a client sobbing almost uncontrollably because it was the first time that she had openly acknowledged how she had alienated most of her family and friends with her abrupt, aggressive style. Many therapists would have insisted that a "can of worms" had been opened and some closure was necessary to instill hope in this client. We are of the exact opposite opinion: By ending the session on such a powerful affective note, the client had to leave with her emotions fully before her. It would be that moment of genuineness to which she would refer for the rest of the week. It provided a potent sensitization that would set the tone for the rest of her treatment.

Coping: An Unexpected Source of Distress

It is evident that the elements of our model of psychotherapy are interconnected and interdependent. The dynamic and mutually influential relationship between coping and avoidance cannot be overstated. Not only must clients acknowledge their avoidance in order to cope, acknowledgement is the seed bed of coping in and of itself.

In chapter 7, we discussed the importance of the therapist being able to identify both the coping and avoidant reactions of the client. This is a major task in the therapy process and can create major problems if not done carefully. It should be remembered that therapy is essentially in the service of providing clients with highly personalized experiential learning events that teach the benefits of coping over avoidance. Consequently, the therapist must continually be mindful of arranging the therapeutic hour so that the client is required to demonstrate the attributes associated with coping (personal responsibility, risk taking, and forthrightness) a process that requires considerable focus.

A lack of focus occurs on the part of the therapist when, for example, the client is evasive several times when asked a pointed question and the therapist does not question the evasiveness. On the other end of the spectrum, when a client has faced a very difficult issue and the therapist does not engage him in the self-evaluative process, an opportunity to make the coping process explicit has been lost. These therapeutic sins of omission are not uncommon.

Client misconceptions also impede the effective implementation of this fourth part of the model. We frequently have clients experience the benefits of a powerful coping response in therapy that seems to catapult them into a healthier mental state. Typically, dependent people assert themselves. Guarded people become more open. Selfish people become more sharing. However, when they return the following week, they report how they were batted down, rejected, and ripped-off. When this happens, many clients are ready to abandon therapy. "If this is what coping is, I'll take avoidance any time!" is their sentiment. How this is handled can be a very important therapy juncture, and one that many therapists often miss.

The need to understand the theory that drives the appropriate response to such a dilemma is probably more important than the ability to execute its application. (The differentiation between the remedial task of identifying and labeling avoidance and the developmental task of identifying and labeling coping responses is discussed in chapter 7.) When clients arrive at a general understanding of how they avoid and begin to apply coping responses in its stead, as is the case described here, many therapists will make the mistake of returning to a remedial stance when the clients report their trials and tribulations between sessions. This can result in a loss of therapeutic momentum as previously identified avoidant patterns are recycled in an affective environment that lacks the impetus that previously accompanied it. At this juncture, a developmental approach characterized by increasing the cognitive awareness of the client should be used. Unless a new and alarming form of avoidance has been identified, a remedial approach is contraindicated.

In returning to our disillusioned clients, let us now apply our theoretical understanding of our approach by casting this as a developmental problem. The characteristic shared by each of the aforementioned clients is a need for external approval. Their sense of disappointment also seems to share the common misunderstanding that choosing a coping response will guarantee a positive response from others when, in fact, it is just as likely that the exact opposite may occur. The therapist must explore the clients' conceptions and expectations of coping.

What coping is to the clients can be reiterated at this point. Did the clients seek self-approval or the approval of others when they felt hurt or betrayed? Based on their definition of being the kind of person that they wanted to be, how close to that image did they come at the moment of personal conflict? How great is the discrepancy? Having clients recall the incident and substituting their coping selves for the ones that responded negatively can serve to reinforce how they want to be and behave at moments of difficulty and conflict. It is also important to emphasize that coping may require clients to stand alone, that discomfort may result, and that they ultimately must ask themselves whether they approved of the way in which they behaved regardless of the outcome. This is the essence of coping.

Clients may also experience moments of avoidance of which they disapprove and will so vocalize in therapy. It should be emphasized that coping and avoidance are not dichotomous, all or nothing concepts. Consequently, when a client begins a session with a confession of the previous week's avoidant response, the therapist should understand and communicate to the client, that such "relapses" are inevitable and do not necessarily define the client as either coping or avoiding.

Another quandary in which both therapist and client may find themselves in the process of learning to cope is the misinterpretation of avoidance as a coping response and, conversely, misperception of coping as avoidance. The following case illustration clarifies this conundrum.

Morris. Morris was a soft-spoken, intelligent business major at a prestigious university. Although consistently at the top of his class in academic ranking, he had received feedback, mostly in his practicum experiences, that his mild manner could curtail, if not preclude, him from a successful career in a world in which "dog-eat-dog" was the prevailing mentality. He consequently enrolled in one of our self-esteem groups hoping to acquire what he thought would be the added confidence and, therefore, the necessary attributes to excel in his chosen vocation.

As he learned about coping and avoiding, he attempted to evaluate his own personality style based on this newly acquired understanding. He was honest and almost brutal in his self-evaluations: he avoided arguments; in class, he would not make comments that were calculated to make his fellow students appear foolish, or use typical tactics that were rampant in his graduate program—from checking out of the library all available materials on class topics to make them inaccessible to other students to starting vicious rumors. Morris perceived his inability to be ruthless as an avoidant response to an environment in which such hostile tactics were expected, and unless he became more aggressive, he was sure to be pushed aside.

Therefore, in addition to joining the self-esteem group, he also read books about power tactics in business, increasing assertiveness, and learning to take care of "number one," without much success. Eventually, he decided that he was no longer willing to do all that was necessary to become a successful corporate star. With this in mind, he announced to his group leader that so long as he was the recipient of other students' conniving, he had decided to cease trying to cope and that he would avoid being as aggressive as he needed to be to complete the business program with high visibility. Is Morris a case of coping or of avoidance?

Therapists with a marginal understanding of the nature of coping and avoidance may not be able to discern which of Morris's behaviors constitutes coping and which, avoidance. At the surface, if Morris avoided competition and conflict, it would be relatively easy to say that leaving his graduate program was avoidant behavior. We have supervised therapists who, subscribing to this line of reasoning, assume that a shy, withdrawn person who takes an assertiveness training course is moving away from avoidance and moving toward coping. This is not necessarily the case. It is all too common for therapists to forget the guiding axiom: to focus on the function that the behavior serves in the total economy of the personality and situation more than on the behavior itself. Is the function to seek the approval of family, of employer, of therapist? All of these are potential sources of external approval. Or is it to avoid the personal risk and responsibility involved in facing or being the person that one truly is?

In Morris' case, his search for a more "macho" self was in the service of his preconceived notion of what it took to be successful. In reality, however, his behavior was a function of doing what he saw others do even though he thought less of himself for doing so. This is a case in which learning assertive behavior might provide external rewards, but not internal ones.

However, there is a more subtle consideration involved. The core of Morris's avoidance ran deeper than his approval or disapproval of learning assertiveness tactics. As a matter of fact, all the time he spent in attending classes and reading books on self-esteem and success were a sophisticated but unintentional charade to avoid asking himself the question that he should have asked in the first place: Did he like his soft-spoken, mild mannered ways? Was he already the kind of person of which he approved? By avoiding these questions, which can only be answered by the self, he was able to postpone defining himself as acceptable to himself because that would mean he would be unacceptable as a viable candidate in his program. He would have to abandon some fantasy of power and prestige that, once he truly evaluated, he discovered was not truly important to him. In many ways, Morris for a time, was an introvert masquerading as an extrovert—certainly a switch from the more predominant external individuals posing as internal ones.

Had Morris's group leader focused on Morris quitting his program rather than requiring him to become intensely self-evaluative, Morris may have been persuaded to continue his assertiveness training and complete his program. Instead, he discovered that he had liked himself all along and was just too hesitant to acknowledge it to himself or to others.

Summary

> *How can one ever hope to build a system that*
> *anticipates all possible problems.*
> Douglas R. Hofstadter

Although scientist / philosopher Douglas R. Hofstadter (1985) was referring to systems as they pertain to computers, the question is relevant when discussing systems or models of psychotherapy. In the process of designing and implementing a therapeutic approach, the number of variables that cannot be anticipated and accommodated far exceed those that can. In fact, defining and specifying a set of variables as a model creates boundaries that can potentially cause problems of restriction and constriction, wherein the therapist limits his responses to the client based on the parameters of a model that can neither be complete nor completely anticipatory of all contingencies.

The first inherent difficulty that arises from the "building of a system" is constriction. The therapist's theoretical perceptions are narrowly compressed into one model or theory that is omni-applicable. No problem is too big and no client too pathological for "the" approach. Prochaska (1984) called this the therapist developmental stage of *dualism* and described these therapists who suffer from constriction as those who

> believe they have had the truth revealed to them. Dualistic therapists are the *true believers* among us who think that a particular system of therapy is correct and all others are in error. Data are of little concern since the true system of therapy is already assumed to be known and data would only document the obvious (p. 365).

Constricted therapists may either fastidiously hold to one theoretical orientation and weather out their entire careers with a delimiting sense of security, or they may leap head on into the gale of a continuing proliferation of therapy approaches, drifting from one camp to the next, ever aspiring to find the ultimate therapy. In either case, constriction may result in the therapist forcing a fit between approach and client where a goodness of fit does not exist. It has been amply demonstrated that clients and their presenting problems are perceived by the therapist on the basis of theoretical orientation as well as on other unique therapist variables, such as value base, education, gender, and so forth. The only way to guard against the unwanted influences that these constricting considerations can introduce in the therapy process is to acknowledge them openly and to keep them available in a larger conceptual framework that allows the therapist to select the most appropriate conceptual tools for the specific needs of a client.

The problem of restriction is a second concern. It is typified by therapists who seek "recipe card" approaches to therapy. They attempt to reduce a therapeutic orientation down to a series of steps that, when applied, will reap a benefit that is readily discernable in the client. An understanding of the theoretical framework that gives rise to any prescribed interventions is circumvented to obtain the "tools" that workshop goers covetously accumulate to place in their "therapeutic toolbox." Although certain basic techniques are essential to any therapy approach, in the absence of understanding the relationship between these techniques and the theoretical underpinnings from which they originate, therapists run the risk of, "executing new and unfamiliar techniques without really understanding their value or without a sense of internal ownership" (Loganbill, Hardy, & Delworth, 1982). We interpret this to mean that, in the absence of a sound conceptual grasp of *why* what is done is done, a simplistic cause and effect expectation of therapy may result by which the therapist will not be prepared to react appropriately to a client whose responses do not "fit" within the therapist's preconceived notions.

Restriction is typified by the technical rigidity of the therapist. Leon Salzman (1977) stated, "'when the therapist is rigid, inflexible, insecure, and essentially a technician following rules of procedure,' the process of therapy itself may become 'an obsessional ritual'" (quoted in Strupp, Hadley, & Gomes-Schwartz, 1977, p. 75). Our earlier caveat regarding the implementation of the steps and techniques in our model, in the absence of a strong understanding of their underlying principles, is particularly relevant to our present discussion. When a therapist is unsure of his or her skill level and, as is the case most frequently with beginning therapists, there is a lack of practical experience and therapy know-how, and strict adherence to procedure becomes a safety net that may appear to save the therapist but, regrettably and typically, at the expense of the client. A limited theoretical understanding of our model can not only transmogrify therapy into an obsessional ritual, but it can also create circumstances in which the client may suffer psychological harm.

Theoretically, we have discussed a model that emphasizes underlying processes more than observable content or behavior, internal self evaluations more than socially mediated external influences, and coping with integrity, in spite of the immediate difficulties that it can create instead of avoidance and the immediate though temporary relief that it can provide. Our guiding assumption is that clients that are guided by personal values and principles, the importance of which transcend the moment, will reap the benefits of personal well-being and emotional health.

To this end, we have discussed the predictable problems that a therapist is likely to encounter if they use our treatment model without a clear and incisive understanding of why what is done is done. Our discussion was limited to the four fundamental levels of intervention. In each area, we have emphasized the importance of conceptual clarity as a prerequisite for the flexible and appropriate use of the core treatment considerations that we have proposed.

Afterword

In this volume we have described our ideas about the role of self-esteem in the treatment of emotional problems. Although a number of theorists emphasize the importance of self-esteem in their work, to the best of our knowledge, the mode of therapy that we have described here is unique.

Any mode of treatment, like science itself—indeed, like therapy itself—is an evolving, growth-oriented process. We fully expect to refine our model further as we continue to work with clients and as other clinicians who apply our methods report their experience. It is our sincere hope that, by pursuing the issue of self-esteem and making it the core of our model, we have been able to build a credible, viable mode of treatment that will eventually take its place alongside other major therapeutic strategies.

References

Adler, A. (1964). *Superiority and social interest* (H. L. Ansbacher & R. R. Ansbacher, Eds. and Trans.). Evanston, IL: Northwestern University Press.

Adler, A. (1979). *Superiority and social interest* (H. L. Ansbacher & R. R. Ansbacher, Eds. and Trans.). New York: Norton.

Allport, G. W. (1937). *Personality: A psychological interpretation.* New York: Holt.

Allport, G. W. (1961). *Pattern and growth in personality.* New York: Holt, Rinehart & Winston.

Allport, G. W. (1962). Psychological models for guidance. In R. F. Carle, C. D. Kehas, & R. L. Mosher (Eds.), *Harvard Educational Review, 32*(4), 373–381.

Ansbacher, H. L., & Ansbacher, R. R. (1956). *The individual psychology of Alfred Adler.* New York: Basic Books.

Bandura, A. (1977). Self-efficacy: Toward a unifying theory of behavioral change. *Psychological Review, 84,* 191–215.

Bandura, A. (1986). *Social foundations of thought and action: A social cognitive theory.* Englewood Cliffs, NJ: Prentice-Hall.

Bateson, G., Jackson, D., Haley, J., & Weakland, J. (1956). Toward a theory of schizophrenia. *Behavioral Science, 1,* 251–264.

Baumrind, D. (1963). Authoritarian vs. authoritative parental control. *Adolescence, 3,* 255–272.

Baumrind, D. (1966). Effects of authoritative parental control on child behavior. *Child Development, 37,* 857–907.

Baumrind, D. (1971). Current patterns of parental authority. *Developmental Psychology Monographs, 41*(1), Part 2.

Baumrind, D. (1975). Some thoughts about childrearing. In U. Bronfenbrenner & M. Mahoney (Eds.), *Influences on human development.* Hinsdale, IL: Dryden Press.

Beck, A. T., Rush, A. J., Shaw, B. F., & Emery, G. (1979). *Cognitive therapy of depression.* New York: Guilford Press.

Bednar, R. L., Burlingame, G. M., & Masters, K. S. (1988). Systems of family treatment: Substance or semantics? *Annual Review of Psychology, 39,* 401–434.

Bednar, R. L., & Kaul, T. J. (1978). Experiential group research: Current perspectives. In S. L. Garfield & A. E. Bergin (Eds.), *Handbook of psychotherapy and behavior change: An empirical analysis* (2nd ed.). New York: Wiley.

Bednar, R. L., & Lawlis, F. (1971). Empirical research in group psychotherapy. In A. E. Bergin & S. L. Garfield (Eds.), *Handbook of psychotherapy and behavior change.* New York: Wiley.

Bednar, R. L., Melnick, J., & Kaul, T. (1974). Risk, responsibility, and structure: Ingredients of a conceptual framework for initiating group counseling and psychotherapy. *Journal of Counseling Psychology, 21,* 31–37.

Bem, S. L., & Lenney, E. (1976). Sex-typing and the avoidance of cross-sexed behaviors. *Journal of Personality and Social Psychology, 38,* 48–54.

Benedict, R. (1934). *Patterns of culture.* Boston: Houghton Mifflin.

Benjamin, L. S. (1993). *Interpersonal diagnosis and treatment of personality disorders.* New York: Guilford Press.

Beutler, L. E., & Clarkin, J. F. (1990). *Systematic treatment selection: Toward targeted therapeutic interventions.* New York: Brunner / Mazel.

Cannon, W. B. (1939). *Wisdom of the body.* New York: Norton.

Carp, F. M., & Carp, A. (1981). Mental health characteristics and acceptance-rejection of old age. *American Journal of Orthopsychiatry, 51*(2), 230–241.

Cooley, C. H. (1902). *Human nature and the social order.* New York: Scribner's.

Coopersmith, S. (1967). *The antecedents of self-esteem.* San Francisco, CA: Freeman.

Coopersmith, S. (1969, February). *Implications of studies on self-esteem for education research practice.* Paper presented at the American Educational Research Association Convention, Los Angeles, CA.

Covington, M. V., & Beery, R. G. (1976). *Self-worth and school learning.* New York: Holt, Rinehart, & Winston.

Daly, M. J., & Burton, R. L. (1983). Self-esteem and irrational beliefs: An exploratory investigation with implications for counseling. *Journal of Counseling Psychology, 30*(3), 361–366.

Eliot, T. S. (1940). *T. S. Eliot: The complete poems and plays.* New York: Harcourt, Brace.

Ellis, A. (1962). *Reason and emotion in psychotherapy.* New York: Lyle Stuart.

Ellis, A. (1973). *Humanistic psychotherapy: The rational and curative approach.* New York: McGraw-Hill.

Epstein, S. (1973). The self-concept revisited: Or a theory of a theory. *American Psychologist, 28,* 404–416.

Epstein, S. (1979a). Natural healing processes of the mind: I. Acute schizophrenic disorganization. *Schizophrenia Bulletin, 5*(2), 313–321.

Epstein, S. (1979b). The stability of behavior: I. On predicting most of the people much of the time. *Journal of Personality and Social Psychology, 37,* 1097–1126.

Erikson, E. (1963). *Childhood and society* (2nd ed.). New York: Norton.

Erikson, E. (1968). *Identity: Youth and crisis.* New York: Norton.

Festinger, L. (1962). *A theory of cognitive dissonance.* Stanford: Stanford University Press.

Fish, B., & Karabenick, S. A. (1971). Relationship between self-esteem and locus of control. *Psychological Reports, 29*(3), 784.

Flaherty, J. F., & Dusek, J. B. (1980). An investigation of the relationship between psychological androgyny and components of self-concept. *Journal of Personality and Social Psychology, 38,* 984–992.

Flavell, J. (1985). *Cognitive development* (2nd ed.). Englewood Cliffs, NJ: Prentice-Hall.

Ford, D., & Urban, H. (1963). *Systems of psychotherapy.* New York: Wiley.

Frank, J. D. (1973). *Persuasion and healing* (Rev. ed.). Baltimore: Johns Hopkins University Press.

Frank, J. D. (1982). Therapeutic components shared by all psychotherapies. In J. H. Harvey & M. M. Parks (Eds.), *The master lecture series: Vol. I. Psychotherapy research and behavior change* (pp. 5–38). Washington, DC: American Psychological Association.

Freud, S. (1937). Repression. In J. Rickman (Ed.), *A general selection from the works of Sigmund Freud.* Garden City, NY: Doubleday Anchor Books. (Original work published 1915).

Freud, S. (1957). Recommendation to physicians practicing psychoanalysis. In J. Strachey (Ed. and Trans.), *The standard edition of the complete psychological works of Sigmund Freud* (Vol. 12, pp. 109–120). London: Hogarth Press. (Original work published 1912).

Freud, S. (1961). On the grounds for detaching a particular syndrome from neurasthenia under the description "anxiety neurosis." In J. Strachey (Ed. and Trans.), *The standard edition of the complete psychological works of Sigmund Freud* (Vol. 3, pp. 87–117). London: Hogarth Press. (Original work published 1924).

Friedenberg, W., & Gillis, J. (1977). An experimental study of the effectiveness of attitude change techniques for enhancing self-esteem. *Journal of Clinical Psychology, 33*(4), 1120–1124.

Friedenberg, W., & Gillis, J. (1980). Modification of self-esteem with techniques of attitude change: A replication. *Psychological Reports, 46*(3), 1087–1095.

Garfield, S. L. (1986). Research on client variables in psychotherapy. In S. L. Garfield & A. E. Bergin (Eds.), *Handbook of psychotherapy and behavior change* (3rd ed.) (pp. 213–256). New York: Wiley.

Gauthier, J., Pellerin, D., & Renaud, P. (1983). The enhancement of self-esteem: A comparison of two cognitive strategies. *Cognitive Therapy and Research, 7*(5), 389–398.

Goldenberg, I., & Goldenberg, H. (1985). *Family therapy: An overview.* Monterey, CA: Brooks / Cole.

Greenberg, J., Solomon, S., Pyszczynski, T., Rosenblatt, A., Burling, J., Lyon, D., Simon, L., & Pinel, E. (1992). Why do people need self-esteem? Converging evidence that self-esteem serves an anxiety-buffering function. *Journal of Personality and Social Psychology, 63,* 913–922.

Greenson, R. R. (1967). *The technique and practice of psychoanalysis.* New York: International Universities Press.

Greenwald, A. G., & Breckler, S. J. (1985). To whom is the self presented? In B. R. Schlenker (Ed.), *The self and social life.* New York: McGraw-Hill.

Hallie, P. O. (1971). Justification and rebellion. In N. Sanford & C. Comstock (Eds.), *Sanctions for evil* (pp. 176–185). San Francisco: Jossey-Bass.

Hamachek, D. F. (1978). *Encounters with the self* (2nd ed.). New York: Holt, Rinehart & Winston.

Harmm, M. H. (1980). The Barron Ego Strength Scale: A study of personality correlates among normals. *Journal of Clinical Psychology, 36*(2), 433–436.

Harper, J. M., & Hoopes, M. M. (1990). *Uncovering shame: An approach integrating individuals with their family systems.* New York: Norton.

Harter, S. (1982). The perceived competence scale for children. *Child Development, 53,* 87–97.

Harter, S. (1983). Developmental perspectives on the self-system. In E. M. Hetherington (Ed.), *Handbook of child psychology, Vol. 4. Socialization, personality, and social development* (4th ed.). New York: Wiley.

Hetherington, E. M., & Parke, R. D. (1986). *Child psychology: A contemporary viewpoint.* New York: McGraw-Hill.

Higgins, E. T. (1983). *A theory of discrepant self-concepts.* Unpublished manuscript, New York University, New York.

Higgins, E. T., Klein, R., & Strauman, T. (1985). Self-concept discrepancy theory: A psychological model for distinguishing among different aspects of depression and anxiety. *Social Cognitions, 3,* 51–76.

Hoffman, M. A., Levy-Shiff, R., & Ushpiz, V. (1993). Moderating effects of adolescent social orientation on the relation between social support and self-esteem. *Journal of Youth and Adolescence, 22,* 23–32.

Hofstadter, D. R. (1985). *Metamagical themas: Questing for the essence of mind and pattern.* New York: Basic Books.

Iseberg, R., Hauser, S., Jacobson, A., Powers, S. (1989). Parental contexts of adolescent self-esteem: A developmental perspective. *Journal of Youth and Adolescence, 18,* 1–23.

James, W. (1890). *Principles of psychology.* New York: Holt.

James, W. (1981). *Principles of psychology.* Cambridge, MA: Harvard University Press. (Original work published 1890).

Johnson, A., Giffin, M., Watson, E. J., & Beckett, P. (1956). Studies in schizophrenia at the Mayo Clinic: II. Observations on ego functions in schizophrenia. *Psychiatry, 19,* 143–148.

Kaul, T. J., & Bednar, R. L. (1986). Experiential group research: Results, questions, and suggestions. In S. L. Garfield & A. E. Bergin (Eds.), *Handbook of psychotherapy and behavior change* (3rd ed.). New York: Wiley.

Kazdin, A. E. (1980). *Research design in clinical psychology.* New York: Harper & Row.

Kelley, G. (1955). *The psychology of personal constructs.* New York: Norton.

Kennedy, J. F. (1956). *Profiles in courage.* New York: Harper.

Kolb, B., & Wishaw, I. Q. (1985). *Fundamentals of human neuropsychology* (2nd ed.). New York: Freeman.

Korchin, S. J. (1976). *Modern clinical psychology.* New York: Basic Books.

Kroll, J. (1988). *The challenge of the borderline patient: Competency in diagnosis and treatment.* New York: Norton.

Lepper, M. R. (1983). Extrinsic reward and intrinsic motivation: Implications for the classroom. In J. M. Levine & M. C. Wang (Eds.), *Teacher and student perceptions: Implications for learning*. Hillsdale, NJ: Erlbaum.

Lidz, T. (1987). *The person*. New York: Basic Books.

Lieberman, M., Yalom, I., & Miles, M. (1973). *Encounter groups: First facts*. New York: Basic Books.

Linton, R. (1956). *Culture and mental disorders*. Springfield, IL: Charles C. Thomas.

Loevinger, J. (1976). *Ego development: Conceptions and theories*. San Francisco: Jossey-Bass.

Loganbill, C., Hardy, E., & Delworth, U. (1982). Supervision: A conceptual model. *Counseling Psychology, 10*(3), 42.

Lynn, D. B. (1959). A model man for applied psychology. *American Psychologist, 14*, 630–632.

Mahoney, M. J., & Thoresen, C. E. (1985). *Self-control: Power to the person*. Monterey, CA: Brooks / Cole.

Markus, H., & Wurf, E. (1987). The dynamic self-concept: A social psychological perspective. In M. R. Rosenszeig & L. W. Porter (Eds.), *Annual Review of Psychology, 38*, 299–337.

May, R. (1953). *Man's search for himself*. New York: New American Library.

May, R. (1983). *The discovery of being*. New York: Norton.

May, R., Angel, E., & Ellenberger, H. (Eds.). (1958). *Existence*. New York: Basic Books.

McCall, R. J. (1975). *The varieties of abnormality*. Springfield, IL: Charles C. Thomas.

McKee, J. P., & Sherriffs, A. C. (1957). The differential evaluation of males and females. *Personality, 25*, 356–371.

Mead, G. H. (1934). *Mind, self, and society*. Chicago: University of Chicago Press.

Meichenbaum, D. B. (1977). *Cognitive-behavior modification*. New York: Plenum.

Millon, T. (1969). *Modern psychopathology: A biosocial approach to maladaptive learning and functions*. Philadelphia: Saunders.

Millon, T. (1981). *Disorders of personality: DSM III Axis II*. New York: Wiley.

Moretti, M., & Higgins, E. T. (1990). Relating self-discrepancy to self-esteem: The contribution of discrepancy beyond actual self-ratings. *Journal of Experimental and Social Psychology, 26*, 108–123.

Orlinsky, D. E., & Howard, K. T. (1986). Process and outcome in psychotherapy. In S. L. Garfield & A. E. Bergin (Eds.), *Handbook of psychotherapy and behavior change* (3rd ed.). New York: Wiley.

Patrick, J. (1984). Predicting outcome of psychiatric hospitalization: A comparison of attitudinal and psychopathological measures. *Journal of Clinical Psychology, 40*(2), 546–549.

Peck, M. S. (1983). *People of the lie: The hope for healing human evil*. New York: Simon & Schuster.

Pelham, B. W., & Swann, W. B. (1989). From self-conceptions to self-worth: On the sources and structure of global self-esteem. *Journal of Personality and Social Psychology, 57*, 672–680.

Prochaska, J. O. (1984). *Systems of psychotherapy: A transtheoretical analysis.* Homewood, IL: Dorsey Press.

Rimm, D. C., & Masters, J. C. (1979). *Behavior therapy techniques and empirical findings* (2nd ed.). New York: Academic Press.

Rogers, C. R. (1950). The significance of the self-regarding attitudes and perceptions. In M. L. Reymert (Ed.), *Feelings and emotions: The Mooseheart Symposium.* New York: McGraw-Hill.

Rogers, C. R. (1951). *Client-centered therapy.* Boston: Houghton Mifflin.

Rogers, C. R. (1957). The necessary and sufficient conditions of therapeutic personality change. *Journal of Consulting Psychology, 21,* 95–103.

Rogers, C. R. (1959). A theory of therapy, personality, and interpersonal relationships as developed in the client-centered framework. In S. Koch (Ed.), *Psychology: A study of a science: Volume III. Formulations of the person and the social context* (pp. 184–256). New York: McGraw-Hill.

Rogers, C. R. (1961). *On becoming a person.* Boston: Houghton Mifflin.

Rogers, C. R. (1980). *A way of being.* Boston: Houghton Mifflin.

Rosenberg, M. (1979). *Conceiving the self.* New York: Basic Books.

Sandler, J. (1985). *The analysis of defense.* New York: International Universities Press.

Sathyavathi, K., & Anthony, T. (1984). An attributional approach to locus of control, self-esteem, and alienation: A clinical study. *Psychological Studies, 29*(1), 76–82.

Satir, V., Stachowiak, J., & Taschman, H. A. (1975). *Helping families to change.* New York: Aronson.

Schlenker, B. R. (1985). Identity and self-identification. In B. R. Schlenker (Ed.), *The self and social life.* New York: McGraw-Hill.

Seeman, J. (1959). Toward a concept of personality integration. *American Psychologist, 14,* 633–637.

Selman, R. L. (1980). *The growth of interpersonal understanding.* New York: Academic Press.

Shoben, E. J. (1957). Toward a concept of the normal personality. *American Psychologist, 12,* 183–189.

Singh, U. P., Prasad, T., & Bhagalpur, U. (1973). Self-esteem, social-esteem, and conformity behavior. *Psychologia: An International Journal of Psychology in the Orient, 16*(2), 61–68.

Steger, J. H., Simmons, W. L., & Lavelle, S. (1973). Accuracy of prediction of own performance as a function of locus of control. *Psychological Reports, 33*(1), 59–62.

Stockton, R., & Moran, D. C. (1982). Review and perspective of critical dimensions in therapeutic small group research. In G. M. Gazda (Ed.), *Basic approaches to group psychotherapy and group counseling.* Springfield, IL: Charles C Thomas.

Strauss, A. (Ed.). (1964). *George Herbert Mead on social psychology.* Chicago: University of Chicago Press.

Strupp, H. H., Hadley, S. W., & Gomes-Schwartz, B. (1977). *Psychotherapy for better or worse: The problem of negative effects.* New York: Jason Aronson, Inc.

Sullivan, H. S. (1962). *Schizophrenia as a human process.* New York: Norton.

Thomas, A., & Chess, S. (1977). *Temperament and development.* New York: Brunner / Mazel.

Thomas, A., Chess, S., & Birch, H. G. (1968). *Temperament and behavior disorders in children.* New York: New York University Press.

Tice, D., Baumeister, R., & Hetherton, T. (1993). When ego threats lead to self-regulation failure: Negative consequences of high self-esteem. *Journal of Personality and Social Psychology, 64,* 141–156.

Truax, C. B., & Carkhuff, R. R. (1967). *Toward effective counseling and psychotherapy: Training and practice.* Chicago: Aldine.

Tyler, L. (1978). *Individuality: Human possibilities and personal choice in the psychological development of men and women.* San Francisco: Jossey-Bass.

Wegrocki, H. J. (1939). A critique of cultural and statistical concepts of abnormality. *Journal of Abnormal and Social Psychology, 34,* 166–178.

Wiener, N. (1948). *Cybernetics, or, Control and communication in the animal and the machine.* New York: Wiley.

Wylie, R. (1961). *The self-concept: A critical survey of pertinent research literature.* Lincoln, NE: University of Nebraska Press.

Wylie, R. (1974). *The self-concept: A review of methodological considerations and measuring instruments* (Vol. 1, Rev. ed.). Lincoln, NE: University of Nebraska Press.

Wylie, R. (1979). *The self-concept: Theory and research on selected topics* (Vol. 2). Lincoln, NE: University of Nebraska Press.

Yalom, I. D. (1985). *The theory and practice of group psychotherapy* (3rd ed.). New York: Basic Books.

York, P., York, D., & Wachtel, T. (1982). *Tough love.* New York: Doubleday.

Author and Subject Index

419

About the Authors

Richard L. Bednar, PhD, is professor of psychology at Brigham Young University. Prior to that, he was director of the Clinical Psychology Training Program at the University of Kentucky. He has published consistently for over 20 years, with recent chapters in the *Annual Review of Psychology* and the *Handbook of Psychology and Behavior Change.* His research has appeared in numerous journals, such as the *Journal of Consulting and Clinical Psychology* (for which he has also been a consulting editor), the *Journal of Counseling Psychology,* and the *Journal of Applied Behavioral Science.* A noted guest speaker, he has been invited to Hebrew University (Israel), Beijing University, and to many international conferences.

Scott R. Peterson, MSW, was with Research and Staff Development of Latter Day Saints Social Services for 15 years and in private practice. He is currently an instructor in the Graduate School of Social Work at Brigham Young University and a writer and producer with the *Video Journal of Education.* He has developed and presented experiential and video-based training programs for clinical social workers on the diagnosis and treatment of psychological disorders. He had primary training responsibility for field application of *DSM-III-R,* marriage and family communications, treatment of personality disorders, and emotional implications of infertility.